OTHER A TO Z GUIDES FROM THE SCARECROW PRESS, INC.

1. *The A to Z of Buddhism* by Charles S. Prebish, 2001.
2. *The A to Z of Catholicism* by William J. Collinge, 2001.
3. *The A to Z of Hinduism* by Bruce M. Sullivan, 2001.
4. *The A to Z of Islam* by Ludwig W. Adamec, 2002.
5. *The A to Z of Slavery and Abolition* by Martin A. Klein, 2002.
6. *Terrorism: Assassins to Zealots* by Sean Kendall Anderson and Stephen Sloan, 2003.
7. *The A to Z of the Korean War* by Paul M. Edwards, 2005.
8. *The A to Z of the Cold War* by Joseph Smith and Simon Davis, 2005.
9. *The A to Z of the Vietnam War* by Edwin E. Moise, 2005.
10. *The A to Z of Science Fiction Literature* by Brian Stableford, 2005.
11. *The A to Z of the Holocaust* by Jack R. Fischel, 2005.
12. *The A to Z of Washington, D.C.* by Robert Benedetto, Jane Donovan, and Kathleen DuVall, 2005.
13. *The A to Z of Taoism* by Julian F. Pas, 2006.
14. *The A to Z of the Renaissance* by Charles G. Nauert, 2006.
15. *The A to Z of Shinto* by Stuart D. B. Picken, 2006.
16. *The A to Z of Byzantium* by John H. Rosser, 2006.
17. *The A to Z of the Civil War* by Terry L. Jones, 2006.
18. *The A to Z of the Friends (Quakers)* by Margery Post Abbott, Mary Ellen Chijioke, Pink Dandelion, and John William Oliver Jr., 2006.
19. *The A to Z of Feminism* by Janet K. Boles and Diane Long Hoeveler, 2006.
20. *The A to Z of New Religious Movements* by George D. Chryssides, 2006.
21. *The A to Z of Multinational Peacekeeping* by Terry M. Mays, 2006.
22. *The A to Z of Lutheranism* by Günther Gassmann with Duane H. Larson and Mark W. Oldenburg, 2007.
23. *The A to Z of the French Revolution* by Paul R. Hanson, 2007.
24. *The A to Z of the Persian Gulf War 1990–1991* by Clayton R. Newell, 2007.
25. *The A to Z of Revolutionary America* by Terry M. Mays, 2007.
26. *The A to Z of the Olympic Movement* by Bill Mallon with Ian Buchanan, 2007.

56. *The A to Z of Feminist Philosophy* by Catherine Villanueva Gardner, 2009.
57. *The A to Z of the Early American Republic* by Richard Buel Jr., 2009.
58. *The A to Z of the Russo–Japanese War* by Rotem Kowner, 2009.
59. *The A to Z of Anglicanism* by Colin Buchanan, 2009.
60. *The A to Z of Scandinavian Literature and Theater* by Jan Sjåvik, 2009.
61. *The A to Z of the Peoples of the Southeast Asian Massif* by Jean Michaud, 2009.
62. *The A to Z of Judaism* by Norman Solomon, 2009.
63. *The A to Z of the Berbers (Imazighen)* by Hsain Ilahiane, 2009.
64. *The A to Z of British Radio* by Seán Street, 2009.
65. *The A to Z of The Salvation Army* edited by Major John G. Merritt, 2009.
66. *The A to Z of the Arab–Israeli Conflict* by P R Kumaraswamy, 2009.
67. *The A to Z of the Jacksonian Era and Manifest Destiny* by Terry Corps, 2009.
68. *The A to Z of Socialism* by Peter Lamb and James C. Docherty, 2009.
69. *The A to Z of Marxism* by David Walker and Daniel Gray, 2009.
70. *The A to Z of the Bahá'í Faith* by Hugh C. Adamson, 2009.
71. *The A to Z of Postmodernist Literature and Theater* by Fran Mason, 2009.
72. *The A to Z of Australian Radio and Television* by Albert Moran and Chris Keating, 2009.
73. *The A to Z of the Lesbian Liberation Movement: Still the Rage* by JoAnne Myers, 2009.

Tha A to Z
of Marxism

David Walker
Daniel Gray

The A to Z Guide Series, No. 69

The Scarecrow Press, Inc.
Lanham • Toronto • Plymouth, UK
2009

Published by Scarecrow Press, Inc.
A wholly owned subsidiary of
The Rowman & Littlefield Publishing Group, Inc.
4501 Forbes Boulevard, Suite 200, Lanham, Maryland 20706
http://www.scarecrowpress.com

Estover Road, Plymouth PL6 7PY, United Kingdom

British Library Cataloguing in Publication Information Available

Library of Congress Cataloging-in-Publication Data

The hardback version of this book was cataloged by the Library of Congress as
follows:

Walker, David M. (David Martin), 1963–
    Historical dictionary of Marxism / David Walker, Daniel Gray.
        p. cm. (Historical dictionaries of religions, philosophies, and movements ;
    no. 74
    Includes bibliographical references.
    1. Communism—Dictionaries. I. Gray, Daniel, 1981–. II. Title. III. Series
HX17.W36 2007
335.403—dc22   200602047

ISBN 978-0-8108-6852-6 (pbk. : alk. paper)
ISBN 978-0-8108-7018-5 (ebook)

⊗™ The paper used in this publication meets the minimum requirements of
American National Standard for Information Sciences—Permanence of Paper
for Printed Library Materials, ANSI/NISO Z39.48-1992.

Printed in the United States of America

To Deborah and Rachael.
For everything and for always.
—DMW

To Mum and Dad,
for all your love and support.
—DG

Contents

Editor's Foreword

Marxism was initially a philosophy, one that could be debated and refined freely, but it soon became a movement, with organizations and even governments adhering to it and coming into conflict with the contending philosophy of capitalism. For some it became a religion, something believed in implicitly, which they would die to defend. What is most extraordinary, however, is that Marxist governments eventually ruled the Soviet Union, much of Eastern and Central Europe, China and other parts of Asia, and even bits of Africa and Latin America while being advocated by numerous political parties and guerrilla movements. This vast empire, initiated in 1917, rapidly subsided in the 1990s but still includes the world's most populous country, China.

Thus *The A to Z of Marxism* must explain and consider philosophical terms and concepts, political organizations and parties, and the several dozen countries that both adopted and adapted Marxism. The chronology traces the long period between Karl Marx's birth to the present; the introduction attempts to define Marxism, consider it in both theory and practice, and above all determine what value it still has; the wide-ranging dictionary contains entries on significant philosophers, politicians, and activists; and the bibliography points to further reading.

This book was written by David M. Walker and Daniel Gray. Dr. Walker is a lecturer in politics at the University of Newcastle and has been teaching political theory for the past 15 years. He specializes in socialism and Marxism and has written extensively on both, including the book *Marx, Methodology and Science* and a booklet on historical materialism. He is currently editing a book on 20th-century Marxist thought. Daniel Gray received a degree in politics and history from the University of Newcastle, has written on the Welsh socialist pioneer Robert Owen and is currently doing research for "Marxism in the Twentieth

Century: A Critical Survey." Together they have produced an extremely useful reference work.

Jon Woronoff
Series Editor

Acknowledgments

A book is always a collaborative effort and this one is no exception. In writing this work we had help and support from many quarters, most directly in the authorship of some of the entries. Jennifer Hay did invaluable research on a range of topics and wrote items on British and American political parties. Paul McFadden contributed entries summarizing Karl Marx's *Economic and Philosophical Manuscripts*, the *Communist Manifesto*, and the *Grundrisse* as well as some on aspects of Marx's philosophy. Matthew Johnson proved the breadth of his knowledge with his piece on Tuva, and Dr. James Babb generously provided expert entries on Japanese Marxism. Heartfelt thanks to all these contributors. In addition, we are grateful to Newcastle University, and to our families, friends, and colleagues for support and encouragement throughout the compiling of the dictionary. Finally, thanks to the series editor, Jon Woronoff, for his helpful and constructive comments and his limitless patience. Although a collective effort the responsibility for any deficiency of content lies with the two authors of the book. We hope, though, that any such failings will not prevent the dictionary being of interest and value to readers.

Acronyms and Abbreviations

ACP	Albanian Communist Party
ADM-19	*Alianza Democrática M-19*/Democratic Alliance M-19 [Colombia]
ANAPO	*Alianza Nacional Popular*/National Alliance Party [Colombia]
ANC	African National Congress [South Africa]
ASWP	American Socialist Workers Party
AVNOJ	Anti-Fascist Council of National Liberation of Yugoslavia
BKP	*Balgarska Komunisticeska Partija*/Bulgarian Communist Party [BCP]
BNMAU	*Bügd Nayramdakh Mongol Ard Uls* /Mongolian People's Republic [MPR]
BR	*Brigate Rosse*/Red Brigade [Italy]
BSP	British Socialist Party
CCP	Chinese Communist Party
CGT	*Confédération Générale Du Travail*/General Confederation of Workers [France]
CHEKA	All-Russian Extraordinary Commission [Soviet Union]
CIS	Commonwealth of Independent States
CND	Campaign for Nuclear Disarmament [Great Britain]
CNR	*Conseil National de la Révolution*/National Council of the Revolution [Congo]
Comecon	Council for Mutual Economic Assistance
Cominform	Communist Information Bureau
Comintern	Third International or Communist International
COPWE	Commission for Organizing the Party of the Working People [Ethiopia]

CPGB	Communist Party Great Britain
CPI	Communist Party of India
CPI-M	Communist Party of India-Marxist
CPSA	Communist Party of South Africa
CPUSA	Communist Party USA
CPV	Communist Party of Vietnam
CPY	Communist Party of Yugoslavia
DPRK	Democratic People's Republic of Korea
DRK	Democratic Republic of Korea
DRV	Democratic Republic of Vietnam
DSOC	Democratic Socialist Organizing Committee [United States]
ELG	Emancipation of Labor Group [Europe]
ELS	*Ejército Libertador del Sur*/Liberation Army of the South [Mexico]
ELZN	*Ejército Zapatista de Liberación Nacional*/Zapatista Army of National Liberation [Mexico]
EPLF	Eritrea People's Liberation Front
EPM	Economic and Philosophical Manuscripts
EPRDF	Ethiopian People's Revolutionary Democratic Front
EPRP	Ethiopian People's Revolutionary Party
First International	International Workingmen's Association
FLN	Algerian National Front
FLN	*Front de Libération Nationale*/National Liberation Front [Algeria]
FRELIMO	*Frente de Libertação de Moçambique*/Front for the Liberation of Mozambique
FRG	Federal German Republic
FSLN	*Frente Sandinista de Liberación Nacional*/Sandinista National Liberation Front
GDR	German Democratic Republic
Gulag	Main Camp Administration
IASD	International Alliance of Socialist Democracy [Europe]
ICP	Indochinese Communist Party [Vietnam]
ILP	Independent Labour Party [Great Britain]
IMF	International Monetary Fund
INC	Indian National Congress

IU	*Izqierda Unidad*/United Left [Peru/Spain]
IWUSP	International Working Union of Socialist Parties
IWW	Industrial Workers of the World
IWW	International Workers of the World
KCP	Korean Communist Party
KGB	Committee for State Security
KMT	*Kuomintang* [China]
Komsomol	Communist League of Youth [Soviet Union]
KOR	*Komitet Obrong Robotników*/Workers' Defense Committee [Poland]
KPD	*Kommunistiche Partei Deutschlands*/German Communist Party
KPRP	Kampuchean People's Revolutionary Party
KPSP	Korean People's Socialist Party
KPSS	*Kommunisticheskaia partiia Sovetskogo Soiuza*/ Communist Party of the Soviet Union (CPSU)
KSC	*Komunistická strana Československa*/Communist Party of Czechoslovakia (CPCz)
KWP	Korean Workers' Party
LDP	Liberal Democratic Party [Japan]
LPDR	Lao People's Democratic Republic
LRG	Labour Representation Committee [Great Britain]
LWMA	League of Working Men's Association
M-19	*Movimento 19 de Abril*/April 19 Movement [Colombia]
MAKN	*Mongol Ardyn Khuv'sgalt Nam*/Mongolian Revolutionary Party (MRP)
MCR	Military Council of the Revolution [Benin]
MDA	Movement for Democracy in Algeria
MM	*Magyar Mankáspárt*/Hungarian Workers Party (HWP)
MNR	*Mouvement National de la Révolution*/National Movement of the Revolution [Congo]
MPLA	*Moviemento Popular de Libertação Angola*/Popular Movement for the Liberation of Angola
MPLA-WP	*Moviemento Popular de Libertação Angola-Partido de Trabalho*/ Popular Movement for the Liberation of Angola-Workers' Party

MSM	*Magyar Szocialista Mankáspárt*/Hungarian Socialist Workers Party (HSWP)
NAM	Non-Aligned Movement
NATO	North Atlantic Treaty Organization
NEP	New Economic Plan
NK	*Nihon Kyosanto*/Japanese Communist Party (JCP)
NKVD	People's Commissariat for Internal Affairs
NKWP	North Korean Workers Party
NLA	National Liberation Army [Yugoslavia]
NLF	National Liberation Front [Yemen]
OLAS	*Organización Latinamericana de Solidaridad*/Latin American Solidarity Organization
PAICV	*Partido Africano da Indêpendencia da Cabo Verdo*/African Party for the Independence of Cape Verde
PAIGC	*Partido Africano da Indêpendencia da Guiné e Cabo Verdo*/African Party for the Independence of Guinea and Cape Verde
PC	*Partido Communista*/Communist Party [Chile]
PCC	*Partito Comunista de Cuba*/Communist Party of Cuba (CPC)
PCE	*Partido Comunista de España*/Spanish Communist Party
PCF	*Parti Communiste Français*/French Communist Party
PCI	*Partito Comunista Italiano*/Italian Communist Party
PCP	Polish Communist Party
PCP	*Partido Comunista Peruano-unidad/*Peruvian Communist Party
PCP-BR	*Partido Comunista Peruano-Bandero Roja*/Peruvian Communist Party-Red Flag
PCP-PR	*Partido Comunista del Peru-Patria Roja*/Communist Party of Peru-Red Fatherland
PCR	*Partidad Comunist Român*/Romanian Communist Party [RCP]
PCT	*Parti Congolais de Travail*/Congolese Workers' Party
PDG	*Parti Démocratique de Guinée*/Democratic Party of Guinea

PDPA	People's Democratic Party of Afghanistan
PDRE	People's Democratic Republic of Ethiopia
PDRY	People's Democratic Republic of Yemen
PDS	*Partei des Demokratischen Sozialismus*/Party of Democratic Socialism [Germany]
PLA	People's Liberation Army [China]
PMAC	Provisional Military Administrative Council [Ethiopia]
Politburo	Political Bureau
POS	*Partido Obrero Socialista*/Socialist Workers Party [Chile]
PPPL	*Phok Paxaxon Patixat Lao*/Lao People's Revolutionary Party (LPRP)
PPR	*Polska Partia Robotnicza*/Polish Workers' Party
PPSh	*Partia e Punës e Shqipërisë*/Albanian Party of Labor
PRC	People's Republic of China
PRC	People's Republic of Congo
PRL	*Pouvoir Révolutionnaire Local* [Guinea]
PRPB	*Parti de la Révolution Populaire du Benin*/Popular Revolutionary Party of Benin
PRRG	People's Revolutionary Republic of Guinea
PS	*Parti Socialiste*/Socialist Party [France]
PSI	*Partito Socialista Italiano*/Italian Socialist Party
PS-NPSI	*Partito Socialista-Nuovo PSI*/Socialist Party-New PSI [Italy]
PTE-UC	Workers Party of Spain-Communist Unity
PUM	*Partido Unificado Mariateguista*/Unified Mariateguista Party [Peru]
PzPR	*Polska zjednoczona Partia Robotnicza*/Polish United Workers' Party
RENAMO	*Resistência Nacional Moçambiçana*/National Resistance Movement of Mozambique
RSDP	Russian Social Democratic Party
RSDRP	*Rossiiskaia Sotsial-demokraticheskaia Rabochaia Partiia*/Russian Social Democratic Labor Party
SACP	South African Communist Party
SDA	*Sozial Demokratische Arbeiterpartei*/Social Democratic Workers Party [Germany]

SDF	Social Democratic Federation [Great Britain]
SDF	Social Democratic Foundation [Great Britain]
SDPJ	Social Democratic Party of Japan
SED	*Sozialdemokratische Einheitspartei Deutschlands/* Socialist Unity Party of Germany
SFIO	*Section française de L'Internationale Ouvrière/* French Section of the Workers International
SI	*Socialisti Italiani/*Italian Socialists
SKJ	*Savez Komunista Jugoslavije/*League of Communists of Yugoslavia
SOVROM	Soviet Romanian
SPA	Socialist Party of America
SPD	*Sozial Demokratische Partei Deutschlands/*Social Democratic Party [Germany]
SPDA	Social Democratic Party of America [United States]
SPÖ	*Sozialdemokratische Partei Österreichs/*Austrian Social Democratic Party
SPÖ	*Sozialistische Partei Österreichs/*Austrian Socialist Party
SRV	Socialist Republic of Vietnam
SWRP	Scottish Workers' Republican Party
UFNSK	United Front for the National Salvation of Kampuchea
UFO	Unidentified Flying Object
USPD	*Unabhängige Sozialistiche Partei Deutschlands/* Independent German Socialist Party
UWS	*Umkhonto we Sizwe/*Spear of the Nation [South Africa]
VWP	Vietnamese Workers' Party
WB	World Bank
WPE	Workers' Party of Ethiopia
YAR	Yemen Arab Republic
YSP	Yemen Socialist Party
ZANU	Zimbabwe African National Union
ZANU-PF	Zimbabwe African National Union-Patriotic Front
ZAPU	Zimbabwe African Patriotic Union

Chronology

1818 Birth of Karl Marx.

1844 Karl Marx, *Economic and Philosophical Manuscripts*, outlines his theory of alienation and human nature.

1845 Karl Marx, *Theses on Feuerbach*, sketches a terse account of Marx's materialist outlook.

1846 Karl Marx and Friedrich Engels, *The German Ideology*, contains the fullest account of Marx's materialist conception of history in contrast to a philosophically idealist approach.

1847 Karl Marx, *The Poverty of Philosophy*, a riposte to Pierre-Joseph Proudhon's *System of Economic Contradictions*, focuses particularly on Proudhon's theory of value and his abstract and philosophically idealist methodology. It also provides a statement of Marx's own materialist approach.

1848 Karl Marx and Friedrich Engels, *The Communist Manifesto*, provides the clearest and briefest statement of the views of Marx and Engels, including specific policy proposals.

1850 Karl Marx, *The Class Struggles in France*, represents Marx's first attempt to explain specific historical events using his materialist conception of history.

1852 Karl Marx, *The Eighteenth Brumaire of Louis Bonaparte*, is the further application of Marx's method to recent events, specifically focusing on Louis Bonaparte's 1851 coup d'état.

1859 Karl Marx, *Preface to a Critique of Political Economy*, famously gives the most succinct account of the materialist conception of history.

1864   Foundation of the First International (dissolved 1876).

1867   Karl Marx, *Capital* vol. I, is of all his works Marx's greatest theoretical achievement. It includes his theory of surplus value and exploitation.

1869   Foundation of German Social Democratic Party.

1871   **France:** Paris Commune; Karl Marx, *The Civil War in France*, sells thousands of copies throughout Europe and earns Marx notoriety for its praise of the revolutionary character of the Paris Commune. It includes interesting indications of Marx's vision of the future communist society.

1872   Hague Congress of the First International.

1875   Gotha Congress.

1884   Death of Marx.

1887   **Great Britain:** Independent Labour Party (ILP) formed.

1889   Foundation of the Second International (collapsed 1914).

1892   Friedrich Engels, *Socialism: Utopian and Scientific*.

1895   Death of Engels.

1898   **Russia:** Foundation of Russian Social Democratic Labour Party (RSDLP); Georgii Plekhanov, *The Role of the Individual in History*.

1899   Lenin, *Development of Capitalism in Russia*; Eduard Bernstein, *Evolutionary Socialism*; Rosa Luxemburg, *Social Reform or Revolution*.

1900   **Great Britain:** Foundation of British Labour Party.

1901   **United States:** Foundation of Socialist Party of America.

1902   Second Congress of RSDLP: Bolshevik–Menshevik split; Lenin, *What Is to Be Done?*

1905   **Russia:** Uprising provoked by "Bloody Sunday" massacre in St. Petersburg. It is eventually quelled after use of military force and promise of various political reforms.

1916   Lenin, *Imperialism: The Highest Stage of Capitalism*.

1917 **Russia:** February and October Revolutions in Russia; Lenin, *State and Revolution*.

1918 Karl Kautsky, *The Dictatorship of the Proletariat*.

1919 Nikolai Bukharin and Evgeny Preobrazhensky, *ABC of Communism*. **Germany:** Rosa Luxemburg murdered by right-wing German army officers; Foundation of the Third International also known as the Comintern (dissolved 1943).

1921 **Czechoslovakia:** Czechoslovak Communist Party founded. **China:** First Chinese Communist National Congress.

1923 **Russia:** United Socialist Soviet Republic (Soviet Union) established; Georgii Lukács, *History and Class Consciousness*; Karl Korsch, *Marxism and Philosophy*.

1924 **Soviet Union:** Death of Lenin; Josef Stalin, *Foundations of Leninism*; Union of Soviet Socialist Republics (USSR) officially formed. **Mongolia:** Mongolian People's Republic comes into being.

1925 **Cuba:** Cuban Communist Party founded.

1927 **Soviet Union:** Leon Trotsky and Grigory Zinoviev expelled from Communist Party of the Soviet Union (CPSU).

1929 **Soviet Union:** Trotsky expelled from Soviet Union; Antonio Gramsci, *Prison Notebooks* (1929–1935).

1930 **Soviet Union:** Collectivization of agriculture. **Vietnam:** Indochinese Communist Party founded.

1934–35 **China:** Long March; Trotsky, *The Revolution Betrayed*.

1937 Mao Zedong, *On Practice* and *On Contradiction*.

1938 Josef Stalin, *Dialectical and Historical Materialism*; Foundation of the Fourth International.

1940 **Mexico:** Trotsky murdered by an agent of Stalin.

1942 **China:** Rectification movement (Zhengfeng) begins marking start of "Mao Zedong Thought."

1944 **Yugoslavia:** Josip Tito's Communist government recognized by British Government. **Albania:** Envar Hoxha forms Provisional

Democratic Government. **Greece:** Greek Communist uprising defeated by British forces. **Bulgaria:** Communist coup. **Poland:** Red Army intervention to support Polish communists in struggle for power.

1945 Poland: Communist-dominated Polish Committee for National Liberation recognized by Soviet Union as government of Poland. **Romania:** Communist coup supported by Soviet Union. **Germany:** Founding of Communist Party of Germany. **Vietnam:** Ho Chi Minh proclaims Democratic Republic of Vietnam. **Korea:** Liberated from Japanese rule with Soviet army occupying much of North Korea.

1946 Korea: Kim Il Sung chairman of North Korean Interim People's Committee. **Albania:** People's Republic of Albania formed.

1947 Theodore Adorno and Max Horkheimer, *Dialectic of Enlightenment*; Foundation of Communist Information Bureau also known as Cominform (dissolved 1956).

1948 Yugoslavia: break with Soviet Union (expelled from Cominform). **Germany:** Berlin Blockade (ended 1949). **Czechoslavkia:** Communist coup. **Korea:** Democratic People's Republic of Korea founded by Kim Il Sung.

1949 China: People's Republic of China established; New Democracy Period begins. **Germany:** German Democratic Republic (GDR) formed; Theodore Adorno et al., *Authoritarian Personality*.

1950 Yugoslavia: Workers' self-management established. **Tibet:** Chinese People's Liberation Army invades; Stalin, *Marxism and Linguistics*.

1952 Yugoslavia: Yugoslav Communist Party renamed League of Communists and workers' self-management officially identified as the distinctive contribution of Yugoslavia to socialist theory and practice.

1953 Soviet Union: Death of Stalin. **Hungary:** New Prime Minister Imre Nagy introduces "new course." **China:** Start of first Five Year Plan.

1955 Hungary: Nagy expelled from Communist Party and reforms ended; Herbert Marcuse, *Eros and Civilization*.

1956 Soviet Union: 20th Congress of CPSU: Denunciation of Stalin. **Hungary:** Hungarian Revolution and Soviet invasion. **China:** The

Hundred Flowers Period begins. **Angola:** Movimento Popular de Libertação de Angola (MPLA) founded.

1957   Ghana (formerly Gold Coast): Becomes independent under Kwame Nkrumah's Convention People's Party (CCP); Mao Zedong, *On the Correct Handling of Contradictions Among the People*; Milovan Djilas, *The New Class*.

1958   Poland: Yugoslav League of Communists adopts program asserting unique Yugoslav road to socialism. **China:** Great Leap Forward. **Guinea:** Becomes independent under Sékou Touré's Parti Démocratique de Guinée (PDG).

1959   Cuba: Revolution resulting in overthrow of Fulgencio Batista regime and establishing of Fidel Castro's leftist regime.

1960 Beginnings of Sino–Soviet split. **Mali:** Becomes independent under Modibo Keita's Soudanese Union Party. **Kampuchea:** Communist Party of Kampuchea founded; Jean-Paul Sartre, *Critique of Dialectical Reason*.

1961 Building of Berlin Wall. **Tanzania (formerly Tanganyika):** Becomes independent under Julius Nyerere's Tanganyika African National Union (TANU).

1962   Algeria: Becomes independent under Ahmed Ben Bella's Front de Libération Nationale.

1963 Soviet and Chinese communist party relations broken. **Congo:** Military coup and new president Alphonse Massemba-Débat declares Congo/Brazzaville to be a Marxist–Leninist state.

1964   Soviet Union: Downfall of Nikita Khrushchev, replaced by Leonid Ilyich Brezhnev; Herbert Marcuse, *One-Dimensional Man*.

1965 Louis Althusser, *For Marx*; Che Guevara, *Socialism and Man in Cuba*.

1965   Algeria: Ben Bella's socialist government overthrown.

1966   China: Beginning of Cultural Revolution (ends 1969). **Ghana:** Nkrumah and the CPP overthrown.

1967 Régis Debray, *Revolution in the Revolution*. **Yemen:** People's Republic of South Yemen founded (became People's Democratic Republic of Yemen in 1970). **Mali:** Keita overthrown by military.

1968 **Czechoslavkia:** Prague Spring and Soviet invasion. **France:** May events in Paris. **Congo (Brazzaville):** New president, Major Marien Ngouabi, oversees creation of People's Republic of Congo; Congo notable as Africa's first lasting regime with Marxism–Leninism as its political outlook.

1969 **Somalia:** Colonel Mohamed Siad Barre comes to power in coup and creates increasingly pro-Soviet Marxist–Leninist regime. **Sudan:** Colonel Gaafar Nimeri overthrows elected government and bans all political parties except Sudanese Communist Party which plays key role in new regime. **Libya:** Colonel Muammar Qaddafi comes to power. **Vietnam:** Death of Ho Chi Minh.

1970 **China:** Disappearance of Lin Biao.

1972 **Benin:** Lieutenant Colonel Mathieu Kérékou seizes power.

1973 **China:** Rehabilitation of Deng Xiaoping. **Guinea Bissau:** Independence declared under leadership of Partido Africano da Independencia da Guiné e Cabo Verde.

1974 **Benin:** Kérékou declares Marxism–Leninism to be the regime's framework for theory and practice. **Ethiopia:** Military seizes power and allows country to become "client state" of Soviet Union.

1975 **Mozambique:** Becomes independent under Samora Machel's Frente de Libertação da Moçambique (FRELIMO) which begins transition from national liberation movement to Marxist–Leninist vanguard party. **Angola:** MPLA led by Agostinho Neto takes power and begins change from national liberation movement to Marxist–Leninist vanguard party.

1975 **Laos:** Lao People's Democratic Republic formed, led by Prince Souphanouvong.

1976 **China:** Death of Mao; Death of Zhou Enlai; Deng Xiaoping dismissed; Gang of Four arrested. **Vietnam:** Following military victory in 1975, unified Vietnam is renamed Socialist Republic of Vietnam. **Kampuchea:** Pol Pot's Khmer Rouge creates new Democratic Kampuchea regime. **Somalia:** Barre's Supreme Revolutionary Party changes into Somali Revolutionary Socialist Party, a Marxist–Leninist vanguard party.

1977   Leonid Ilyich Brezhnev, *A Historic Stage on the Road to Communism.*

1978   **China:** Deng Xiaoping endorsed by Third Plenum as leader; Gerry Cohen, *Karl Marx's Theory of History.*

1980   Yugoslavia: Death of Tito. **Zimbabwe (formerly Rhodesia):** Becomes independent under Robert Mugabe's Zimbabwe African National Union–Patriotic Front (ZANU-PF).

1981   **China:** Hu Yaobang elected Chairman of Central Committee.

1982   **Soviet Union:** Death of Brezhnev; Yuri Andropov becomes general secretary of the Central Committee of the Communist Party and Chief of State.

1984   **Guinea:** Touré dies and PDG overthrown.

1985   **China:** "Document No.1" endorses new enterprise agricultural policies. **Soviet Union:** Mikhail Gorbachev becomes general secretary of the Central Committee of the Communist Party of the Soviet Union.

1987   **China:** Hu Yaobang ousted from power.

1989   **China:** Tiananmen Square massacre. **Poland:** Solidarity-led government formed. **Berlin:** Berlin Wall breached. **Czechoslavakia:** Government of National Understanding formed. **Romania:** Nicolae and Elena Ceausescu executed.

1991   **Soviet Union:** Collapse of Soviet regime; Comecon dissolved.

1994   **Mexico:** Zapatista rebels rise to prominence.

1997   **China:** Death of Deng Xiaoping. **Cuba:** Communist Party of Cuba reaffirms commitment to Marxism–Leninism at party conference. **Vietnam:** Le Kha Phieu becomes Communist Party of Vietnam leader, Tran Duc Luong president and Phan Van Khai prime minister (all reappointed July 2002). **Mongolia:** People's Revolutionary Party candidate Bagabandi wins presidential contest (re-elected 2001).

1998   **Laos:** Khamtai Siphandon becomes president and two years later leads celebrations of 25 years of communist rule. **China:** Zhu Rongji succeeds Li Peng as premier. **North Korea:** Deceased Kim Il Sung affirmed "eternal president."

2001 **Vietnam:** Man Duc Manh becomes Communist Party of Vietnam leader.

2002 **Laos:** Elections return to power the Lao People's Revolutionary Party which fields 165 of the 166 parliamentary candidates. **Vietnam:** Unopposed Communist Party of Vietnam returned to power in National Assembly election. **China:** Hu-Jintao appointed head of the Chinese Communist Party in place of Jiang Zemin.

2003 **Mexico:** Zapatistas announce complete establishment of their own "state within a state" in Chiapas. **China:** Hu-Jintao replaces Jiang Zemin as president.

2005 **Mongolia:** People's Revolutionary Party candidate Nambaryn Enkhbayar wins presidential contest.

Introduction
History of a Word

"What is certain is that I am not a Marxist."

—Karl Marx

The history of the word *Marxism* tells us something of the history of Marxism itself. The development of the word, of linked words and of qualifying terms is the surface trace of deep struggles within the radical labor movement. Marxism as a movement and as an ideology has always involved fierce controversies, partly as a result of the great richness, not to mention ambiguities, of Marx's writings, but also reflecting the fact that Marxism has always been rooted in political struggle. Schisms have occurred and factions arisen out of real political, and sometimes personal, disputes. From battles with other socialists and with anarchists to fights between rival Marxist camps, the Marxist vocabulary has grown acting as a set of signposts pointing to the twists and turns of Marxist history.

Initially the term *Marxism* and the closely related terms *Marxian* and *Marxist* were used by *opponents* of Marx and his followers.[1] As early as the 1840s opponents of Marx referred to the *Marx party*, and by the 1850s the term *Marxian* was being used by supporters of Wilhelm Weitling to refer to those they saw as blindly following Marx's teachings. Within the First International (1864–1876) the anarchist Michael Bakunin and his disciples used the terms *Marxian*, *Marxids*, and *Marxists* to refer disparagingly to Marx and his adherents, and to their outlook and deeds. For example, Bakunin's followers would typically use the term *Marxist* in such phrases as *Marxist falsifications*, always with some negative connotation.

The word *Marxism* seems to have appeared first in the 1880s, and, although its originator cannot be clearly identified, it was certainly used in 1882 by the anarchist Paul Brousse in a pamphlet criticising *Marxists* entitled *Le Marxisme dans l'Internationale*. In the 1880s the term

Marxism also started to be used in a more positive sense in radical circles in Russia to refer to the movement inspired by Marx. Elsewhere, again shaking off the negative associations the term *Marxist* was used by many to describe the 1889 International Workers' Congress in Paris, and the terms *Marxist* and *Marxism* were used with increasing frequency from the 1880s on by groups, parties and activists wishing to associate themselves with Marx. At this stage those calling themselves *Marxists* or *Marxians* did not necessarily embrace Marx's theoretical position, being swayed more by Marx's personal authority and standing.

Marx's intellect, strong personality, and tactical maneuvering within the First International made him dominant within the European labor movement of the time, and he achieved wider fame through the aligning of the International with the Paris uprising and the Paris Commune in 1871. Marx was identified by the press of the time as the head of the dangerous International giving him a wider reputation. Marx's actual theories and ideas were more slowly disseminated. Initially, the main vehicle for propagating Marx's ideas was the set of basic documents of the First International that Marx wrote and/or edited. Among these were the *Inaugural Address*, Congress resolutions, and the *Addresses to the Council* of the First International including the important addresses on the civil war in France at the time. Gradually the ideas and language of Marx's theoretical standpoint permeated the socialist movement, mixing with the existing and competing arguments and terms.

Marxism as a distinct and dominant ideology also developed slowly but steadily. Friedrich Engels played a key role in creating a Marxist movement and system of ideas. His *Anti-Dühring* published in article form during 1877–1878 clearly demarcated Marx's ideas from those of his rivals who, notably Karl Dühring and the "utopian socialists," were subjected to scathing criticism. This enormously influential work helped to make Marxism the dominant ideology of European socialism, and, in particular, to make it the ideology of the preeminent European socialists, the German social democrats. The German Social Democratic Party (SPD) leaders, August Bebel, Karl Liebknecht, Eduard Bernstein and Karl Kautsky, all embraced Marxism, via Engels, as a system of ideas, and as a label to apply to themselves and the movement they headed. Kautsky in particular took up the terms *Marxist* and *Marxism* and used them in a systematic and positive way to refer to the views he advocated and the system of ideas he sought to further within the social democratic movement. Fighting against the "eclectic socialism" of the time that mixed various ideas and viewpoints, Kautsky more than anyone created an explicit and distinctive Marxist school and program. As editor of the SPD's theory journal *Neue Zeit* Kautsky sought to advance the Marxist school and the idea of Marxism as a science of history.

By 1895 the *Encyclopaedia Meyer* included the word *Marxist*, and in 1897 the first socialist encyclopaedia, *Handbuch des Sozialismus*, referred to *Marxist socialism*. By the new century *Marxism* and *Marxist* were in common usage, being particularly strongly identified with the German Social Democratic Party and organizations of a similar outlook. The Russian Marxists, especially Vladimir Ilich Lenin, commonly used the term as well, although some Marxists, for example Rosa Luxemburg, still favored other labels such as *scientific socialism* or *social democracy*.

In the 20th century the history of the terms *Marxism* and *Marxist* becomes the history of Marxism's divisions and developments. Qualifying terms abound, such as Marxism–Leninism, Marxism–Leninism–Maoism, Austro-Marxism, analytical Marxism, structural Marxism, and even post-Marxism. Also, alternative terms have been created to distinguish schools and sides within the Marxist camp, for example, revisionism, Bolshevism, Menshevism, Trotskyism, Stalinism and Castroism.

So, the neologisms based on Marx's name were born out of the struggle within the socialist movement, initially terms of denunciation that became proud labels. They referred to movements, ideas and individuals, and with their acceptance came the divergence in their usage. They have always been contested terms with some of the fiercest battles being between rival Marxists questioning what was authentic Marxism.

As for Marx and Engels themselves, they avoided or resisted the use of such terms as *Marxist* or *Marxism*. Marx feared that the use of such terms would marginalize his ideas and supporters by encouraging the view that they were a sect centered on Marx. Marx and Engels preferred terms such as *critical materialist socialism*, *critical and revolutionary socialism*, or *scientific socialism*. It is worth mentioning in this context Marx's remark quoted by Engels. Marx purportedly said, "What is certain is that I am not a Marxist," a comment intended to distance Marx from some of the ideas and groups in France claiming to be Marxist and indicative of his distaste of such labels in the first place.

The other words most often used to label Marx's ideas and his followers are *communist* and *communism*, and the most famous work of

Marx and Engels is titled *Communist Manifesto*. The words were not and are not exclusively used to refer to Marxism and Marxists, both being used and claimed by other socialists, including during Marx's time Louis Blanqui and his supporters. Marx and Engels used the word communism in two related ways: to refer to the political movement of workers; and as a name for the society that would follow capitalism. *Marxism* and *communism* are more often than not used interchangeably, and most Marxist-inspired organizations employ the word *communist* to describe themselves. One final lexical clarification that should be made regards the term *social democratic*. Today it usually refers to moderate, reformist center-left ideas and organizations, but in the late 19th and early 20th century it was a term adopted by German and Russian Marxists (among others) to denote their political outlooks and parties.

HISTORY OF A MOVEMENT

In commenting on the history of a word something of the history of the movement has been indicated. In providing a little more of this history the geographical starting point must be Europe and, in particular, Germany. Initially, Marxism had its greatest impact in Europe dominating the European socialist movement at the end of the 19th century and beginning of the 20th century. The largest and politically most successful socialist party of the time was the German SPD. The SPD was formed in 1875, and assumed a Marxist outlook in 1891. As a Marxist party it was the battleground for crucial ideological and political schisms within Marxism. Three major interpretations that emerged were the orthodox advocated by Karl Kautsky, the revisionist espoused by Eduard Bernstein, and the radical led by Rosa Luxemburg. Kautsky defended what he believed to be "pure" Marxism, true to Marx and Engels, and committed to revolution at least in theory. Sustained by a belief in the inevitability of socialism, Kautsky and his followers developed a strategy of political gradualism; they followed a path of legislative reform whilst continuing to proclaim revolutionary principles. Bernstein made the bold leap to embrace reform not just in practice but in principle too. He saw a need to update Marxism in the light of recent evidence that suggested key predictions of Marx were wrong. For example, Bernstein noted that there had not been a polarization of classes, or an increase in the misery of the workers, or a trend toward ever greater economic crises. Luxemburg took the lead in attacking Bernstein's views as an abandonment of Marxism, and she continued to advocate revolutionary theory and practice.

Of the three camps, Bernstein's revisionism may ultimately be said to have triumphed within the SPD. The SPD moved from a fully revolutionary party in 1891 to be revolutionary in theory but reformist in practice in the early 1900s, and ultimately evolved into a thoroughgoing reformist party abandoning its Marxism altogether shortly after World War II. As a Marxist party it achieved some measure of success gaining, for example, 35 percent of the vote in 1912 and having a membership of some 983,000 in 1913. However, its successes fell short of achieving governing power.

Elsewhere in Europe Marxism also made significant advances, though not until after World War II. In France the French Communist Party had a membership of over 700,000 in the late 1970s and had representatives in the government in the 1980s. In Italy membership of the Italian Communist Party was around 1.5 million in the mid-1980s and the communists have been influential at both a local and national level particularly in the 1970s and 1980s. Even in countries such as the United Kingdom, which developed a different socialist tradition largely impervious to continental ideas, a Marxist presence in the form of a variety of small parties and organizations has been maintained since the end of the 19th century. However, in terms of grasping state power the European Marxists have not achieved great success, with the dubious exceptions of the Eastern Bloc countries where the Soviet Union essentially did the grasping.

At least as significant, though, has been the place of Europe as home to many of the great thinkers and innovators in the Marxist tradition. Significant contributors to Marxist thought have included Rosa Luxemburg (Poland); Eduard Bernstein, Karl Korsch, Herbert Marcuse, and the Frankfurt School (Germany); Antonio Gramsci (Italy); Georgii Lukács (Hungary); Jean-Paul Sartre and Louis Althusser (France). Marxist theorizing in Europe has not been bound by the constraints of serving the interests of those in power, for example, fulfilling a role as official state ideology as in the Soviet Union. As a result European Marxists have been the most adventurous and advanced theoretically of any of the Marxist schools of thought. European Marxists have tended to be open to non-Marxist influences, and, simultaneously, have had a significant influence on non-Marxist intellectual life. Humanist, structuralist and reformist Marxism, concepts of hegemony and relative autonomy of the superstructure, combining of Marxism with psychoanalysis, and development of Marxist theories of art, literature and aesthetics have all had their origins in European Marxism along with many other innovations in Marxist thought.

While the German SPD and later European communist parties took the social democratic route, in Russia the Bolsheviks pursued the revolutionary road, and, unlike the Europeans, they did achieve political power. Marxism appeared in Russia in the 1880s, its earliest notable exponents being Georgii Plekhanov, Paul Axelrod and Vera Zasulitch. They led the Russian Social Democratic Party, which was formed in 1898, and it was this party that split into the Menshevik and Bolshevik factions, the latter led by Lenin. From the outset, Marxism in Russia had to be adapted to the unique Russian conditions, conditions very different from those found in Europe at the time. Russia's economy was primarily agricultural and technologically backward; in class terms it possessed a vast peasantry, minuscule working class, small and politically weak middle class, and conservative aristocracy; in political terms Russia was an incompetently ruled authoritarian Tsardom.

The Russian Marxists, aware of the significant differences between the Europe in which Marxism was formulated and the Russia of their time, modified Marx's ideas. In particular, Lenin introduced crucial innovations to Marxism while claiming to be true to Marx. Where Marx and European Marxists saw peasants as essentially reactionary, Lenin ascribed revolutionary potential to them. While the German Marxists all viewed a mass workers' party as essential, Lenin advocated and created a small, professional revolutionary party to lead the masses, and insisted on the enforcement of discipline and obedience via the principle of "democratic centralism." He also laid stress on the need for the dictatorship of the proletariat, a temporary, interim stage of socialism in which a workers' state was necessary before Engels' famous "withering away of the state" took place. The doctrines of the vanguard party and democratic centralism contributed to turning the dictatorship of the proletariat into the dictatorship of the party.

The great success of the Bolsheviks under Lenin occurred in 1917 when they seized power as the already rotten Russian state and fragile economy reeled under the impact of World War I. Surviving civil war and the intervention of foreign troops, the fledgling Marxist state grew stronger politically and economically. However, the death of Lenin in

1924 saw political infighting increase as rivals with conflicting views sought to gain the ascendancy. Most famously Leon Trotsky and his theory of permanent revolution were defeated by Josef Stalin and his doctrine of Socialism in One Country. Stalin ruled Russia as its supreme leader from 1929 until his death in 1953.

In many respects the greatest spread of Marxism, or at least of one form of Marxism, was orchestrated by Stalin. Just as he controlled the Soviet Communist Party and through it the Soviet Union, so he controlled the Communist International and through it most of the Marxist organizations around the world. Marxists from numerous countries came to the Soviet Union for training and education, and Marxist organizations outside of the Soviet Union could rely on support from Moscow provided that Moscow could rely on loyalty from them. It was Stalin who oversaw the takeover of Eastern Europe after World War II, introducing Marxist regimes to a cluster of countries virtually at a stroke. While the Soviet Union made remarkable progress economically and militarily under Stalin, its people also underwent terrible deprivations and experienced the most brutal repression. Stalinism will be remembered primarily as a form of totalitarian dictatorship some way removed from the workers' paradise envisaged by Marx. While the distance between Marx's aims and the realities of Stalinism are evident, it remains a matter of debate as to the link between Marxism and Stalinism.

The success of the 1917 Revolution in Russia inspired the growth of Marxism elsewhere. In Asia outside of the Russian empire, the first growth of Marxism occurred in the Dutch East Indies (later Indonesia) in 1920 when the Indonesian Communist Party was founded by a Dutchman called Sneevliet. The same Dutchman in 1921 helped establish the Chinese Communist Party along with representatives of the Communist International from Russia. Initially close to and supported by the Soviet Communist Party, the Chinese Communist Party grew apart from the Soviet Union and a gulf opened up between them in the 1960s. Leader of the People's Republic of China from 1949 until his death in 1976, and the single most important figure in Chinese Marxism, Mao Zedong gave his name to yet another neologism in the Marxist lexicon, Maoism.

Mao and the Chinese Marxists, like the Russian Marxists before them, had to adapt Marxism to the conditions of their own country. For example, the economic determinism that characterized much of European Marxism had to be replaced with a voluntarism that emphasized political will and consciousness over economic development as prerequisites for revolution. Mao stretched the Marxist theory of class to encompass the social stratification found in China, a class structure very different from that of Europe. Mao also introduced the strategy of guerrilla warfare as part of the revolutionary struggle. The "sinification" of Marxism introduced a flexibility and an emphasis on the peasantry and the countryside that suited not just the Chinese, but other developing countries. The success of communism in China, and in particular the flexible ideology and tactics of Mao, helped the spread of Marxism in the Third World. Furthermore, the Chinese communists supported communist organizations around the world and sometimes directly intervened in other countries to aid like-minded communists, for example in Vietnam.

One significant factor in the spread of Marxism in the developing world was its anti-imperialist stance. From Lenin's theory of imperialism onwards Marxists saw a link between capitalism and imperialism and supported struggles against colonial powers as struggles against capitalism. This encouraged the Soviet and Chinese regimes to support national liberation movements, notably in southeast Asia, Latin America, and Africa. Third World countries were also drawn to Soviet and Chinese Marxism because of the models for rapid industrialization and modernization that they offered. By 1950 the Soviet Union and the People's Republic of China constituted two powerful Marxist states that could provide support and aid to Marxist parties and national liberation movements throughout the Third World. Perhaps the most notable beneficiary of such support has been Cuba, which up until the collapse of the Soviet Union received sustained and substantial aid.

It is noteworthy that the greatest successes of Marxism in terms of achieving power have largely occurred in the developing world: Afghanistan, Angola, Benin, China, Congo, Cuba, Ethiopia, Guinea-Bissau and Cape Verde, Kampuchea, Laos, Mongolia, Mozambique, North Korea, Russia, Somalia, Vietnam, and Yemen. None of these countries could be counted among the most advanced economically at the time they turned to communism.

As Marxist ideas have spread to different parts of the globe, so they have changed. "Russified" in Russia and "Sinified" in China, Marxism has been adapted elsewhere too. For example, Che Guevara, who was active in Cuba and Bolivia, followed on from the Chinese in stressing the importance of creating the conditions necessary for revolution, rather than waiting for the correct objective economic and social conditions to emerge. He rejected any idea of historical stages through which a country must pass before creating communism. He also elaborated a theory of guerrilla warfare suited to developing countries. Amilcar Cabral, the noted African Marxist, emphasized the importance of local conditions in developing revolutionary theory. Frantz Fanon, active in the Algerian liberation movement in the 1960s, incorporated a racial and psychological dimension into Marxist theory as he applied it to Africa. The history of Marxism as a movement and as a theory is a history of diversity and change.

THEORY AND PRACTICE

As a movement then, Marxism has spread to virtually every part of the globe, and as an ideology it has spread to a vast and diverse array of disciplines and subjects. In terms of political influence the former Soviet Union and the People's Republic of China must count as the most significant areas of impact. It is of course debatable how truly Marxist, or to be more precise, how true to Marx's ideas either of these countries has been, and, as has been suggested, Marx's theory of revolution did not point to either of these places as likely candidates for Marxist revolutions. Nevertheless, both claimed to act on the basis of Marxist principles, and for many the failings of these countries suggest failings in Marxism itself.

While the practice of these and other countries claiming to be Marxist would seem to be at odds with much of what Marx wrote, for example about freedom and the future stateless, classless communist society, it would be facile to dismiss any link between Marxism in theory and communist practice. For example, there is a case to be made for suggesting that Marx and subsequent Marxists neglected the individual, individual rights, constitutional checks and balances to power, and democratic institutions and procedures. This stemmed, perhaps, partly through too optimistic a view of human nature and a failure to observe Lord Acton's dictum that "Power corrupts; absolute power corrupts absolutely." The omission in the theory suggests a reason for the totalitarian tendencies displayed in communist practice.

For Marxists the "unity of theory and practice" is a tenet of faith, so the practice of avowedly communist countries has greatly exercised

Marxist writers seeking to understand, explain and assess "Marxism in action." Some commentators, including some Marxists, see the Soviet Union and communist China as distortions of true Marxism, using terms such as *degenerate workers' state*, *deformed workers' state*, or even *state capitalism* to describe them. Trotsky and his followers have propounded such a viewpoint laying much of the blame for the corruption of Marxism at the doorstep of Stalin. Others have seen Lenin as the culprit; even during his lifetime Lenin had his critics within the Marxist movement, for example the Mensheviks who saw him as ignoring the laws of history, and Rosa Luxemburg who criticized him for putting party above the people. The distortions and, at times, horrors of communism in practice have led other Marxists to pursue an "authentic Marxism" looking to recover the "true Marx" with the corruptions of later Marxism scraped away. For example, Cyril Smith, a committed Marxist, writes in his *Marx at the Millennium* that he wishes "to establish what were Marx's real ideas" in contrast to the debased interpretations of subsequent Marxisms.[2]

It is doubtful that a project to uncover a single authentic Marxism could ever be definitively achieved. The history of Marxism has thrown up an irreducible plurality of Marxisms, all linked in some way to the writings and ideas of Marx, but no single interpretation being the one true Marxism. Marxism in practice has led to changes in Marxist theory, and any living ideology must change itself in response to changing conditions and the lessons of practice.

THE DEATH OF MARXISM?

In 1989 the Berlin Wall was breached, marking the end of the Marxist regime in East Germany. In 1991 the Marxist regime in the Soviet Union collapsed, its communist empire in Europe already fallen. In 1992 Francis Fukuyama published a book, *The End of History and the Last Man*, in which he argued that Marxism was defeated, and capitalism had triumphed over its ideological adversary. Fukuyama described Marxist doctrine as "discredited" and "totally exhausted."[3] In 1999 Andrew Gamble, who is not entirely unsympathetic to Marxism, nevertheless began a book on it with a chapter titled "Why Bother with Marxism?" in which he wrote, "Marxism is widely perceived to be in crisis, and many believe the crisis is terminal. Marxism it is said had had a long run and now its energies are spent and its usefulness is long past. It is time to return Marx to the nineteenth century where he belongs."[4] In other words, for many the final destruction of the Soviet Union marked the death of Marxism.

This would seem to imply that a book such as *The A to Z of Marxism* is purely an exercise in history, albeit a useful and interesting exercise. The death of Marxism thesis suggests that the story of Marxism has come to an end and that any lingering doubts about the futility and falsity of Marxism have now been dispelled. Marxist theory and practice have been discredited. Furthermore, Marx died well over 100 years ago, and he wrote the *Communist Manifesto* over 150 years ago. The world of Marx was very different from the world of today, politically, economically and socially, so there can be little of interest in Marxism now. The *Communist Manifesto* must be seen for what it is, simply a historical document, and any truth there may have been in Marx's ideas no longer applies in the vastly changed world of today.

Proponents of the death of Marxism argument overlook several points. First, Marxist governments continue to exist, most notably, at the time of writing, China and Cuba, and Marxist parties and Marxist-influenced organizations continue to be active around the world, the Zapatistas in Mexico to name but one significant example. Secondly, in many former communist countries there is a growing nostalgia for the days of communist rule when there was stability, security, full employment, welfare and a strong central authority. This is manifesting itself in increased support for the old communist parties such as the Party of Democratic Socialism (*Partei des Demokratischen Sozialismus*—PDS), the successor to the East German Communist Party (SED) that ruled in the German Democratic Republic.[5] Thirdly, Marxism is a living tradition that has changed and spread in different directions, so that while 19th-century Marxism may be dated, just as 19th-century liberalism is, 21st-century Marxism is not so easily dismissed as irrelevant. Fourthly, the influence of Marxist ideas in a vast range of fields should not be underestimated. Geography, anthropology, literature, the arts, criminology, and ecology are just some of the less obvious fields in which Marxism has made, and continues to make, an impact. In other words, both politically and ideologically Marxism has not yet breathed its last. Finally, there is the issue of the discrediting of Marxism by the practice of communist regimes. That is to say, those pronouncing the death of Marxism argue that the failings and fall of the Soviet Union show the falsity of Marxism. At the very least, proponents of this view need to show that Marxist theory entails the practice seen in the Soviet Union, and also that the failings and ultimate collapse of the Soviet Union were due to its Marxism and not to other factors. However, it is fair to say that contemporary Marxists face a greater challenge than that faced by their predecessors. For now they are confronted with either defending or explaining the deeds done in the name of Marxism: the Great Terror of Stalin's purges, the brutalities of Mao's Cultural Revolution, and the Killing Fields of Pol Pot. Now the absence of a successful and sustained Marxist revolution and the continuing presence of capitalism must be explained.

So the announcement of the death of Marxism may be premature. History may not have vindicated Marx, but nor has it clearly disproved him yet either. The point being made here is not that Marx was right and that Marxism is true, but that Marxism remains significant politically and as a source of ideas. Marxism, as has been noted, has its own challenges to meet, but it also still represents one of the great challenges to capitalism and to liberal ideas and it will continue to do so for some time to come.

—David Walker

NOTES

1. This account of the development of *Marxism* and related words draws on the excellent "Marx and Marxism" by George Haupt in *The History of Marxism*, vol. 1, edited by Eric J. Hobsbawm, Brighton, England: Harvester Press, 1982.

2. *Marx at the Millenium* by Cyril Smith, London: Pluto Press, 1996.

3. *The End of History and the Last Man* by Francis Fukuyama, London: Penguin, 1992, p. 296.

4. *Marxism and Social Science*, edited by Andrew Gamble, David Marsh, and Tony Tant, London: Macmillan, 1999, p. 1.

5. The PDS secured close to 9 percent of the vote in the 2005 general election, including over 25 percent of East German votes cast. Electoral support for communism is also to be found in other former communist countries. To give just a few examples: in the Czech Republic the Communist Party of Bohemia and Moravia polled 18.5 percent of the vote in the 2002 parliamentary elections; in Russia the Communist Party of the Russian Federation polled 12.6 percent in Duma elections in 2003; in Moldova the Communists' Party of the Re-

public of Moldova holds power, having polled 46 percent in 2005. In East Germany the growing nostalgia for life under the former communist system, particularly prevalent among the over-sixties, is called *Ostalgie*, and opinion polls point to significant nostalgia for the "good old days" elsewhere also with a poll of over 2000 Russians in 2004 by the reputable Yuri Levada Analytical Center showing that 67 percent "regretted the fall of the Soviet Union." In another survey 71 percent of Russians "strongly" or "somewhat" approved of the former communist regime with 41 percent responding either "somewhat agree" or "strongly agree" to the statement "We should return to communist rule" (*New Russia Barometer XIV: Evidence of Dissatisfaction Studies in Public Policy No. 402*, ed. Prof. Richard Rose, Glasgow, University of Strathclyde, 2005).

The Dictionary

– A –

ADLER, MAX (1873–1937). Adler was born and died in Vienna, and his greatest significance is as a leading figure in the **Austrian Social Democratic Party** (SPÖ) and as a major contributor to **Austro-Marxism**. He studied jurisprudence at the University of Vienna and became a lawyer, but his real time and attention were devoted to sociology, philosophy and his political activities. In 1903 he helped to establish a workers' study circle with **Karl Renner** and **Rudolf Hilferding**, and in 1904 he co-founded the *Marx-Studien* with Hilferding. Adler was also a frequent contributor to the **German Social Democratic Party** journal *Der Klassenkampf*. He served in the Austrian Parliament from 1920 to 1923 and from 1920 to 1937 he was Professor of Sociology at the University of Vienna.

Adler was on the left of the SPÖ. He viewed parliamentary democracy as a mask for the dictatorship of the **bourgeoisie** and advocated its replacement by a **dictatorship of the proletariat**. However, he called for this dictatorship of the proletariat to be achieved via legal means and with the minimum of violence. He was also critical of the **Bolsheviks** for having established nothing but the dictatorship of a minority. He supported the workers' council movement as part of his strategy for achieving **communism** peacefully. His theoretical contribution to Austro-Marxism consists in his application of neo-Kantian and positivist ideas to **Marxism**. He sought to elaborate epistemological foundations for Marxism as a sociological theory.

ADORNO, THEODOR W. (1903–1969). Adorno was a key figure in the influential Marxist **Frankfurt School**, and wrote extensively on a variety of subjects, including several works widely considered to be classics in their fields. Born in Germany, Adorno studied at the

University of Frankfurt, developing an interest in philosophy, music and psychology. He taught philosophy at Frankfurt before leaving Germany when the Nazis came to power. After four years in England he moved to the United States where he joined the Institute for Social Research in New York in 1938. The Institute had had a previous incarnation in Frankfurt, Germany before relocating to the United States in response to the rise of the Nazis. After World War II Adorno along with the Institute returned to Frankfurt. Adorno became director of the Institute in 1959 and was a key contributor to the "critical theory" developed there.

Adorno's key publications include *Dialectic of Enlightenment* (1947 with **Max Horkheimer**), *The Authoritarian Personality* (1950), and *Negative Dialectics* (1966). In these and other works Adorno applied and developed **Karl Marx**'s ideas particularly relating to the dominance of **commodity** production in the contemporary world and its impact on culture. Adorno sought to highlight the destruction of personal freedom and the capacity for critical thinking in a world characterized by authoritarianism, bureaucracy, administration, technocracy and instrumental reason. In his work he aimed to help stimulate and cultivate independent critical thought and a desire for and belief in the possibility of radical change. For example, he described the creation of a "culture industry" based on the commodification of art and culture. The culture industry standardized culture, impeded the development of individual critical thinking, diverted and distracted people, and generally served the ends of the existing social order. For Adorno, the pervasiveness of political economy in all aspects of society meant that **Marxism** must focus not just on the economic **base**, but also on the **superstructural** elements of ideas and culture. In this and in his openness to non-Marxist theorists such as Sigmund Freud and Max Weber, Adorno departed from orthodox Marxism. Adorno, along with his Frankfurt School colleagues, was also prepared to criticize the authoritarian Marxism of **Josef Stalin**.

AFGHANISTAN, DEMOCRATIC REPUBLIC OF. The April 1978 "Saur Revolution" in Afghanistan heralded the creation of a Marxist government whose 11-year reign was to be perennially beleaguered by the country's position as something of a Cold War pawn between the **Soviet Union** and the **United States**.

Afghanistan had partially embraced Soviet politics under the then-presidency of Muhammad Daud, who had initiated five- and seven-year economic plans underwritten with financial and military aid from Moscow. The center-left Daud, who assumed control of the country from his cousin the king in 1973 and declared Afghanistan a republic, was overthrown in the Saur Revolution by the People's Democratic Party of Afghanistan (PDPA), a **Marxist** group containing many of his own supporters. The PDPA pronounced the birth of the Democratic Republic of Afghanistan, which was to be governed by a "Revolutionary Council" under the guardianship of inaugural leader, President Nur Muhammad Taraki. The PDPA, buoyed by a freshly signed 20-year treaty of friendship with the Soviet Union, soon announced their **revolutionary** program of reforms. They called for the abolition of **feudal** power in rural areas and the transformation of Afghanistan from feudalism to **socialism**. In addition, the PDPA proposed, and often delivered, the introduction of free healthcare, a mass education scheme, the release of 13,000 political prisoners, freedom of religion, and, significantly, equality for women. However, these rapid innovations were not wholeheartedly embraced in many rural areas, and, further motivated by PDPA repression of perceived "opponents," armed resistance to the government soon manifested itself. The resistance movement was led by the Mujahedin guerrilla faction, which obtained covert funding from the United States.

The events of 1979 paved the way for those of the next decade, beginning with the February assassination of the U.S. ambassador to Kabul, and the murder of President Taraki by supporters of his deputy Hafizullah Amin the following month. By October, Amin had ascended to the position of president, and immediately begun repairing relations with Washington. This proved an anathema to the Soviet Union which, having already increased its military presence on the appointment of Amin, in December sent in further troops and abetted his assassination. Amin's replacement was the pro-Soviet Babrak Karmal. By now, in the eyes of oppositional fighters the presence of vast numbers of Soviet soldiers had turned a factional civil war into an all-out liberation movement. Mujahedin guerrillas, their ranks swelled by those released from prison as part of the PDPA general amnesty, were for the next decade and beyond to maintain a sustained attack upon the Marxist government which inhibited their reformist agenda entirely. Coupled with consistent U.S. aid and aggressive Soviet military tactics that saw vast areas of agricultural land leveled and a legacy of starvation left in their place, the Mujahedin made rapid ground.

Having failed to quell the Mujahedin movement's progress, President Karmal made way in May 1986 for Dr. Muhammad Najibullah. Najibullah displayed reformist tendencies early on in his term of office, dropping the government's nascent **Marxism–Leninism** in favor of a watered down, general socialist orientation. In Moscow, **Mikhail Gorbachev**'s *glasnost* and *perestroika* modification programs meant that by 1987 Soviet troops began to disengage. By February 1989, they had withdrawn entirely, and though Najibullah held on to power for three more years under vaguely socialist auspices, the Marxist era in Afghanistan was over. In 1992, the finally victorious Mujahedin ousted the leader, and proclaimed the beginning of the Islamic State of Afghanistan.

The development of Marxism in Afghanistan was stunted by the double thorns of foreign interference and war, and the progressive reforms made in the late 1970s were soon undermined by bureaucratic Muscovite influence, and the government's basically **Stalinist** approach to political opponents. Before these distortions the PDPA aimed to shun orthodox Marxist stage theory and take Afghanistan straight from feudalism to socialism, a doctrinal belief echoing to an extent those of **Fidel Castro** in **Cuba**. However, internal turmoil accentuated by external intrusion meant ideological development was difficult.

AFRO-MARXISM. A term used to refer to movements that attempt to apply **Marxist** ideas to African conditions. It is also used to refer to the ideology of Afro-Marxists and Afro-Marxist regimes. Afro-Marxism is particularly influenced by **Marxism–Leninism**, although in adapting to African conditions it departs from various aspects of the **Soviet** model of **socialism**. The typical features of Afro-Marxism are a stress on ideology, a central role for the party as a **vanguard party**, and a central role for the **state** particularly in the economic sphere where there is a commitment to a centrally planned economy. **Angola**, **Mozambique**, **Ethiopia**, **Benin** and **Congo** might all be termed Afro-Marxist regimes, and **Samora Machel** and **Haile Mengistu** might be seen as examples of Afro-Marxists.

ALBANIA, SOCIALIST PEOPLE'S REPUBLIC OF. The 1944 liberation of Albania from the Third Reich led to the inauguration of a **communist** government led by the hugely influential leader **Enver Hoxha**. Over the next half century the Albanian regime was fairly successful in pursuing an independent path to communism, shunning other **Marxist** countries including the **Soviet Union** from 1961, and the **People's Republic of China** from 1978.

Given that the country was comprised mainly of vast agrarian lands inhabited by an illiterate **peasantry**, that communism took hold in Albania was something of a surprise, and as of 1941 the Marxist **Albanian Party of Labor** (PPSh) numbered just 130 members. Yet the PPSh gained popularity in World War II as it became intrinsically linked with the resistance movement. With German withdrawal imminent, the party turned its attentions to defeating royalist factions loyal to the Zog monarchy inside Albania. The PPSh was soon victorious and the monarchy was abolished in early 1945. The communists won an emphatic victory in elections held toward the end of the year, so forming a huge majority in the Albanian National Assembly. As 1946 began, the assembly announced that the country was to be renamed the People's Republic of Albania, and though Hoxha wished Albanian communism to be relatively independent from the start, in order to gain economic assistance for his plans to modernize the country, a friendship treaty with **Yugoslavia** was signed.

However, in a move that was later to be replicated with both the Soviet Union and China, Hoxha denounced the agreement and severed all ties with **Josef Tito**'s country in 1948, using the split between the Yugoslav leader and Moscow as a veil to eject Yugoslavians from Albania and commence a series of purges inside the PPSh. What followed was a period of concerted "**Stalinization**," with Hoxha using an Albanian constitution that had been remodeled on Soviet lines in 1946 to implement extensive change. Engineered elections in May 1950 gave the PPSh a gargantuan 98 percent of votes and signaled the final phase of Stalinization in Albania. By the following year industry and business had been forcibly and briskly nationalized, the first of several centralized five-year plans begun, land **collectivized**, and the subordination of **state** to party and party to leader completed. Culture and education were adopted by the regime as weapons with which to indoctrinate the masses with the virtues of **Marxism–Leninism** and "communist patriotism," a form of Albanian nationalism that the PPSh was to use as a core value and motive behind its fierce independence in latter years.

It was such fierce loyalty to the Stalinist route to communism that led Hoxha to call an official halt to friendly relations with the Soviet Union in December 1961. Unlike other East European countries, Albania steadfastly refused to de-Stalinize upon the Soviet leader's death in 1953, with Hoxha blaming the 1956 **Hungarian Uprising** on the regional break with orthodoxy. The PPSh was constantly at odds with Stalin's successor and condemner **Nikita Khrushchev** over this issue, and relations hit a nadir when Hoxha furiously denounced the new Soviet general secretary's demand that Albania and **Romania** concentrate on agriculture rather than industry, a policy switch that would contradict the Albanian chief's Stalinist plan of rapid urbanization. With Soviet–Albanian interactions formally ceased Hoxha brokered an alliance with China, tellingly at the same time as Beijing and Moscow severed ties.

The new alliance brought much needed technical help to Albania, as well as military and economic assistance, and China opened its university doors to Albanian students. The bond was further strengthened when Hoxha determined that **Mao Zedong**'s 1966 **Cultural Revolution** should be replicated in Albania. The aim, as in China, was to rid the country of "deviationists" in order to reaffirm the authority of the PPSh over state and country. Scores of senior army, civil service, and cabinet officials were removed from power, and intellectuals' work meddled with. In early 1967, Hoxha declared that the second phase of the Albanian Cultural Revolution was to begin, the cause this time the reinstatement of Marxist–Leninist ideological purity in opposition to the Moscow-style "**bourgeois** bureaucratism" that had infiltrated the country. As in China **Red Guards** were encouraged to pursue and vilify enemies, and by the middle of the year the **revolution** had climaxed, its aims, declared the regime, fulfilled. Hoxha's adherence to Marxist–Leninist orthodoxy led to his pronouncement shortly after the Cultural Revolution that Albania was the first constitutionally atheist state on the planet. Instead, the deifying cult of leadership constructed around Hoxha meant that he was effectively the God the Albanian people should turn to. In 1968 Albania achieved another first, as it became the sole Eastern Bloc nation thus far to withdraw from the **Warsaw Pact**, as Hoxha berated as "imperialist" the **Brezhnev Doctrine** that had been used to justify Soviet interference in the **Prague Spring**.

Suitably isolated from the Soviet Union and its allies, Albania continued good relations with China into the 1970s. Yet, as with the previous two international alliances, this was to come to an acrimonious end as a consequence of Hoxha's **ideological** rigidity. From 1973, China had begun economic relationships with the **capitalist** West, in particular the **United States**. This proved to be anathema for Hoxha, and after repeated calls for China to halt this deviation from orthodoxy, Beijing slowed aid. By 1978, Chinese assistance had been completely halted, and Albanian unwillingness to bend from an entrenched, Stalinist approach to communism had rendered the country an international pariah. Hoxha declared that Albania, as the only pure Marxist–Leninist nation left, would pursue a policy of self-reliance, and announced a new wave of economic drives and initiatives.

In tandem, he instigated a series of repressive measures to again reassert his and the PPSh's authority, calling for the execution of high-ranking military figures and even the murder in 1981 of one of the forefathers of the Albanian communist movement, Mehmet Shehu. Such actions emphasized Hoxha's strong adherence to the Stalinist mantra of eliminating potential opponents to ensure ideological purity, a motive that resulted in a tangible degree of paranoia among the Albanian government just as it had during Stalin's term of office in the Soviet Union. Accordingly, Hoxha prompted a mass fortification scheme between 1978 and 1981 that saw 100,000 pillboxes erected and conscription introduced. A common enemy, whether internal, external or nonexistent, could bind the Albanians together in a frenzy of nationalism, or communist patriotism, in turn preserving the PPSh regime.

Hoxha passed away in April 1985, leaving behind an Albanian economy in tatters, a state as pervasive as ever, and a crippling international isolation. His regime had, though, greatly modernized the once fully peasant land, brought about healthcare and literacy for all, and advanced the cause of **women**. The task of replacing the monolithic leader went to Ramiz Alia, something of a pragmatist who realized that ideological stubbornness was no longer an option if communist Albania was to endure. Alia set about reforming to preserve, allowing a renewal of relations with the West, albeit on a strictly limited basis. The watershed came in 1990, as Tirana began to communicate with both Washington and the rapidly democratizing Moscow, while domestically consent was given to the privatization of collectivized lands and the legalization of religion. The tide of instability sweeping through the rest of the Eastern Bloc and the Soviet Union in 1989 had proven irresistible for the Albanian government, despite their isolationism. Alongside this ran an economic crisis that left the country saddled with the unhappy fact that it possessed both the fastest growing population in Europe and the lowest living standards. In this intense climate, Alia's reforms simply did not go far enough, and in December 1990 the Albanian people spilled onto the streets to protest against the regime and demand the introduction of a multi-party system. Having initially ordered the army to violently suppress the demonstrations, Alia realized the will of the people would eventually prevail, especially given the atmosphere in neighboring parts of the region, and consented to free elections. In spite of the antipathy toward the regime, the first general elections, in March 1991, returned a communist government. However, turmoil still reigned in Albania, and so it was no real surprise a year later that with communist implosion imminent, the electorate voted in the oppositional Albanian Democratic Party. The result meant the collapse of the last bastion of Marxism–Leninism in the Eastern Bloc as Albania mirrored the course of adjacent nations and headed for democratization.

In pursuing a flexible foreign policy that eventually led to isolationism, unlike many other governments in the region, Hoxha's regime was able to construct its own track to communism without Soviet interference. The Marxism–Leninism Albania pursued was essentially Stalinist to the core, but with a few nationalistic deviations necessitated by the fractious relationship with Moscow, and far less brutality.

ALBANIAN PARTY OF LABOR. The Albanian Party of Labor (*Partia e Punës e Shqipërisë*—PPSh) was inaugurated in 1941 as the Albanian Communist Party, changing its name seven years later. The PPSh was dominated by a steadfast adherence to **democratic centralism**, and the cult of personality constructed around untouchable leader **Enver Hoxha**. From 1978, courtesy of its ultra-orthodox approach to **Marxism**, the party offered ideological inspiration for **Chinese Communist Party** members loyal to the doctrines of **Maoism**. With the introduction of democracy in **Albania**, the party reinvented itself as the social democratic Socialist Party, and as of 2005 once again found itself forming a government.

ALIENATION. Karl Marx developed his theory of alienation in his early writings, particularly in the *Economic and Philosophical Manuscripts* (1844). Using the German words *Entfremdung* (to estrange, make alien, rob) and *Entäusserung* (to alienate, part with, sell, externalize), Marx outlined various ways in which human beings become alienated in their lives, particularly in the course of the labor process. According to Marx, human beings experience a loss of control over their lives and over the creations that constitute the basic institutions and processes of society, such as the **state** and work. This alienation or estrangement means that human beings have a sense of living in a world that is alien and hostile, and they experience their lives as meaningless, unsatisfying and worthless. Ultimately human beings live their lives in a way that is less than fully human; they are dehumanized.

Marx derived his theory of alienation from **Georg Wilhelm Friedrich Hegel**'s notion of alienation and his own critique of Hegel. For Hegel alienation referred to the process of "Spirit" (*Geist*) externalizing itself in the creation of reality, but failing to grasp that the world was not something external to Spirit. Spirit, through human consciousness, gradually comes to realize that the world is the creation of Spirit, and in so doing overcomes alienation. Marx, treading in the footsteps of the "Young Hegelians" and Ludwig Feuerbach critiqued and moved away from this notion of alienation rooted in **idealist** philosophy. Following the line of thought developed by the Young Hegelians and by Feuerbach in particular, Marx identified the problem of religious alienation where human beings create the notion of God and attribute to this creation idealized features of themselves. Having created God and projected on to it our most essential features, we then give it an independent existence and bow down to worship this entity that is entirely our own creation. This process sees the externalization of our essential features and the fashioning of an alien entity out of them which then has a power over us.

In religious alienation we become separated from our essential selves, and this occurs in an even more significant way in the labor process. Human productive active is fundamental to us, not just as the way in which we produce our subsistence, but also as the way in which we develop and express our human potential. However, in **class** society, and in **capitalism** in particular, the process of production is a process by which individuals become alienated. First, individuals are alienated from what they produce. For example, a worker in a factory creates a product which is then sold by the factory owner when, where, to whom and at what price he sees fit. The worker has no control over the product that he has created. Secondly, an individual is alienated from the conditions of the work process, that is, he has no control over the process of production, does not own the tools of production and, increasingly under capitalism has to perform dull, repetitive tasks requiring little imagination, skill or creativity. Thirdly, an individual is alienated from his "species-being," that is to say, he is unable to develop and express his essential human characteristics.

Human beings, according to Marx, are essentially productive creatures and it is in the course of producing that we distinguish ourselves from animals. Unlike animals human beings produce consciously, planning their actions and using imagination and creativity. Human beings can exercise their will and not just act according to instinct, and they are also essentially social and cooperative, but all these characteristics are denied in the labor process in capitalism. The restrictions placed on us by a class society where the majority do not have free access to the **means of production**, where there is a highly specialized **division of labor**, and where control is exercised over our labor by bosses and impersonal market forces serve to prevent work from being the enriching and fully human activity it should be. For Marx the solution to the problem of alienation is **communism**; the overthrow of capitalism with the abolition of the division of labor and private **property** will make de-alienation possible.

The theory of alienation is controversial among Marxists and Marxist commentators with some, for example **Stalinists** and **structuralist Marxists** such as **Louis Althusser**, viewing it as essentially a product of Marx's immature thought and a theory that he left behind as he developed his more sophisticated and scientific notions of **historical materialism** and of **exploitation** in particular. However, **Georgii Lukács**, **Herbert Marcuse**, **Jean-Paul Sartre**, **Erich Fromm** and **Gajo Petrovic** are notable Marxists who have accorded a place of importance to the theory of alienation in Marx's thought.

ALLENDE GOSSENS, SALVADOR (1908–1973). Marxist president of Chile from 1970 to 1973 and founder of the Chilean Socialist Party, he died in the course of a **United States** Central Intelligence Agency-backed coup against his government. He was born in Santiago and before his full time involvement in politics he trained (at the University of Chile) and worked as a doctor. In 1937 he was elected to the Chilean congress, served as minister of health from 1939 to 1942, and from 1945 until 1970 served in the Chilean senate. He was the presidential candidate for a leftist coalition in the 1952, 1958 and 1964 elections before his successful bid in 1970. His government put into effect various **socialist** measures, such as nationalization of major industries and land reform, but it could not be described as Marxist, despite Allende's own Marxist sympathies.

ALL UNION COMMUNIST PARTY. *See* RUSSIAN SOCIAL DEMOCRATIC LABOR PARTY.

ALTHUSSER, LOUIS (1918–1990). A hugely influential French **Marxist** theorist, Althusser put forward an innovative **structuralist** reading of **Karl Marx**. He portrayed Marxism as a science, rejecting **humanist** interpretations of Marx, and promoting the view that there is a radical break between Marx's early humanist writings and his later scientific works. Born in Birmandreïs, Algeria, Althusser studied in Lyons and later at the prestigious École Normale Supérieure in Paris, where he became a professor of philosophy. He was an activist in the Catholic youth movement in the 1930s, imprisoned in a German prison of war camp during World War II, and joined the **French Communist Party** in 1948.

Althusser's most significant publications are *For Marx* (1965), *Lenin and Philosophy and Other Essays* (1971), *Essays in Self-Criticism* (1976), and *Reading "Capital"* (1970 with Étienne Balibar). In these and other works he advanced the thesis that Marx's work could be divided into two: the pre-1848 writings which were concerned with human nature, **alienation** and self-realization; and the writings of 1848 and after which outlined a scientific theory of history and society. These later works superceded the earlier pre-scientific ones and involved a rejection of any notion of human nature or of human beings as the crucial active agents of change in society. Rather, Althusser argued, society is composed of different structural levels that determine human actions and outlooks. The early works were separated from the mature works by what Althusser called an "epistemological break." This break demarcated two distinct "problematics" or theoretical frameworks characterized by different concepts, presuppositions, values, and questions. The early works, according to Althusser, represented an **ideological** pre-history of the Marxist science that followed.

Althusser, though, did not embrace some form of **economic determinism**, but instead offered a much more complex and sophisticated model of society and change based on multiple determining factors. Specifically, he introduced the notion of "relative autonomy," suggesting that the different levels of the social whole were decentered and operated with relative autonomy. In terms of the orthodox Marxist model of society as composed of an economic **base** that determined the noneconomic **superstructure**, Althusser's approach understands the superstructure to be relatively autonomous from the economic base and to act back upon it.

AMERICAN SOCIALIST WORKERS PARTY (ASWP). Founded in 1938, the American Socialist Workers Party was established by the **Trotskyist** James P. Cannon following his expulsion from the **Socialist Party of America**. The ASWP's political orientation throughout its history has been Trotskyist, although in the late 1980s it moved toward the politics espoused by the **Cuban** leader **Fidel Castro**. It has also undergone many splits and factional struggles.

The party was opposed in principle to World War II, which resulted in the imprisonment of Cannon and 17 other leading members under the Smith Act. As one of the original members of the **Fourth International**, the ASWP withdrew its formal membership to comply with the Voorhis Act, while maintaining an **ideological** affiliation. When the Fourth International split in 1953, the ASWP joined the International Committee under the new leadership of Farrell Dobbs. In the 1960s the ASWP influenced the left through its Young Socialist Alliance, which mobilized many university students, causing membership to rise as high as 10,000 by the early 1970s. Factional disputes however occurred over the **Cuban Revolution**. Cannon and other leaders, such as Joseph Hansen, viewed Cuba as categorically different from the **Stalinist** states of Eastern Europe. The ASWP moved closer to the ideological position of the International Secretariat of the Fourth International from which it had split in 1953, rejoining the organization in 1963. A faction called The Revolutionary Tendency, however, opposed this re-joining, and produced a critical analysis of the Cuban Revolution. Its leaders, James Robertson and Tim

Wohlforth, were expelled from the party and went on to form the **Spartacists**.

The party's membership grew throughout the 1970s mainly as a response to its campaign against the Vietnam War. Jack Barnes became National Secretary in 1972, by which time membership had begun to stall. Barnes focused the party's energies on industry, arguing mass struggles were coming, and urged members to uproot and take jobs in industry. Many of the older and younger members opposed this policy and left. In 1982 the party formally parted from its Trotskyist ideology, resulting in a loss of one third of its membership. Former member Weinstein established Socialist Action, and the Breitman–Lovell group formed the Fourth International Tendency.

By the late 1980s the ASWP and its supporters internationally reconstituted themselves in each country as the Communist League. In 1990 the ASWP formally left the United Secretariat of the Fourth International. The ASWP's international formation is sometimes referred to as the Pathfinder Tendency, as each member of the Communist League operates a bookstore which sells ASWP's Pathfinder publications. Since 1948 the ASWP has entered every presidential election, receiving its highest number of votes in 1976 (91,314). The party membership has declined to several hundred in recent years, and in 2003 it sold its New York headquarters.

ANALYTICAL MARXISM. A school of thought that emerged in the late 1970s, largely prompted by the publication of Gerry Cohen's *Karl Marx's Theory of History: A Defence*. In this book Cohen drew on the Anglo–American analytical philosophical tradition to raise the standards of clarity and rigor in **Marxist** theory, a move that led him to distance Marxism from continental European philosophy, and to reject much of the **Hegelian** and **dialectical** tradition attached to **Marx**'s writings. Other important figures in this essentially academic school are Jon Elster, John Roemer, Adam Przeworski and Erik Olin Wright, who developed Marxist theory in the direction of a **rational choice Marxism**. Analytical Marxism emphasizes methodology, and the utilizing of analytical philosophy, rational choice theory and methodological individualism (the doctrine that all social phenomena can only be explained in terms of the actions, beliefs, etc of individual subjects) has led many Marxists and scholars of Marxism to argue that analytical Marxism represents a departure from Marx's approach.

ANGOLA, PEOPLE'S REPUBLIC OF. When Portugal relinquished its colonial hold on Angola in 1975, the **socialist Popular Movement for the Liberation of Angola** (*Movimento Popular de Libertação de Angola*—MPLA) successfully fought off opposition groups to emerge as the leading post-independence power. They immediately announced the creation of the People's Republic of Angola and under the guidance of **Agostinho Neto** set about transforming the West African country along **Marxist–Leninist** lines. Though the MPLA remains in governance 30 years on, long-serving ruler José Eduardo dos Santos eradicated any last vestiges of Marxism–Leninism from party doctrine in the early 1990s.

The decisive factors in the MPLA's victory over rival factions vying for control of Angola were aid from the **Soviet Union** and **Cuba**, and the halting of assistance from the **United States** to those other groups. By 1976 Neto's MPLA was widely recognized as the legal government of the newly founded republic, and Angolan admission to the United Nations followed in December. Though the MPLA had not previously claimed to be of a Marxist–Leninist orientation, it soon became clear that the course it had mapped for Angola heavily leaned toward that taken by the Soviet Union. This became apparent through 1976, firstly with the introduction in March of the Law on State Intervention, paving the way for the nationalization of 80 percent of private industry and enterprise, and then the signing in October of a Treaty of Friendship and Cooperation with Moscow. The treaty meant Angola's fortunes became inextricably linked with those of the Soviet Union, and though Neto had initially argued for the transformation of the country through the implementation of an African socialism similar to that advocated by **Amilcar Cabral**, the MPLA soon formally adopted the scientific creed of Marxism–Leninism as its official **ideology**.

At the 1976 plenum of the Central Committee, orthodox Soviet-style measures were undertaken, with the creation of a secretariat, a commission to direct and control the newly founded Department of Political Orientation, and a Department of Information and Propaganda. A year later at its first congress, the MPLA, previously thought of as a movement rather than a formal political organization, transformed itself into a **vanguard party** with strictly limited membership as propounded by **Vladimir Ilich Lenin,** elongating its name to the Popular Movement for the Liberation of Angola–Workers'

Party (*Movimento Popular de Libertação de Angola–Partido de Trabalho*, MPLA-WP). Though the MPLA-WP instigated measures to encourage mass participation and mobilization similar to those adopted in Cuban Marxism (for instance, in promising "broad and effective participation in the exercise of political power" and creating neighborhood committee groups), genuine authority remained in the hands of the closed, party-based Council of the Revolution.

Owing to its ailing infrastructure, however, Angola could not feasibly embrace Marxism–Leninism with the relish of, for example, Eastern European countries, and to this end trade with the **capitalist** West never halted. Indeed, the country came to rely on western investment in its oil fields for survival, a fact which hastened the smooth transition to market capitalism in the early 1990s. The beginning of the end for Angolan Marxism–Leninism came as early as 1979 with the replacement of the cancer-stricken Neto by the moderate dos Santos. While attempting to remain on the road to socialism, the MPLA-WP was constantly bumped off course as its former enemies, with backing from the Marxism-loathing South Africa, waged a bloody civil war throughout Angola. Resources intended for mass education and health programs instead went on military arms, and with an increasing number of party officials expressing disgruntlement at Angolan adherence to Soviet economic policies, hard-line Moscow cadres were ejected from the government and replaced with moderate nationalists. Pragmatism was beginning to win the inner-party ideological battle against idealism.

As the civil war dragged on amidst numerous short-lived peace agreements, continuous economic decline, compounded by a world oil crisis and combined with the desire of new Soviet leader **Mikhail Gorbachev** to be free of third world entanglements, meant the end of Angolan Marxism was nigh. 1987 saw reforms to reduce the role of the state sector, and moves to seek membership of the International Monetary Fund. In December 1990, at its Third Party Congress the MPLA-WP voted to transform itself into a social democratic party, pledge Angola to a free market future, and introduce a multi-party democratic system. The Angolan experiment with Marxism–Leninism was over before it had barely begun, though the MPLA-WP has continuously held power ever since its cessation.

Throughout Neto's short term in office, the Angolan commitment to Marxism–Leninism remained apparent. In his tenure Angola officially adopted and espoused classic Marxist–Leninist **scientific socialism**. The MPLA-WP advocated the existence of two distinct groups in Angolan society, the workers, representing the "leading force" of the **revolution**, and the **peasants**, who represented the "principal force." The two would come together in a worker–peasant alliance to execute the revolution and bring about socialism. This socialism was only rendered feasible by the implementation of a planned economic framework, which in turn would allow for planning to permeate each and every aspect of society. All of this would be underpinned by the righteousness of the cause of Marxism–Leninism. However, given the exhausting civil war dos Santos was met with when he replaced Neto in 1979, there was simply no scope for ideological purity, and pragmatism meant the end of Angola's once deep-seated devotion to scientific socialism.

APRIL 19 MOVEMENT. When populist candidate Rojas Pimilla of the National Popular Alliance party (*Alianza Nacional Popular*— ANAPO) was defeated in the Colombian presidential elections of 1970, outraged **socialist** party members who insisted the result was fraudulent formed a break-away anti-government group. Naming themselves after the date on which the election result was declared, the April 19 Movement (*Movimiento 19 de Abril*, M-19) pledged itself to a guerrilla battle for political reform and the alleviation of poverty in Colombia. Though ANAPO explicitly repudiated suggestions of links with the group, M-19 regarded itself as the military wing of the nonviolent party. M-19 became renowned for audacious stunts that ranged from the theft of Latin American liberator Simon Bolivar's sword and spurs from their museum home, to the seizure and occupation of the Dominican Republic's Bogotá embassy. Its motivation was to highlight the impoverished nature of their country, and M-19 protests soon took on the form of economic sabotage as it sought to rid foreign **capitalist** business and interest from Colombia.

In 1985, with its influence at its apex given its status as the largest left-wing guerrilla group in the **state**, it forceably occupied the chief power base of Colombia's judiciary, the Palace of Justice in Bogotá. One hundred people from either side perished during the occupation, prompting moves two years later by M-19 to begin the process of negotiations toward peace with the government. By March 1989, M-19 had pledged to demobilize and become a political party in mainstream society. As the Democratic Alliance M-19 (*Alianza Democrática M-19*, ADM-19) it enjoyed early local electoral success and played a pivotal role in the 1991 reshaping of the traditionalist Colombian constitution into a more modern document. In 2003, ADM-19 became part of the Independent Democratic Pole coalition. M-19 never explicitly committed itself to **Marxism**, offering instead a hybrid **communistic** interpretation of **ideology** that mixed **revolutionary** left-wing ideas drawn directly from the Marxist canon with deeply nationalistic elements motivated by populism. In this manner, like the **Zapatistas** after it, M-19 presented a post-modernist take on Marxism.

ASIATIC MODE OF PRODUCTION. **Karl Marx** outlined the chief stages of historical development based on different **modes of production**. Initially he identified three stages of development: the ancient period based on slavery, **feudal** society based on serfdom, and **capitalist** society based on wage labor. To these he added the Asiatic mode of production, mentioning and discussing it in the *Grundrisse* (1857–1858), the *Preface to A Contribution to the Critique of Political Economy* (1859), and *Capital*, volume I (1867). Marx elaborated different features of the Asiatic mode of production in different writings, but the chief characteristic of it is that it is a stagnant society. There is no private ownership of **property**, with ownership of property, and land in particular, in the hands of the **state** or taking a communal form. Marx also attributed to the Asiatic mode of production an essentially despotic form of government and very low-level technology with the economy centered around agriculture and simple handicrafts. He also suggested that a dependency on irrigation requiring a centralized administrative apparatus to organize it gives the Asiatic state enormous power. The state characteristic of the Asiatic mode of production is exceptional in that it does not represent the power of a dominant property-owning **class** as in other modes of production, but instead has an independent, autonomous character.

Critics argue that Marx's notion of an Asiatic mode of production is a product of a European (even Eurocentric) viewpoint, implying that the European course of development is the norm and Asian society represents a departure from this. Furthermore, it also provides a justification for **imperialism** and colonization by more developed countries of Asian ones, and this is evidenced by Marx's arguing for the progressive role of the British conquest of India. However, it also introduces an element of flexibility into Marx's view of development, by undercutting the notion of a single linear **deterministic** view of history where each society must pass through primitive, feudal and capitalist stages before attaining socialism. The notion of the Asiatic mode of production was raised in debates on the possible transition of "semi-Asiatic" Russia to socialism.

AUSTRIAN SOCIAL DEMOCRATIC PARTY. Founded in the mid- to late 18th century under the guidance of Victor Adler, the Austrian Social Democratic Party (*Sozialdemokratische Partei Österreichs—* SPÖ) was modeled on its German namesake, which it later joined in the **International Working Union of Socialist Parties.** In its early years, the SPÖ was plagued by factional infighting between advocates of orthodox **Marxism** such as **Max Adler** and **Karl Kautsky,** and reformists led by **Karl Renner,** but by 1919 had unified enough to form a government under the latter. It was 1945 before the SPÖ was to govern again, largely because of the ban placed on the party by the Third Reich. The SPÖ reemerged in 1945 as the Austrian Socialist Party (*Sozialistische Partei Österreichs—* SPÖ), and governed Austria until 1966. The SPÖ affiliated to the non-Marxist Socialist International in 1951, and by 1958 had dropped explicit mentions of Marxism from its program entirely. The newly moderate SPÖ took the reins of government again from 1971 until 1983, and subsequently as a partner in various coalition administrations. In this era, the party softened its policy on nationalization and advocated privatization and free market economics. In 1994 it polled its lowest total in the post–World War II period, still a healthy 35 percent of all votes cast. Into the 21st century, the firmly non-Marxist SPÖ held the Austrian presidency under Heinz Fischer and remained the second largest party in parliament.

AUSTRO-MARXISM. A school of thought centered on Vienna from the late 19th century until the mid-1930s, Austro-Marxism has been influential on **Marxism** understood as a sociological theory. **Max Adler**, Otto Bauer, **Rudolf Hilferding** and **Karl Renner** were all members of this school and wrote on topics ranging from economics to law, all from a sociological perspective. Methodologically they drew on positivism, marginalist economics and also found inspiration in neo-Kantian philosophy.

AVELING, EDWARD BIBBINS (1849–1898). Aveling has achieved a certain notoriety for the apparently unscrupulous and even cruel way in which he conducted his personal life. He lived with **Karl Marx**'s daughter **Eleanor Marx** for 14 years, during which time he had numerous affairs. After leaving Eleanor and marrying another woman he assisted a despairing Eleanor to commit suicide, but only after he had ensured her will was changed in his favor.

Personal life aside, Aveling was active for many years in the labor movement helping link the British labor movement to continental Marxists through the **Second International**. He was involved in the **Social Democratic Federation** and **Socialist League**, and was a founder member of the **Independent Labour Party**. For a brief time he was viewed as a if not the leading interpreter of **Marxism** in Great Britain. His most significant contribution, though, is perhaps as co-translator of the first English edition of the first volume of *Das Kapital* (*Capital*).

AXELROD, PAUL B. (1850–1928). One of the founders (with **Georgii Plekhanov** and **Vera Zasulich**) of the first Russian Marxist organization, the **Emancipation of Labor Group** (1883). A close collaborator with Plekhanov, he also joined the **Russian Social Democratic Labor Party**, and in the crucial split in the party in 1903 he sided with the **Mensheviks** against **Vladimir Ilich Lenin** and the **Bolsheviks**.

– B –

BARRÉ, MUHAMMAD SIAD (1919–1995). President of the **Somali Democratic Republic** from 1969 until 1991, and chairman of the Somali Socialist Revolutionary Party, Barré espoused an idiosyncratic **Marxism** that incorporated elements of nationalism and Islam, and increasingly moved away from Marxism to "Somali socialism." Born in Lugh (Kana Dere) district in southern Somalia to a nomadic camel herder, Barré joined the police force during the British military administration of Somalia (1942–1950) becoming chief inspector. In 1950, during the Italian-administered United Nations trusteeship administration, he won a scholarship to study at a military academy in Italy and in 1954 became an officer in the Somali security forces. With the creation of the independent Somali Republic in 1960 he became a colonel and deputy commander of the army, and in 1966 he became general and commander of the army. He led the military coup of 1969 and was president of the Supreme Revolutionary Council until 1976 when he became president of the country. His time in power was marked by hostilities with Ethiopia and an increasingly autocratic rule against which a rebellion was initiated leading to his fleeing the country in January 1991.

BASE AND SUPERSTRUCTURE. In describing his **materialist** conception of history **Karl Marx** suggests that a society is like a building consisting of a foundation on which is erected the more visible structure. The foundation is the economic **mode of production**, that is the organization and process of economic production. On top of this sits the social and political system. Marx labels these two elements the economic base and the superstructure. The economic base consists of the **forces** and **relations of production** and Marx's theory of **historical materialism** identifies these as being crucial in conditioning the superstructure. The superstructure consists of the noneconomic aspects of society and includes laws, political and legal institutions, philosophy, religion, morals, culture, and the dominant or prevailing ideas more generally which Marx calls the "social consciousness."

The exact relation between the base and superstructure is unclear and has been disputed by **Marxists**, some taking a more deterministic or reductionist viewpoint, where the superstructure is seen as secondary and derivative and the economic base as primary and determining, while others have stressed the interaction between the two. The imprecision of the metaphor allows for a range of different and conflicting constructions to be placed upon it.

BEBEL, AUGUST (1840–1913). A major figure in the German and European labor movement during the late 1800s and early 1900s, Bebel led both the League of Working Men's Association (LWMA) and the Social Democratic Workers Party (*Sozial Demokratische Arbeiterpartei*—SDA), as well as being involved in the **First International**. He was also an early and significant contributor to the subject of **women**'s emancipation, writing *Women and Socialism* in 1883.

Born in Cologne, Bebel worked as a joiner and then as a lathe operator before devoting himself full-time to politics. In 1886 he and

Wilhelm Liebknecht held a workers congress at Chemnitz which led to the creation of the LWMA, of which he was elected president in 1867. In 1869 he helped to found the SDA and in 1871 he became a member of the new German parliament, the Reichstag, in which he served from 1871 to 1881 and 1883 to 1913. He was sent to prison for two years for treason in 1872 and was again imprisoned in 1886. He also helped to bring together the SDA and General Association of German Workers at Gotha in 1875 to form a party that became the **German Social Democratic Party** (*Sozial Demokratische Partei Deutschlands*—SPD) at the Erfurt Congress in 1891. Bebel played a key role in the adoption of an essentially **Marxist** program by the SPD at the same Congress in Erfurt, and was also involved in the founding of the **Second International** in1889.

A committed Marxist, he nevertheless sought a peaceful road to achieving **socialism**, a theme he pursued as editor of the influential socialist journal *Vorwärts*, which also condemned militarism and **imperialism**.

BEN BELLA, AHMED (1916–). Ben Bella was the first president of Algeria in 1963 and founder member of the Algerian National Liberation Front (*Front de Libération Nationale*—FLN). Born in Marnia, the son of a peasant, he was conscripted to the French army in 1937 and fought in the French army in World War II. He became involved in the struggle for Algerian independence shortly after the war, helping to found the FLN in 1952. He was arrested and imprisoned in 1956, and released in 1962 after France agreed to Algerian independence. He became independent Algeria's first prime minister in 1962 before being elected president in 1963. He was overthrown in 1965 by a former ally, Houari Boumedienne, and placed under house arrest until 1980. After a period abroad he returned to Algeria in September 1990 to become the leader of the Movement for Democracy in Algeria (MDA), and he presented himself as the bearer of the original **revolutionary** spirit of Algeria.

The FLN, particularly in the **ideology** put forward by another key figure, **Frantz Fanon**, incorporated **Marxist**-inspired doctrines. Ben Bella as president pushed through **socialist**-style measures such as expropriating the majority of foreign-owned land and encouraging widespread social and economic reforms especially in the areas of land and education. He did not, though, ally Algeria to the **Soviet**

Union and his one-party authoritarian rule became increasingly autocratic. A significant figure in 20th-century politics, Ben Bella was more marginal within the Marxist tradition.

BENIN, PEOPLE'S REPUBLIC OF. Following 12 years of instability caused when France relinquished its colonial hold on Benin (then named Dahomey), in 1972 a coup d'état allowed military leader Major **Mathieu Kerekou** to assume power in the northwest African country. Kerekou oversaw the immediate creation of the People's Republic of Benin, and directed the young nation's **ideological** allegiance to **Marxism–Leninism**.

Having seized power in October 1972, Kerekou and his supporters installed the 11-man Military Council of the Revolution (MCR) in government. Kerekou himself was to be executive president, and he oversaw the official adoption of Marxism–Leninism in November 1974, a move that prompted a wave of nationalization of private enterprise, and overtures to **communist** countries in Eastern Europe and Asia for financial aid. A year later, the name Dahomey was formally abandoned and the People's Republic of Benin asseverated. The MCR' also announced the creation of the avowedly Marxist–Leninist Popular Revolutionary Party of Benin (*Parti de la Révolution Populaire du Benin*—PRPB), a marriage of far-left "La Ligue" **Leninists** and members of the decentralist *Jeunesse Unie du Dahomey*. A new constitution, enshrining the blending of military and civil authority, and asserting Kerekou's unassailable position as leader of the sole political party, the PRPB, was pronounced.

Under Kerekou's stewardship, the PRPB immediately undertook further moves that signaled its adherence to Marxism–Leninism. Foreign-owned businesses were taken into **state** control, industry and agriculture were nationalized, and measures to undermine the authority of the church introduced. To accomplish this, the government initiated a number of campaigns, chiefly against "**feudalism**" in the majority countryside. This amounted to the replacing of regional leaders, who remained in power from the colonial era, with party approved henchmen. Their job was to oversee the application of the government's development program, which aimed to **collectivize** rural land and expropriate crops for the state. In urban areas, the government's interpretation of Marxism–Leninism meant the creation of a monolithic state sector that, though guaranteeing university graduates employment, left the budget massively unbalanced. Accordingly, by 1977 both civil and social spheres were largely controlled and subject to the direction of party and state.

In common with each of the 12 governments that had attempted to control Benin after French withdrawal, the Kerekou regime was exposed to a number of coup attempts, principally the short-lived mercenary assault led by Bob Denard in 1977. While the government's authority was rapidly reaffirmed on that occasion, it spurred Kerekou into further strengthening his grip on power. He did this by dissolving the MCR in 1979 and replacing it with the unicameral legislative National Revolutionary Assembly. In its opening sitting in February 1980, this pseudo-parliament elected Kerekou president of Benin. The constitutional changes prompted Kerekou's resignation from the army amid proclamations that his was now officially a civilian government rather than a military one. In effect, it also heralded the end of the **revolutionary** period, and with growing economic unease resulting in the concurrent re-privatization of a number of state enterprises, the gradual repealing of Marxism–Leninism as the government's official **ideology** had begun.

As pragmatists emerged and began to assume positions of influence in the PRPB, this gravitation toward the political center was accentuated. Furthermore, with government borrowing levels escalating to subsidize a budget deficit caused by the gigantic public sector, and a crash in oil prices in neighboring Nigeria, the economy was at breaking point. A deep recession consumed Benin from the mid-1980s, and with the country's chief donors threatening to withhold aid until the budget was balanced, state employees were subject to mass redundancies. Those who retained their positions frequently went unpaid, and the number of university places available was vastly reduced. Inevitably, 1989 saw strikes and demonstrations break out across the nation, and with bitter disputes inside the government, Kerekou was forced to approach the International Monetary Fund/World Bank (IMF/WB) for aid. The IMF/WB consented to finance a rescue package so long as Kérékou agreed to drive Benin toward free market economics and democratization. Thus, in December 1989 the president proclaimed that he and the government had renounced Marxism–Leninism, the PRPB had been liquidated, and that multi-party elections were to be held imminently. The 1991 presidential election in the newly renamed Republic of Benin saw

Kerekou soundly beaten, though he startled African politics by emerging victorious in both 1996 and 2001, albeit on a centrist ticket.

That Kerekou announced his apostasy of Marxism in 1989 came as little surprise to those on both the right and the left of the Beninese political landscape, who regarded him as little more than a centrist military dictator. While there were some genuine attempts to implement Marxist–Leninist measures in the mid to latter parts of the 1970s, the PRPB government was neither consistently nor vigorously committed to the ideology. This was reflected through the 1980s, when pragmatism regularly and increasingly assumed primacy over idealism. The Marxism practised in Benin was one of rhetoric rather than genuine commitment to the practical application of Marxian economic and social concepts.

BENJAMIN, WALTER (1892–1940). Benjamin has been described as "possibly the most important cultural theorist within the Marxist tradition." Closely associated with **Bertolt Brecht** and the **Frankfurt School** he produced a range of works on culture, aesthetics, drama and literature that has had an enduring influence. Born in Berlin, Germany, Benjamin studied philosophy at Freiberg University and language at Munich, before writing his doctoral thesis on the *Origin of German Tragic Drama*. Partly as a result of the rejection of his thesis by Frankfurt University, Benjamin turned away from academic life and earned a living as a journalist and art critic. He also wrote a number of pieces for the Frankfurt Institute for Social Research journal. Benjamin traveled extensively, particularly after leaving Berlin when the Nazis came to power, and lived for a time in Paris, ending his days in Port Bou, Spain. Significant in his travels was a trip to Moscow in 1926–27 that stimulated an already existing interest in Soviet cultural life and prompted a number of articles on the topic.

Benjamin's most important writings include his *Origin of German Tragic Drama* (1925), *The Work of Art in the Age of Mechanical Reproduction* (1936), *Charles Baudelaire: A Lyric Poet in the Era of High Capitalism* (1938), *Illuminations* (1968), and *Theses on the Philosophy of History* (1940). The main idea expressed in these works is that ideas and culture have no autonomous existence or history, but are rooted in and conditioned by the prevailing technology and **class** background. He also explored themes of liberation, the centrality of human action and history in understanding art and culture, and **Karl Marx**'s notion of **fetishism of the commodity**. Other themes of religious mysticism, utopianism and pessimism, particularly in his last work, *Theses on the Philosophy of History*, suggest a departure from Marxist doctrines, and leave an ambiguous, inconsistent, but nevertheless profound legacy.

BERLIN WALL (1989). When the infamous Berlin Wall was surprisingly opened and then torn down in November of 1989, what ensued was the unification of the **communist German Democratic Republic** (GDR) with the **capitalist** Federal Republic of Germany (FRG), the end of the communist regime in East Germany, and the eventual unraveling of the stranglehold of the **Soviet Union** on Eastern and Central Europe. The event symbolized something of a death knell for **Marxism–Leninism** throughout the Soviet Union and Eastern Bloc.

The wall was erected to divide the communist east of Berlin from the capitalist west on 12 August 1961, initially as an impromptu network of barbed wire and cinderblocks, and eventually as over 160 kilometers of concrete walls, guard towers and mine fields. The GDR administration ordered the erection of the partition to stem a tide of refugees that had seen some two to three and a half million people defect from East Germany to West since the conclusion of World War II. Such large-scale desertion caused ideological embarrassment for the GDR hierarchy, as citizens fled west to escape the authoritarian rule of the **East German Communist Party** (SED). In addition fiscal difficulties arose, as workers with highly sought-after skills joined the drain west in search of greater financial reward, placing a further dent in the depressed eastern economy. The formation of the Berlin Wall did not, however, altogether halt the defections, with approximately 5,000 easterners making it through between 1961 and 1989. Yet many met a far more unpleasant end, with up to 350 killed trying to cross the heavily guarded wall, and thousands more ending up wounded, captured or both. The Berlin Wall became an almost literal manifestation of the "iron curtain" that had sprung up between communist and capitalist states following the end of World War II, and for those in the Cold War–fixated West, stood to represent the ailments of Soviet communism.

While continued economic relations with the Federal Republic of Germany (FRG) meant that the GDR withstood economic pressures more easily than other communist states in the region, by 1989 the

East German economy was nonetheless ailing. The SED rejection in 1986 of **Mikhail Gorbachev**'s ideas for economic reform, and a growing international distaste for the command economy countries of Eastern and Central Europe, left the GDR to cope with falling living standards and dwindling growth rates. The GDR had become increasingly reliant on aid from the Soviet Union, and so when in October of 1989 Soviet Foreign Minister Eduard Shevardnadze announced that Moscow would now take a noninterventionist stance toward its allies in Eastern Europe, and on a visit to Berlin Gorbachev firmly stated that the Soviets would not back a repression of the campaign for reform in the GDR, Eric Honecker's SED regime was desperately weakened. Power was undermined further in a wave of pro-democracy demonstrations in the GDR and beyond, as isolation from capitalist states and the Soviet Union, and the resultant harshening of economic conditions for communist populations prompted widespread upheaval and demands for reform.

Revolt in the GDR had been brewing throughout 1989. During the summer, scores of East German tourists in **Hungary** had scattered west over the recently demilitarized border with Austria, while others besieged East German embassies in Prague and Warsaw. The result of this was ballooning popular pressure and opposition to the ruling regime in the GDR. This materialized in the re-founding of the **German Social Democratic Party** (SPD), the establishment in September of the Neues Forum, the growth in civil rights action groups, and mass demonstrations on the streets of Berlin (where 500,000 gathered to call for an end to communist rule), Dresden, Leipzig and elsewhere. All of this prompted hasty changes in the highest echelons of the SED hierarchy. Between June and November, nearly 2 percent of the population of the GDR migrated west, and decades of solidarity between Eastern Bloc communist leaders vanished as Budapest allowed tens of thousands of East Germans to pass through Hungary, where previously regimes had maintained the grip on power of one another by compelling visitors to return to their country of origin. With such an air of change permeating the GDR, the government was forced to seek desperate measures to ensure the regime's survival, halt the population hemorrhage, maintain order and quell unrest. Dramatically and unexpectedly, the government of the GDR saw fit on 9 November to open up the Berlin Wall under the supposition that if the people of the east were given the concession of freedom of travel, the breakup of the country could be averted. The opening of the wall was hastened along with gusto by thousands of jubilant Germans who gathered amid wild celebrations to tear down the wall and all it stood for. While the SED leaders hoped this concession to the clamor for reform would ensure the survival of their regime and the GDR, the collapse of communism and the reunification of East and West Germany were in fact imminent. Just weeks after the opening of the wall, the SED was compelled by overwhelming pressure to renounce its "leading role" in politics, economy and society, to enter into roundtable negotiations with opposition factions and parties, and to set up a timetable for the implementation of free elections. On 18 March 1990 the first and last free elections in the GDR took place. The victory of the Alliance For Germany coalition, with backing from FRG leader Helmut Kohl, laid down a clear mandate for reunification of East and West, and the GDR joined the FRG in October 1990 under Article 23 of the West German Basic Law. Within a year of the fall of the Berlin Wall the communist regime of the GDR had ceased to exist, and the SED party fragmented into smaller "successor" parties such as the **Party of Democratic Socialism**. The events of 1989 sparked a remarkable and unexpected end to the great experiment of Marxism–Leninism that had begun in Russia in 1917. As the year began, there existed a general consensus in the West that communism's grip on the Soviet Union and Eastern and Central Europe would last into the new millennium. However, by the end of 1989, communist regimes throughout that region had collapsed or were on the verge of collapse, with partially free elections in **Poland** and fully free ones in Hungary, the resignation of the hardline regime in **Czechoslovakia**, and the deposing of Nicolae Ceaucescu in **Romania**.

BERLINGUER, ENRICO SASSARI (1922–1984). A leading **Eurocommmunist** and figure in the **Italian Communist Party** (PCI) Berlinguer is particularly associated with the "historic compromise" with the Italian Christian Democrats. Born in Sardinia he joined the resistance to the fascists and the Italian Communist Party in 1943. From 1950 to 1956 he was head of the PCI youth organization and in 1968 he was elected to the Italian Parliament. From March 1972 until his murder in 1984 by an extreme monarchist he was secretary general of the PCI.

As PCI secretary general he sought to build on the strategies of **Antonio Gramsci** and **Palmiro Togliatti**, especially in his advocacy of a "national–popular" strategy. In practice this meant abandoning the **revolutionary** road to **socialism** and following a parliamentary route, taking into account distinctive Italian conditions. He advocated the embracing of democratic pluralism and a distancing of Italian **communism** from the **Soviet** model, which he saw as discredited. In 1981 the PCI broke completely with the **Communist Party of the Soviet Union** over the issue of martial law in **Poland**. He believed a third path between the Soviet approach and the social democratic reformist road could be navigated, encompassing both a commitment to pluralist parliamentary democracy and the revolutionary socialist goal of overcoming **capitalism**. He expressed his views in his book *The Italian Communists Speak for Themselves* published in 1978.

The "historic compromise" with the ruling Christian Democratic Party began in 1973 and was an attempt to maximize support, avoid divisive splits and push through democratic reforms en route to a fully socialist society. It was also an acknowledgement of the particular Italian situation where much of the working **class** was Catholic and looked to a Catholic political party for representation and leadership. The alliance held until 1980 when previous electoral gains began to be reversed and the limits of cooperation with the Christian Democrats seemed to have been reached.

BERNSTEIN, EDUARD (1850–1932). Bernstein is one of the most significant Marxists in terms of his political and theoretical contributions to **Marxism**, and in terms of his lasting influence. He has been both condemned and lauded as a **"revisionist**," and was bold enough to try to challenge and change major aspects of **Karl Marx**'s thought. Bernstein argued for a reformist and moral Marxism that favored constitutional legislation over revolutionary action and supplemented science with ethics. He advocated a gradual democratization and socialization of **capitalist** society. His Marxism was evolutionary, ethical and democratic, and his views have been a key influence on the development of the European social democratic movement.

Born in Berlin, Bernstein had a limited formal education and threw himself into labor movement politics from an early age. In 1872 he joined the Eisenacher Socialist Group which merged with the Lassallean Socialist Group in 1875 to become the **German Social Demo-**

cratic Party (SPD). Apart from a brief move to the more left-wing **Independent Social Democratic Party** (USPD) in 1917 in protest at the party's support for the war, Bernstein remained in the SPD for the rest of his life. Between 1881 and 1890 he edited the SPD newspaper, *Der Sozialdemokrat*, and, on and off, for some 18 years between 1902 and 1928 Bernstein represented the SPD in the German Parliament. Bernstein lived in Switzerland and London between 1878 and 1901 to avoid arrest under Prince Otto von Bismarck's anti-**socialist** laws. While in London he worked closely with **Friedrich Engels**, and after Engels' death he was named as executor of his estates and, with **Karl Kautsky**, his literary executor. Partly as a result of this close collaboration with Engels, Bernstein had great influence within the European Marxist movement.

In 1899 Bernstein wrote a book called *Die Voraussetzungen des Sozialmus* (first published in English as *Evolutionary Socialism*), in which he put forward a revised interpretation of Marxism, which rejected the orthodox, economic **determinist** interpretation of Marxism. Bernstein argued that Marxism needed to be revised in light of the empirical evidence, the statistics and facts about society, gathered since Marx's death. According to Bernstein, Marx had predicted a number of important things which were now proved to be false. These predictions included that **classes** in capitalist society would polarize into just two, the **bourgeoisie** and the **proletariat**; that there would be a steady increase in the poverty and misery of the proletariat; that the number of unemployed would continually grow; that ownership and control of industry would become concentrated in fewer and fewer hands; and that economic crises in capitalism would become more acute until there was a catastrophic crash which would mark the end of capitalism.

Bernstein said that the evidence did not support any of these predictions, and in particular there was no sign of the imminent collapse of capitalism. He argued that capitalism had developed certain self-stabilizing mechanisms, what he called "means of adaptation," and these means of adaptation allowed it to stave off collapse indefinitely. The development of things like the credit system and cartels, according to Bernstein, meant that capitalism was a stable system able to avoid catastrophic crises. He also argued that there was every sign of a steady improvement in the situation of the working class through the efforts of the trade unions and the SPD in getting the government to pass measures to improve its welfare and working conditions. He suggested that Marxism as a science could be divided into two: the pure science which consists of the general laws and principles, and which he believed to still hold true, and the applied science, which consists of laws and predictions based on the application of the pure science, of the general laws, to specific circumstances. Applied science he saw as fallible and was where modifications were required.

The key revisions Bernstein argued for were, first, that Marx's science must be supplemented with ethics; the case for socialism, since its occurrence was not inevitable, had to be made on ethical grounds. Second, he argued that revolutionary change should be rejected in favor of reform. Bernstein believed in the steady advance of the working class by gradual reform and democratic socialization of political institutions and private **property**. By piecemeal reform there would be a gradual transition to socialism, but there was no definite line to cross from capitalism to socialism. In an evolutionary process capitalism would be increasingly permeated by socialism through reform. For Bernstein, the process of change was of much greater importance than the end goal. Socialism requires no predetermined goal to guide the tasks of socialists, only a general sense of direction. The shape of the future socialist society was of little consequence to Bernstein; what was important was the pursuit of socialist reforms in the here and now. Bernstein wrote, "The movement means everything for me and what is usually called the final aim of socialism is nothing."

BLOCH, ERNST (1885–1977). Bloch was a German Marxist academic whose chief contribution to **Marxism** lies in his work in the field of philosophy. He utilized ancient Greek thought in his unorthodox and original portrayal of Marxism as an "act of hope" and, in a certain positive sense, a utopian philosophy. Born in Ludwigshafen Bloch lived and worked in Germany for most of his life. He studied a range of subjects including philosophy, music, and physics in Munich, Wurzburg and Berlin, and by 1919 had established himself as an important political and cultural writer. In 1933 he fled Nazi Germany to the United States via Switzerland. He returned to Germany after the war, first seeking to settle in the German Democratic Republic. He was appointed to teach at Leipzig University in 1949, where, as well as developing his own interpretation of Marxism, he defended **Stalinism**. However, his unorthodox Marxism got him into trouble with the government authorities and he moved to Tubingen in West Germany in 1961, where he espoused an anti-Stalinist outlook and broke with his previous support for the Soviet system.

Bloch's major works are *Geist der Utopie* (*Spirit of Utopia*, 1918), *Thomas Munzer als Theologe der Revolution* (*Thomas Munzer as Theologian of the Revolution*, 1921), *Das Prinzip Hoffnung* (*The Principle of Hope*, 1959), and *On Karl Marx* (1971). In these he elaborated his view that the material universe evolves through an internal dynamic toward perfection, and that redemption is possible for humanity in the here and now. He took religious and Platonic themes, but transformed them to produce secular, **materialist** ideas that offered an attainable vision of a utopian free and equal society characterized by an absence of **class** and **alienation**. He advocated **revolutionary** struggle in pursuit of "the persistently indicated" future. His distinctive interpretation of Marxism understood it as a "concrete utopia." By this he meant that Marxism represented a theory of utopia, a future paradise, but one grounded in the historical process. Marxism, as a concrete utopia, is not an abstraction or a speculative dream, but, rather, a future anticipated in the present which Marxist theory shows us how to attain via revolutionary action. This utopianism, according to Bloch, is based on scientific analysis of history and society, albeit a scientific analysis some way removed from positivist or other standard conceptions of science. Marxism, for Bloch, is a wholly future-oriented philosophy that incorporates utopia as a central category within itself.

BOLSHEVIKS. The name Bolsheviks derives from the Russian word *bol'shinstvo* meaning the majority, and refers to the faction of the **Russian Social Democratic Labor Party** led by **Vladimir Ilich Lenin** that achieved a majority on the Central Committee of the party at its 1903 congress. The opponents of Lenin at this congress came to be known as the **Mensheviks**. Bolshevik was officially used in the party title in 1917, and continued in subsequent party name changes until 1952. The term is often used loosely to refer to supporters of Lenin or to Russian **communists** more generally. Under Lenin Bolshevism was associated with the notions of the **vanguard party** and **democratic centralism**; under **Josef Stalin** it came to be linked to policies of **socialism in one country**, rapid industrialization, a **collectivized** agricultural sector, and centralized **state** control.

BONAPARTISM. This term derives from **Karl Marx**'s analysis of the rule of Louis Bonaparte who became Napoleon III after seizing power in France in 1851. In his *The Eighteenth Brumaire of Louis Bonaparte* (1852) Marx argued that the different warring **classes** were at an impasse with no one class having sufficient strength to gain control of the **state**. In this situation it was possible for a single individual to grasp control of the executive of the state and to achieve a dictatorship over society as a whole. A Bonapartist state is an exception to the basic Marxist conception of the state as an instrument of class rule in that the state becomes semi-autonomous representing the interests of no single class. However, Louis Bonaparte's dictatorship did not constitute an entirely independent state with no class connection according to Marx. Marx stated that Bonaparte in some sense represented the largest class in France at the time, the small-holding **peasantry**, but that this did not mean it was a peasant state. Objectively Bonaparte's state actually helped the development of **capitalism** according to Marx, and at the same time also served its own interests. Bonapartism is an important notion in more recent Marxist writings on the state that stress the state's "relative autonomy," for example the work of **Nicos Poulantzas**.

BOURGEOISIE. A term used by **Karl Marx** to refer to the economically dominant **class** in **capitalist** society. Essentially a synonym for "capitalists," the bourgeoisie owns the **means of production**, employs wage labor and controls the **state**, and as such constitutes the ruling class. Marx describes the bourgeoisie as standing in opposition to the other great class of modern times, the **proletariat**. Locked in struggle the bourgeoisie and proletariat can never be reconciled, and the only possible outcome of the struggle is **revolution** and defeat for the bourgeoisie. Although the term has largely acquired a pejorative tone, for Marx the bourgeoisie was a revolutionary class in itself, which overthrew the old **feudal** order and achieved great and admirable things in the spheres of industry and technology. Marx viewed the bourgeoisie as a great force for progress, although ultimately it acted to oppress the mass of people and had to be overthrown.

BRECHT, BERTOLT (1898–1956). German playwright, poet and theorist of theater and literature, Brecht was a committed **Marxist**

who sought to apply Marxist ideas to the theater. His most famous plays include *Mother Courage*, *St. Joan of the Stockyards*, *The Resistible Rise of Arturo Ui*, *Caucasian Chalk Circle*, *A Man is a Man*, *The Three-Penny Opera* and *Galileo Galilei*. In general he focused on the contradictions and dilemmas of modern **capitalist** society, its dehumanizing and isolating effects, and the need for **revolutionary** transformation to create a moral caring and cooperative community beyond capitalism. He fled Germany for the United States in 1933 when Adolf Hitler came to power, returning to Europe in 1950 to work for the Berlin Ensemble Company in the **German Democratic Republic**. Commercially unsuccessful, his uncompromising **socialist** approach to theater (what he called "epic" or "dialectical" theater), nevertheless, has had a profound influence on later theater.

BREZHNEV, LEONID ILYICH (1906–1982). Brezhnev was a crucial figure in the leadership of the **Soviet Union** from 1964 when he became first secretary of the **Communist Party of the Soviet Union**, until his death in 1982, and was the central figure in the Soviet leadership from the 1970s on. The main themes associated with his leadership were "developed socialism," "scientific and technological revolution," "peaceful coexistence" and the "**Brezhnev Doctrine**." The first of these, "developed socialism," was a theoretical innovation used to describe the then current status of the Soviet Union. **Socialism** had been achieved and gradual change was transforming this "developed socialism" into **communism**. The "scientific and technological revolution" was the primary driving force that would bring about communism, and, as a worldwide phenomenon, would heighten the inherent contradictions of **capitalism** leading to its collapse. "Peaceful coexistence" describes the détente between the Soviet Union and the capitalist world (primarily the **United States**), although it did not preclude continued ideological competition, the arms race, and widespread economic and military intervention including "proxy wars" in the Third World. The "Brezhnev Doctrine" outlined in 1971 describes the Soviet Union's position on change in the socialist world. It made clear that any attempt to depart from the Soviet Union's view of socialism in Eastern Bloc countries would not be tolerated, and, if necessary, would be dealt with by military intervention as in **Czechoslovakia** in 1968 (*see* PRAGUE SPRING).

BREZHNEV DOCTRINE. In broad terms this refers to policies put forward by **Leonid Brezhnev** as general-secretary of the **Communist Party of the Soviet Union.** In particular, it refers to the policies of peaceful coexistence and détente with the **capitalist** world, but with grounds outlined for Soviet intervention in other **socialist** countries where the socialist regime was threatened. This doctrine was put forward by Brezhnev in a speech to the **Polish Communist Party** in 1968, and it was used to justify the invasion of **Czechoslovakia** in the same year.

BRITISH SOCIALIST PARTY. The British Socialist Party (BSP) was formed in 1911 mainly drawing its members from the **Independent Labour Party** (ILP) and outside sympathizers who opposed the "Labour alliance," and the **Social Democratic Federation** (SDF), whose veteran leader **Henry M. Hyndman** became chairman of the organization. It included many individual Labour Party rebels and even whole branches from the ILP, as well as other **socialists,** such as those belonging to the Clarion fellowship (sponsored by Robert Blatchford's *Clarion Newspaper*). The BSP was launched in the immediate aftermath of the 1911 strike movement and at the end of its first year was claiming a membership of 15,000. Thereafter BSP membership dwindled until the outbreak of the war in 1914, by which time it had declined to about 300 members in 15 branches.

There was conflict within the BSP, for example between those such as Leonard Hall, an ex-ILP stalwart, who saw the object of the party as to exploit the socialist potential of the labor unrest at the time, and others such as Hyndman and the "old guard" of the SDF, who retained control over the BSP, and who insisted the party had no cause to interfere with the industrial responsibility of the trade unions. Conflict between the pro- and anti-**syndicalists** was a cause of BSP membership decline, which fell by nearly two-thirds between 1912 and the outbreak of World War I. Hyndman and a minority of supporters continued to control the party until Hyndman was ousted in 1916 for his support for the war and replaced by Theodore Rothstein.

Notable BSP members **John MacLean** and Will Gallacher were active in the Clydeside Workers Committees, which called for the organization of the workers and the continuation of struggle until the wage-labor system was abolished. This movement took on a national character through the National Committee of Shop Stewards established in 1917. When the **Bolsheviks** took power in the **Soviet Union** in October 1917 the BSP gave the Russian workers unconditional support and expressed its firm belief in the inevitability of world **revolution** in the immediate future. The BSP supported the "Hands off Russia Campaign" which was successful in halting British intervention. In 1919 the BSP affiliated with the **Communist International** after a party referendum (local organizations voted 98:4 to seek affiliation). The BSP, together with the Communist Unity Group (pro unity members of the Socialist Labour Party) and various other smaller left-wing groups, formed the core of the Communist Party of Britain in 1920, on the basis of support for the Russian Bolsheviks. At the first Unity Congress in 1920 almost all local BSP organizations entered the **Communist Party of Great Britain** (CPGB), claiming to have contributed some 10,000 members (in reality they probably only contributed about 2,500).

BUKHARIN, NIKOLAI I. (1888–1938). An important figure in the **Bolshevik** Party and described by **Vladimir Ilich Lenin** as "a most valuable and major theorist," Bukharin contributed several works of note to **Marxist** theory and was active in the Bolshevik leadership from the 1917 **Russian Revolution** until he was ousted in the 1930s. He became an opponent of **Josef Stalin** from the late 1920s on for which he paid the price of being expelled from the party in 1937, and was tried and executed for treason and espionage in one of the notorious Moscow show trials in 1938.

Bukharin's key works include *Imperialism and World Economy* (1917–18), *ABC of Communism* (1919) written with **Evgeny Alexeyevich Preobrazhensky**, and *Historical Materialism: A System of Sociology* (1921). In the first he argued that **capitalist** competition was increasingly between "state capitalist trusts" rather than between individual capitalist firms. *ABC of Communism* was a standard introduction to Marxist ideas, and *Historical Materialism* was a clear exposition of **Marxism** as sociological theory and a critique of the ideas of prominent non-Marxist sociologists such as Max Weber. Bukharin was initially seen as a "leftist," a position that included advocating, in opposition to Lenin, the continuation of the war against Germany in 1917. He then revised his views coming to favor the New Economic Policy and a gradualist strategy of "growing into **socialism**."

He opposed the forced **collectivization** in agriculture and the over-centralized authoritarian control exercised by Stalin. He was eventually rehabilitated in the Soviet Union in 1988 when the Soviet Supreme Court quashed his 1938 conviction, and the Soviet **Communist Party** restored his party membership. In general Bukharin's stock as a Marxist and thinker rose in the post-Stalin period, as he was seen as representing a genuine Marxist alternative to the Stalinist path.

BULGARIA, PEOPLE'S REPUBLIC OF. With heavy assistance from the **Soviet Union**'s **Red Army**, a coup d'état in September 1944 saw the installation of a **communist** government in Bulgaria. The regime was to last until 1989, and was one of the most loyal to the Soviet line of thinking throughout its tenure.

From 1945 Bulgaria entered into a period of Sovietization. To establish a monopoly of political power "**class** enemies" were executed and exiled, and in November dubious elections were held that saw a 90 percent vote for the Bulgarian National Front, in reality an orthodox communist party. Further elections in October 1946 gave the communists an absolute majority in the national assembly, and left **Stalinists** Georgy Dimitrov and Vulko Chervenkov as prime minister and party general secretary respectively. To ensure absolute political dominance, by August 1948 they had forced the Social Democratic party into a merger in order to create the all-encompassing **Bulgarian Communist Party** (BCP).

Throughout the latter half of the 1940s and into the 1950s, the BCP proceeded with a rapid Stalinization of the country. Industry, commerce and economic institutions were breathlessly nationalized, central-planning organs introduced, foreign trade appropriated and diverted only to Eastern Bloc countries and the Soviet Union, and a brutal **collectivization** program heralded. Political institutions were overhauled and remodeled along Soviet lines, with the dominance of the BCP over the Bulgarian **state** enshrined, and the centralization of power guaranteed, both measures allowing for the emergence of an all-powerful, cult worshiped general secretary. The education system was heavily infiltrated and became an ideological breeding ground for the BCP. Repression grew commonplace with high profile show trials and the introduction of concentration camps. Victims of this repression included intellectual and cultural figures as the government sought to introduce "**socialist** realism" as the only appropriate art form in revolutionary Bulgaria. In 1955 Bulgaria pledged its allegiance to the **Warsaw Pact**, confirming its status as an adherent of Moscow-led **Marxism–Leninism**, and formally recognizing the complete subservience of Bulgarian foreign policy to the direction and rule of the Soviet government.

Progress toward complete Stalinization had begun to stutter following the death of its father ideologue, **Josef Stalin**, in 1953. The BCP began to grow weary of General Secretary Chervenkov's Stalinist orthodoxy, and erred toward a system of collective leadership like that under construction in Moscow after Stalin perished. Chervenkov was soon ousted, and Todor Zhivkov emerged to take his place as general secretary for the next 35 years. As elsewhere in the Eastern Bloc, the 1956 20th Party Congress of the **Communist Party of the Soviet Union** had a galvanizing effect on Bulgaria, with **Nikita Khrushchev**'s denouncement of the excesses of Stalin's rule providing a license for reform. As such, at its 1956 April Plenum the BCP offered a number of liberalizing measures, and even allowed the resumption of trade with the **capitalist** West. The Plenum's decrees led to a relaxation of the BCP stranglehold on the arts and intellectual life, allowed for self-management units within nationalized industry similar to those in **Yugoslavia**, and legalized the underground private economy. These reforms, though, in reality amounted to a strengthening of the BCP's grip on power, and allowed Zhivkov, as the man widely associated with diverting Bulgaria away from the orthodoxy of Chervenkov, to gain increased legitimacy and infallibility as leader.

In essence, little changed except party and leader had been seen to offer reform, in turn increasing their popularity. No matter what management initiatives were promoted on the ground, the state remained in formidable control of the economy through its ownership of the national bank and emphasis on centralized planning. The BCP continued to be as committed to regime self-preservation as it was to a policy of absolute fidelity to the whims of the Soviet Union, and as if to further emphasize the lack of devotion to genuine reform, the communists responded to the 1956 **Polish** and **Hungarian Uprisings** with full support for Warsaw Pact intervention and a tightening of domestic societal control. The BCP's reformist façade had been abandoned fully by 1964, with the death of Khrushchev signaling a return to ideological orthodoxy, a state heightened following the events of the 1968 **Prague Spring**. But with living standards generally and gradually rising, the Bulgarian people were near content to live under repressive conditions; it was when an economic downturn occurred as in the 1980s that opposition manifested itself.

The return to Stalinist orthodoxy began to slow toward the middle of the 1970s, with the catalyst coming in the surprising form of the chair of the Committee for Science and Culture, Lyudmila Zhivkova. In loosening party control of science and the arts, Zhivkova was able to improve relations with Western Europe, the **United States**, India and Japan through cultural connections. This encouraged the BCP to reap the gains of (albeit modest) liberalization, and by the time Zhivkova died in 1981 Bulgarians had gained a number of civil liberties previously unheard of, such as the right to travel abroad, which stood to further legitimize Zhivkov and his party's hold on power. Economic reforms had also been attempted by the regime, as poor performance toward the conclusion of the 1970s led to the announcement of the New Economic Mechanism (NEM), a system restructuring elements of the economy and even introducing free market principles. However, the reforms offered by the NEM were consistently curtailed owing to Bulgaria's ever-increasing budget deficit, and whether offering cultural, civil, or economic changes, the BCP stopped short of allowing anything leading to political alteration.

The death of Soviet leader **Leonid Brezhnev** in 1982 and his eventual succession in 1985 by the reformist **Mikhail Gorbachev** undermined the position of orthodox leaders such as Zhivkov across the Eastern Bloc. Faced with a legitimization crisis, the deteriorating Bulgarian economy and awkward international relations, the BCP resolved that the creation of a common enemy would rally the population behind it and mask its perilous position. The "regeneration campaign" declared by the government in 1984 used Bulgarian nationalism to facilitate widespread hostility toward the country's one million strong Turkish population. By 1989 310,000 Turks had been forced to flee the country, with those who stayed left to inhabit a landscape of prejudice or hope to go unnoticed by changing their names to Bulgarian sounding ones. The party leadership, for a time, had ensured the regime's survival by uniting even oppositional factions in the cause against the invented Turkish "threat." Though appearing in public to follow Gorbachev's *glasnost* and *perestroika* reforms, there was anger at Moscow's reluctance to supply raw materials until commitment to its change programs became tangible, and the BCP began to disassociate itself from the Soviet Union for the first time in its history.

With such isolation the Bulgarian economy was left at breaking point, and it was no surprise that the clamor for widespread reform intensified. Perceived liberalization in surrounding communist countries led Bulgarians to demand civil liberties and found independent groups that stood to undermine the legitimacy of the BCP. A succession of anti-government protests broke out, with the issue of nuclear power in particular uniting the Bulgarian people following the 1985 Chernobyl disaster. The final push for regime change was stimulated by the publication of the July Theses in 1987, a document that laid down principles of economic reform along the lines of *glasnost* and *perestroika*, and called for a "new model of socialism" that contravened the entire ethos of Zhivkov's reign. In the spring of 1989, intellectual opponents of the BCP added to the air of mutiny by defiantly voting against party candidates in academic and cultural congresses. Finally, in November 1989 a peaceful "palace coup" put an end to Zhivkov's staunchly orthodox period of rule, as he was replaced, apparently with the acquiescence of Moscow, by Petúr Mladenov.

Mladenov inherited all the problems of and animosity toward the BCP, and unable to steer party and state away from their legitimacy problem, he was replaced in February 1990 as general secretary by Alexander Lilov. The communist regime had already begun to accept that Bulgaria would inevitably become a free market country, and in April, faced with the realization that it could no longer maintain political monopoly and ideological orthodoxy, renamed and remodeled itself as the Bulgarian Socialist Party (BSP). The party had finally embraced the constituent principles and ideas of *glasnost* and *perestroika*. Multi-party elections in June 1990 perhaps surprisingly returned the BSP to office, but it was to be only a matter of time before the party was defeated in October 1991 the Bulgarian people voted in the oppositional Union of Democratic Forces, ending the communist experiment begun in 1944.

The Marxism embraced and promulgated by the Bulgarian communist regime was hugely loyal, until the Gorbachev era, to whatever course the Soviet Union pursued. The BCP initially followed the rapid Stalinist route to communism, before halting to offer piecemeal reform subsequent to the death of Khrushchev, and then stiffening control through the Brezhnev era. Reform slowly reappeared on the agenda until the rise to power of Gorbachev when Zhivkov pursued an increasingly nationalist form of Marxism in order to remain in power. There always remained a strong ideological commitment to **Marxist–Leninist** tenets and to a strong leader at the head of a party totally in control of government and state espousing ideas and initiatives from the center. Ultimately the regional tide of change proved uncontainable, and as it had done throughout most of its existence, communist Bulgaria followed the Soviet Union, only this time into extinction.

BULGARIAN COMMUNIST PARTY. Having been created in 1919, the Bulgarian Communist Party (*Balgarska Komunisticeska Partija*—BKP) held office from 1944 until the collapse of **communism** in **Bulgaria** in 1989/90. Under its uncompromising leader Vulko Chervenkov, the BKP embraced **Stalinism**. From 1954 to 1989 the tutelage of Todor Zhivkov saw the party remain close to the **Soviet Union** and mirror the policies of **Nikita Khrushchev, Leonid Brezhnev** and **Mikhail Gorbachev** accordingly. By 1990 the BKP had become as obsolete as the communist system surrounding it, and re-formed as the Bulgarian Socialist Party (BSP). A splinter faction retained the BKP name and now forms part of the Coalition For Bulgaria alliance, victorious in the general election of June 2005.

– C –

CABRAL, AMILCAR (1924–1973). Cabral was a Guinea–Cape Verdean revolutionary who led the *Partido Africano da Independencia da Guiné e Cabo Verde* (PAIGC) from 1959 until his death in 1973. He led the struggle against the Portuguese colonists, a struggle that brought about independence for **Guinea-Bissau** in 1974 and for the **Cape Verde** islands in 1975. He applied **Marxism** in a nondogmatic way, acknowledging the vital role of the colonial **petty bourgeoisie** in leading the **proletariat** and **peasantry** to national liberation. Cabral oversaw the political mobilization of the peasants, the training of party cadres, the prosecution of a politically led guerrilla warfare, and the reconstruction of liberated Guinea (about 60 percent of the country when he died) including the holding of democratic elections in 1972. He advocated gradual rural development toward self-sufficiency in food, and a very slow industrialization, with links maintained to the capitalist world after independence. Cabral opposed any kind of coerced **collectivization** in agriculture and his overall approach was characterized by pragmatism and moderation. He rejected notions of a common black or African culture and stressed specific conditions over generalized theories. Cabral was assassinated in January 1973 before the full independence he sought was achieved.

CAPE VERDE, REPUBLIC OF, AND REPUBLIC OF GUINEA-BISSAU. After a prolonged struggle to free themselves from Portuguese colonial rule, between 1974 and 1975 the twin Northwest African nations of Cape Verde and Guinea-Bissau gained independence. While remaining as separate sovereign states, both were to be governed by the same, **Marxist**-oriented political organization, the African Party for the Independence of Guinea and Cape Verde (*Partido Africano da Indepêdencia da Guiné e Cabo Verde*—PAIGC).

Following its inception in 1956, the PAIGC, led by **Amilcar Cabral**, fought tirelessly for liberation from Portugal and the adoption of a Marxist program. While Cabral's theoretical commitment to Marxism was always evident, he steered the PAIGC toward a fluid approach to **ideology**, and as such circumvented doctrinal splits within the party. That stability was threatened, however, when he was assassinated in January 1973. Yet the inexorable pursuit of independence did not halt, and nine months later the PAIGC, now under the tutelage of Amilcar's brother Luis de Almeida Cabral, announced the end of Portuguese rule over Guinea-Bissau. Cape Verde gained autonomy from Portugal in 1974, and as the sole governing force in both independent countries, the PAIGC committed itself to the aim of their unification. Though each had separate presidents from the offset (Cabral in Guinea-Bissau, Luis de Almeida in Cape Verde), policy and governance were to be inextricably linked in the early postcolonial years.

The PAIGC set about remedying the economic morass they inherited through the implementation of Marxist measures. In each of the two states banking, currency and credit were swiftly nationalized and the monopoly of Lisbon-based business conglomerates emphatically curtailed. Road networks were improved to facilitate the distribution of food and expand the fiscally essential fishing industry. To constitutionally reflect the embracing of Marxism, political structures were overhauled to increase popular participation, culminating in the creation of People's National Assemblies. Given the unusual system of single party rule over twin sovereign states, schisms inevitably meandered below the surface. Disgruntlement came from hard line **Marxist–Leninists**, who fulminated against the decentralist nature of the PAIGC government and the overemphasis on agriculture, and from Guineans who perceived there to be a Cape Verdean hegemony on significant political stations. This feeling was accentuated following the PAIGC's party conference in November 1977. Here a motion to transform the party into a **vanguard** Leninist organization was defeated, paving the way for increased bureaucratization, and allowing Cape Verdeans such as President Cabral the opportunity to further augment their stranglehold on power. Accordingly, the aim of unification was relegated to the status of ultimate possibility.

In Guinea-Bissau, these events occurred against a backdrop of amplified economic discontent. The legacy of the war for independence, the rising price of oil, widespread drought and governmental mismanagement of resources all took their toll, and in tandem fueled opposition to the PAIGC hierarchy. On 11 November 1980 a military coup spearheaded by former guerrilla commander João Bernardo Vieira overthrew and arrested Cabral and his cohorts. The new incumbents were quick to deny their coup was a counter-**revolution** and assert their credentials as loyal apostles of the doctrines of Amilcar Cabral. However, these attestations proved apocryphal, and as the decade progressed the Vieira regime gradually shed all remnants of Marxism and began to embrace the **capitalistic** program of its major creditors, chiefly the International Monetary Fund. Predictably, as the PAIGC formally relinquished its Marxism so it did its political monopoly, and in 1991 multi-party free elections were held. President Pereira reacted to the 1980 rebellion by calling an extraordinary party conference, at which it was decided that Cape Verde would now pursue its goals by liquidating the PAIGC and replacing it with a new organization, the African Party for the Independence of Cape Verde (*Partido Africano da Indepêdencia da Cabo Verde*—PAICV). Despite

11 years of pragmatic, peaceful and internationally accredited solo party rule, the PAICV could not avoid the clamor for democracy engulfing mainland Africa. Thus, plural and free elections were held in January 1991, and the ardently capitalist Movement For Democracy Party elected.

The Marxism of Amilcar Cabral informed much of what the PAIGC undertook through its struggle for liberation and in the early of years of its reign, as solidly Marxist measures were tempered with practical considerations. Amilcar Cabral emphasized the central importance of avoiding ideological rigidity for the sake of ideological rigidity, preferring instead a flexible system that would wield actual gains rather than a pure "to the book" form of Marxism. For Cabral, abstract ideas were always secondary to practical considerations of time, place and context. In the 1980s, though, the rulers of both Cape Verde and Guinea-Bissau were concerned evermore with the pragmatic element of this standpoint to the extent that as the decade wore on, the Marxist core of Cabral's thought was squeezed out entirely.

CAPITAL. The **Marxist** understanding of the meaning of capital is connected to the everyday and non-Marxist economist use of the term to refer to an asset owned by an individual which is capable of generating income. For **Karl Marx**, capital is better understood as a social relation than as a thing, and it is a social relation that is specific to a particular historical formation of society, namely, **capitalism**. So, as with the more usual usage, capital does refer to assets that generate income, but in what amounts to a critique of non-Marxist economists and their use of the term, capital can only be seen as historically specific and not as something found in all societies, and also it is not a thing but a social relation. In describing it as a social relation, Marx intends to convey the idea that capital, while appearing to be a thing, actually embodies the predominant social relation in capitalism where the **means of production** are owned and controlled by a tiny minority to whom the vast majority must sell their labor power. Capital may take different forms including the form of money, credit for the purchase of labor power and other requirements for production, machinery and stocks of goods.

Marx distinguishes between what he terms "constant capital" and "variable capital," and these terms are important in his theory of **exploitation** and his law of the tendency of the rate of profit to fall.

Constant capital refers to machinery and raw material used up in the process of production, and variable capital refers to labor power. The former is referred to as constant because its value does not vary in the course of production; it does not create or increase value and represents what Marx calls "dead labor." Labor power, because it is capable of generating value is called variable: its value can vary (*see* LABOR THEORY OF VALUE). The ratio of constant to variable capital changes over time according to Marx, with an ever greater proportion of constant capital in what Marx calls the "organic composition of capital." This increase in the ratio of constant to variable capital results in a reduction in surplus value (because only variable capital, or labor power, creates surplus value), and ultimately in a decline in the rate of profit. The tendency of the rate of profit to fall leads to economic crises and ultimately the collapse of capitalism.

Marx also talks about what he calls the "circuit of capital." He suggests that in a relatively underdeveloped exchange economy individuals produce goods (**commodities**) to sell for money which they then use to buy other commodities, such as food and clothes, that they need to live. This process Marx calls the "circuit of commodities" and he represents it as the formula C-M-C, with C standing for commodity and M for money. In a more developed industrial capitalist economy the starting point is money, which is advanced to purchase commodities such as machinery and labor power in order to create new commodities that are in turn sold for a greater amount of money than was originally invested. Marx represents this with the formula M-C-M', where M is money, C is commodity and M' is the increased amount of money obtained from the process. It is this circuit of capital that highlights the issue of the source of profit: if everything exchanges for its value, where does profit come from? The answer lies in the special nature of labor power and is explained in Marx's theory of **surplus value** and notion of exploitation.

CAPITAL (DAS KAPITAL). The culmination of **Karl Marx**'s life's work, *Capital* (volume I, 1867; volume II, 1885; volume III, 1894), contains Marx's analysis of **capitalism**. In his theory of **historical materialism** Marx identified the economic structure of society, and in particular the **forces** and **relations of production**, as the crucial factors in shaping the nature and character of society, and in *Capital* Marx applies this insight to the system of capitalism, in his words, "to lay bare the economic laws of modern society." Marx's analysis of capitalism is not a straightforward descriptive account of the capitalist economic model, and it is not pure economic theory. Rather, *Capital* examines capitalism as a historical epoch, a **mode of production**, the origins, development and decline of which he seeks to trace. He sees capitalism as a form of economic organization that has arisen and developed only recently in historical terms, and which contains tendencies and contradictions that will inevitably lead to its decline and collapse. *Capital* is also, according to Marx, a scientific and critical work, based on solid research and rigorous reasoning, and containing a critique of both capitalism and the bourgeois political economists who have misdescribed capitalism as a harmonious, efficient and stable system.

CAPITALISM. A term rarely used by **Karl Marx** and not at all until 1877 (Marx favored the adjective "capitalist"), "capitalism" refers to a **mode of production** characterized by **commodity** production and the private ownership of **capital** or the **means of production** by the capitalist **class** to the exclusion of the vast majority of the people. The capitalist mode of production, based as it is on the commodity, involves production primarily for exchange or sale rather than for direct use by producers, a market in labor, a monetary rather than barter system, the pursuit of profit by producers and competition between producers.

For Marx, capitalism is a stage in history preceded in Europe by serfdom and, he predicts, to be succeeded by **communism**. Emerging from **feudalism**, capitalism first took the form in the 15th to 18th centuries of merchant capitalism where overseas trade and colonization was central in its development. In the 19th century the technological advance marked by the industrial revolution saw the industrial capitalism of Marx's day develop and flourish with the corresponding theories of political liberalism and classical economics typified by Adam Smith and David Ricardo. As capitalism has developed and changed since the time of Marx new terms have been employed to describe different phases, including "monopoly capitalism" (**Paul Sweezy**), the era of "finance capital" or "organized capitalism" (**Rudolf Hilferding**), "imperialism" (**Vladimir Ilich Lenin**), "late capitalism" (**Ernest Mandel**) and "state capitalism."

Capitalism, according to Marx, is inherently unstable, riven by internal contradictions and liable to collapse at any time. One of its key internal contradictions is embodied in the tendency of the rate of profit to fall. In their pursuit of profit capitalists will increase their use of machinery, making use of any new technology that becomes available, and reduce their use of labor in order to keep costs down and in an effort to gain a competitive edge. However, **surplus value**, which is the ultimate source of profit, is only created by the labor power of workers, and in making progressively greater use of machinery in place of workers the amount of surplus value generated is reduced, and hence the rate of profit declines. Alongside the fall in the rate of profit there is also a decline in the relative standard of living of the worker. As more workers are replaced by machines so unemployment increases and real wage levels decline as the supply of labor exceeds demand. With profits and wages falling and unemployment increasing, economic crisis inevitably ensues. Production exceeds consumption as demand falls alongside the fall in workers' incomes, and this leads to goods being dumped on the market and many firms going bankrupt. However the crisis will help to restore the equilibrium between production and consumption, and there will be firms, particularly larger firms, that ride out the crisis and are able to benefit from the bankruptcies of their competitors, and which will gradually employ more workers at lower wages thus increasing the generation of surplus value leading to a restoration of profits.

Inevitably, though, the pursuit of profit will see the same cycle repeated again and again, except that the crisis will be worse each time until the entire system ultimately collapses. In other words, capitalism will collapse as a result of its own contradictions; the very forces that drive it forward—competition and the pursuit of profit—will cause it to collapse, having created an agent of **revolution** in the industrial **proletariat** and the necessary conditions for the socialist society that will succeed it.

CARILLO, SANTIAGO (1915–). Born in Gijón, Spain, Carillo's place in the history of Marxism is as one of the chief architects of **Eurocommunism**, an outlook he expressed in his book *Eurocommunisimo y Estado* (*Eurocommunism and the State*) published in 1977. Carillo joined the Communist Party of Spain (PCE) in 1936, became secretary of the Communist Youth International in 1939, and by 1942 had taken on responsibility for organizing the PCE. He spent a number of years living abroad, mainly in the **United States** and South

America, following the triumph of General Francisco Franco and the nationalists in the Spanish Civil War. From 1960 until 1982 he was secretary-general of the PCE, and during his period of office the party gradually moved away from the **Soviet Union**'s influence and outlook, moving closer to the **Italian Communist Party** (PCI), and coming to embrace the alternative approach of Eurocommunism. Carillo's time as secretary-general was also characterized by regional and factional disputes, expulsions and efforts by Carillo to maintain his position. Among the high-profile expulsions were party intellectuals Fernando Claudin and Jorge Semprún in 1964, Soviet loyalists Eduardo García and Agustín Gómez in 1969, and faction leader Enrique Lister in 1970. Carillo himself suffered the same fate being expelled from the central and executive committees of the PCE in April 1985 and replaced as parliamentary leader by Gerardo Iglesias.

Key events during Carillo's period of office included the joint declaration by the PCE and PCI at Livorno in July 1975 which provided a blueprint for Eurocommunism. 1975 also saw the death of Franco in 1975 leading Carillo to focus his energies on campaigning for the legalization of the PCE, a campaign that culminated in the PCE legally participating in the 1977 election. Results in three general elections were poor and Carillo resigned as secretary-general in 1982 after the party polled just over 3 percent. Following his expulsion in 1985 he formed the dissident Communist Unity group and then the Workers' Party of Spain–Communist Unity (PTE-UC) in 1986.

Carillo's Eurocommunism drew on ideas put forward by **Antonio Gramsci**, and incorporated the views that socialism and democracy are interconnected, that socialism can be achieved peacefully through the establishment of "advanced democracy," and that the **dictatorship of the proletariat** and the Soviet model should be rejected.

CASTRO RUZ, FIDEL (1927–). Recognized around the world the bearded, cigar-smoking Castro in his trademark military fatigues led the guerrilla struggle that overthrew the Cuban government of the dictator Fulgencio Batista y Zaldívar in 1958, and has been leader of the country ever since. Criticized by orthodox **Marxists** for leading a revolutionary **vanguard party**, the *July 26 Movement*, that was not **Marxist–Leninist**, he nevertheless declared the **Cuban Revolution** a **socialist** one in 1961, and aligned Cuba with the **Soviet Union**. Under Castro Cuba also has given military and economic support to socialist independence movements in the Third World. He oversaw the nationalization of industry, the **collectivization** of agriculture, the creation of a one-party **state**, and the imprisonment and exile of political opponents and "undesirables."

Castro's Cuba has had a particularly antagonistic relationship with the **United States**, which had supported Batista, backed an unsuccessful invasion attempt in 1962 (the Bay of Pigs), imposed and continues to impose economic sanctions on Cuba, and which has been behind several unsuccessful attempts to assassinate Castro. Since the collapse of the **Soviet Union**, which provided economic support to Cuba, Castro has modified policies to permit some private enterprise. *See also* COMMUNIST PARTY OF CUBA.

CHINA, PEOPLE'S REPUBLIC OF. Having come to power in the 1949 **Chinese Revolution, Mao Zedong**'s **Chinese Communist Party** (CCP) set about steering the world's most densely populated country toward his and their own vision of **Marxism**. Eternally influenced by the tenets of **Maoism** and its practical application, or **Maothought**, the course of Chinese history was altered dramatically following the revolution. From 1949 until the late 1970s, the entire economy was under **state** direction and ownership, as a planning system similar to the one employed in the **Soviet Union** was implemented. Vast industrialization and the **collectivization** of rural land were accentuated, and the adoption of an autarkic approach to foreign policy led to the restriction of trade to Soviet Bloc countries only. It was self-interest too which led to the Sino–Russian split that occurred through the 1960s. The CCP government curtailed relations with Moscow due to territorial and ideological tensions that overspilled into violent border skirmishes in 1966 and 1969.

The Mao era was characterized firstly by a number of Soviet-style five-year plans, and then a series of mobilization campaigns, such as the 1958 "Great Leap Forward." This amounted to an attempt to rapidly increase production while eschewing the five-year plan paradigm, chiefly through placing a greater emphasis on localized economic authority, establishing rural "communes," and encouraging light industry and agriculture. The results, however, were disastrous. The gross economic mismanagement of the "Great Leap" brought about little in terms of advancement in the pursuit of full industrialization, allowed state brutality and coercion costing countless lives, and gave birth to an endemic and enduring famine. Seemingly just as the Great Leap Forward period came to its sorry denouement, the CCP announced a new crusade in the form of the 1966 **Cultural Revolution**. The Cultural Revolution brought about further chaos and disaster, and left the reputation of Chairman Mao indelibly scarred. In 1976, with his grip on power tenuous and undermined by the **Gang of Four** plot to succeed him, the once venerable leader died.

In the wake of Mao's death, **Deng Xiaoping** eventually emerged as his outright successor. Deng had been purged from party life for his criticisms of the Cultural Revolution, and as the new chief he immediately displayed a propensity to negate aspects of orthodox Maoism in his actions. He helped drive out the hard-line Gang of Four who had been expected to take the reins from Mao, and set the country on the road to the "Four Modernizations," namely of the **state**, the economy, armed forces and in scientific research. The Four Modernizations were underpinned by the pragmatic motivation of rapid industrialization and improved trade with the capitalist West. This allowed for concessions to **capitalism** that contradicted established Marxist and moreover Maoist principles, including the creation of a (planned) market economy, stock markets, and Special Economic Zones buttressed by a largely free trade ethos. Consequently, the 1980s were characterized by increased economic and social freedoms.

However, the CCP maintained a strong and totalitarian system of governance, and this inherent contradiction with those freedoms led to an era of tension between government and public. This manifested itself in the pro-democracy protests of 1986, and more infamously 1989. On both occasions, the CCP regime used brutal violence instigated by Premier **Zhao Ziyang** to quash the dissent, most notably in the Tiananmen Square massacre of June 1989. In that same period, the **collapse of the Soviet Union** and the governments of the other Eastern Bloc countries spurred the CCP into further pragmatic and un-ideologically motivated actions, as it sought to extend economic entente with the **United States** and Japan. Until his death in 1997, Deng, along with **Jiang Zemin**, his ultimate successor as overall leader and CCP general secretary from 1989, turned China further toward capitalist economics, decommissioning state-owned enterprises in pursuit of a controlled market economy. Jiang has continued to pursue similar pragmatic fiscal policy, allowing the PRC to embrace a period of unbridled economic growth, though allegations of a patent disregard for human rights still plague the CCP regime.

Chinese Marxism, or more accurately Maoism, borrowed from **Karl Marx** the theories of **historical materialism, class** struggle and **dialectical materialism**, and from **Vladimir Ilich Lenin** the concepts of **imperialism** and the **vanguard party**. However, Mao and the CCP supplemented these doctrines with a number of their own, some of which, primarily the notion of the "Mass Line" in its negation of Lenin's distrust of the "spontaneity" of the **proletariat**, contradicted orthodox **Marxist–Leninist** thought.

CHINESE COMMUNIST PARTY. The Chinese Communist Party (CCP) was constituted between 1920 and 1921, and has ruled in the **People's Republic of China** (PRC) since the 1949 **Chinese Revolution**. Between its foundation and rise to power, the CCP aligned with the **Third International** and waged a rural civil war against nationalist forces, with **Mao Zedong** and his loyalists able to take control of areas of the Chinese countryside and run them as CCP **soviets**. Throughout this time, the CCP grew in size and momentum, and regrouped after the **Long March** of 1934 ready to begin the quest for power over the entire country. This came in the form of the 1949 revolution, after which the CCP effected changes in the newly created PRC according to its **Marxism–Leninism–Maoism**. This often took the form of party-led initiatives such as the "Great Leap Forward" and the **Cultural Revolution**. The latter of these destroyed the CCP's organizational structures entirely, and left the once proudly **vanguard party** in chaos. It took the succession of Mao by **Deng Xiaoping** to restore normality, and from 1978 he began to move the party away from its rigidly ideological position and toward an acceptance of free market-based economic reforms. While the PRC continued to pursue these reforms with zeal, however, the authoritarian rule of the CCP did not come under threat, and it remained into the 21st century a gigantic presence in Chinese life, and with a reported 66 million members the largest political party in the world.

CHINESE REVOLUTION (1949). Following civil and world war, in 1949 Chairman **Mao Zedong**'s **Chinese Communist Party** (CCP) swept into power and proclaimed the beginning of the **People's Republic of China**. The route from rule by dynasty to rule by **Maoism**

began long before 1949, chiefly with the instability caused by the Opium Wars (1839–1842) that had coerced China into opening its ports to Western merchants. Toward the conclusion of the 19th century and into the 20th, China's attempts to rapidly modernize had been accompanied by turmoil, as witnessed in the Taiping Rebellion, the Boxer Uprising and most prevalently the Chinese Republican Revolution of 1911. Here, economic stasis, a demographic imbalance between rural and urban, and increased militancy from a number of independent social forces proved enough to bring an end to dynastic rule in China. Nonetheless, the change this brought about was merely superficial, transforming political rule from imperial to republican and doing little to quash simmering tensions within a China still split by intense fighting between warlords and their factions. Intellectuals in the country demanded that the political **revolution** be accompanied by a cultural one that sought to rid China of its entrenched, seemingly backward values symbolized by Confucianism. This demand for change found voice in 1919 in the guise of the May Fourth Movement, named after a mass student rally against **imperialism** that broke out on that date following the end of World War I. The May Fourth Movement became a vehicle for the expression of radical ideas, and together with the 1917 **Russian Revolution**, contributed to a rising climate of radicalism in China that eventually led to the formation of the CCP in 1921.

At its second party congress in 1922, the CCP voted to join the **Comintern**, and at its third a year later to obey an order from the **Soviet Union** to merge with the nationalist party, the Kuomintang (KMT) under the leadership of Dr. Sun Yatsen, in order to bring about a national revolution. Though this inflated the CCP from being a fringe movement to performing a role in a mass incendiary association, its subordination to the KMT within the alliance diluted its ability to bring about **communism**. This subordination was brutally highlighted from 1925 following the death of Sun and his replacement with the right-wing anti-communist Chiang Kai-shek.

The KMT-CCP had fought together to defeat the warlords and reunify Southern China as part of Chiang's "Northern Expedition," but with that objective achieved, the KMT leader ordered the mass slaughter of CCP members, and was able to establish dictatorial nationalist rule over China by 1929. The diminished and beleaguered CCP fled to the countryside and took the decision to pursue the support of the rural masses rather than that of the relatively small number of urban dwellers as it had previously. This strategy proved to be successful from an early stage, enabling CCP groups to build strongholds in a number of areas including the southeast where Mao came into prominence. This was enough to stir the KMT into action, and in 1934 with the nationalist army encircling their base at the Jiangxi Soviet, 100,000 communists embarked on the legendary **Long March**, in essence a retreat to avoid horrendous reprisals and annihilation at the hands of vast opposition forces. A year later just 50,000 of them arrived in Shanxi to find haven and set up a new base, and with the KMT distracted by the need to repel Japanese expansionism, the CCP were able to regroup and build.

Japan's occupation of Manchuria and the subsequent Sino–Japanese War (1937–1945) was a deep distraction for the KMT, which was intent on quelling the communist threat and preserving its own rule. Chiang was forced to devote most of his resources to fighting the Japanese, and the CCP did much to exploit this state of affairs, creating what it termed "liberated areas" in northern China and taking control. In order to do this it had garnered heavy support among the **peasantry** by protecting them from Japanese invasion, and waging a war on the rural elite that included a redistribution of landlord wealth to the destitute. Once Japan had become embroiled in battle with the **United States** in World War II, the CCP was again quick to manipulate its opponents' diverted attention and consolidate its rule in northern China, laying in wait for the recommencement of civil war with the KMT. As World War II drew to a close, the communist grip on large areas of the country tightened in the face of an ever-weakening KMT government, and the stock of Mao, now the main leader of the movement, rose accordingly. Between 1946 and 1949, the CCP was able to increase its influence yet further, and again by mobilizing the local rural peasantry, it captured the hugely significant area of Manchuria. With KMT forces demoralized, depleted and crippled by hyperinflation, the CCP finally emerged victorious when the nationalist government fled to Taiwan, and on 1 October 1949 Chairman Mao's communist People's Republic of China was proclaimed.

Chairman Mao and his Prime Minister **Zhou Enlai** set about transforming China through their own interpretation of **Marxism**, Maoism. Beijing was designated capital and a "Common Program" was formulated to decree how widespread change would be accomplished. Toleration of noncommunist political parties and private enterprise was declared, and an alliance with the Soviet Union that guaranteed economic aid for China was announced following a visit by Mao to Moscow. Also, the new regime intervened in the Korean War to protect its communist comrades in **North Korea**, and instigated in 1953 the first five-year plan to nationalize and **collectivize** rural land. In 1958 the "Great Leap Forward" was initiated. This was a program aimed at bringing about rapid urban industrialization and local authority for rural communities. However, the primary consequence of the Great Leap was famine and an enormous number of fatalities, and the chaotic and disastrous **Cultural Revolution** of 1966 to 1976 was also in part a consequence. In between the end of the Great Leap and the commencement of the Cultural Revolution, the People's Republic completely broke off relations with the Soviet Union and continued to designate its own path to communism.

The 1949 revolution in China was to some extent a cousin of that in Russia 32 years previously, in that 1917 had provided a framework to follow for bringing about Marxism and it too had originated from a ruling power's failure in war. However, the CCP's insurrection sprang more from a conjuncture of internal factors running back over the previous 100 years of Chinese history. While employing a **vanguard party** of "professional revolutionaries" as **Marxism–Leninism** decreed, Mao deviated from that orthodox path by substituting the peasantry for an industrialized working **class**. While Marx had argued, for example in his analysis of the 1848 **revolutions**, that **socialist** upheaval was impossible without a strong urban **proletariat**, Mao attempted to prove otherwise by adopting his theory of revolution according to conditions in contemporary China.

CLASS. Although, surprisingly, **Karl Marx** did not elaborate a systematic theory of it, nevertheless the concept of class is central in **Marxist** theory. In the *Communist Manifesto* Marx wrote, "The history of all hitherto existing society is the history of class struggles." For Marx, the most prominent feature of history is class conflict and in all but the most primitive of societies Marx believed that classes had existed, and that throughout history classes had been locked in conflict. Marx did not invent or discover classes, and there is nothing inherently radical or revolutionary about a theory of class. Many other writers very different in political outlook from Marx had written about classes including Niccolò Machiavelli and Adam Smith to name but two, but what Marx did was to put classes and class conflict center-stage, and to give a new understanding of what classes are. Marx defined classes in a new and distinctive way that related them to the **means of production**, and he argued that the class to which we belong influences our consciousness, the ideas and outlook we have. Furthermore, Marx argued that class conflict was not only inevitable but also necessary for history to progress.

Classes are defined by Marx in terms of their relationship to the means of production, or to the prevailing mode of production. The fundamental factor in defining class is whether or not the members of a class own the means of production, and what kind of means of production they own. For example, feudal lords or landowners are defined as a class by their ownership of land, and capitalists are defined by their ownership of **capital**. Other classes are defined by their non-ownership of the means of production, for example, serfs in **feudal** society or workers in capitalist society. Workers own nothing but their capacity to work or their labor power, and in order to live they sell their labor power to those who do own the means of production, namely the capitalists. In the *Communist Manifesto* Marx identifies two great classes in capitalist society, the **proletariat** and the **bourgeoisie**. According to Marx, society is becoming increasingly polarized into these two classes. The proletariat consists of the workers or working class, those who own nothing but their capacity to work, and the bourgeoisie consists of those who own the means of production, specifically those who own capital, in other words the capitalists.

In *Capital* Marx identifies three rather than two main classes, and he defines them in terms of their source of revenue. These three classes are: workers or wage laborers who own nothing but their labor power, and this is their source of revenue or income which they receive in the form of wages; capitalists who own capital, and this is their source of revenue, which they receive in the form of profit; and landowners, whose source of revenue is their land, which they receive in the form of rent. Marx is aware of the existence of other classes, various intermediary classes that do not exactly fit into any of the three main classes noted already. These include the petty bourgeoisie (for example shopkeepers) and **peasant** smallholders. These smaller classes blur distinctions between the main classes, but are of little importance, having no significant role to play in the development of society. The capitalists and landowners by contrast are important because they constitute the ruling classes in society, and the workers are important because they constitute the majority class in society and have the capability to overthrow the ruling classes.

According to Marx, all classes develop out of common conditions, common interests and common antagonisms. They have a common experience and develop a common outlook, and they only gradually emerge as fully fledged classes. The proletariat gradually developed as a class out of the remnants of old feudal classes, peasants and artisans who were pressed into service in the newly created factories. These new industrial workers became a class in course of conflict and struggle with the equally new capitalists, a struggle that first occurred in single factories or workplaces, and then, as unions developed, spread to a whole trade, eventually widening until it included all workers. The proletariat as a whole became aware of itself as a single class with a common interest and with a common enemy in the capitalist. This development of an awareness of a class identity is the process of the formation of **class consciousness**, and proletarian class consciousness is a vital prerequisite for **revolution**.

A distinction is suggested in Marx's writings between class membership and class consciousness. A worker may belong to the working class by virtue of his owning nothing but his labor power, but not have a subjective awareness of his class identity. He will only have full subjective awareness, that is full class consciousness when he is aware of belonging to the working class, and is aware of the common interest and common enemy of that class. This is the difference between what Marx calls a "class in itself" and a "class for itself," the former being when the workers still lack class consciousness, and the latter being a class that is engaged in class struggle and is conscious of its interests in opposition to the interests of other classes. The proletariat only truly becomes a class for itself when its members organize themselves politically on class lines and when they realize that the only way they can be free is to overthrow capitalism.

Later Marxists have struggled to outline a coherent theory of class that addresses the problems and omissions in Marx's comments. For example, **Eduard Bernstein** and **Nico Poulantzas** have both focused on the problem of the growth of the middle classes and the conflict of this phenomenon with Marx's prediction of an increasing polarization of classes into the proletariat and the bourgeoisie. This problem points to a central omission in Marx's writings on class, namely a precise definition of the proletariat. Managers, professionals, housewives/husbands, service workers are all groups that pose problems for delineating the boundaries of the proletariat. Further difficulties concern the application of the theory outside of Europe (*see* ASIATIC MODE OF PRODUCTION), particularly the role of the peasantry in the revolutionary process, the classification of classes in the "socialist" **Soviet Union** where there was no private ownership of the means of production, and the relation of class struggle to other forms of struggle such as that of nations, races and **women**.

CLASS CONSCIOUSNESS. Classes, according to **Karl Marx**, inevitably develop their own identity, interests and outlook. Class consciousness is the development of an awareness of belonging to a class, of that class's interest and its enemy. The **proletariat**, although defined essentially by its nonownership of the **means of production**, only becomes a class in the full sense when it gains class consciousness. This class consciousness manifests itself in a sense of solidarity and the formation of separate political organizations based on class identity. With the development of class consciousness the proletariat turns from being a "class in itself," where class identity is essentially passive, to being a "class for itself," where class identity is conscious and active. For the proletariat class consciousness means **revolutionary** consciousness since only through revolution and the overthrow of **capitalism** can the true interests of the proletariat be achieved.

For Marx class consciousness develops more or less spontaneously in the course of class conflict. However, later Marxists, notably **Karl Kautsky** and **Vladimir Ilich Lenin**, argued that revolutionary class consciousness had to be brought to the workers from the "outside," that is to say, **socialist** intellectuals or a **vanguard party** with a highly developed class consciousness had to educate and guide the proletariat to avoid a lapse into a reformist, "trade union consciousness" that failed to move beyond demands for better pay and conditions to the call for an outright revolution.

CLASS STRUGGLE. The importance of the concept of class struggle to **Marxism** is affirmed by its appearance in the very first line of the *Communist Manifesto* (1848): "The history of all hitherto existing society is the history of class struggles." For **Karl Marx**, the class struggle is an inevitable conflict process out of which emerges a revolutionary **proletariat** instilled with a fully developed sense of **class consciousness** and ready to overturn **capitalism** in favor of **socialism**.

The conflict between classes begins with the emergence of distinct classes, which, in turn, is the product of the development of productive forces and the social division of labor. When a society enters a stage of surplus production, one class, in Marx's time the **bourgeoisie**, is able to benefit via the expropriation of the surplus created by another, in Marx's day the proletariat. Inevitably, this leads to class-based tensions as the two fall into direct conflict with one another, and so begins the process of the class struggle. As the proletariat, with its ever-developing sense of class consciousness, starts to realize its interests are pitted in direct opposition to those of the bourgeoisie, so begins the process of workers uniting to fight for their common cause, namely the replacement of capitalism with socialism and ultimately **communism**. Marx saw this struggle as taking various forms: political, economic and violent, with the final overthrow of capitalism most likely requiring violent **revolution**. However, Marx stated that revolution could only happen once the class struggle occurring in the individual factory spread through society to become a more general movement. As he and **Friedrich Engels** postulated in the *Communist Manifesto*, "the numerous local struggles" would have to make way for "one national struggle between classes" to produce revolution. Only at this point would the proletariat have become not merely a class "in itself" but one "for itself," and as such one ready to organize for a socialist revolution, conscious of its identity, its enemy and its purpose. Following the proletarian revolution and the initial period of the **dictatorship of the proletariat**, social classes would disappear and class struggle would fade into history. The withering away of class boundaries would be followed by a withering away of the state and the emergence of a fully communist society characterized in part by the complete absence of classes and class struggle.

COLLAPSE OF THE SOVIET UNION (1991). The 1985 appointment of **Mikhail Gorbachev** as general secretary of the **Communist Party of the Soviet Union** (CPSU) heralded a period of transition in the country that would ultimately lead to its dissolution. Gorbachev's rule was characterized from the outset by "*perestroika*" and "*glasnost*" policies of liberalization and reform that sought to remedy the rapidly deteriorating Soviet economy and polity. This openness and social relaxation in turn gave encouragement to burgeoning independence movements in the **Soviet Union**'s constituent republics. By the end of the 1980s, in a context of successive communist regimes across Eastern Europe foundering under popular pressure, independence groups pushed for and gained constitutional changes legalizing their existence. With the emergence of multi-party politics for the first time since the 1917 **Russian Revolution**, CPSU hegemony was under threat. Wary of this, in August 1991 party hard-liners attempted a coup d'état against Gorbachev but were soon repelled. This further highlighted Gorbachev and the Soviet Union's vulnerability to both internal and external pressures, and on Christmas Day 1991 the leader handed the reigns of government to Boris Yeltsin. The dissolution of the Soviet Union was announced the following day, and its 15 member countries became independent, though some temporarily remained aligned to Moscow in the short-lived Commonwealth of Independent States (CIS). Outside of the Soviet Union, the events of 1991 had marked effects. In Africa and across other parts of the world, **Marxist–Leninist** regimes formerly reliant on Soviet aid were forced to disband or embrace social democratic politics. For critics, the collapse of the Soviet Union signified the end of the Marxist epoch and the triumph of the values of liberalism and **capitalism**.

COLLECTIVIZATION. The policy of collectivization was promoted in the **Soviet Union** by **Josef Stalin** from 1929 onwards, and involved the forcible elimination of small-scale peasant farming and its replacement by a system of large communal farms to which all peasants had to belong. The aim was to create a more efficient agricultural sector able to produce more food, accumulate capital and with fewer workers, so increasing labor available to industry. In addition, collectivization was in keeping with anti-individualist, pro-communal Marxist ideology. The policy was also intended to eliminate conservative and even bourgeois traits within the peasantry, replacing them with a revolutionary communist spirit. Collectivization was extended to **China** and Eastern Bloc countries after World War II, but in the Soviet Union, China and the Eastern Bloc it was not a success.

COMINFORM. *See* COMMUNIST INFORMATION BUREAU.

COMINTERN. *See* COMMUNIST INTERNATIONAL.

COMMODITY. According to **Karl Marx**, the commodity is the cornerstone of **capitalism** and commodity production is a key defining characteristic of capitalism. Marx begins his investigation of capitalism in *Capital* with an analysis of the commodity. A commodity is something that is produced for exchange rather than something produced for immediate use or consumption by the producer. According to Marx, every commodity combines two aspects: use value and exchange value. Use value refers to the power of a commodity to satisfy some human want, or put simply what the commodity is used for. Exchange value refers to what a commodity can be exchanged for, in other words its power to command other commodities in exchange for itself in a particular ratio. The value of a commodity is the amount of labor embodied in it (*see* LABOR THEORY OF VALUE), and the labor that creates a commodity can be viewed as either concrete labor, that is a particular kind of labor (such as weaving) that produces a particular use value (such as cloth), or as abstract labor. Abstract labor represents labor in an undifferentiated way, as just labor that creates exchange value, and only occurs in a system where commodities are exchanged and the labor embodied in them has to be commensurable. Marx identifies one particular commodity as crucial in capitalism because of its unique ability to create value, and this commodity is labor power. Labor power is the source of surplus value and ultimately of profit in capitalism (*see* EXPLOITATION; FETISHISM OF THE COMMODITY; SURPLUS VALUE).

COMMODITY FETISHISM. *See* FETISHISM OF THE COMMODITY.

COMMUNISM. The term communism is often used as a synonym for **socialism** and **Marxism**, and, although most strongly associated with **Karl Marx**, it has a history pre-dating and independent of Marxism. Marx used the term to refer to both the **revolutionary** movement of workers in **capitalist** society, and the future society that would supercede capitalism. For much of the second half of the 19th century, no great distinction, and certainly no systematic or consistent distinction, was drawn between the terms communism and socialism, but after 1917 and the creation of the **Third International** and sprouting of distinct communist parties, communism and socialism came to acquire different meanings and to attach to different movements. With the advent of **Stalinism** this distinction was made stronger with communism unavoidably linked to the totalitarian regime of the **Soviet Union** and later its satellites, and socialism claimed as a label by reformist, more moderate and less statist left-wing parties that were committed to democratic structures and processes. The movement by West European communist parties away from the Soviet line and toward a democratic **Eurocommunism** once again blurred the line between communism and socialism.

In terms of a future, post-revolutionary society, the word communism was used by Marx from the 1844 *Economic and Philosophical Manuscripts* right through to *Capital* III, but at no point did Marx describe in detail what the future communist society would look like. Nevertheless, from various scattered comments, it is possible to discern a number of features: common ownership of the **means of production**; an end to the **division of labor**; an end to **alienation** and **exploitation**; no **classes**; no **state**; no scarcity; transformed conditions of production; and transformed human beings able to achieve true self-realization. In a society with common ownership there can be no classes, and with no classes there will no longer be a state in the sense of centralized power and a coercive body used by one class to suppress another class. Marx suggests there will be no standing army, no police, no bureaucracy, no judiciary, and no clergy. There will, though, be decentralized public and administrative bodies to coordinate production and distribution. With regard to production, the fetters of capitalist relations of production will be removed allowing for the forces of production to be developed and employed to their fullest capacity, resulting in a massive expansion in production so that there is an abundance of goods. Production will be communal, carried out collectively and in the collective interest, and labor will be free activity in the sense that it will be freely engaged in without coercion or the need for financial incentive. Work will be varied, fulfilling and allow for the development and expression of individuals' creativity. The selfish, competitive, aggressive nature characteristic of human beings in capitalist society will be replaced by a communist consciousness that will allow people to live in harmony with one another.

In his *Critique of the Gotha Programme* (1875) Marx distinguished between a higher and a lower phase of communism. In the latter there would still persist certain elements from capitalist society, including payment for work, while in the latter the principle "from each according to his ability, to each according to his need" applies, with everyone contributing as they are able and receiving according to their individual needs.

Vladimir Ilich Lenin in *The State and Revolution* (1917) used the term socialism to refer to Marx's lower phase of communism, and reserved the word communism to describe the higher phase. Both Marx and Lenin have been accused of utopianism in their speculations on the future communist society.

COMMUNIST INFORMATION BUREAU (COMINFORM). More commonly referred to as the Cominform, the Communist Information Bureau was a cabal of nine **Marxist–Leninist** parties inaugurated at the behest of **Josef Stalin** in 1947. The group initially included the **communist** parties of **Bulgaria, Czechoslovakia, France, Hungary, Italy, Poland, Romania,** the **Soviet Union** and **Yugoslavia,** though the last of these was expelled in 1948 owing to its "**Titoism.**" The Cominform sought to bring about communication and cooperation lacking between its constituent members since the 1943 dissolution of the **Comintern.** However, it was not intended as a replacement for that organ, but instead as a means with which to express international solidarity between communist parties, chiefly through the dissemination of pro-**Soviet** propaganda among its members. The Cominform was completed in 1956 upon Soviet rapprochement with Yugoslavia.

COMMUNIST INTERNATIONAL. *See* THIRD INTERNATIONAL.

COMMUNIST LEAGUE. *See* LEAGUE OF COMMUNISTS.

***COMMUNIST MANIFESTO* (1848).** Commissioned by the London Congress of the **Communist League** in November 1847, the *Manifesto of the Communist Party* was written by **Karl Marx** using **Friedrich Engels'** drafts as a basis. It appeared in early 1848 at a time of **revolution** in Europe and has been the textbook of revolutionaries for over 150 years. It is not a simple declaration of principles but an exposition of the fundamental tenets of **Marxism** presented in a polemical form. The influence of **Georg Wilhelm Friedrich Hegel**'s ideas, and Marx's opposition, is clear in his use of "scientific method"—**historical** and **dialectical materialism**—as the fundamental structure of the work; all man's history is social change necessitated by **class struggle**. The relation of the **base** to the **superstructure** is so clear as to suggest Engels' input. A **class** exists by virtue of its relation to the **mode of production** and the emergence of a new **ruling class** is caused by revolutions in production begun in the previous epoch; as the **bourgeoisie** was built in the feudal age, so the **proletariat** turns bourgeois weapons against their bearers. Marx proposes that the elements of the new social epoch exist within the old; his theory of history is that of struggle between classes leading inevitably to the **communist** society.

The character of wage labor is that the minimum wage is that which nourishes the development of **capital** alone; man is subject to **alienation**, he is an appendage of industry. Furthermore, he is a valuable **commodity** only insofar as he is useful for **exploitation** in the service of production and capital. In bourgeois society, the "worker as commodity" is subject to the same laws of supply and demand as every other commodity. Capital is independent and individual, man is not; the living commodity is not enriched by capital as the static commodity is. Man has only bourgeois notions of independence and individuality, i.e., **property** and free trade as independence. Yet only the minority bourgeoisie has this freedom. Bourgeois state and society withhold freedom from the proletarian majority, therefore "working men have no country" because no country is *for* man.

The fundamental opposition of these classes conceals their dialectical interdependence. The bourgeoisie necessarily creates the proletariat, and as the bourgeoisie develops dialectically, so the proletariat develops against it, as a "really revolutionary class." The bourgeoisie depends upon capital, which relies upon wage labor, the division of labor and mass production, creating increasing socialization of the workers and ever-growing solidarity; the bourgeoisie produces its "own gravediggers." Proletarian revolution is the inevitable consequence of the confluence of all the contradictions of the capitalist mode of production and must be violent because, unlike Hegel, Marx argues that systems cannot be changed from within; communism can only be achieved by overthrowing existing conditions. Furthermore, the bourgeois ruling class will not participate in its own destruction. The proletarian revolution is also a further stage in the dialectic of revolution; only this sweeps away the old conditions of class antagonism and abolishes its own supremacy. The abolition of private property, the *Manifesto* proposes, creates a classless society that can be the first age for the truly free development of man.

COMMUNIST PARTY OF. *See* under individual country name for communist parties not listed as "COMMUNIST PARTY OF . . . ," e.g., FRENCH COMMUNIST PARTY.

COMMUNIST PARTY OF CUBA. The Communist Party of Cuba (*Partito Comunista de Cuba*—PCC) has retained single-party control over the **Republic of Cuba** since the 1959 **Cuban Revolution**. Between the **revolution** and 1965, the party was known as the Integrated Revolutionary Organizations, and then the United Party of Cuban Socialist Revolution, both of which contained members of **Fidel Castro**'s 26th of July Movement. Castro was central throughout this period, establishing himself as the first secretary of the PCC at its very inception, and remaining in charge of the party and **state** thereafter. In accordance with its professed **Marxism–Leninism**, the PCC was run by decree from the Politburo and Central Committee, and established strong ties with the **Communist Party of the Soviet Union**.

However, owing to the doctrines of "Castroism," which in contrast to orthodox Marxism–Leninism did not place primacy on the importance of a **vanguard party** to lead the revolution, in terms of membership and influence the PCC was the smallest ruling communist party in the world for the first decade of its existence. This lasted until 1975 when the PCC held its maiden party conference, and from then onwards adopted many characteristics of a mass communist party. Party membership was accelerated, and a PCC youth wing similar to the Soviet Komosol instituted. Externally, the party was keen to support other Marxist movements, sending expertise and aid to revolutionary African regimes such as those in **Angola** and **Mozambique**, and lending support to the **Sandinistas** in Nicaragua.

The **collapse of the Soviet Union** left the PCC in something of a quagmire, and the Fourth Party Conference in 1991 saw critical debate between reformists looking to implement free market economic solutions, and traditionalists who feared for the continued survival of the communist regime in Cuba should such reforms be implemented. The result was limited economic reforms and a redefining of the PCC's status as the "party of the Cuban nation" rather than the "party of the working class." Threatened by a sudden lack of allies and increased pressure from the **United States**, at its Fifth Party Conference in 1997 the PCC reaffirmed its adherence to Marxism–Leninism and the maintenance of single-party rule.

COMMUNIST PARTY OF CZECHOSLOVAKIA. Established in 1921, the Communist Party of Czechoslovakia (*Komunistická strana Èeskoslovenská*—KSÈ) ruled over the **Socialist Republic of Czechoslovakia** from its inception in 1948. Staunch proponents of **Marxism–Leninism**, the KSÈ advocated **democratic centralism** and under **Stalinist** leader Klement Gottwald developed into a carbon copy of the **Communist Party of the Soviet Union**. The KSÈ built for itself a political monopoly and obliterated the separation between party and **state**, meaning its ideas became governmental policies. However, reformist tendencies within the party persisted, and the leadership of **Alexander Dubcek** brought economic and civil reforms as embodied in the 1968 **Prague Spring** and Dubcek's "socialism with a human face." The crushing of the Prague Spring by the **Red Army** curtailed this reformism and Dubcek's 1969 successor, Gustáv Husák, took the party through a period of "normalization" in which reforms were diluted and hardliners within the KSÈ leadership were able to assert their hostility toward tolerance of dissent. Opposition groups, though, were able to continue their activities, and by 1989 the ground swell of popular discord made the KSÈ government's position untenable. Though it continued as a party after the "Velvet Revolution" of that year, the dissolution of Czechoslovakia in December 1992 spelt the end of the KSÈ. The party split into two successor organizations, the Communist Party of Bohemia and Moravia in the Czech Republic, and the Party of the Democratic Left in Slovakia.

COMMUNIST PARTY OF GREAT BRITAIN. Founded in 1920 the Communist Party of Great Britain (CPGB) was for many years the leading **communist** organization in the country, and until 1943 the

British arm of the **Communist International**. The CPGB resulted from the merger of the **British Socialist Party** with the Communist Unity Group and various other small left-wing groups, on the basis of their mutual support for the Russian **Bolsheviks**.

Throughout the 1920s the party was active as a minority movement seeking to organize itself within the left of the trade unions and attempting, but being denied, affiliation with the Labour Party in 1921. Efforts to cooperate with the Labour Party were abandoned in 1927 and the CPGB fought against Labour candidates in the 1929 elections. After Adolf Hitler and the Nazis came to power in Germany in 1932 the CPGB sought to unite all socialist parties against fascism. In 1935 it called for the establishment of a Popular Front of all anti-fascists, including Liberals and Conservatives, to oppose the national government's appeasement policy. The CPGB only put forward two candidates in the 1938 general election, both of whom were elected, and supported all other Labour candidates. Throughout the Spanish Civil War many members of the CPGB fought in the International Brigade, over 250 being killed. The anti-fascist stance of the party raised its membership to 17,756. A month after the outbreak of World War II the CPGB changed its stance, denouncing the war as **imperialist**. General Secretary Harry Pollitt was removed from his position as a result of his opposition to the change, although he was reinstated in 1941. The party's stance on the war and its support of the Nazi–Soviet Pact was extremely unpopular and brought it into conflict with the government which in January 1941 banned its official paper the *Daily Worker*. After the German invasion of the **Soviet Union** the CPGB gave its backing to the war effort. The ban on the *Daily Worker* was lifted in 1942, and the party's membership soared to 56,000.

During the Cold War membership and support for the party steadily declined, with, for example, 97 of the 100 candidates put forward in the 1950 election losing their deposits. The party supported the Soviet Union's suppression of the 1956 **Hungarian uprising**, which, allied to **Nikita Krushchev**'s speech denouncing **Josef Stalin**, resulted in CPGB membership falling from 33,095 in February 1956 to 24,670 two years later. The CPGB opposed both Labour and Conservative government labor policies in the 1960s and 1970s, also moving toward a more **Eurocommunist** position during this time. In 1979 the CPGB condemned the Soviet invasion of

Afghanistan and similarly opposed the Soviet-supported imposition of martial law in **Poland** in 1981. A pro-Soviet minority controlling the party newspaper, the *Morning Star*, continued to fight against the Eurocommunist wing, and in 1987 the party broke with the *Morning Star*, whose supporters then founded the Communist Party of Britain. By 1990 CPGB membership had plummeted to 6,000 with funds of only around £4 million. In 1991 the Eurocommunist leadership broke up to form the Democratic Left, a left-wing think tank, while a small minority reforged the party, now known as the Communist Party of Great Britain (Provincial Central Committee).

COMMUNIST PARTY OF INDIA (CPI). According to its official history, the Communist Party of India was formed in 1925, though it spent its early years as something of a disjointed unit impeded by British-enforced illegality. In 1935 the CPI joined the **Third International**, and in line with **Soviet** popular front advocacy the party dropped its criticism of parliamentary democracy and joined the Indian National Congress by virtue of an alliance with the Congress Socialist Party. Though the CPI was expelled from this union in 1940, it had already attained influence in several Indian states, and party members remained in the National Congress. At the close of World War II, the party was legalized, and its profile was further raised through its involvement in the Quit India campaign, which aimed to end British colonial rule in the country. This aim achieved in 1947, the CPI moved leftwards and began to advocate the use of violence to prompt **revolution**, encouraging **peasant** militias to become embroiled in armed struggles against regional feudal monarchs. This policy came to an abrupt halt in 1951 following the violent crushing of a rebellion in Telangana state.

From this point onwards, the CPI pledged itself to bringing about **communism** via the ballot box and not the barrel of a gun. The early consequences of this decision were positive, with the CPI becoming the largest opposition party at the 1957 general election, and the first to assume control of an entire Indian state, Kerala. However, this buoyancy came to an abrupt halt when the government declared President's Rule in 1959, and CPI gains were annulled. The CPI suffered further turmoil in 1962 as party members entered into a divisive quarrel over the Sino–Indian War. Pro-Muscovite elements backed the Indian government, while other CPI members rallied behind **China** owing to its status as a communist country. Many in the latter group found themselves under arrest, and in 1964 broke away to form the **Communist Party of India (Marxist)**. CPI strength never reached its early 1960s peak again as a result, though the party has continued to exist as a minor opposition group.

COMMUNIST PARTY OF INDIA-MARXIST (CPI-M). Formed by dissenting members of the **Communist Party of India** (CPI) in 1964, the Communist Party of India-Marxist is now the largest and most successful party advocating **communism** in the country. The CPI-M was heavily critical of the CPI's **"revisionism"** in relation to the 1962 Sino–Indian War and has maintained an orthodox approach to Marxism since, with an 85-member central committee still in place to elect an all-powerful 17-strong Politburo. In the general election of May 2004, the CPI-M polled over 5 percent of the vote giving it 43 members in the Indian National Congress.

COMMUNIST PARTY OF PERU. See PERUVIAN MARXISM.

COMMUNIST PARTY OF POLAND. Marxist organization active in Poland from 1918 to 1938, at which point **Josef Stalin** ordered its abolition. The Communist Party of Poland (*Komunistyczna Partia Polski*) was eventually superseded on the left by the Moscow-friendly **Polish United Workers Party**.

COMMUNIST PARTY OF THE SOVIET UNION (CPSU— *KOMMUNISTICHESKAIA PARTIIA SOVETSKOGO SOIUZA*). The Communist Party of the Soviet Union officially came into being in 1952 as the new name for what had been the All-Union Communist Party, and before that the Russian Communist Party (**Bolsheviks**), and before that the Russian Social Democratic Party (Bolsheviks). At its height the CPSU permeated nearly all aspects of Soviet life and was the leading party in the international **communist** movement. Its structure mirrored that of the Soviet **state** with a hierarchical organization headed by the All-Union Congress (the supreme policy-making body on paper), and with the more significant bodies of the Central Committee, the Political Bureau (Politburo) and the Secretariat exercising real power. Party membership was high with some 15 million members even in 1991 on the eve of its dissolution. The breakup of the **Soviet Union** in that year saw the party banned by the new regime headed by Boris Yeltsin.

Originally conceived by **Vladimir Ilich Lenin** as a **vanguard party** of professional revolutionaries, the party under **Josef Stalin** increasingly became a centralized, hierarchical and bureaucratic organization for transmitting the orders of the leadership and elaborating an ideology justifying Stalin and the party's rule. Under **Nikita Khrushchev** during the late 1950s and 1960s the party became more open with new members from the **peasantry** and workers encouraged, and many existing officials replaced. Khrushchev also took steps to decentralize the party, rotate officials, enhance accountability and increase the frequency of meetings of its decision-making bodies and debating forums. Participation and mobilization were key themes for the party during Khrushchev's time as leader. In the 1970s under **Leonid Brezhnev** the party underwent further changes in an effort to modernize by adopting modern methods of scientific management as part of a more technocratic approach while retaining a role of ideological guidance. The next major change in the CPSU occurred under **Mikhail Gorbachev** whose policies of *perestroika* and *glasnost* saw the party move toward a more limited ideological and political role, with greater internal democracy and a more pluralistic political arena. Ideologically the party was moving toward a greater humanism and pluralism, with the 1991 draft party program talking of "Humane Democratic Socialism" and stating "While restoring and developing the initial humanist principles of the teaching of Marx, Engels and Lenin we include in our ideological arsenal all the wealth of our own and world socialist and democratic thought." By 1991, with the Soviet Union on the brink of collapse, the CPSU had effectively abandoned orthodox **Marxism–Leninism** and **scientific socialism** in favor of an ethical socialism, and from being the dominant communist party in the world was soon to lose its existence.

COMMUNIST PARTY OF YUGOSLAVIA. *See* LEAGUE OF COMMUNISTS OF YUGOSLAVIA.

COMMUNIST PARTY OF THE UNITED STATES OF AMERICA (CPUSA). A descendent of the Communist Labor Party and the Communist Party (both formed in 1919), and at different times going under the names of the Workers' Party and the Communist Political

Association, the Communist Party of the United States of America was based on the model of the **Communist Party of the Soviet Union**. Rigidly pro-Soviet, the CPUSA was the largest communist party in the **United States** with membership reaching some 20,000 in the 1980s. Even at the peak of its strength the party had no elected representatives at either state or national level, and today it is little more than a tiny sect active as a protest group for specific causes.

CONFÉDÉRATION GÉNÉRALE DU TRAVAIL (CGT). Formed in 1895, the Confédération Générale du Travail (General Confederation of Workers) remains the largest trade union association in France, numbering over two million members. Fierce advocates of **Syndicalism**, the CGT has sought to bring about an end to **capitalism** by ensuring all workers are unionized in order to facilitate their personal and collective emancipation, and ultimately convert to **Marxism** the social and political systems surrounding them. Historically, central to this has been the ultimate aim of replacing the political party with the trade union. The CGT remains loyal to the *syndicat* ideal, permitting absolute autonomy to each group within the confederation, retaining its traditional commitment to strike action, and attempting to remain apolitical, though involvement with both the **French Communist Party** and **French Socialist Party** has, perhaps inevitably, always persisted.

CONGO, PEOPLE'S REPUBLIC OF (PRC). In 1968, after a flirtation with **socialism** that followed the 1960 end to French rule in Congo, a military coup saw the installation of a **Marxist–Leninist** government and the birth of the People's Republic of Congo. 1963 had witnessed the overthrow of the post-independence government of Fulbert Youlou, and its replacement with the moderately socialist administration of Alphonse Massemba-Débat. Despite the creation a year later of the radical National Movement of the Revolution (*Mouvement National de la Révolution*—MNR), in August 1968 left-wing hardliners, led by Captain **Marien Ngouabi**, overthrew Massemba-Débat's technocratic regime and put in its place the National Council of the Revolution (*Conseil National de la Révolution*—CNR). Ngouabi, as president of the new government, immediately set about wielding **revolutionary** changes, creating the **vanguard** Congolese Workers' Party (*Parti Congolais de Travail*—PCT), and announcing the creation of the People's Republic of Congo, the first outwardly and officially Marxist–Leninist state in Sub-Saharan Africa. Ngouabi also began a nationalization program, and sought to strike up friendly relations with **communist** countries in the Far East. In accordance with the Marxist–Leninist model, the state soon became subordinate to the diktats of the all-powerful PCT.

However, Ngouabi's commitment to Marxism–Leninism as an actual doctrine of rule, rather than an ideological tool with which to bind together the many fractious and disparate groups that made up Congolese society, was questionable. Despite paying lip service to Marxist–Leninist bedrock principles such as widespread nationalization and solidarity with foreign communist governments above all others, the Ngouabi regime left much private industry untouched and in the hands of **capitalist** companies from the Western world. This left the PCT leadership open to criticism from the left of the party, an early embodiment of which was the failed **Maoist** coup attempt launched by Lieutenant Ange Diawara in 1971. The defeat of the attempted usurpation proved only to be a temporary reprieve for Ngouabi and his government, as armed forces members, alarmed by the leader's drift toward the political right, organized his assassination in early 1977. The new head of state, however, was the avowedly un-Marxist army colonel Joachim Yhomby-Opango, and his immediate act was to announce the start of a period of rule by authoritarian Martial Law.

Yhomby-Opango never enjoyed the full support of his party nor complete power over his people, and having handed power over to the PCT he was succeeded in February of 1979 by the Central Committee's overwhelming choice, Colonel Denis Sassou-Nguesso, seemingly a fervent and committed Marxist–Leninist. Sassou-Nguesso initially presided over a leftist renewal, increasing PRC ties with **Cuba**, and announcing a new constitution that reaffirmed and institutionalized Marxism–Leninism as the country's ideological foundation. The constitution also promised huge public sector growth, further nationalization, and the introduction of an elected legislature, the National People's Congress, as well as democratic regional and local councils. The reality, though, was somewhat different, as elections remained tightly monitored and limited to party list candidates. Consequently, the PCT emerged with an increased stranglehold on power and was able to indulge in the occasional purging of those deemed to be in opposition to the government. Additionally, key industries remained in the hands of foreign owners, with the nationalization that did occur bringing only untenable and unprofitable ventures into government possession.

Just as the Congolese economy had benefited enormously from the oil boom of the 1970s, as oil prices plummeted during the following decade, Sassou-Nguesso's government faced a devastating fiscal crisis. When coupled with the burden presented by maintaining an ever-mushrooming **state** sector, and the crushing budget deficit resultantly built up, the PCT was forced to seek methods removed from Marxism–Leninism to preserve rule and country. Thus, the regime accepted the measures required by the World Bank in order to formulate a reconstruction plan for the PRC's debt that would in turn resuscitate its ailing economy. Inevitably, this meant an austerity drive that was to hit the Congolese people hardest, and provoke mass strike action, demonstrations, and the birth of oppositional political groups. It was in this climate that the PCT was forced in July 1990 to officially renounce Marxism–Leninism as its **ideology**, and shortly afterwards preside over democratic multi-party elections and the dismantling of the PRC.

The Marxism of the PCT regime developed into little more than a sustained revolutionary posture aimed merely at cementing together the PRC, rather than steering the country along the path to communist utopia. The commitment to genuine Marxism–Leninism never extended beyond the rhetorical, and this was illustrated by the continuing presence and influence of free market forces throughout the country's supposedly revolutionary epoch.

CONNOLLY, JAMES (1868–1916). Connolly sought to combine **Marxism** with both nationalism and religion, and was one of the leaders of the 1916 "Easter Rising," the nationalist insurrection in Dublin, Ireland, for which he was executed by the British government. His Marxism was orthodox and followed the **Second International** line, except for some **syndicalist** leanings influenced by **Daniel De Leon**. De Leon's influence made Connolly sympathetic to industrial unionism and he spent several years in the **United States** as an organizer for the **Industrial Workers of the World**. His nationalism co-existed alongside his Marxism without ever being properly integrated, and certainly in Ireland his nationalism came to dominate his political activities. He also sought to mix Marxism with Catholicism. Connolly made no significant contribution to Marxist theory, but he wrote two important works of propaganda for the cause of Irish independence, *Labour in Irish History* (1910) and *The Re-conquest of Ireland* (1915).

CRISES. Karl Marx did not compile his theory of crises in any discrete manner but proposed it throughout his major works, notably *Theories on Surplus Value* (1861–1879), the *Grundrisse* (1857–1858), and *Capital* (volume I, 1867). Crises are an expression of "all contradictions of **bourgeois** production." **Revolutions** in production caused by advancing technology, and the great expansion of existing **capital**, necessitate expansion of the market. The surface phenomenon appears as an opposition of overproduction and underconsumption, a conflict that can only be resolved in an economic crisis. The underlying incongruity is actually the expression of the **contradiction** between the social character of production and the mode of capitalist accumulation. Bourgeois production necessarily creates an antagonism between **use value** and **exchange value**; **commodities**, including labor, exchange at prices of production and not at their value, thus, the theory is derivative of the transformation of **surplus value** into profit. In consequence, this contradiction cannot be resolved by market manipulation; "the circulation of capital has no limits" but a market has precise limits.

The separation of purchase and sale, and each entering into contradiction with the other is the precondition for the possibility of crises. The existence of money allows for surplus value and, therefore purchase and sale, but "labor as commodity" makes crisis inevitable. The **division of labor** creates a concentration of production and fosters increasing interdependence. Labor is set against capital, its antithesis, and production separates into two industries, that for the **means of production** (constant capital) and production for consumption (variable capital). This "growing organic composition of capital" develops unequally and results in the intensification of the contradiction of production and consumption. Capital exceeds the **relations of production** and credit accelerates the contradiction, which must be resolved as momentary crisis. However, the root cause remains and the crisis merely creates new expressions of the contradiction that must be resolved. Increasingly severe crises are inevitable in bourgeois production; there is a tendency to the absolute impoverishment of the worker and the degradation of capital with the decline of the rate of profit. The attempts of the market to correct itself by credit and cartels will fail and the contradictions of capitalism will result in ever-growing surplus labor and the violent overthrow of bourgeois rule. However, whether this is a purely economic analysis by Marx or an integral facet of his revolutionary theory remains an enigma.

CROCE, BENEDETTO (1866–1952). Born in Percasseroli, southern Italy, Croce was a leading philosopher and active in Italian politics. Greatly influenced by the philosopher **Georg Wilhelm Friedrich Hegel**, he in turn was a major influence on the great **Marxist** thinker and activist **Antonio Gramsci**. He wrote prolifically, producing some 70 books, including his *Filosofia dello Spirito* (*Philosophy of Spirit*) in four volumes on aesthetics (1909), logic (1917), ethics (1915), and philosophy of history (1921), *Ariosto, Shakespeare, and Corneille* (1920) and *History of Europe in the Nineteenth Century* (1932). Croce also founded the journal *La Critica*, which he edited for some 40 years and in which he published many of his writings. In his writings he elaborated a humanist philosophy which sought to provide a secular substitute for the beliefs of religion, with a commitment to a concept of human creative power at its center. His writings on **Karl Marx** praised his separation of ethical and political considerations, and criticized **Friedrich Engels'** interpretation of Marx.

Croce served as minister of education in 1920–21 and again after World War II, and also as a senator in the Italian government. An opponent of Fascism he was liberal and conservative in political outlook, and stands as an influence on the Marxist tradition rather than an advocate of it.

CUBA, REPUBLIC OF. Following an extended struggle, the 1959 **Cuban Revolution** saw **Fidel Castro**'s left-wing movement oust the dictatorship of General Fulgencio Batista and announce the adaptation of a **Marxist–Leninist** program for the island. The Republic of Cuba remains one of the few states on earth still committed to the **ideology**. In continuously retaining power since 1959, Castro's **Communist Party of Cuba** (CPC) continues to defy world trends and pressure from the **United States**.

Though Marxism–Leninism was not confirmed as the official state ideology in Cuba until 1961, little post-revolutionary dust had settled when Castro set the country on the path to **communism**. With the assistance of his brother, Raúl, and the fabled **Ernesto "Che" Guevara**, the leader announced in August 1960 the confiscation and nationalization of foreign-owned property and the redistribution of rural plantations among the **peasantry**. Plans to imprison and exile "undesirables" were also conceived. Soon after, the large-scale nationalization of industry and **collectivization** of rural plots was ordered, and a gigantic and ultimately successful mass health and education scheme unveiled. The country also struck up close relations with other communist states, in particular the **Soviet Union**, much to the ire of the United States. It was this, along with the American government's repulsion at the idea of communism and its support for Batista, which pushed Washington into action. Economic sanctions that still remain in place today were imposed on Cuba, and the infamous April 1961 Bay of Pigs invasion was only one of the first failed attempts on Castro's life by the U.S. government. The October 1962 Cuban Missile Crisis, when the Cold War almost turned alarmingly hot, was also a direct consequence of Havana's courting of the Soviet Union that the adoption and survival of Cuban Marxism–Leninism necessitated.

Those crises and others safely overcome, Castro and his entourage relentlessly pursued the idea of exporting their revolution abroad, forging close ties with communist groups across the globe and granting economic and military assistance to uprisings in South America and Africa. Domestically, the communist hold on power remained, and remains, secure, owing largely to rapid advances in health and education, but in part as a consequence of the one-party rule that has emerged. This authoritarian system was ratified in the Soviet-style 1976 constitution, which made Castro outright president and *de facto* dictator. The **collapse of the Soviet Union** heralded something of an economic emergency in Cuba, given that events in Moscow and the demise of the rest of the Soviet Bloc brought an abrupt halt to many of the trading avenues open to it. As ever, the seemingly indefatigable Castro and his regime have survived, in part due to partial modifications of policy that have allowed controlled private foreign investment and impelled a growing tourist sector.

Despite Cuba amounting for the majority part of its existence to little more than a Moscow satellite state, Cuban Marxism has developed relatively organically. Castro's approach has always been one of a "revolutionary nationalism," or "Castroism," that has negated both orthodox communism's desire to enforce revolutionary theory on the mass population, and its fanatical promotion and enforcement of the central role of the party. It was this independence of thought and interpretation of Marxism that led to early hostility from orthodox Marxists across Cuba and South America, as Castro and his loyalists sought to prove that a revolutionary **vanguard** group, in this case the "July 26th Movement," could guide the masses toward revolution without being part of a formal Marxist–Leninist party. Informed by the Marxism of his cohort Guevara, Castro's vision of communism for Cuba cited the adoption of military arms as the foremost catalyst for revolutionary change, and looked to circumvent the traditional economic stages on the road to socialism by engendering in the masses a sense of shared moral purpose and patriotic pride. Only once the revolution and regime had been consolidated did Castro look to establish a vanguard party in the form of the CPC.

CUBAN REVOLUTION (1959). Having led a guerrilla war against the regime of President Fulgencio Batista, **Fidel Castro** came to power through a coup in 1959 and set about transforming **Cuba** along **Marxist** lines. Castro had first led an attempted attack on the Batista regime on 26 July 1953. He and 118 other rebels laid siege on the Moncada Barracks in Santiago de Cuba, only to be met with fierce reprisals. On capture Castro was sentenced to 15 years' imprisonment, but saw his sentence quashed after 11 months when Batista pardoned him as part of an amnesty decree to abet his reelection as Cuban president. Exiled in Mexico, Castro formed the 26th of July Movement, a gathering of guerrilla troops who shared the common aim of deposing the repressive Batista, one of whom was **Ernesto "Che" Guevara**. On 2 December 1956 82 members of the movement set sail for Cuba onboard the yacht *Grandma* aiming to bring down the Batista government. On arrival they were met by the brutality of the president's troops, with 70 July 26th members perishing and the remaining 12 fleeing to take refuge in the Sierra Maestro Mountains in Cuba's Oriente Province. However, the three most important figures in the group, Castro, his brother Raúl and Guevara, were among the survivors, and used the retreat into the mountains to recruit and train members for a future guerrilla insurrection, while carrying out sporadic attacks on the Batista government.

The government's response was to attack towns and villages perceived to be pro-Castro, an undertaking that served only to increase the rebels' popularity among the population. Castro mustered considerable rural support from the **peasantry**, while in Cuba's urban areas Frank Pais led the offensive against Batista. After months of guerrilla warfare, on 17 March 1958 Castro declared total war on the Batista regime, prompting the besieged president to launch Operation Verano toward the end of May. The operation saw 17 battalions, tanks, planes and naval vessels besiege the rebel base in the Sierra Maestro Mountains to no avail, as the outnumbered rebels held firm and employed their regional expertise to drive Batista's troops away. Lacking knowledge of how to fight against guerrilla tactics, the Cuban army was regularly caught in disarray with surrender and desertion routine.

Sensing that the government troops were on the back foot, Castro's rebels plotted an offensive of their own. They quickly formed into two groups, with the first led by Castro and his brother Raúl heading for the east of the island and Santiago de Cuba, and the second, under the command of Guevara and Camilo Cienfuegos, bearing westwards for Havana. Guevara's company, having emerged victorious from a crucial battle in Santa Clara, met little resistance in Havana, and by Christmas 1958 the city was under the occupation of Castro's men. Having effortlessly taken Santiago, Castro himself began the journey to Havana, arriving shortly after new year 1959 to declare the victory of the revolution. Batista, meanwhile, was hurriedly seeking exile in the Dominican Republic and then Spain, buoyed by several hundred million dollars gained through dubious means.

As prime minister from 1959, and president from 1976, Castro and his **Communist Party of Cuba** sought to apply Marxist concepts to transform Cuba's political, social and economic landscape. Much to the annoyance of the United States which duly meted out sanctions on Cuba, he embarked upon a program to nationalize all foreign-owned property on the island, and improve literacy and healthcare. Cuba moved ever closer to the **Soviet Union**, resulting most famously in the Cuban Missile Crisis of 1962. Though the human rights record of the Castro government has been criticized in some quarters, Cuba nonetheless stands out as one of few states to have applied Marxist ideas with some success over a sustained period with little threat to the regime's continued existence.

CULTURAL REVOLUTION (1966–1976). A violent campaign of epic proportions demanded by **Mao Zedong** in **China** to renew the atmosphere and ideals of the 1949 **Chinese Revolution**, the Cultural Revolution was a campaign against privilege, party bureaucracy and **revisionism**. Following the failure of the ruinous "Great Leap Forward," Mao faced clandestine criticism from **Chinese Communist Party** (CCP) members over his **ideology**-led actions. Mao's critics wished to see China adopt a more pragmatic, bureaucratic stance similar to that espoused in the **Soviet Union**. The Chinese leader's reaction was to invoke a campaign to reassert his grip on party and state by reinvigorating the **revolution** and defeating revisionism. His tool for doing so would be the "masses" who would aid him in ridding the country of figures deemed to be pillars of the party old guard, and replacing them with a fresh cohort of fanatical revolutionaries. Ideologically, the purpose of the campaign would be to implement a **"permanent revolution"** aimed at repelling the threat of a **capitalist** resurgence. To this end, in 1966 Mao ordered an assault on "capitalist roaders" within the CCP that would in turn become an attack on groups such as intellectuals reckoned to be opponents of the revolution by virtue of their possession of foreign literature, or even their fashion sense.

In May 1966 Mao certified his grip as director of the Cultural Revolution in a politburo circular, and close behind him as figureheads of the action were his wife Chiang Ch'ing and Defense Minister **Lin Biao**. With party opposition to Mao rife, he turned to the outside population and in particular the disgruntled young for assistance in carrying out the renewal of the revolution. They were loosely organized into the "**Red Guards**," a group supported logistically with the aid of Lin Biao's People's Liberation Army (PLA). The Red Guards set about removing principal local and national CCP dignitaries and replacing them with ardent **Maoists**. Targeted too were the managerial and educational elite, and with the acquiescence of the PLA the Guards were able to paralyze most universities and other institutions. Mao was intent on purging China of the privileged bureaucratic class that had emerged out of the 1949 revolution, and for a sustained period in 1966 11 million Red Guard "foot soldiers" were dispersed throughout the country to brutally carry this out.

The Guards' action sent China into a state of frenzied hysteria as people frantically pledged allegiance to Mao, with 350 million copies of *Quotations From Chairman Mao* (Or, *The Little Red Book*) distributed and enormous wall posters adorned with revolutionary messages erected. The immediate goal of the Cultural Revolution had been to remove leading party figures from office, and this was accomplished by 1968, for example with the high-profile sidelining of **Deng Xiaoping** and State Chairman **Liu Shaoqi**. Beyond that, the movement was without a structure or a set of aims, and predictably chaos reigned. Maoists battled both each other and those identified as enemies of the revolution, and with anarchic mob rule taking hold, Mao called on the PLA to stabilize China in 1968, and at the Ninth Party Congress a year later the violent phase of the revolution was formally halted. However, normality did not return to China until 1976 with the death of Chairman Mao and the removal from power of Jiang Qing's "**Gang of Four**."

The decade of turmoil wrought by the Cultural Revolution resulted in the death and torture of hundreds of thousands of Chinese, and by its conclusion the cult of Mao had been destroyed as a myth. The CCP was thoroughly purged and its established order transformed beyond recognition. The education system was crippled, as were numerous communities, and the country's industry came to a grinding halt with the transportation of urban workers to the countryside for party reeducation. This practical manifestation of Mao's **Marxism** stunted and reversed China's political, social, cultural and industrial progress immeasurably.

CZECHOSLOVAKIA, SOCIALIST REPUBLIC OF. In the latter half of the 1940s, Czechoslovakia (since 1993 the Czech Republic and Slovakia) was transformed into a **communist** satellite state of the **Soviet Union**. Up until its collapse following the 1989 **Velvet Revolution**, the Czech regime, other than during the 1968 **Prague Spring**, exclusively followed Muscovite **Marxist–Leninist** rule.

When World War II came to a close in 1945, political limits were enforced in Czech and Slovak lands that restricted the number of parties in each to four. In reality, it was the **Communist Party of Czechoslo-**

vakia (CPCz) that benefited most from regional conditions, as it was able to call in support from the gigantic **Communist Party of the Soviet Union** (CPSU). The postwar government, in pursuing economic recovery via the nationalization of industry and commerce, opened the way for left-wing politics to take hold, and in May 1946 the CPCz won overall control of parliament following a general election. In 1947 Moscow prevented Czechoslovakia from taking part in the **United States'** recovery program, the Marshall Plan, pushing the country further toward orthodox **Stalinist** rule and ensuring its alliance with the communist bloc against the United States in the Cold War.

Soon afterwards, in February 1948, the CPCz forcefully attained complete control of the country and set about invoking Soviet-style reforms. Opposition parties were banned, the economy was rapidly fully nationalized, **collectivization** of agriculture was begun and a series of purges undertaken. On 25 February 1948, the People's Republic of Czechoslovakia was proclaimed under the leadership of Klement Gottwald, becoming the last Soviet satellite state to be born. Marxism–Leninism came to infiltrate all aspects of Czech life, with anti-**bourgeois** measures to rid "enemies" from the fledgling state, a clamp-down on religion, and harsh censorship of intellectual, educational and cultural life in order create ideological monism in all society. In addition to agreeing to place an emphasis on industry as oppose to consumer goods, to ensure full financial subordination to the Soviet machine, Czechoslovakia was forced by Moscow to join the Council for Mutual Economic Assistance (Comecon). As elsewhere in the Soviet Bloc, **state** became subordinated to party, and party to its doctrinaire, deified general secretary.

There was a slight let-up in repression following the passing of **Josef Stalin** in 1953, with a halt brought to the secret police's indiscriminate purges. However, this thaw lasted only until 1956, when the **Polish** and **Hungarian Uprisings** provoked a strong backlash against liberalization. In spite of this, through the following decade **revisionist** tendencies remained relatively strong, with concessions given to those desperate for a relaxation of state intervention in the press and the arts. Additionally, revisionists such as Ota Sik thrived as an economic downturn engendered a sense of collective anxiety among the Czech people, culminating in the replacing of the authoritarian General Secretary Antonín Novotny with the reform-minded **Alexander Dubcek**, and the 1968 Prague Spring. The Prague Spring, though, provoked a repressive Soviet response, and by 1969 the old order had been restored, with Moscow stooge Gustáv Husák put into power, and the period of "normalization" heralded.

Despite the orthodox Marxist–Leninist oppressive culture of normalization, underground opposition movements began to grow, buoyed especially by Czechoslovakia's 1975 signing the Helsinki Accords that appeared to guarantee a new wave of governmental respect for human rights. One such movement was Charter 77, a broad group from across the political spectrum that publicly criticized the Czech government's failure to carry out the pledges of the Helsinki edict. The group's action was met with brutality from the Czech regime, but they nonetheless persisted in its fight and subsequently succeeded in garnering massive public support for the cause of systemic reform. As the 1980s began, the dynamic was changing, and the 1985 ascent to power of **Mikhail Gorbachev** in the Soviet Union accelerated the demise of the Husák administration. The Czechoslovakian command saw its rule undermined and illegitimated by the processes of *glasnost* and *perestroika*, and by the withdrawal of Soviet support for the regime. In Czech and Slovak regions the Civic Forum and the Public Against Violence groups respectively sought to capitalize on the government's uncertainty and bring about its collapse.

In 1987 Miloš Jakeš replaced Husák as general secretary, as antigovernment protests and demonstrations broke out all over the country. Two years later, on 11 November a student protest in Prague was momentarily repressed, but spurred on by events in the rest of the Eastern Bloc, the indefatigable reformist spirit within the country continued, and as 1989 drew to a close Jakeš resigned and the end of communist rule was nigh. The regime peacefully petered out in what is commonly referred to as the Velvet Revolution, and in June 1990 the Czechoslovakian electorate, many of them experiencing a free election for the first time, returned a noncommunist government.

While the People's Republic of Czechoslovakia habitually followed the orthodox Marxist–Leninist line emitted from Moscow, a strong sense of revisionism often meant an undercurrent of dissent existed. Czech theorists such as Zdenek Mlynar sought to reverse **determinist** Stalinist distortions of Marxism and divert **socialism** in the country toward a more democratic, humanist ethos, culminating in the reforms of the Prague Spring. However, orthodoxy was constantly reasserted, never more emphatically so than following the events of 1968, as reforms were reversed, and revisionism extinguished until its reemergence in the form of groups such as Charter 77 toward the end of the 1970s.

– D –

DEBRAY, JULES RÉGIS (1940–). A French left-wing **revolutionary** theorist and intellectual, Debray achieved prominence for his advocacy of guerrilla warfare in advancing **socialist** goals, and his links with and writings on **Fidel Castro**, **Che Guevara** and Latin American **Marxism**. Debray showed early intellectual ability and at the age of 16 he won the philosophy prize in the annual *Concours Général.* He graduated with a 1:1 from Lycée Louis-le-Grand, and then entered the École Normale Supérieure (gaining the highest score in the entrance exam) where he studied with **Louis Althusser** and became a member of the **French Communist Party** (PCF). Debray's interest in Latin America began in 1961 when he visited Cuba and saw Castro's new regime first hand. He followed this with tours of Latin America in 1963 and 1964 during which he studied guerrilla tactics. In 1966 he held a position as a professor in Havana, and in 1967 he went to Bolivia where he worked alongside Che Guevara. He accompanied Guevara on his final fateful expedition and was himself captured, arrested and imprisoned for three years. He subsequently continued his work as an academic, writer and intellectual and in 1981 became an advisor to French President François Mitterand on Latin America.

Debray has written a number of books including *Castroism: The Long March in Latin America* (1964), *Problems of Revolutionary Strategy in Latin America* (1965), *Revolution in the Revolution?* (1967), *A Critique of Arms* (1969), *The Chilean Revolution: Conversations With Allende* (1971), and *Critique of Political Reason* (1984). In the earliest of these he developed his views on the importance of rural guerrilla warfare, as practised by Guevara, which he believed would prompt the evolution of socialist theory. In guerrilla movements Marxist–Leninist **vanguard parties** were not necessary. He became more critical of Guevara for failing to appreciate the vital need for urban **proletariat** support and for his lack of attention to specifics of theory and history in relation to Bolivia. In his writings Debray also praised "Fidelism," the revolutionary nationalist practice of Fidel Castro, and criticized orthodox **communism** with its dogmatic emphasis on the key role of the party and the need to inculcate correct revolutionary theory into the masses. He also rejected the approach of **Eurocommunism**, and even though sympathetic to **Salvador Allende** in Chile, he still saw the need for armed insurrection in much of Latin America. By 1984 he had moved to a further critique of **Marxism** in his *Critique of Political Reason* in which he argued that a reinvigorated Marxism needed to reject its scientific pretensions and, instead, had to connect with people's emotions, hopes and fears.

DEBS, EUGENE VICTOR (1855–1926). Born in Indiana in the **United States**, Debs is one of the most significant and well-known American **socialists**. He was an organizer and leader of various labor organizations and stood as a socialist candidate for the U.S. presidency five times. Initially his activism was in the labor movement, notably as grand secretary and treasurer of the Brotherhood of Locomotive Firemen from 1880 to 1893, and from 1893 to 1897 as organizer and president of the American Railways Union. With the latter he was involved in two major strikes, successfully in 1894 against the Great Northern Railroad, but unsuccessfully later on that year against the Pullman Palace Car Company. The Pullman strike saw Debs imprisoned for six months for conspiring to interfere with the passage of federal mail. While in jail he was introduced to socialism via the visits of American Socialist editor Victor Berger, and through his readings of socialist authors including **Karl Kautsky** and **Karl Marx**.

In 1896 Debs joined the Socialist Brotherhood of Cooperative Commonwealths, and in June 1897 was instrumental in the forming of the Social Democratic Party of America (SDPA). The party demanded nationalization of monopolies, public works for the unemployed, and an eight-hour working day. In 1901 the SDPA merged with other socialist groups to form the **Socialist Party of America** (SPA). Debs stood as presidential candidate for the SDPA in 1900, and for the SPA in 1904, 1908, 1912 and 1920, gaining close to a million votes in the 1920 election. Debs also played an important role in the formation of the **Industrial Workers of the World** (IWW) in

1905, but left in 1908 due to policy disputes. In addition, his political views gained him a further jail sentence in 1918 for a speech expressing his pacifist-inspired opposition to U.S. involvement in World War I that was deemed to be a violation of the Espionage Act. He served three years of a 10-year sentence before being pardoned by President Warren G. Harding in 1921. He spent the remaining years of his life lecturing and promoting the SPA.

Debs was influenced by **Marxism** and its criticisms of **capitalism**. He believed in the necessity of overthrowing capitalism and its replacement by communism. He criticized Marxism for failing to pay attention to the project of constructing a socialist society, and put forward ideas for a socialist state to be created in the west of the United States. This showcase for socialism would be based on common ownership of the **means of production** and distribution according to need, and would demonstrate the superiority of socialism, thus winning workers over to the socialist cause. Debs was also a great advocate of education for the workers as the key element, along with organization, in the emancipation of the working **class**.

DE LEON, DANIEL (1852–1914). Born on the island of Curaçao off the coast of Venezuela, De Leon became an important figure in the history of **Marxism** in the **United States**. He joined the main Marxist party in America, the Socialist Labor Party, in 1890, launched and edited its paper *The People* in 1891, and became its leading propagandist. He translated a number of works by leading Marxists including ones by **Karl Marx, Friedrich Engels, Karl Kautsky,** and **August Bebel**, which, with his own articles, pamphlets and speeches, helped to disseminate Marxist ideas in the United States. He opposed both moderate union demands for higher wages or shorter hours and moderate demands for political reform. Instead, he argued that **capitalism** must be overthrown by spontaneous, peaceful **revolution** by the workers using the strike weapon and leading to a **syndicalist** socialist society based on the industrialist unions. De Leon was involved in the founding of the **International Workers of the World** (IWW). By the time he died the Socialist Labor Party was a tiny sect, his intransigence and sectarianism minimizing the party's appeal. The IWW dissolved in 1925, and it is fair to say that while he was important in the U.S. **socialist** movement during his life, his influence has not been lasting.

DEMOCRATIC CENTRALISM. At the 1906 **Bolshevik** party congress, **Vladmir Ilich Lenin** put forward the principle of democratic centralism. In essence, democratic centralism meant that decisions within the party should be taken democratically, but once made they should be centrally imposed. Democratic centralism allowed completely free discussion before decision-making, and required absolute conformity and discipline afterwards; in Lenin's words, "freedom of discussion, unity of action." The democratic aspect in practice took second place to the centralist aspect of the principle. Democratic centralism was formerly adopted by the Bolshevik party at the 6th party congress in 1917, and the 1920 *Twenty-One Conditions of Admission to the Comintern* stated it should be the basis of party organization. It was only implicit in **Josef Stalin**'s 1936 **Soviet** constitution, becoming explicit in **Leonid Brezhnev**'s 1977 constitution, and various **Marxist** parties and organizations have embraced the principle.

DEMOCRATIC FEDERATION. *See* SOCIAL DEMOCRATIC FEDERATION.

DEMOCRATIC REPUBLIC OF. *See* under country name, e.g., AFGHANISTAN, DEMOCRATIC REPUBLIC OF.

DENG XIAOPING (1904–1997). Deng Xiaoping was the paramount leader of the **Chinese Communist Party** (CCP) throughout the 1980s and a key figure before and after. Arguably he was the person who did most to overturn the policies of the **Cultural Revolution** and to guide China toward economic modernization and growth. Deng joined the Communist Party in the early 1920s while a student in France, and took this ideological commitment back with him to China. Centrally involved in the **revolutionary** struggle against the nationalists in China, he held various posts in the **Red Army** and took part in the Long March in 1934–35. He opposed **Mao Zedong** at the time of the Cultural Revolution, leading to Mao purging him from the party, but emerged as the key leader after Mao's death. Deng's leadership focused on the development of China and was characterized by its pragmatism and emphasis on organizational efficiency. He encouraged elements of **capitalism** and the replacement of revolutionaries with managers in the party in the drive for economic development, while keeping a tight bureaucratic–authoritarian political control. He was also behind the establishing of closer links with both the **United States** and Japan.

DETERMINISM. Karl Marx's theory of **historical materialism**, his predictions (for example concerning the increasing immiserization of the poor and the collapse of **capitalism**), and **Marxist** laws of history/capitalism all lead to the issue of determinism. Within Marxism this issue concerns the extent to which events are inevitable, predictable and alterable.

One interpretation of historical materialism that constituted the orthodoxy within the Marxist movement at the end of the 19th and beginning of the 20th century has come to be known as economic determinism. This view, associated particularly with **Karl Kautsky** and the **Second International**, asserted that the ultimately determining factor in history and society was the economic **base**. Within the economic base, according to this view, the **forces of production**, or more narrowly still technology, determined the **relations of production**, and these in turn (possibly in combination with the forces of production) determined the character of society as a whole. Hence, a change in technology or the forces of production would ultimately change the character of the whole of society. Kautsky and his followers saw the collapse of capitalism and the advent of **communism** as inevitable, and all that Marxists and the labor movement could do was to help hasten this eventuality. **Georgii Plekhanov**, who similarly approached Marxism from a determinist perspective, suggested in his *The Role of the Individual in History* (1908) that individuals did have an active role to play in shaping history, but they could not change the general trend of history.

However, other Marxists, even when acknowledging a determinist aspect to Marx's writings, have suggested the role of human agency is much greater than the economic determinism of the Second International approach allows. The school of **Western Marxism**, the **Marxist humanists**, and **Jean-Paul Sartre** in particular have suggested nondeterminist interpretations, and **Mao Zedong** and Chinese Marxism with such slogans as "Politics in Command" have put forward a much more voluntarist interpretation of Marxism. There remains, though, a genuine ambiguity in Marx's writings with regard to the inevitability of the collapse of capitalism and its replacement by communism, and about the extent to which human action can influence the course of history.

As regards the predictability of events, Kautsky, Plekhanov and Eduard Bernstein all take the scientific status of Marxism seriously and their interpretation of science is strongly colored by positivism. This means they understand Marxism as a theory that is capable of generating predictions, but other Marxists and a close reading of Marx both indicate this interpretation to be wrong.

DEUTSCHER, ISAAC (1907–1967). Born in Poland, Deutscher became a major **Marxist** scholar and writer, producing classic biographies of **Josef Stalin** and **Leon Trotsky**. He joined the **Polish Communist Party** (PCP) in Warsaw in 1927, but was expelled in 1932 for dissenting from the official party line that fascism was no bigger a threat to the working class than social democracy. He then joined the Polish Socialist Party which was associated more with Trotsky's views, and he remained sympathetic to **Trotskyism** and critical of **Stalinism** throughout the rest of his life. From 1940 to 1942 he served in the Polish army, and after the war he devoted much of his time to writing and broadcasting.

Despite Trotskyite sympathies Deutscher did not endorse the Trostkyite **Fourth International**, and despite vehement criticism of Stalinism he did not condemn the **Soviet Union** entirely, instead acknowledging what he saw as its achievements and describing the 1917 **Russian Revolution** as an unfinished **revolution**. Among his many works are: *Stalin: A Political Biography* (1949); his three volumes on Trotsky, *The Prophet Armed: Trotsky 1879–1921* (1954), *The Prophet Unarmed: Trotsky 1921–1929* (1959), and *The Prophet Outcast: Trotsky 1929–1940* (1963); and *The Unfinished Revolution: Russia 1917–1967* (1967).

DIALECTICAL MATERIALISM. Representing the influence of **Friedrich Engels** and in particular his book *Anti-Dühring* (1878), dialectical materialism became the dominant **Marxist** philosophy in the **Second International** and official **ideology** in the **Soviet Union**. A term probably first used by **Georgii Plekhanov**, dialectical materialism combined the dialectical approach of **Georg Wilhelm Friedrich Hegel** with philosophical **materialism**. The materialist aspect of dialectical materialism consists in the tenets that: the material world exists independently of our perception of it or of any thought, mind or spirit; the material world is basic or has primacy over the ideal, mental or spiritual world; and the sole reality is the natural world. The dialectical aspect is contained in Engels' three laws and can be summed up as asserting that the world is characterized by constant change, including revolutionary change, and by the presence of contradictory tendencies and entities that drive forward the changes. As a philosophy dialectical materialism, or "diamat" as it was called for short, tended to the dogmatic and to be both reductionist and **deterministic** suggesting a mono–causal approach to understanding society and the world. With the general ossification of philosophy in the Soviet Union from **Josef Stalin** onwards, dialectical materialism failed to develop and found little favor elsewhere. *See also* DIALECTICS.

DIALECTICS. Marxists are divided on the issue of dialectics and the question of the extent to which **Karl Marx** embraced the theory of dialectics. Dialectics (or the dialectic, or dialectical philosophy) is a philosophical approach the roots of which can be traced back to the ancient Greeks—Socrates, Plato, Aristotle. Of more direct influence on Marx, though, was the philosophy of **Georgii Wilhelm Friedrich Hegel**, which had dialectics at its heart. According to the dialectical approach, reality is characterized by three key features: change, contradiction and connection. All reality is in a state of flux, nothing is static; all reality contains and is driven forward by internal contradictions; and all reality is interconnected, nothing exists in isolation. Hegel based his philosophical method on dialectics, his philosophy of history and his political philosophy, for example, being clearly structured to incorporate the notions of change, contradiction and connection.

Marx was initially a disciple of Hegel and a member of the group of Left Hegelians that sought to interpret Hegel's writings in a radical way. However, he broke with the Hegelians and wrote a critique of Hegel's political philosophy (*Critique of Hegel's Philosophy of Right*, 1843), but Marxists have disputed to what extent this represented a complete break with dialectics. **Eduard Bernstein, Louis Althusser** and the **analytical Marxists** for example reject the notion of a place for dialectics in Marx's thought, but **Vladimir Ilich Lenin, Mao Zedong, Georg Lukács** and **Herbert Marcuse** are notable for the prominence they give to dialectics in Marxism. The weight of evidence in Marx's later writings, particularly in the *Grundrisse*

(1857/58), would seem to support the argument for Marx continuing to incorporate dialectical themes into his theories throughout his life. It is fair to say that Marx accepts the validity and importance of dialectics, but rejects Hegel's treatment of it. Marx talks about Hegel having turned dialectics on its head, and he writes, "It must be inverted, in order to discover the rational kernel within the mystical shell." From this it may be inferred that Marx rejects Hegel's metaphysics, in particular his philosophical **idealism** and notion of *Geist* as the driving force in the universe.

Instead, Marx adopts a **materialist** approach, seeing dialectics as a true description of the nature and structure of material reality. He retains the notion of contradictions, often identifying opposites that are in one sense united, but in another in conflict with one another. For example, Marx identifies the forces and relations of production as opposites constituting a contradiction. **Forces of production** are not static and in the course of developing come into conflict with the **relations of production** leading to crisis and change. Marx's method of investigation of social reality is dialectical in that he seeks to identify and analyze different forms of development, the inner connections of different phenomena, and the latent contradictions within things. This gives Marx's method a sense of history and context, so that, for example, he sees **capitalism**, its economic and political structures and institutions, its value and concepts as transient (change), as containing hidden connections between such aspects as production and politics (connections), and as conflict-ridden rather than a harmonious system (contradictions).

Friedrich Engels described dialectics as "the science of the general laws of motion and development of nature, human society and thought," and formulated three main laws of dialectics: (i) the transformation of quantity into quality, by which is meant gradual quantities changes at a certain point cause sudden and revolutionary qualitative change; (ii) the unity of opposites, by which is meant that all reality contains opposites or contradictions bound together as unities; and (iii) the **negation of the negation**, by which is meant that when opposites clash one negates the other and is then itself negated and superceded by another opposite, but with previous negations all in some sense preserved. Engels' emphasis on dialectics as universal scientific laws led to a rigid, dogmatic interpretation of it that became known as **dialectical materialism**

and dominated Marxist dialectical theory in the **Second International** and the **Soviet Union**. **Josef Stalin** dropped the law of the negation of the negation with its potential revolutionary implications a threat to his regime, and Mao Zedong made the transformation of quantity into quality a form of the law of the unity of opposites, and he made contradictions the central focus. **Western Marxists** have been bolder in their interpretations of dialectics and willingness to depart from Engels' laws and Soviet/Second International orthodoxy.

DIALECTICS OF NATURE. One of the areas of debate among Marxists relating to **dialectics**, philosophy and science concerns the dialectics of nature. **Friedrich Engels** wrote about the dialectics of nature claiming that dialectics, and his three laws of dialectics in particular, represented an ontology of both the social and the natural world. In other words, Engels argued that the same processes relating to change and contradiction could be observed in both the social and the natural world. This view, accepted by the **Second International** and **Soviet Marxism**, has been challenged by many other Marxists, even those sympathetic to dialectics notably **Georgii Lukács** and **Jean-Paul Sartre**, on the grounds that the natural and social spheres are vastly different and that dialectical categories and concepts have been derived from and formulated in relation to the social world. Dogmatically applied in the **Soviet Union** it is questionable if the notion of dialectics of nature, at least in the form it assumed, contributed anything to philosophy of natural science or to scientific practice.

DICTATORSHIP OF THE PROLETARIAT. This term is used by **Karl Marx** to refer to the transitional period between **capitalism** and **communism**. A specific definition of the term is lacking, but from various references in *The Class Struggles in France* (1850), *The Civil War in France* (1871), *Critique of the Gotha Program* (1875) and elsewhere a picture can be constructed. During this period **classes** still exist and the **state** still exists, but the **proletariat** has taken control, smashing the existing **bourgeois** state and replacing it with a workers' state. This workers' state is the rule of the immense majority and retains coercive powers to use against the old economically privileged classes which might seek to restore capitalism and the rule of a minority. The dictatorship is temporary, only existing so long as significant vestiges of capitalism and capitalist consciousness remain. The term is misleading insofar as it implies an authoritarian government. For Marx, dictatorship of the proletariat meant a temporary concentration of political power in the hands of a single class, but, given that the class in question is composed of the overwhelming majority of the people, this is not a case of a minority of people wielding dictatorial power over the masses. Furthermore, Marx suggests that the dictatorship of the proletariat will resemble the **Paris Commune** of 1871, a revolutionary organization with democratic features, and he also explicitly mentions decentralized, local and regional communes as possible structures for it. The 10-point program given in the *Communist Manifesto* (1848) indicates the kind of measures the dictatorship of the proletariat will implement, and these include: abolition of private ownership of land; the use of all rents for public purposes; the implementation of a heavy, progressive income tax; abolition of the right of inheritance; nationalization of factories and instruments of production; centralization of powers of credit in the hands of a national bank; state control of the means of communication and transport; and free education for all children in state schools. In addition, the dictatorship of the proletariat will be characterized by the requirement that all must work and distribution of income and rewards will be according to how much people work.

Vladimir Ilich Lenin wrote about the dictatorship of the proletariat in *The State and Revolution* (1917), and elsewhere discussed the use of violence by the proletariat against the bourgeoisie. This developed into the use of violence and repression by the state justified by its aim of maintaining proletarian power. This repressive dimension has come to be identified with the notion of the dictatorship of the proletariat to the exclusion of all its other features.

DIETZGEN, JOSEF (1828–1888). A German-born self-taught intellectual, he was credited by **Friedrich Engels** with the independent discovery of materialist dialectics (*see* MATERIALISM and DIALECTICS), and described by Engels and **Karl Marx** as the **First International**'s philosopher. He was also praised by **Vladimir Ilich Lenin** for his materialist philosophy. Dietzgen worked in his father's tannery until forced to flee Germany in 1848 as state repression increased after the revolutionary events of that year. He spent time in the **United States** and Russia, before returning to Germany where he wrote for **communist** journals and involved himself in **socialist** politics including the First International.

In *The Nature of Human Brainwork, Described by a Working Man* (1864) and *The Positive Outcome of Philosophy* (1906) Dietzgen outlined a monist dialectical theory of reality that stressed the unity of mind and matter, the interconnectedness of everything and the centrality of sensory experience as the basis of our understanding of the world. Little read now, he was viewed as a major contributor to the development of the philosophical foundations of **Marxism** during and immediately after his lifetime.

DIVISION OF LABOR. **Karl Marx** discusses the division of labor at various points in his writings, and it clearly is a topic of particular significance in his thought. In his earlier writings, notably *The German Ideology* (1846), Marx talks about it in fairly loose terms referring to the various divisions of labor, for example, between mental and manual work and between town and country. Private **property**, **class** relationships, the **state** and **ideology** are all identified as consequences of the division of labor, and the claim that **communist** society will involve the abolition of the division of labor is strongly made in *The German Ideology*. Later, in *Capital* I, Marx makes a distinction between the social division of labor and the division of labor in manufacture or production. The former refers to the separation of functions in society as a whole, constituting a system of independent producers linked only in the course of exchange. In **capitalism** different entrepreneurs produce different commodities in what Marx sees as an unorganized form of "anarchy." The division of labor in manufacture refers to the "despotic" organization of workers, each allocated a very specific function, and none wholly responsible for the manufacture of a **commodity**, only of a part of a commodity. As machinery advances and becomes more widespread in capitalist production, the worker becomes more and more an automaton, an appendage of the machine, crippled in mind and body, and possessing limited or no skills.

Slightly more circumspectly than in his early works, Marx in *Capital* acknowledges the need for some technical division of labor and specialization, but the division of labor will no longer involve the individual being subject to structures and processes created but no longer controlled by human beings, and being dehumanized in work that denies the possibility of self-realization.

DJILAS, MILOVAN (1911–1995). Born in Pobišcé, Montenegro, Djilas was a leading member of the Yugoslav Communist Party (YCP) and a minister in the **communist** government of Yugoslavia after the war, becoming vice president to **Josef Tito** and viewed as his likely successor. However, his chief contribution has been as a critic of communism and in particular of **Stalinism**.

Djilas came from a **peasant** background, but gained a place at Belgrade University in 1929 to study literature. Here he became a communist agitator against the ruling dictatorship of King Alexander, and in 1932 was arrested, tortured and imprisoned. While in prison he met other communist thinkers and activists which reinforced his communism and led him to embrace a pro–**Josef Stalin/Soviet Union** outlook. In disputes within the YCP during the 1930s he sided with Josef Tito and **Edvard Kardelj**. In World War II Djilas was important in organizing guerrilla resistance to the Axis powers between 1941 and 1944. Djilas grew increasingly disillusioned with Stalin and Soviet communism, and his growing critical stance was given further impetus by the Soviet Union's expulsion of the YCP from the **Cominform** in 1948. Between 1948 and 1953 Djilas, along with Kardelj and Boris Kidri, developed the idea of "self-management" which became a key part of the distinctive Yugoslav approach to communism sometimes known as "Titoism." Self-management involved workers managing their own workplaces and the use of the market in the economic sphere. In 1950 the legislation creating workers' self-management was passed, and at the Sixth Congress of the YCP in 1952 Djilas was involved in the change of the party name to the **League of Yugoslav Communists** (SKJ), along with its decentralization.

However, in spite of these major changes in the theory and practice of Yugoslav communism, Djilas grew increasingly unhappy with the continuing power of the bureaucracy and authoritarian nature of the regime. He used his position as editor of the party newspapers *Borba* and *Nova Jugoslavija* to criticize Tito and Titoism, and this resulted in his being stripped of all his party and government positions at an extraordinary Third Plenum of SKJ in 1953–1954. Djilas resigned from the SKJ in 1954 and continued to be a dissident voice leading to his imprisonment between 1956 and 1961 (for his support of the **Hungarian uprising**), and again between 1962 and 1966. On his release in 1966 he was allowed to return to Belgrade and to travel abroad, and in 1972 he was permitted to have his writings published again in Yugoslavia.

Djilas' key writings include the enormously influential *The New Class* (1957) in which he described and criticized the growth of a new bureaucratic **class** in Stalinist countries. He used the Soviet Union as his model, but included other communist countries such as Yugoslavia. The new class, he argued, was composed of communist party members, some of whom were also part of the bureaucracy and as such formed a super elite. The absence of private ownership of the **means of production** meant the power of the elites was based on their control of state resources and institutions which they used to bolster and maintain their position and to ensure obedience to their rule. Power, privilege and a higher standard of living was passed on to their children who benefited from better educational opportunities. This new class became corrupt and alienated from the people, ultimately displaying the key characteristics of a class in the Marxist sense. Djilas saw this form of communism—Marxism/Leninism/Stalinism—as a particularly Russian form of communism that other countries had adopted or had had imposed upon them. He suggested that communism could and should take different national forms in different countries reflecting the different conditions, histories and cultures.

Djilas' other book of particular note is *The Unperfect Society: Beyond the New Class* (1969) in which he extended his critical view of existing communisms to suggest that **Marxism** itself, as an ideological goal, was impossible. A "rational core" of Marxism, based on the notions of a classless society and the economic dependence of man, remained, but communism, like **capitalism**, had become corrupted by the conditions in which it developed and the way ahead now lay with different national versions of democratic socialism and social democracy. He placed particular emphasis on freedom, human rights and pluralism in his revised vision of a socialist future. *See also* YUGOSLAVIA, PEOPLE'S REPUBLIC OF.

DOBB, MAURICE HERBERT (1900–1976). Dobb was a prominent British **Marxist** and one of the most important contributors to

Marxist economic thought. He wrote extensively on a wide range of economic subjects, in particular the history of **bourgeois** economies, **socialist** planning, value theory and the rise of **capitalism**. Showing academic talent from an early age, Dobbs gained a master's degree in 1922 from Pembroke College, Cambridge, and studied for his doctorate at the London School of Economics, before he began teaching at Cambridge University in 1924. In 1948 he was elected a fellow and lecturer at Trinity College, Cambridge, and in 1959 the university appointed him reader in economics. He also held visiting positions at the University of London School of Slavonic Studies (1943–1946) and the University of Delhi (1951). He retired from teaching in 1967.

From 1922 until his death Dobbs was a member of the British Communist Party (BCP). He was active in the party, particularly in anti-fascist work in the 1930s and contributing to the debates on **Soviet Marxism** during and following the events in **Hungary** in 1956. He grew increasingly critical of the **Soviet Union** and its dogmatism, but remained loyal to Marxism and the BCP. His publications include *Capitalist Enterprise and Social Progress* (1925), *Wages* (1928), *Political Economy and Capitalism* (1937), *Studies in the Development of Capitalism* (1946), *On Economic Theory and Socialism* (1955), *An Essay on Economic Growth and Planning* (1960), *Welfare Economics and the Economics of Socialism* (1969), *Socialist Planning: Some Problems* (1970), *Theories of Value and Distribution Since Adam Smith* (1973), and *Random Biographical Notes* (1978). The titles give some indication of Dobbs' areas of interest: classical economics and the development of capitalism, and socialist economic planning. The latter in particular show his commitment to bridging the gap between the theoretical and the practical, between academia and politics. He criticized Soviet attempts at planning and contributed to debates on the relationship and roles of plan and market. He also made a seminal contribution to Marxist theorizing of the transition from **feudalism** to capitalism.

DUBCEK, ALEXANDER (1921–1992). Dubcek's name will forever be associated with the **Prague Spring**, an attempt to democratize and liberalize communist **Czechoslovakia** in 1968. At the time Dubcek was first secretary of the Central Committee of the **Communist Party of Czechoslovakia**, having gradually worked his way up through the party since joining in 1939. The reform program he initiated was described as "**socialism** with a human face," and involved increasing and guaranteeing the democratic rights and civil liberties of Czechoslovakian citizens. It included a relaxation of censorship laws and institutional reforms to permit greater participation of the people in government policy-making. The reforms crystallized in the "Action Program," and this provoked military intervention by the **Soviet Union** and five **Warsaw Pact** countries, the Soviet Union fearing that Czechoslovakia might leave the Warsaw Pact and inspire instability in the remaining countries of the Pact. The military invasion immediately brought the reforms to an end, with Dubcek being pressured to sign the "Moscow Protocol" in October 1968, in effect renouncing the path of reform. Dubcek held on as leader until April 1969, then becoming chair of the Federal Assembly and ambassador to Turkey before being expelled from the Communist Party in 1970. The "Velvet Revolution" of 1989 when communist rule was overthrown saw Dubcek return from obscurity to give his support and he took up the largely ceremonial role of Federal Assembly chair.

– E –

EAST GERMAN COMMUNIST PARTY. *See* SOCIALIST UNITY PARTY OF GERMANY.

EAST GERMANY. *See* GERMAN DEMOCRATIC REPUBLIC.

ECONOMIC AND PHILOSOPHICAL MANUSCRIPTS **(1844).** Written during **Karl Marx**'s exile in Paris after the proscription of the *Rheinische Zeitung* by the Prussian authorities, the *Economic and Philosophical Manuscripts* (EPM) is often called *The Paris Manuscripts*. Not intended for publication, the manuscripts were rediscovered and published in 1930 by the Institute of Marxism–Leninism in the **Soviet Union**, which also gave the title and some chapter headings, finally reaching the West in 1953.

Consisting of three interlinked texts, the second being incomplete, the manuscripts are a critique of **Georg Wilhelm Friedrich Hegel**'s views, a simultaneous endorsement of the importance of Hegel's "theoretical revolution," and a demystification of the Hegelian **dialectic**, to truly show the **material** condition of man. In essence, the manuscripts represent Marx's first major declaration of his lifelong critique of **capitalism** and his most discrete conceptualization from which **humanist** condemnation of the **commodity** system arises. Marx uses an analysis of the classical political economists Adam Smith, David Ricardo and Jean-Baptiste Say to achieve this.

Labor is not a constant value, it is contingent upon the dialectic of **capital**. Capitalism necessarily creates "two great **classes** opposing one another" because the character of the bourgeois **superstructure** and the nature of capital itself inevitably create monopolies. The **bourgeoisie** narrows, the **proletariat** is enlarged, the worker suffers, existentially and economically, in both the booms and **crises** caused by the contradictions of capital, thus labor is contingent. Marx uses Ludwig Feuerbach's positive, humanistic criticism to further undo Hegel's abstraction of man and condemns his classical political economy as noncritical. While the classical political economists recognize man as "the most wretched of commodities," they also conceal his **alienation**.

The most distinctive feature of the EPM is the comprehensive and systematic account of Marx's theory of alienation as the social, psychological, and physical human consequence of capitalism. His conception of alienation is a whole theory, which contains factors with inter-transferable relations. Each manifestation of the concept across four different spheres of man's life—relation to product, relation to activity, relations between men, and relation to his species life—appears in a different way because of its causal factor but is actually the same phenomenon. In capitalist society man is a commodity and in his labor he is lost to himself; he has a contingent existence that is manifested in capital.

As well as a descriptive analysis, Marx also offers a normative program. Ideas are propelled by the material condition of humanity and there exists a dialectical movement of estrangement from the first annulment of private property to the "positive transcendence of private property," the **negation of the negation**. In the opposition to Hegel's speculative philosophy, the thesis of the subjectivity of man's objective powers, that man can only be independent when he only owes his existence to himself, Marx suggests a sublation of **idealism** and materialism. The content of this early work is further expanded and made systematic in Marx's later works, notably the *Grundrisse* and *Capital*.

EMANCIPATION OF LABOR GROUP. The first Russian **Marxist** organization, the Emancipation of Labor Group (ELG) was formed by **Georgii Plekhanov, Paul Axelrod** and **Vera Zasulich** in 1883. Plekhanov was the leading intellectual figure in the group, and the group itself was the leading Marxist organization in Russia in the late 19th century and helped to both propagate Marxism and shape its character in the country. The ELG opposed its radical rivals, the populists, who based their revolutionary **socialism** on the existing communes in Russia.

ENGELS, FRIEDRICH (1820–1895). Engels was **Karl Marx**'s closest friend and political collaborator. He co-authored a number of works including *The Holy Family, German Ideology* and *The Communist Manifesto*, and worked with him as a political organizer and activist in the **Communist League** and **First International**. Engels also assisted Marx financially for much of his life, allowing Marx to continue his writing. After Marx's death Engels edited volumes two and three of *Capital*, helped to establish the **Second International**, and acted as the leading authority on Marx's ideas. He also wrote numerous works of his own, most notably *The Condition of the Working Class* (1845), *Anti-Dühring* (1878), *Dialectics of Nature* (1878–1882), and *Ludwig Feuerbach and the End of Classical German Philosophy* (1886). His wide-ranging interests took in philosophy (as evidenced in *Anti-Dühring, Dialectics of Nature* and *Ludwig Feuerbach*), science (see *Anti-Dühring*), anthropology (see *Origins of the Family*), history and military affairs. Engels' distinctive contributions lie particularly in the area of philosophy where he wrote extensively on **materialism, idealism**, and **dialectics**, supplying **Marxism** with an ontological and metaphysical foundation. There has been some controversy over the extent to which the views of Marx and Engels were in accord, with some commentators suggesting that Engels oversimplified and distorted Marx's views, giving an un-Marxian, positivist character to Marxism particularly as espoused by the Second International.

ETHIOPIA, PEOPLE'S DEMOCRATIC REPUBLIC OF. When Emperor Haile Selassie was deposed in 1974, a left-wing military junta assumed control of Ethiopia. Under the leadership of Colonel **Mengistu Haile Mariam**, the East African state advocated a

Marxist–Leninist path of development until the close of the 1980s. Soon after the September toppling of Selassie, the in-coming regime pronounced the creation of the Provisional Military Administrative Council (PMAC), also known as the "Derg." The PMAC was to become the government of Ethiopia, and despite initially appearing cautious toward the idea of wholesale adoption of Marxism–Leninism, it implemented a statist program that borrowed heavily from that of **Soviet** leader **Leonid Brezhnev**. The motives for this were as much pragmatic as ideological; such a system would allow for the creation of a reorganized **state** that could eliminate the ruling bureaucracy of the Selassie era and tighten the new regime's hold on power. The PMAC decreed a series of orthodox Marxist–Leninist measures, instigating a **peasant** literacy program to engender **revolutionary** verve in the majority countryside, nationalizing vast amounts of industry and commerce, and **collectivizing** both urban and rural land. The price of this was increased political and personal censorship, a clamp down on trade union powers and measures to eliminate anti-government demonstrations.

The drive toward **socialism** had been initiated by head of state General Tafari Benti, but when in 1977 he proposed negotiations with the PMAC's main political rivals, the apparently **Maoist** Ethiopian People's Revolutionary Party (EPRP), he was arrested and shot under the charge of collaboration with the enemy. Benti was replaced by Mengistu whose opening move was to instigate a "Red Terror" campaign against enemies of the PMAC regime, namely the EPRP, and Tigrayan and Eritrean nationalists who desired independence for their respective provinces. Mengistu was able to garner support and aid from his ideological brethren in the Soviet Union, and this became pivotal in repelling attacks from neighboring **Somalia**, as well as from the aforementioned nationalist movements within Ethiopia.

With such military opposition a constant threat, despite resistance to the idea in the early years of his reign, Mengistu realized a robust political organization was required to protect the regime. In December 1979 the Commission for Organizing the Party of the Working People of Ethiopia (COPWE) was launched to act as a Marxist–Leninist **vanguard party** charged with holding the country together and executing revolutionary strategy. COPWE spent the next five years presiding over a mass expansion of Ethiopian bureaucracy and ensuring that state power became subordinate to party will. Having constructed an unassailable position at the helm of government and country, in 1984 despite a horrendous countrywide famine COPWE channeled efforts into giving birth to its own replacement, the Workers' Party of Ethiopia (WPE). The effect of this was a further centralization of power, with former regional COPWE organs distorted to become mere mouthpieces of the WPE's central committee, politburo, secretariat, and most crucially general secretary, Mengistu. The party was structured like those of the monopoly regimes in the Soviet Union and Eastern Europe, strongly adhering to a centralist agenda aimed at transforming Ethiopia via the means of **scientific socialism**. In reality, it amounted to an ideological legitimatization of sustained one-party military rule, and stood to offer constitutional backing for Mengistu's place as the venerable and sagacious leader of the country. Ignoring a background of insurrectionary provincial violence, Mengistu and the WPE announced further structural alterations embodied in the constitution of 1987. This represented the regime's final and unequivocal adoption of orthodox Marxism–Leninism, with the liquidation of the PMAC it entailed presaging the creation of the People's Democratic Republic of Ethiopia (PDRE). The PDRE was to exist under the tutelage of a centrally elected president, with the first incumbent of that post unsurprisingly Mengistu. However, rather than acting as a democratizing measure, the constitution's foremost effect was the further ossification of the grasp on power of both the new president and the WPE.

This concentration on rapid centralization meant a mollification of tensions with radical groups that had desired and fought for autonomy throughout Ethiopian independence remained distant. One such group, the Eritrea People's Liberation Front (EPLF) continued to make territorial advances as the government's overstretched troops floundered. The effects of this were accentuated by the formation of the Ethiopian People's Revolutionary Democratic Front (EPRDF), who in collaborating with the EPLF contrived to test the WPE's authority over the country further through 1987 and 1988. Simultaneously, Ethiopia's command economy was stuttering and on the verge of collapse, and with the Soviet Union, in the throes of **Mikhail Gorbachev**'s *glasnost* and *perestroika* initiatives, refusing aid, Mengistu was forced to appeal to the World Bank and the International Monetary Fund for an urgent financial remedy.

From the fall of 1989 through to the beginning of 1990, with widespread famine, sweeping territorial gains by oppositional groups and an absence of assistance from **communist** regimes now crumbling across Eastern Europe and indeed the Soviet Union, Mengistu announced his government's renunciation of Marxism–Leninism and the extinction of the WPE. The party became the Ethiopian Democratic Unity Party, but before it had had a chance to act upon its **capitalist**-oriented reformist agenda Mengistu and his government had been forced to flee. Free elections were held in May 1991, with the EPRDF assuming control of Ethiopia, and the EPLF taking over in the imminently independent Eritrea. Both, despite their former commitment to an **Albanian** creed of **Leninism**, quickly began implementing free market economics and attempting to create a pluralistic society unthinkable of during Marxist–Leninist military rule.

The Marxism–Leninism employed in the PDRE was always more theoretical than actual. **Ideology** was used to justify measures that would ensure continuing and hegemonic rule, rather than because of a deep-seated commitment to Marxian scientific socialism. While there were occasional bouts of Soviet-style schemes, these were undertaken with practical motivations. This was exemplified by the government's nationalization and collectivization programs, which were primarily aimed at quelling unrest and achieving disassociation from the previous regime, and in their early reluctance to create a vanguard political party, a mainstay of orthodox Marxism–Leninism. The regime was above all a military one that sought to employ Marxism as an ideological tool with which political supremacy could be secured and maintained.

EUROCOMMUNISM. A briefly important school of **Marxism** that flourished in the 1970s, but which had effectively ceased to exist by the early 1980s. The movement and its ideas are primarily associated with the three largest European communist parties of the time: the **Italian Communist Party**, the **French Communist Party** and the **Spanish Communist Party**. Its key thinkers and practitioners were **Enrico Berlinguer**, Jean Ellenstein and **Santiago Carrillo**. The distinguishing features of Eurocommunism were a critical perspective on the **Soviet Union** and the Soviet model of **socialism**, a pluralist view of Marxism as taking different forms in different countries, and a commitment to human and civil rights and to a parliamentary road to socialism. The very pluralism of Eurocommunism entailed a lack of homogeneity within the movement and a lack of coherence in its theoretical outlook. *See also* LONGO, LUIGI.

EXCHANGE VALUE. *See* COMMODITY.

EXPLOITATION. This term is important in **Karl Marx**'s theory of **historical materialism** and in his analysis of **capitalism** in particular. For Marx, exploitation in one sense is a technical term denoting the extraction of **surplus value** from one section of the population by another section, and typically this will take the form of a subordinate **class** producing surplus value that a dominant or **ruling class** appropriates with the use or threat of force. In slave and serf societies the exploitation is visible with direct force and threats of force used in compelling the subordinate classes to produce and relinquish to the dominant classes a surplus. In capitalist society the extraction of surplus value is more subtle with workers selling their labor power to the capitalists who then use this labor power to generate surplus value which they then own. According to Marx, the extraction of surplus value from the worker by the capitalist involves no robbery and is not unjust, because both worker and capitalist only receive what they are entitled to. The worker is entitled to the value of his labor power, and, as with any **commodity**, this is the amount of labor required to produce it. The labor required to produce labor power is the amount required to keep the worker alive and in a position to perform the work for which he is paid. In other words, the value of labor power is the amount of labor required to produce the food, housing, clothes, training and so on that the worker needs. In essence the worker is entitled to no more than a subsistence wage in the capitalist system of exchange, although historic conditions may see a higher wage paid.

Despite Marx's theory of historical materialism (according to which justice and morality are relative to specific historical modes of production), his claims to be scientific and various comments he makes suggesting exploitation is not used as a term of condemnation, the term and the theory point to a critique and denunciation of capitalism. *See also* LABOR THEORY OF VALUE.

– F –

FANON, FRANTZ (1925–1961). A revolutionary **socialist** activist and major theoretician of Third World liberation, Fanon was strongly influenced by **Marxism**, but both developed it and departed from it in his analysis of colonialism. Born in French colonial Martinique, he attended schools both there and in France. He volunteered to serve in the French army in 1944, and subsequently studied medicine and psychiatry at the University of Lyons in France. In 1953 he was made head of the psychiatric department at Blida-Joinville hospital in the French colony of Algeria. When the Algerian war of independence began in 1954 Fanon helped the rebels, gradually becoming more involved in the rebel cause. He resigned from his hospital post in 1956 and became editor of the Algerian National Front's (FLN) newspaper. In 1960 he was appointed ambassador of the Algerian Provisional Government to Ghana. In the same year he was diagnosed with leukemia for which he was treated in the **Soviet Union** and the **United States**. He died in a hospital in Washington, D.C. in 1961 and was buried in Algeria.

Fanon has through his writings and example been influential in the Third World and among black activists in the United States. His most important writings are *Peau noire, masques blancs* (*Black Skin, White Masks*, 1952), *L'an V de la révolution algérienne* (published in English under the title *Studies in a Dying Colonialism*, 1959), *Les damnés de la terre* (*The Wretched of the Earth*, 1961), and *Pour la révolution africaine* (*For the African Revolution*, 1964). Of these *The Wretched of the Earth* is the most famous, and notable for its advocacy of and emphasis on violence in the process of national liberation. In addition, Fanon portrayed the **peasantry** rather than the **proletariat** as the key revolutionary **class**, and saw psychological liberation as a fundamental part of national liberation.

FETISHISM OF THE COMMODITY. In his analysis of **capitalism** in *Capital* **Karl Marx** introduces his notion of the fetishism of the **commodity**. Drawing an analogy with religious fetishes where a power is falsely attributed to an object, Marx argues that in capitalism the commodity is given the appearance of being the natural source of value by the prevailing social relations. Commodities appear to have a natural and intrinsic value rather than being the value of the labor power invested in their manufacture. Marx attributes a similar fetishism to wages, profit and rent, which in capitalism have the appearance of being revenue derived from labor, **capital** and land respectively, but are in fact derived from different amounts of labor power. Marx sees capitalist social relations as mystifying, as obscuring the true relations between people and things, for example wages conceal **exploitation**, and overall capitalism appears as natural rather than a historically specific social form.

FEUDALISM. Karl Marx identified feudalism as the **mode of production** coming between slavery and **capitalism**, characterized by the antagonistic **class** relationship between landlords and **peasants**, and by a low level of technology, essentially still at the manual and simple tool stage. In feudalism **surplus value** is extracted from the peasants by the landlords in the form of feudal rent. In drawing the broad differences between feudalism and capitalism Marx writes, "The handmill gives you society with the feudal lord; the steam mill, society with the industrial capitalist." What he means by this is that when technology is at the level of the handmill, or in other words at a relatively simple nonmechanized level, then the typical relation of production is that of lord and serf. The lords own the land and the serfs work on it to produce food and other essentials. Tied to the land and bound to serve their lord, the serfs' freedom of movement is severely restricted. As for the small number of skilled workers, a system of guilds serves to organize them and to limit competition between them. On this economic **base** rests a **superstructure** that includes an authoritarian, hierarchical political structure headed by a monarch with vast and often arbitrary powers. This political and social structure is supported by religious, moral and social ideas that all serve to legitimize it. In the sphere of religion the clergy preach the divine right of kings and acceptance of one's lot in the here and now with a promise of better things to come in the afterlife as a reward for such acquiescence. The dominant moral ideas and social attitudes espouse obedience, loyalty, deference and social immobility, all of which again serve to sanction and bolster the existing political, social and economic system.

Marx sketches the transition from feudal society to capitalist society. The key factor in this transition is technological development and specifically the advent of steam power and mechanization. This is a

radical change in the **forces of production**, which leads to a transformation of the **relations of production** and the superstructure. For
steam power and machinery to be used efficiently it is no use having
serfs tied to the land and spread out over the countryside. What is
needed instead is a concentration of laborers in towns to work in the
factories that use the new machines. The new machines and factories
require laborers who are free to move to the towns, and free to become workers in factories. The feudal relations of production, principally the relationship between lord and serf, become redundant, particularly as they hold back the development and utilization of the new
technology. The new productive forces cannot operate efficiently and
develop to their full potential while feudal relations of production
still prevail. The conflict between the old relations of production and
the new forces of production can only last so long before a **revolutionary** change in society takes place, and feudal relations are replaced by the more appropriate capitalist relations of production; instead of serfs there are workers, and instead of lords there are
capitalists. This in turn requires a change in the political and legal institutions, and in the religious, moral and social attitudes of society.

Hence, political power and influence begin to swing to the newly
born class of industrialists which is rapidly becoming the wealthiest
class in society. The monarchy and aristocracy, with their economic
power on the wane, find themselves engaged in a political struggle
with this new class of capitalists, a struggle that they are historically
destined to lose. Parliamentary democracy supersedes absolute
monarchy; kings lose their power and sometimes their heads too.
New constitutions and laws are made by the new ruling class. New
political ideas concerning the rule of law, liberty of the individual,
freedom of conscience, freedom of contract, the free market and
competition emerge and gradually come to dominate society. In religion the clergy no longer insists on the divine right of kings, but
preaches Puritanism and a work ethic in keeping with the virtues
most useful to the new ruling class and society. For Marx, feudalism
serves to highlight that modes of production, including capitalism,
are historically specific and neither natural nor eternal.

FIRST INTERNATIONAL. Officially the International Working
Men's Association, the First International was an organization of
working **class** groups from Western and Central Europe, with which

Karl Marx and **Friedrich Engels** were heavily involved. Formed in 1864 it initially lacked both a firm structure and organization, and an overall political program. This reflected the diverse groups and views represented in the International, including nationalist followers of Guiseppe Mazzini, Anglo–French positivists, English former Chartists, Proudhonists, supporters of Michael Bakunin and German **socialists**. The International had both individual members and group affiliations, and when it began had five affiliated national sections: English, French, German, Italian and Polish. Marx, who sat on the International's General Council, drafted the Inaugural Address and Rules and the moderate and minimal character of the program he wrote reflected the compromises required to produce anything that would gain agreement from so broad a range of groups and views.

Gradually, Marx was able to influence the International in a more socialist direction, so that by 1868 it was committed to collective ownership of mines, railways, communications and some land. In 1871 the International gave its support to the **Paris Commune**, with Marx's *The Civil War in France* being issued as an Address on behalf of the General Council. In the same year at the party's conference the goal of creating a working-class party was endorsed, and the following year the "conquest of political power" by the **proletariat** was announced as an objective at the Hague Congress. This Congress was also notable for both its size (65 delegates from 15 countries including the **United States** and Australia) and the expulsion of Bakunin who had opposed Marx and the General Council on issues of political action and the "growing authoritarianism" of the Council. In addition, the Hague Congress decided in favor of moving the General Council from London to New York, a move that contributed to the end of the First International, which was formally dissolved at a conference in Philadelphia in 1876. The First International was notable for its support of the Polish national uprising of 1863 and of the Paris Commune. It also represents one of the earliest attempts to forge international links between socialist groups, and helped Marx to spread his influence and ideas among the European labor movement. The International also saw the deepening of the divide between anarchists and socialists, embodied in the battle between Marx and Bakunin, and it led Marx to view international organizations (at least at the time of the demise of the First International) as "impossible" and "useless," and to move instead toward the strategy of promoting workers' (**Marxist**) parties with the aim of conquering political power.

FORCES OF PRODUCTION. The term "forces of production" or "productive forces" refers to a crucial element in **Karl Marx**'s theory of **historical materialism**. It is used by Marx to refer to a broad range of factors involved in the process of production. For example, he includes under the heading "forces of production" tools and machines such as ploughs and steam engines, factories and workshops, raw materials, roads and canals, knowledge and skills, and even classes directly involved in production, such as the working class in capitalist society. The forces of production along with the **relations of production** constitute the economic **base** of society, and the economic base is crucial in shaping the nature of the rest of society, its **superstructure**. Some interpreters of Marx, such as Gerry Cohen, attribute a causally determining role to the forces of production, suggesting that the nature of the forces of production ultimately determines the nature of society as a whole. This interpretation is known as technological **determinism**.

FOURTH INTERNATIONAL. Founded in 1938 by **Leon Trotsky** and his supporters, it positioned itself in opposition to the **Third International** and **Stalinism**. Parties and organizations belonging to it are linked by their commitment to Trotsky's brand of **Marxism**, but it has seen numerous disagreements and splits often relating to how Trotsky should be interpreted. It continues to function, but remains small and unsuccessful so far in fomenting **revolution**.

FRANKFURT SCHOOL. A school of **Marxism** associated with the Frankfurt Institute for Social Research founded in 1923. Among the many significant figures linked with the school are **Max Horkheimer, Herbert Marcuse, Theodor Adorno, Erich Fromm, Jürgen Habermas** and **Walter Benjamin**. Spanning a range of research interests, these and other academics associated with the institute sought to create a critical Marxism that addressed and responded to the conditions of the time. In particular the lack of success of revolutionary working-**class** movements, the degeneration of the **Bolshevik** revolution into **Stalinism**, and the rise of fascism were key issues underlying much of the work of the school. Perceiving the limitations of orthodox Marxism they sought to reinvigorate and develop it in new directions drawing on non-Marxist thinkers such as Immanuel Kant, **Georg Wilhelm Friedrich Hegel**, Max Weber and Sigmund Freud, as well as the writings of **Georgii Lukács**. The Frankfurt School is a major strand of **Western Marxism** and a significant influence on the New Left, as well as providing the environment for the writing of some of the "classics" of Marxist literature.

The Frankfurt School really began to emerge when Horkheimer became director of the institute in 1930 and assembled the outstanding academics who became the "membership" of the school. Horkheimer oversaw the transfer of the school to the United States in 1934 after the Nazis came to power in Germany. He was still director of the institute when it returned to Frankfurt in 1949. Addressing the key question of why revolution had not occurred in Western Europe members of the school explored areas of culture, philosophy, social psychology and sociology. They investigated and theorized the stabilizing features of **capitalism** that prevented revolution. They tended to move away from the Marxist commitment to class struggle and turned on its head Marx's Promethean faith in science and technology taming nature and providing the basis for human emancipation. The outlook of the Frankfurt School was critical of rationalism and saw technological progress as a potential obstacle to human freedom in its denial of the truly human, our individuality, creativity and spirituality. The Frankfurt School was only a school in a very loose sense with individual researchers expressing a range of differing ideas and political perspectives. It was partly this pluralism and lack of dogma that made the school such a successful generator of innovative ideas and research. Academic rather than activist the school's impact has been more in the intellectual than the political realm.

FRENCH COMMUNIST PARTY. The French Communist Party (*Parti communiste français*—PCF) was established in 1920 by **Marxist–Leninist** members of the **French Socialist Party** who supported the **Bolsheviks** in the 1917 **Russian Revolution** and opposed World War I. The PCF became a member of the **Comintern**, and accordingly in the 1920s went through a period of concerted **Stalinism**, accentuated by the 1930 appointment of the Muscovite **Maurice Thorez** as general secretary. External political opponents and those within the party advocating **Trotskyism** were sidelined, and the PCF was organized as a mirror of the **Communist Party of the Soviet Union**. However, owing to the growing threat posed by the National Socialists in Germany, the PCF was instructed by the Comintern to seek political alliances with other Marxist and **socialist** groups in France. The result was a Popular Front alliance that sailed to victory in the 1936 general election, but imploded soon after. The PCF, at the behest of a Moscow that had freshly ratified the Nazi–Soviet Pact, initially opposed World War II and collaborated with the Germans upon the invasion of France. The 1941 German invasion of the **Soviet Union**, though, triggered a reversal of this policy, and the PCF became central to the resistance movement, to the extent that by 1944 it found itself a member of Charles de Gaulle's government, and a year later with a 25 percent share of the French vote.

The PCF was removed from office in 1947, prompting a three-decade period in which it consistently polled in excess of 20 percent of the popular vote but was prohibited from entering government. In between, it supported the general strike of 1968 but opposed what it labeled the "Trotskyite and **Maoist**" actions of those taking part in the Paris demonstrations of May in the same year, using its close relationship with the **Confédération Générale du Travail** to broker an end to the disorder. From the 1970s, the PCF sought alliances with other left-wing groups to facilitate an end to its period outside of office. It duly became a member of François Mitterrand's socialist administrations of 1981 and 1984, with party leaders holding ministerial positions for the first time since 1947. Mitterrand's socialists, however, were able to assume primacy over the PCF as the recognized party of the left, and by the 1986 elections the party was already on its way to electoral oblivion. The 1991 **collapse of the Soviet Union** brought about a repudiation of the party's Stalinist past, though concurrently a re-affirmation of its commitment to **communism**. The PCF was given hope anew by its inclusion in Lionel Jospin's socialist administration of 1997, but at the 2002 National Assembly elections it gained less than 5 percent of the vote.

Marxism in the PCF has appeared in a number of different guises, though a Stalinist core, more pronounced in the first half of the party's life than in the second, has remained constant. This was challenged in the 1970s, as moderate general secretary Georges Marchais drove the party to advocate **Eurocommunism**. By the late 1990s the

PCF openly advocated "socialism in French colors," a program that supplemented its Marxism with a fervent nationalism. Today, the party is rife with disputes from adherents of each of these ideologies, though it remains committed to "rescuing" France from **capitalism** through Marxism–Leninism.

FRENCH REVOLUTION (1789). Events in the summer of 1789 heralded the transition of France from the rule of monarchy and *ancien régime* to that of "liberty, equality and fraternity," and, eventually, the First Republic. Opposition to the *ancien régime* and the privileged establishment it maintained mounted throughout 1789, with **peasants** attacking their landlords' estates in the countryside and anti-monarchy agitation in Paris. Economic hardship was the central cause of nationwide disillusionment with the status quo, as high prices and food shortages conspired to create a state of famine in many areas, and the sheer poverty of a majority of citizens led to a yearning for political change. The American Revolution and the impact of the Enlightenment movement enhanced this rebellious climate. The paucity of finance ran right through to state level, and with those within the establishment unwilling to compromise any of their own personal wealth, on 5 May 1789 King Louis XVI summoned the Estates General to thrash out a solution.

The Estates General consisted of three groups, the Clergy, the Nobility and the Commoners (or Third Estate), and despite convening to discuss fiscal matters it soon became affected by the clamor for reform throughout France. Having quarreled with the other two groups over the system of voting that the Estates General would employ, the Commoners made a dramatic decision to declare themselves the sole governors of France, and on 17 June announced the creation of the National Assembly to enable them to bring about rapid change. With political violence threatening to spill over, radicals inside the National Assembly were able to pass far-reaching reforms as moderates feared anarchy should the French population not be placated. On 20 June members of the Third Estate gathered and vowed not to disband until they attained for France a written constitution, in what became known as the Tennis Court Oath (forbidden to enter the Palace of Versailles, the rebels had gathered in an adjacent tennis court). With popular pressure escalating, the king saw fit to recognize the legitimacy of the National Assembly and ordered the Clergy and the Nobility to join.

The National Assembly immediately set about transforming France's political, social and economic landscape, adopting a succession of radical reforms. Between 4 August and 12 August, feudal rights and privileges were swept away, the *ancien régime* confined to the history books and legal and fiscal equality between all proclaimed. At the same time, the Assembly was working on a new constitution limiting monarchical powers and installing a unicameral elected legislative. The Declaration of the Rights of Man was drafted and adopted on 26 August, marking the birth of egalitarian France, and the Nobility was abolished to reaffirm this. The Clergy, having possessed so much of France's wealth, fell victim to the **revolutionary** tide as its estates were confiscated and nationalized to solve the government's financial predicament in November, and early in 1790 the Civil Constitution of the Clergy was forced upon them, reorganizing relations between church and state and decreeing that Clerics be paid by the government. In December the Assembly eradicated provincial divisions and parliaments, and divided the country into departments whose rule would come from elected assemblies.

Despite these radical reforms, as **Karl Marx** would later observe, the revolution remained at this stage essentially the preserve of a moderate **bourgeoisie** which sought to create a constitutional monarchy rather than a republic. This propagated in France a suspicion among the **proletariat** and peasantry that the Royals and the Assembly were both against the revolution, and unrest continued to manifest itself, for instance in the storming of the Bastille on 14 July, and the forceful removal of the royal family from Versailles to the capital following agitation by the "Paris Mob" on 6 October.

France remained in a constant state of volatility, and in 1791 events came to a head that would eventually see the full abolition of the monarchy. On 20 June 1791, King Louis XVI, fearing the insurrectionary masses, attempted to flee abroad, but got only as far as Varennes, at which point he was returned to Paris with his popularity and trustworthiness at a new low. With France fighting the Revolutionary Wars against hostile foreign states abroad, and constant turmoil domestically, the bitter factional disputes characterizing the country were accentuated, and rioting was widespread. The National Assembly was supplanted by the Constituent Assembly in September 1791, and in an atmosphere of such instability radicals came to dominate the government. In 1792 the monarchy was formally abolished, with the king executed the following year, and the First Republic established, while the National Convention replaced the year-old Constituent Assembly, an event that sparked the beginning of the so-called Reign of Terror. The Reign of Terror was characterized by the National Convention's suppression of bitterly split factions such as the Jacobins and the Girondins, and of counter-revolutionary royalist forces.

Violence ceased midway through 1794, and a year later the Convention remolded itself into the government of the Directory. However, such cosmetic changes only stood to mask the split administration of the young republic, and in 1799 Napoleon Bonaparte put down the government in the Brumaire coup d'état and began his rule. Subsequently, many of the reforms made following the revolution were reversed, but the long-term legacy for France could not be erased, as the concepts of liberty, equality and fraternity had entered the nation's psyche and shaped what it later became.

Marx considered the French Revolution of 1789 to be a classic example of a bourgeois revolution as **feudalism** had been replaced with a **capitalism** able to prosper via more suitable improved legal conditions. As the revolution favored the bourgeoisie, so it was a bourgeois revolution, a characterization Marx applied too to the 1848 **Revolutions**. The French Revolution was thus to be the first stage of an eventual worldwide proletarian revolution.

FRENCH SOCIALIST PARTY. Though there had been socialist parties in France since the 1880s, the first mass **Marxist** organization was launched in 1905 under the leadership of **Jean Jaurés** as the Socialist Party–French Section of the Workers International (*Section française de L'Internationale Ouvrière*—SFIO). The SFIO was destabilized in 1920 when members defected to form the **French Communist Party** (FCP), a group whose pro-**revolution** stance sat uncomfortably with the democratic Marxism of the socialists. By 1936, the two had joined together in the Popular Front coalition and formed a government under socialist leader Léon Blum. The Popular Front served for just two years before collapsing, and by 1940 the SFIO had been banned by the occupying German National Socialists. For the rest of World War II, the party played a key role alongside the communists in the resistance.

In the decade after the war, the SFIO regularly polled 25 percent of the vote to the FCP's 26 percent, though by the 1960s the party was locked into an irreversible decline. It was in this context that General Secretary Guy Mollet appealed for the formation of a new socialist party. The Socialist Party (*Parti Socialiste*—PS), a collection of various left-wing forces, was inaugurated in December 1968. Under François Mitterand's stewardship as first secretary, which began in 1971, the party championed a progressive program bereft of any mention of Marxism. With the help of coalition partners including the FCP, in 1981 the PS with Lionel Robert Jospin at its head won both presidential and national elections, and proceeded to implement an economic recovery plan underpinned by left-wing ideals. Banks and insurance companies were nationalized, a wealth tax introduced, and social benefits and wages were increased. However, this failed to overturn France's fiscal decline, and in 1984 the PS abandoned its commitment to socialist principles and remolded itself into a social democratic, free market–friendly party. Though defeated in the 1986 elections, the party formed governments from 1988 until 1993, and from 1997 until 2002. The PS has all but renounced its commitment to socialism and their Marxist traditions are, it seems, consigned to history.

FROMM, ERICH (1900–1980). An important contributor to modern psychoanalytical thought, Fromm combined psychoanalysis and **Marxism**. He espoused a **humanist Marxism** placing particular emphasis on **Karl Marx**'s early writings.

Born in Frankfurt-am-Main, Germany, Fromm studied psychology, sociology and philosophy at the universities of Frankfurt (where he also studied law) and Heidelberg, receiving his PhD from the former in 1922. He trained in psychoanalysis at the Berlin Institute and became associated with the Institute of Social Research (*see* FRANKFURT SCHOOL) during the 1920s. In 1933 he fled Nazi Germany and settled in the **United States** where he became a citizen in 1934. Here he lectured at the New School for Social Research, Yale University, Columbia University and Bennington College, spent time as chairman of the faculty of the William Alanson White Institute of Psychiatry, Psychoanalysis and Psychology, and in 1951 became a professor at the National University of Mexico where he founded the Mexican Institute of Psychoanalysis. Fromm's political activities included writing the manifesto for the Socialist Party of the United States in 1959 and being a leading activist in protests against the Vietnam War and in favor of nuclear arms control.

Among Fromm's many publications were his essay on Marxism and psychoanalysis, *The Method and Function of an Analytical Social Psychology: Notes On Psychoanalysis and Historical Materialism* (1932), *Escape From Freedom* (1941) in which he described the social and cultural influences on human personality, *The Fear of Freedom* (1942) in which he theorized the underlying psychology of fascist supporters linking it to **capitalism**, and *The Sane Society* (1956) in which he analyzed the dehumanizing effects of both capitalist and socialist modern industrial societies and their bureaucratic institutions. He also wrote specifically on Marxism in *Marx's Concept of Man* (1961) and *Socialist Humanism: An International Symposium* (1965). Fromm interpreted Marx as a humanist and argued that capitalism **alienates** and debilitates human beings, preventing the development of their authentic, creative and loving selves, of their potentialities. Instead, capitalism fosters the development of personality types that prevent human realization. He believed that the contradictions of capitalism, psychological as well as economic, would lead to the workers overthrowing the system and creating a humanist socialist society in its stead. He criticized the dehumanizing institutions and structures of **Soviet**-style socialism along with its emphasis on the attainment of material affluence.

FRONT FOR THE LIBERATION OF MOZAMBIQUE. The Front for the Liberation of Mozambique (*Frente de Libertação de Moçambique*—FRELIMO) came to power on Mozambican independence in 1975, having spent the first 13 years of its existence in a protracted guerrilla struggle against Portuguese colonial occupation. After the creation of the **People's Republic of Mozambique**, under the guidance of President **Samora Machel** FRELIMO sought to apply the **Marxism–Leninism** that had informed its liberation struggle to the wider state, **collectivizing** production, affirming its single-party status and disseminating its ideology across the country through "dynamizing groups" of party cadres. In 1977, FRELIMO declared its status as a **vanguard party**, increasing the size of the Central Committee and moving closer to the **Soviet Union**. However, the party's leaders acknowledged the necessity of applying Marxism to the concrete conditions surrounding them, acknowledging the primacy of agriculture and the **peasantry** over industry and the **proletariat**. As a result, FRELIMO allowed rural private enterprise to continue, an economic necessity given the ruinous civil war in which it was engaged with the anti-communist National Resistance Movement (*Resistência Nacional Moçambicana*—RENAMO). By 1989, with widespread recession and a heartfelt desire to bring about an end to the civil war, at its Fifth Party Congress FRELIMO renounced Marxism–Leninism, and moderate leader Joaquim Chissano moved the party toward social democratic status. The distinctly non-Marxist FRELIMO has formed continuous government ever since.

– G –

GANG OF FOUR. Consisting of Jiang Qing, Zhang Chunqiao, Wang Hongwen and Yao Wenhuan, the Gang of Four was a group of Chinese **communist** leaders who were arrested in 1976 accused of trying to seize power after **Mao Zedong**'s death. They were convicted of a number of crimes against the state. All members of the Politiburo, the Gang of Four were hard-line radicals and leading proponents of the **Cultural Revolution**. Jiang, who led the group, was Mao's wife and had had great power and influence in China while Mao was alive. The arrest and conviction of the Gang of Four was seen as a victory for more moderate communists in the country.

GARAUDY, ROGER (1913–). A French **Marxist**, born in Marseille, Garaudy was a leading figure and theorist in the **French Communist Party** (PCF) from the 1950s until his expulsion from the party in 1970. His chief contribution to Marxism lies in his increasingly liberal, humanistic and pluralistic interpretation of Marxism and his critique of **Soviet Marxism**.

Garaudy's humanistic interpretation of Marxism was apparent in his *Perspectives de l'homme: existentialisme, pensée catholique, marxisme* (1959) in which he also made positive comments regarding existentialism, phenomenology and Christianity. He continued these themes, moving away from all dogmatism and criticizing the Soviet system in further works such as *From Anathema to Dialogue: A Marxist Challenge To The Christian Church* (1966), *Initiative in History: A Christian–Marxist Dialogue* (1967), *Crisis In Communism* (1970) and *Marxism in the Twentieth Century* (1970). Garaudy rejected Marxist orthodoxy and advocated the de-Stalinization and opening up of Marxism to nonorthodox and even non-Marxist points of view. For him Marxism was not an absolute truth but rather an intellectual truth aiding us in making the world intelligible rather than dictating our actions. Marxism helped to explain other theories and perspectives, but Garaudy rejected claims for it providing absolute knowledge.

Garaudy's academic career began at the Faculty of Letters of the University of Paris where he gained his doctorate in philosophy, and it continued with academic posts at the University of Albi (Algiers), the Lycée Buffon in Paris (1958–1959), the University of Clermont-Ferrand (1962–1965), and the University of Poitiers (1965, 1969–1973). He was also director of the Centre for Marxist Research and Study from 1960 to 1970. Politically Garaudy was an official in the political bureau of the PCF from 1956 until 1970, and his political posts included deputy to the First National Assembly (1946–1951), communist deputy to and vice president of the National Assembly (1956–1958), and communist member of the National Senate (1959–1962). In addition, he became editorial head of the radical French journal *Alternatives socialistes* in 1974.

GERMAN COMMUNIST PARTY. The German Communist Party (*Kommunistische Partei Deutschlands*—KPD) was a splinter group from the *Unabhängige Sozialistische Partei Deutshlands* (Independendent German Socialist Party—USPD), which was itself a breakaway party from the *Sozialdemokratische Partei Deutschlands* (**German Social Democratic Party**—SPD). Formed 1 January 1919 it consisted of members of the **Spartacus League**, most notably **Rosa Luxemburg** and **Karl Liebknecht**. In 1920 it gained just 2 percent of the vote, but after merging with the left wing of the USPD to form the United Communist Party of Germany it increased both its membership and its vote so that by 1932 it had 17 percent of the vote. Following the line of the **Comintern** to which it belonged, the KPD condemned the SPD as "social fascism." It found itself the victim of Nazi terror, and after World War II sought to unite with the SPD, but its close ties to the Soviet Union led to this being rejected by the SPD, and it failed to make a significant electoral impact subsequently.

GERMAN DEMOCRATIC REPUBLIC (GDR). At the end of World War II in 1945, the **Soviet Union** was left in control of the eastern half of Germany. By 1949 the Soviets had managed to convert the zone into a fully fledged, independent **communist** country, one that was to rigidly follow the **Marxist–Leninist** schema until its demise in 1989. The German Democratic Republic became one of the most orthodox, authoritarian countries in the Eastern Bloc, following the policies of the **Stalinist** era even past 1985 as surrounding countries subscribed to **Mikhail Gorbachev**'s reformist *glasnost* and *perestroika* programs.

Initially, the Soviet-controlled area was run by the military with little sign of political intervention. However, the Soviets quickly moved to reeducate the east German population in anti-fascism and the merits of Marxism–Leninism. German communists, exiled in the Soviet Union throughout the tenure of the Third Reich, were drafted back into the country and handed control of local government and the media to disseminate the communist mantra. Among these was Walter Ulbricht, a hard-line Stalinist who oversaw the Soviet-enforced merger into the **Socialist Unity Party of Germany**, or, *Sozialdemokratische Einheitspartei Deutschlands* (SED) of the **German Communist Party** and the **German Social Democratic Party** in East Germany in April 1945. Moscow stooge Ulbricht, as the first SED general secretary, immediately began work to sideline other political parties by wresting control of the east German political machine for the communists, so that as the 1950s approached all opposition was rendered impotent. As the Cold War began to take hold, differences between the communist-occupied east of Germany and **capitalist**-held west were exacerbated. With such tangible tensions abounding, and given the strong position of the heavily Soviet-backed SED, the proclamation of the east as an independent communist state came on 7 October 1949 when a new constitution was approved by the 3rd People's Congress creating the GDR. Wilhelm Pieck became the infant state's first president, though in common with the Soviet Union and its other satellite states, real power rested with the party general secretary, in this case Ulbricht.

The SED was quick to proceed with the Sovietization of the GDR. It rapidly asserted its political will as the sole one in the country, embarking upon a centralization program that in 1952 saw five self-autonomous Länder abolished in favor of ceding control to the party organs of Berlin. The SED became one of the most pervasive political parties in the communist Eastern Bloc, with every element of society infiltrated and under the influence of party *nomenklatura*. To support this vigilant grip on the GDR the "Stasi" secret police was created, which rapidly accumulated detailed files on several million unsuspecting East Germans. The economy was remodeled according to the Soviet Stalinist prototype, with strict central planning, target setting and the implementation of Five Year Plans overseeing a newly nationalized industrial and commercial landscape. In addition, agriculture was **collectivized** and also subject to centrally ordained targets. To eradicate any ideological competition for Marxism–Leninism, as well as the liquidation of political rivals, religion came under harsh repression, with religious meetings and organizations outlawed at the start of the 1950s. The cultural sphere faced SED interference too, with the regime acutely aware of the importance of propaganda to legitimize its rule in the eyes of the public. Finally, General Secretary Ulbricht sought to underpin the education system with the concept of the "new socialist man," demanding a rewrite of the curriculum along Marxist–Leninist lines in order to cleanse the GDR of "bourgeois" culture, and create pupils devoted to the noble cause of communism. In the space of a few years, the GDR had been forcibly sculpted by the all-powerful SED into a Moscow-oriented "People's Republic."

The death of **Josef Stalin** in 1953 created pressure from reformist groups, which aspired to see adherence to the Stalinist course relaxed throughout the Soviet satellite states. Though the orthodox Ulbricht did not wish to hand down genuine reform, he did, under pressure from Moscow, reluctantly consent to the introduction of a "New Course" scheme. This purported to pay heed to errors made toward, among other persecuted groups, small farm holders and artisans, and offered as a solution to resultant problems a price freeze and an increase in the production of consumer goods. To fulfill this pledge, demands to raise productivity levels were meted out to industrial workers. What followed was widespread protest, beginning in Berlin in June 1953 and soon engulfing most of the GDR, and only quelled by the intervention of Soviet troops on the government's behalf. The reforms proposed in the New Course were annulled, and with Moscow, given that the alternative was a distinct undermining of the communist regime, now firmly behind the anti-reformist Ulbricht, and de-Stalinizing tendencies within the SED defeated, the leader emerged with a firmer grip on power than ever.

Further integration with the Soviet Union followed, and in 1956 a National People's Army was formed to work closely with the **Red Army** under the auspices of the freshly signed **Warsaw Pact**. That same year, **Nikita Khrushchev**'s "secret speech" denouncing Stalin had caused shockwaves throughout the communist world, and emboldened reformist thinkers to propound liberalizing measures. In the GDR, however, these "revisionists" were condemned by the regime in the strongest terms, and faced long-term imprisonment. The SED was not going to allow widespread demands for reform such as those which occurred during the 1956 **Polish** and **Hungarian Uprisings** to seep through and spread in the GDR. Where other Soviet brother states undertook measures to turn away from Stalinist orthodoxy, Ulbricht and the SED embraced the doctrine with renewed vigor. The erection of the **Berlin Wall** in August 1961 stood as further affirmation of the SED government's commitment to communist orthodoxy, officially and literally sealing the GDR from the capitalist West.

With Pieck now deceased, in abolishing the position of president and placing himself at the helm of the new Council of State, Ulbricht was able to confirm and accentuate his status as the monolithic strong leader in accordance with Soviet Stalinism. The SED had become the most unbendingly loyal apostle of Moscow rule and Marxist–Leninist orthodoxy, a fact illustrated by the strong assistance lent to the Soviet-led crushing of the 1968 **Prague Spring**. Inside the country, with living standards rising continuously, disquiet toward the regime was rare, and where dissent existed it faced harsh institutional repression. Yet Ulbricht's unflinching devotion to orthodoxy meant his position as general secretary came under intense scrutiny as the 1970s began. Moscow, perhaps sensing the need for the GDR to reform in order to preserve, demanded that Ulbricht steer his country toward closer relations with its neighbors in the Federal Republic of Germany (FRG, or West Germany). Ulbricht vehemently opposed any such alliance with a capitalist country, and was duly replaced in 1971 by another Moscow partisan, Erich Honecker.

Honecker, though never attempting to alter the climate of state-led repression, managed to increase the legitimacy of the SED government by offering social reform programs, for example, creating a fully developed welfare state and introducing measures to end societal gender inequalities. Primarily through improved relations with the FRG, the economy rapidly grew to the extent that the GDR became something of a beacon for communist economic development. Such progress (in comparison with the other communist Eastern Bloc states) coupled with the SED's deep-seated commitment to ideological orthodoxy gave Honecker the confidence to reject in 1985 Gorbachev's landmark *glasnost* and *perestroika* reform initiatives. The SED general secretary argued that as the GDR had already undergone significant economic reforms in the 1970s, a new wave of changes was not necessary. It was these reforms that allowed the GDR to avoid the economic slump afflicting surrounding Soviet satellite countries, as its trading relationship with the FRG underpinned a relatively healthy performance. The decision to assuage Gorbachev's proposals was also ideologically motivated; if the GDR adopted strict market economics it would in effect cease to be any different from the FRG, thus ending its life as a separate, communist, state. To reaffirm the supremacy of orthodox Marxist–Leninist doctrine the SED ignored calls for political reform, banned the circulation of reformist Soviet newspapers, and in February 1989 stated its intention to tread its own path to communism, one that would allow for continued political monopoly and state ownership of industry and commerce. Having been ceaselessly loyal to the **Communist Party of the Soviet Union** for over 40 years, the SED now found itself vainly attempting to resist edicts emanating from Moscow. The party had become one of the few left in the world still steadfast in its faithfulness to the ideological orthodoxy of mid-20th-century Soviet communism.

Inevitably, such isolation left the GDR on the brink of collapse. As communist regimes throughout Eastern Europe began to weaken, fatigued by decades of communist repression, jealous of perceived higher living standards enjoyed in the FRG and sensing the tide of revolution elsewhere, large numbers of the GDR population began to desire change. From September 1989, the restless natives were able to flee west as **Hungary** demilitarized its border with Austria, and a widespread protest movement was born. In a hasty October reshuffle the SED replaced Honecker with Egon Krenz, but regime and party were already aboard the inexorable slide toward oblivion. The following month saw the epoch defining opening of the Berlin Wall, an event that sparked the rapid decline of both the SED and the GDR, and the creation of modern Germany. As Gorbachev had warned the SED on the 40th and final anniversary of its inauguration, the price of ignoring the need for reform was the death of party and state, and furthermore the extinction of orthodox Marxism–Leninism as a ruling ideology in Eastern Europe.

GERMAN INDEPENDENT SOCIALIST PARTY. *See* GERMAN SOCIAL DEMOCRATIC PARTY.

GERMAN SOCIAL DEMOCRATIC PARTY. The German Social Democratic Party (*Sozialdemokratische Partei Deutschlands*—SPD) was established in everything but name in 1875 when it existed as the Socialist Workers' Party of Germany (*Sozialistische Arbeiterpartei Deutschlands*). At this time the party was an amalgamation of the followers of **Ferdinand Lassalle** and the supporters of **August Bebel** and **Wilhelm Liebknecht.** At its founding conference at Gotha it produced a program that, while in some respects **Marxist**, also drew severe criticism from **Karl Marx** in his *Critique of the Gotha Program* (1875). Two years after its creation the party received 493,000 (9 percent) of the votes cast in a general election, and by 1890 this had risen to 1,427,000 votes (nearly 20 percent), the largest share of the vote for a single party. In 1891, at its Erfurt conference, it renamed itself the *Sozialdemokratische Partei Deutschlands* and **Karl Kautsky** and **Eduard Bernstein** revised its program to give it a firmly Marxist basis and including in it a commitment to fight "for the abolition of **class** rule and classes themselves." The SPD continued to increase its share of the vote in elections receiving 4,250,000 votes (35 percent) in 1912, when it finally became the largest party in the Reichstag having been handicapped by unfavorable constituency boundaries. At a local level the SPD also gained electoral success with some 13,000 local and municipal councilors in 1913.

World War I saw the SPD turn from a commitment to international brotherhood and against war to supporting the "fatherland" in its war of "national defense." A minority within the party opposed the war including notable figures such as **Karl Liebknecht, Rosa Luxemburg,** Karl Kautsky and Eduard Bernstein. In 1917 the growing split between the pro- and anti-war groups within the SPD led to the creation of the *Unabhängige Sozialistische Partei Deutschlands* (German Independent Socialist Party—USPD). In 1918 the SPD joined a new government that introduced parliamentary government and sought a negotiated peace. With Germany clearly losing the war a revolutionary impulse swept across the country leading to the declaration of a republic under the SPD leader Friedrich Ebert and the creation of a Council of People's Representatives which ruled with extensive powers. A new national assembly was formed in 1919 and elections to it gave the SPD 165 seats (38 percent of the vote) and the USPD won 22 seats (over 7.5 percent of the vote). The SPD represented the majority party in a ruling coalition that introduced the Weimar Constitution in August of that year along with various social reforms. The general election of 1920 saw support for the SPD drop and the party was only ever a junior partner in coalition governments that governed up until the Nazis came to power. In spite of this, aided by the return of the bulk of the USPD in 1922, SPD membership rose to 1,261,072 in 1923. The SPD also continued to exercise power and influence at a local level, both in municipalities, rural districts and even states. With the onset of Nazi rule the SPD became the target of increasingly repressive and violent actions, and in 1933 it was banned and its deputies removed from the Reichstag. Many of its leaders and members were forced to flee and an SPD executive-in-exile continued the party's activities chiefly working to publicize the true nature of the Nazis.

With the end of World War II the SPD re-founded itself in Germany, but from the outset clearly differentiated itself from both the *Kommunistische Partei Deutschlands* (**German Communist Party—KPD**) and **Soviet** communism. The party conference at Bad Godesberg in 1959 essentially marked the final break with Marxism as the party adopted a program based on social justice, individual liberty, parliamentary democracy, pluralism, the recognition of the value and validity of competition and profit, and a rejection of wholesale public ownership of the **means of production** and of **revolution**.

In one way the Bad Godesberg conference may be seen as the overdue acknowledgement of a path down which the party had been moving for many years. In the late 1890s Eduard Bernstein had recognized a separation between revolutionary Marxist theory and reformist practice in the party's activities, and in the **revisionist** debate he had battled Kautsky and Luxemburg in an effort to revise the party's Marxist theoretical foundation. Bernstein lost his battle, but the party, while retaining its Marxist theory, pursued a reformist practice and made little reference to Marxist thought in its decision and policy-making. While the pre–World War II social democrats, including Bernstein, remained committed to Marxism, the postwar German social democrats ended that commitment.

GLASNOST. Along with *perestroika glasnost* was one of the two key themes of **Mikhail Gorbachev**'s leadership of the **Soviet Union**. Meaning "openness," it entailed greater freedom of expression, including criticism of the government bureaucracy, and a wider and fuller disclosure of information by the government.

GOLDMANN, LUCIEN (1913–1970). Goldmann followed in the footsteps of **Georgii Lukács** in expounding a form of Hegelian **Marxism** that placed great emphasis on **dialectics**, though he also advanced his own notion of "genetic structuralism." He was born in Bucharest, **Romania**, but spent most of his life in France, particularly Paris where he died. His career as a scholar began with the study of law at his hometown university, before he moved on to study philosophy, economics and German philology at Vienna, Lwów and Paris. It was in Vienna that he began his lifelong study of the ideas of Lukács. During World War II Goldmann spent time as an internee in France before moving to Switzerland where he worked as an assistant to the psychologist Jean Piaget. Piaget's ideas and in particular his "genetic epistemology" were, after those of Lukács, a second great influence on Goldmann's thought. While in Zurich he wrote a doctoral thesis on Kant, following this with a second doctoral dissertation on Racine and Pascal written in Paris after the war.

In his second period in Paris Goldmann worked first in the Centre National de Recherche Scientifique and then in the École Practique des Hautes Études. He also spent a little time at the Sociology Institute of the Université Libre de Bruxelles. As an academic rather than an activist, Goldmann's chief contribution lies in the realm of ideas, particularly his elaboration of a structuralist and dialectical interpretation of (some would say revision of or even departure from) Marxism. He sought to combine **structuralism** with the historical/genetic approach found in the **dialectical** tradition of **Georg Wilhelm Friedrich Hegel**, **Karl Marx** and Lukács. Goldmann's works include *Immanuel Kant* (1948), *Sciences Humaines et Philosophie* (1952), *Le Dieu Caché* (1955), *Recherches dialectiques* (1959), *Pour une sociologie du roman* (1964), and *Marxisme et sciences humaines* (1970). Of these *Le Dieu Caché* (published in English as *The Hidden*

God) is arguably his most important work, although *Pour une sociologie du roman* (published in English as *Towards a Sociology of the Novel*) proved to be his most popular. Among the themes stressed by Goldmann are the notions of totality, **class consciousness**, worldview and **reification**. The notion of totality is drawn from dialectical philosophy and Goldmann uses it to suggest that facts must be understood within the context of "significant structures." These "significant structures" give facts their meanings. Furthermore, things cannot be considered in isolation because they constitute interrelated parts of a whole; human communities constitute totalities and different aspects of the communities, such as economics or literature, do not have independent existences or histories, but express the whole. Goldmann was particularly interested in the key social group of class. Classes have a worldview that unites and distinguishes them, and also have both an existing class consciousness and a "potential consciousness" that expresses a clear, unmystified view of a class's position and interests. Economics, literature and so on represent expressions of worldviews and must be studied in relation to these worldviews and not as if they were independent areas with their own separate histories. Marx's view of reification Goldmann believed to be valid and relevant, but he did not follow Marx's (not to mention Lukács') view that the **proletariat** would develop a **revolutionary** class consciousness. Developments in production allowed many material needs of the workers to be met, thus dulling any revolutionary zeal. Instead, Goldmann looked hopefully to greater democratization and the development of workers' self-management to de-reify society and achieve **socialism**.

GORBACHEV, MIKHAIL SERGEYEVICH (1931–). The last president of the **Soviet Union**, Mikhail Gorbachev oversaw radical changes in both the **Communist Party of the Soviet Union** (CPSU) and the country as a whole. He presided over the abandonment of the **Brezhnev doctrine**, and played a major role in bringing about the collapse of **communist** rule in Eastern Europe and the end of the Cold War.

Born in Stavropol, southern Russia, Gorbachev began work as a tractor driver and farm laborer at the age of 14. He went on to study law at Moscow University before returning to Stavropol where he rapidly moved up the CPSU hierarchy. Having joined the party in

1952, he became the local head of the Komsomol (Young Communist League) on his return from university, and in 1966 became the first secretary of the Stavropol City party committee and took charge of collective farms. By 1971 Gorbachev was a full member of the Central Committee of the Communist Party and in 1978 he moved to Moscow to become agriculture secretary of the Central Committee of the Communist Party. In 1980 he was elected as the youngest ever member of the Politburo, and in 1985, following the death of Konstantin Chernenko, he took over as general secretary of the CPSU, in effect the new (and youngest since **Josef Stalin**) leader of the **Soviet Union**. Partly due to changes in the political structure of the Soviet Union Gorbachev acquired several further titles of the next few years: he became chairman of the Supreme Soviet Presidium in 1988, chairman of the Supreme Soviet in 1989, and president of the Soviet Union in 1990. In 1991, following an attempted coup, Gorbachev resigned as general secretary of the CPSU and by December of that year the Soviet Union had ceased to exist.

Gorbachev's rise was assisted by a series of mentors, the most important of which was Yuri Andropov who took over from **Leonid Breznhev** as leader in 1982. The deaths in quick succession of Andropov and Chernenko cleared the way for the younger Gorbachev who soon established his reformist agenda based on the principles of *perestroika* (restructuring) and *glasnost* (openness). These reforms included: greater freedom of expression, for example, the establishment in 1989 of the Congress of People's Deputies as a forum for debate; greater religious tolerance; multi-candidate elections; fewer restrictions on foreign travel; and the shifting of authority from party to state, for example, by giving power held by the CPSU to elected legislatures in the republics. Despite, or for some because of, these reforms Gorbachev was unpopular, doing enough to anger conservatives and hard-liners, but not enough to please reformers and nationalists seeking change.

Abroad, though, Gorbachev achieved much greater respect and popularity. The withdrawing of troops from Afghanistan, the normalizing of relations with **China**, allowing the ousting of communist regimes in Eastern Europe, ending support for wars in **Angola** and Nicaragua, the halting of Soviet subsidies to Third World communist regimes, signing arms control treaties with the **United States** (1987 and 1990), and cooperation with the West in the first Gulf War to prevent Iraq from taking over Kuwait all won over Western politicians, commentators and peoples. He was even awarded the Nobel Peace Prize in 1990 for his efforts to end the Cold War and bring peace to countries such as Afghanistan.

GRAMSCI, ANTONIO (1891–1937). One of the most important and influential of Marxist thinkers. Antonio Gramsci outlined an interpretation of **Marxism** that offers an alternative to **Leninism** and suggests imaginative innovations and revisions to orthodox Marxism. In particular Gramsci offered insights into the nature of the **state**, and the concept of **ideology**, wrote on factory councils and the role of intellectuals, and developed the concept of **hegemony**. Along with **Georgii Lukács** Gramsci is at the forefront of Hegelian Marxists drawing on the philosophy of **Georg Friedrich Wilhelm Hegel** in their interpretation of Marx. **Humanist Marxism** and **Eurocommunism** have both drawn inspiration from Gramsci's writings.

Gramsci was born in the small town of Ales, Sardinia in 1891. His intellectual ability was evident when he won a scholarship to Turin University in 1911. Here he was influenced by the tradition of Italian philosophical **idealism** and the writings of **Benedetto Croce** in particular. In 1913 he joined the **Italian Socialist Party** (PSI) and began writing articles for socialist publications. In 1919 he helped to found the socialist weekly *Ordine Nuovo* in Turin, which supported the growing factory council movement in the city. In January 1921 Gramsci was active in establishing the **Italian Communist Party** (PCI). He worked for the **Comintern** in Moscow and Vienna between 1922 and 1924, and it was in 1924 that he was elected to the Italian Parliament and assumed leadership of the PCI. In November 1926 the fascist government had Gramsci arrested and sentenced to 20 years' imprisonment. It was in prison that he wrote what became his most famous writings, the *Prison Notebooks*. Suffering from ever-worsening health Gramsci was temporarily released from prison at the end of 1934 and spent most of the rest of his life in a hospital in Rome where he died on 27 April 1937 from a cerebral hemorrhage.

Perhaps the most influential of Gramsci's ideas is his notion of hegemony which he expounded in the *Prison Notebooks*. For Gramsci hegemony referred to the means by which the **bourgeoisie** established and maintained its dominance and rule. Gramsci saw that the rule of the bourgeoisie was not based on force or the threat of force alone. A crucial aspect of bourgeois rule was the manufacturing of consent through a combination of judicious compromise and alliance building, and the propagation of bourgeois ideas, values and culture throughout society via such institutions of socialization as schools, churches and the media. For Gramsci the rule of the bourgeoisie and the role and nature of the state was far more complex than orthodox and Leninist Marxists suggested. Control was exercised as much through ideas (ideology) as through force, and this gave a key role to intellectuals in what Gramsci called a "war of position," a battle of ideas in which revolutionary forces must engage with bourgeois intellectuals. The function of intellectuals in **capitalism** is to organize beliefs and persuade the masses to embrace and accept the leadership and views of the bourgeoisie. Revolutionary intellectuals must disrupt and subvert this process of hegemony, thus making the sphere of ideology a battlefield, an arena of struggle. In the advanced capitalist countries the war of position must precede the overthrow of the state through a frontal assault (the "war of maneuver"). Broadly speaking, the political state organizes force and civil society creates consent; both must be combated.

Gramsci was more orthodox in his emphasis of production and technology as a key element in human emancipation. Like Marx he saw the future communist society as one based on the expansion and development of productive forces. However, he did not endorse an economic **determinist** or "scientific" interpretation of Marxism that understood history as governed by iron laws. He described the **Bolshevik Revolution** in Russia as "The revolution against *Capital*" because it showed history did not have to progress through rigid stages, that revolutionary will could bring about socialist transformation even if a country had not yet gone through a capitalist stage of development.

Gramsci also eschewed absolute and final truths, even viewing Marxism as only "true" in a historically relativist sense. In other words, for Gramsci Marxism was true in a historical, pragmatic sense; it grasped and expressed the needs and historical tendencies of the time better than any other theoretical viewpoint. The function of intellectuals in capitalism is to organize beliefs and persuade the masses to embrace and accept the leadership and views of the bourgeoisie. Revolutionary intellectuals must disrupt and subvert this process of hegemony, thus making the sphere of ideology a battlefield, an arena of struggle.

GRUNDRISSE (1857–1858). Consisting of seven notebooks intended as a discrete work, the writing of the *Grundrisse* was stimulated by the general economic crisis of 1857 and borne on the failure of the European **revolutions** in 1848–50. Not intended for publication, the notebooks are essentially a clarification of **scientific socialism**, specifically a commentary upon the contradiction between the **forces of production** and the **relations of production** in preparation for *Critique of Political Economy* and *Capital* and was described by **Karl Marx** as the "result of fifteen years of research, thus the best period of my life." The title was given when the Marx–Engels–Lenin Institute published the books in 1939, as were the chapter names and breaks. The *Grundrisse* is a difficult read because of its very nature as Marx's personal notes and not as a publishable work. It does, however, give the reader great insight into Marx's methodology and the influence of **Georg Wilhelm Friedrich Hegel** upon it. In a letter to **Friedrich Engels** during the writing, Marx comments upon how Hegel's *Logic* contributed to his theory of profit being subordinate to **surplus value** in the **dialectic** of **exploitation**, but the extensive Hegelian terminology that appears here is discarded and the method less apparent in *Capital*.

The dialectical movement within money and **capital**, and the opposition and relation between the two is the essence of *Grundrisse*. Marx uses "The Chapter on Money" to uncover the secrets of capital and his method of **historical materialism** is extremely clear in the uncovering of the **contradictions** of money and exposing the sociohistorical importance. In expanding and systematizing his earlier works, Marx illustrates the oppression of man by the alien power he creates, but does so in terms of the **superstructure** relation of **bourgeois** morality, religion, law and economics, which, as a result of their derivation from the contradictory **base**, are each one-sided spheres attempting to form a totality. Money is social, and its superstructural significance will inevitably change. Marx penetrates the surface phenomenon that is money in order to study its underlying contradiction, capital: the exchange of labor as **commodity**.

As in other works, Marx confronts classical political economy while simultaneously developing his own theory. As well as a critique of the inherently contradictory **labor theory of value** in terms of the vicissitudes of wage labor, Marx expands his earlier theory of **alienation** to scientific categories, yet retains its **humanism**. The key antithesis of **use value** and **exchange value** is first identified in the *Grundrisse*. Contrary to classical political economy, Marx believes the capitalist purchases labor for its exchange value and obtains its use value, thus consuming labor. Labor power is a living thing and **surplus value** can be extracted from it; labor can be exploited, therefore the worker cannot be enriched, only the antithesis of the worker, capital, is nourished by **wage labor**. Capital is a process, which at first appears static but is a one-sided unity of contradictions, i.e., the surface phenomenon of money is the object of "the law of equivalence" yet capital is the object of the law of exploitation.

The contradictions of capital are also fundamental to the theory of revolution. The highest development of productive power and the greatest expansion of existing wealth cause not only the degradation of the worker but the depreciation of capital. This contradiction causes ever-worsening economic **crises** which, juxtaposed with the inevitability of the "absolute impoverishment" of the worker, will ineluctably result in the violent overthrow of bourgeois rule.

GUEVARA DE LA SERNA, ERNESTO (CHE) (1928–1967). Born in Rosario, Argentina, Che Guevara trained in medicine but spent his life engaged in various political struggles in Latin America. In 1954 he was involved in the struggle against the Central Intelligence Agency–inspired overthrow of President Jacopo Arbenz. Between 1956 and 1965 he was involved with **Fidel Castro** and Cuban affairs, first in the struggle against Batista and then, after the rebels won power, as president of the National Bank, minister of industries, and director of the Industrial Development Section of the National Institute of Agrarian Reform. In 1965 he went to Bolivia in an attempt to foment revolution against the military authorities. He led a guerrilla band that was captured by the Bolivian army, who executed him the day after his capture.

Guevara's **Marxism** consisted of applying Marxism to Latin American conditions and modifying it in light of those conditions. He rejected any "stageist" understanding of Marxism that required the workers to wait for a **bourgeois** revolution before they could create a **socialist** revolution. He believed in forcing through **revolution**s with individuals and **vanguard** groups, and not in "iron laws of history" inevitably resulting in revolution. Change in consciousness precedes development of the **forces of production**, and moral incentives must drive the revolution not material ones. The masses, and Guevara stressed the role of the **peasantry** here, must be led by those in the vanguard who had the necessary political consciousness. He was a strong advocate of guerrilla warfare in Latin America, arguing that guerrilla bands could be catalysts for revolution, and he stressed the importance of military action over political action in the various struggles in which he was involved. In terms of socialist society he believed it must be based on new non-**capitalist** structures, with the old destroyed, and a planned economy replacing the capitalist market economy. Ultimately, **communism** for Guevara was about the creation of a new human being with a new consciousness, free and complete.

GUINEA, PEOPLE'S REVOLUTIONARY REPUBLIC OF (PRRG). After colonial rule by France ended in 1958, revolutionary leader **Ahmed Sékou Touré** oversaw the transition of Guinea to **socialism** and frequently propounded a **Marxist** course for the country. The experiment with socialism formally ended with Touré's death in 1984, making the government of the People's Revolutionary Republic of Guinea one of the longest serving socialist administrations in Africa.

Touré became general secretary of the pro-independence Democratic Party of Guinea (*Parti Démocratique de Guinée*—PDG) in 1952, and his first discernible achievement was steering the party to an overwhelming victory in territorial elections staged five years later. With momentum gathered, in 1958 the electorate again bolstered the PDG cause by rejecting French Prime Minister Charles de Gaulle's "community" constitution in a referendum, making Guinea the only colony to do so. This enraged de Gaulle who demanded the withdrawal of French personnel and aid from the West African country with immediate effect. Consequently, on 2 October 1958 Guinean independence was proclaimed with Touré the inaugural president of the sovereign state.

Touré began his reign with a number of socialist-style measures including a colossal nationalization push, but it was not until 1967 that he announced the adoption of **Marxism–Leninism** as the official bedrock of the **revolution**. The PDG government accordingly heralded a program to move power away from the bureaucratic and cautious center, and toward radical regional groups named the *Pouvoir Révolutionnaire Local* (PRL). Further moves were made to push the

PRRG toward Touré's interpretation of Marxism in 1975, with the **state** criminalizing private trading and launching a **collectivization** initiative to bring rural areas into communalized state ownership. Reality, though, bore little resemblance to this constitutional and theoretical framework. Touré became increasingly dictatorial as time progressed, with an already existing paranoia of French plots to overthrow him augmented by perceived domestic threats to his hegemony. The PDG government rapidly deteriorated into a centralized and despotic organ, with the village cell groups of the PRL merely disseminators of the iron will that emanated from the capital Conakry, and systematic terror meted out on scores of "enemies" of Touré.

Inevitably, the Touré administration's popularity plummeted, and with a mounting economic crisis resulting from the continued foreign ownership of the country's most lucrative natural resources, the PDG had little choice but to discard its rigid and essentially **Stalinist** doctrine. In 1978 Marxism was formally dropped as the guiding light of the revolution, a move that enhanced efforts earlier on in the decade to improve relations with the **capitalist** West, as did the furtive steps taken toward implementing a free market system. When Touré passed away in March 1984, with him went PDG rule, as a military junta led by Lieutenant Lansana Conté bloodlessly took power in April of the same year.

While Touré and the PDG had initially subscribed to the relationship between party and state as espoused by **Vladimir Ilich Lenin**, where a proletarian **vanguard party** would lead an urban **proletariat** class towards a revolution that was then to be extended outwards, their Marxism became one of the all-encompassing "mass party." The PDG was initially and fundamentally a catchall rather than a **class**-based organization. It worked for the collective interest of the **peasantry**, the working class, trade unionists and the petty **bourgeoisie**; namely an end to colonial rule and the survival of an independent Guinean state. This explains both the early reluctance to openly adopt Marxism and the lack of hesitation in abandoning it. When coupled with Touré's insistence that the inherently atheistic philosophy of Marxism was compatible with Islam, it becomes clear that genuine commitment to the application of **scientific socialism** was, like the leader's ideological persuasions in general, fleeting and aimed only at maintaining power.

GUINEA-BISSAU, REPUBLIC OF. *See* CAPE VERDE, REPUBLIC OF, AND REPUBLIC OF GUINEA-BISSAU.

– H –

HABERMAS, JÜRGEN (1929–). One of the great thinkers of the 20th century, Jürgen Habermas is viewed by many as the leading light in the second generation of the **Frankfurt School**. Far from an orthodox **Marxist**, Habermas may best be described as influenced by **Karl Marx** rather than a disciple of Marxism; he has criticized it as much as he has drawn on it. His philosophy has gradually moved further and further away from Marx and toward an outlook based on hermeneutic and linguistic philosophy with a focus on the communicative interaction between human beings. In this he has moved beyond the school of **Western Marxism** in which his work could once be located.

Born in Düsseldorf, Germany, Habermas studied philosophy, history, psychology and German literature at the University of Göttingen, and then in Zurich and Bonn, where he obtained a doctorate in 1954. He then worked as a journalist from 1954 to 1956, before working as **Theodor Adorno**'s assistant at the Institute for Social Research in Frankfurt from 1956 to 1959. A brief period as a professor of philosophy at Heidelberg was followed by a return to Frankfurt in 1964 as a professor of philosophy and sociology. In 1971 Habermas left Frankfurt to become the director of the newly formed Max Planck Institute for the study of the Conditions of Life in the Scientific-Technical World at Sturnberg, Bavaria.

A prolific writer, Habermas has produced a number of very influential works including: *Structural Transformation of the Public Sphere* (1962), *Theory and Practice* (1963), *Knowledge and Human Interests* (1968), *Toward a Rational Society* (1970), *Legitimization Crisis* (1973), *Communication and the Evolution of Society* (1979), *Theory of Communicative Action* (1981), and *The Philosophical Discourse of Modernity* (1985). In these and other works he explores a number of themes including how the Enlightenment turned from a source of emancipation to one of barbarism and enslavement, and, linked to this, the role of science and technology in society and the conditions necessary in society for rational discussion. For Habermas science has developed a purely instrumentalist form, no longer freeing human beings from ignorance and superstition, but instead becoming a form of tyranny treating human beings as objects for manipulation, as something less than human. He develops this argument into a general critique of modernity and in particular of positivism, including Marxism's positivist and **determinist** tendencies in this critique.

Habermas does not wish to reject the achievements of modernity and rationality, and of science and technology, but he does reject the instrumentalist rationality that has taken hold, and the ideological role of science based on its supposed value-free status. Habermas turns toward a more hermeneutic-inspired view of knowledge, and seeks to outline the conditions for "domination-free communication" between human beings. For Habermas, liberation must go beyond the Marxist emphasis on mastery of nature and an abolition of the division of labor, and requires the elimination of all obstacles to rational communication, not all of which are located in the process of production.

HARRINGTON, MICHAEL (EDWARD) (1928–1989). Born in St. Louis, Missouri, Harrington was a prominent **Marxist** political activist. He advocated a thorough-going democratic, peaceful, humanist, ethical Marxism, and sought to work with liberal groups, notably the Democratic Party, in the **United States**. He was educated at Holy Cross College, Worcester, Massachusetts, Yale University Law School (briefly), and the University of Chicago, graduating from the last of these in 1949 with a master's degree in English Literature. Moving to New York in 1951 he worked for the Catholic Worker movement writing for and editing the organization's newspaper. Harrington embraced the movement's pacifism and was a conscientious objector to the Korean War. In 1953 religious doubts led Harrington to leave the church and the Catholic Worker movement, and to become leader of the Young People's Socialist League (the youth group of the American Socialist Party). Between 1960 and 1968 he was a member of the Socialist Party's National Executive Committee, editing the official party paper *New America* from 1961 to 1962, and serving as the party's national chairman from 1968 to1972. Harrington developed a close political relationship with the American Socialist Party leader Norman Thomas, who came to regard him as his successor (although Thomas rejected Harrington's conscientious objector stance on the Korean War).

However, a series of political setbacks and a nervous breakdown which left him unable to speak in public thwarted any ambitions to become leader. He did though become co-chairman of the Socialist Party, a position from which he resigned in 1972 over the issue of the Vietnam War to which he was opposed. In the same year he became professor of political science at Queens College, City University of New York. In 1973 he led a few hundred of his anti-war followers into a new organization, the Democratic Socialist Organizing Committee (DSOC). This group was determined to be the "left wing of the possible" and tried to influence the Democratic Party to be as liberal as possible. In 1983 the DSOC merged with the New American Movement to form the Democratic Socialists of America. At the start this group had 5,000 members with Harrington as co-chair. It continued the project of the DSOC in working with the Democratic Party, although with little success. Throughout the 1980s Harrington became increasingly occupied with the Socialist International, attending many of its conferences and drafting many of its resolutions. He was involved with many other political groups, most notably the A. Philip Randolph Institute (an organization committee to establishing links between the black and labor communities) and the League for Industrial Democracy.

Harrington wrote a great many articles, pamphlets and other publications, the most significant being his *The Other America: Poverty in the United States* (1962), a piece that influenced John F. Kennedy's "War on Poverty" program and other democratic socio-economic policies, and his *Socialism* (1972).

HEGEL, GEORG WILHELM FRIEDRICH (1770–1831). A German **idealist** philosopher and one of the most important thinkers of the 19th century, Hegel was one of the key influences on **Karl Marx** and his thought. Born in Stuttgart, Germany, Hegel studied philosophy and theology at the University of Tübingen, and after a brief period as a private tutor in Bern, Switzerland, he went on to study further and became a lecturer at the University of Jena. The seizure of Jena by French troops forced him to flee and he worked for a period as a newspaper editor and then as a school headmaster before becoming professor of philosophy at the University of Heidelberg in 1816. In 1818 he moved to the prestigious University of Berlin, where he remained until his death from cholera in 1831.

Among Hegel's major philosophical works are *The Phenomenology of Mind* (1807), *The Science of Logic* (1812, 1813, 1816), *The Philosophy of Right* (1821) and *The Philosophy of History* (1830–31). In these and other writings Hegel outlined a comprehensive philosophical system that covered both the natural and social worlds with particular emphasis on religion, philosophy, culture, history and politics. For Hegel the whole of reality represents the expression and unfolding of "Absolute Spirit," and the whole of reality is an interconnected totality. Every aspect of reality reflects Absolute Spirit and gives us a means of grasping the nature of it. For example, in his philosophy of history and political philosophy Hegel shows that the history of the world is nothing other than the history of the development of the "Idea" of freedom, and freedom is the essence of Spirit. Gradually human freedom has developed, both in terms of human understanding of freedom and in terms of the development of political and legal structures, institutions and processes allowing greater freedom.

It was this that Marx first embraced as a disciple of Hegel's thought and then rejected notably in his *Critique of Hegel's Philosophy of Right* (1843). Marx was critical of Hegel's conservatism, his belief that freedom could be attained in a **class** society with a market economy and a constitutional **state**. Marx argued that Hegel's philosophy was abstract, passive and lacked a critical perspective, so that it ended up endorsing the profoundly unfree Prussian state of Hegel's day. Many of the flaws in Hegel's thought stemmed from his philosophical idealism that gave primacy to Spirit and the realm of ideas instead of concentrating on the **material** world, the world of human activity. Marx embraced a materialist outlook that essentially saw ideas as born out of human activity, and in particular as reflecting the level of economic and technological development in any given society. Nevertheless, Marx still acknowledged the profundity of Hegel's thought and incorporated a form of Hegel's **dialectic** into his thought. Marxists and commentators on Marx dispute the degree of influence of Hegel on Marx, but there is strong evidence to suggest that Marx's thought embodied dialectical themes from his early through to his later writings.

HEGEMONY. A key concept developed by **Antonio Gramsci** in his *Prison Notebooks* (1929–1935), hegemony refers to the domination achieved by a **ruling class** through force and, more importantly, through moral and intellectual leadership and alliances with other classes in what Gramsci calls a "historic bloc." For Gramsci, ideology plays at least as important a role in maintaining the rule of the **bourgeoisie** as does force. Schools, churches and the media are key institutions in the creation of consent to bourgeois rule. The implications of Gramsci's notion of hegemony include a key role for intellectuals both on the side of the bourgeoisie in developing and propagating an **ideology** that engenders consent, and on the side of the **proletariat** in disputing bourgeois ideas and developing an alternative. Hegemony also implies an expanded notion of the **state** as an institution that is more than simply an instrument of repression, and a greater significance attributed to the arena of civil society where much of the ideological struggle for hegemony takes place.

HEKMAT, MANSOOR (ZHOOBIN RAZANI) (1951–2002). One of the leading lights of Iranian **Marxism**, Mansoor Hekmat co-founded the Worker-Communist parties of Iran and Iraq in 1991. Hekmat was born Shoobin Razani in Tehran and did not develop his revolutionary politics until coming to London in 1973, having previously studied economics at Shiraz University. He studied in Britain at Kent, Bath and London before returning to Iran in 1979 when the **revolution** broke out. The coming to power of Ayatollah Khomeni put the Iranian Left into disarray and internal conflict. In 1982 Hekmat left Tehran for Kurdistan, where he helped to found the Communist Party of Iran. He returned to Britain in the mid-1980s where he continued to analyze and write on Marxism and Iran until his death from cancer in 2002. He rejected the Marxisms of the **Soviet Union, China** and Eastern Europe as well as **Trotskyism** and social democratic Marxism, advocating instead a more humanist, less sectarian approach.

HILFERDING, RUDOLF (1877–1941). Born in Vienna, Hilferding trained and worked as a doctor before becoming involved full-time in politics, with a particular interest and expertise in political economy. He wrote frequently on economics for the *Neue Zeit*, edited by **Karl Kautsky**, taught in the **German Social Democratic Party** (SPD) school, and at different times edited the SPD newspaper *Vorwärts*, the Independent Social Democratic Party (USPD) paper *Freiheit*, and the socialist journal *Gesellschaft*. He was briefly minister of finance in 1923 in the Gustav Streseman coalition government and again in 1929 under Chancellor Herman Müller, and was a member of the Reichstag from 1924–1933. With the Nazi takeover Hilferding fled to Switzerland, then Austria and then France, but was captured and committed suicide while being held by the Gestapo.

Hilferding's major contribution to **Marxism** lies in his two works *Bohm-Bawek's Marx-Critique* (1904) and *Finance Capital* (1910). In the former he replied to Bohm-Bawek's criticism of Marx's economic theory and in the latter he analyzed what he called "the latest phase of capitalist development." There were several key points in his defense of Marxist economic theory and his account of contemporary **capitalism**. First, finance **capital** (the banks) was becoming much more closely involved with industrial capital and playing a dominant role. Secondly, capital was becoming increasingly concentrated and centralized in ever more powerful corporations. Thirdly, there now existed what Hilferding called "organized capitalism" by which he meant that there was much more planning and regulation of the economy and of relations between states to create a stable capitalism. Finally, he concluded from his analysis that the workers must wrest control of the planning and organization of the large corporations by winning political power through democratic elections.

HISTORICAL MATERIALISM. "Historical materialism" is not a term that **Karl Marx** himself used, but it has become the commonly used label for what Marx called his "materialist conception of history." The key idea of historical materialism is that the basis of society and of social change is production or productive activity. According to historical materialism the way in which we produce our food, clothing, shelter and goods for exchange is the basis of society, or to put this another way, the basis of society and social change is economics and technology. Consequently, if we want to understand history and society we must look first at production, because human beings are fundamentally producers, and human society is fundamentally a productive system and process. In order to understand the politics, the philosophy, the religion, morality, laws, institutions, culture and so on of a society, we must examine the way in which that society produces.

Marx, in the 1859 *Preface to a Contribution to Political Economy*, used a building metaphor to explain his materialist conception of history. He divided society into its economic **base**, consisting of **forces and relations of production**, and the **superstructure** consisting of the legal and political institutions, laws, ideas and culture of society. The economic base conditions or shapes the superstructure, hence making production, economics and technology (or the **mode of production**) all important in determining the ideas, and the political, legal and social arrangements of society.

Marx states that the forces of production develop, essentially as technology develops, and when this happens they come into conflict with the existing relations of production which now become a hindrance to the progress of the former. This conflict takes the form of a struggle between **classes** that are tied to either the new forces of production or the old relations of production. **Revolutionary** change will be the ultimate outcome with new relations of production and a new superstructure matching the new forces of production. Presented in these stark terms Marx appears to be putting forward a rigid form of **determinism**, where the forces of production determine the relations and these in turn produce a corresponding superstructure. It is clear, though, from Marx's historical analyses and various comments he makes that the process is far more complex, that the forces of production are not always the dominant determining factor, and that aspects of the superstructure may act back upon the economic base and even initiate change.

The schematic nature of Marx's outline of historical materialism, the ambiguity of key terms and the difficulty of reconciling the theory of actual historical development have led to divergent interpretations of historical materialism by later Marxists, with particular argument over the nature of Marx's determinism. Different Marxists and schools of Marxism can be characterized in terms of their interpretations of historical materialism, for example as determinist (**Karl Kautsky, Georgii Plekhanov**), voluntarist (**Mao Zedong**), **structuralist** (**Louis Althusser**), **analytical**/rational choice (Gerry Cohen, Jon Elster), and **dialectical**/non-determinist (**Frankfurt School, Antonio Gramsci**).

HO CHI MINH (NGUYEN TAT THANH AND NGUYEN AI QUOC) (1890–1969). Ho Chi Minh was founder and leader of Vietnamese **communism** and first president of North Vietnam. Born at Kim-Lien in central Vietnam, Ho developed his politics when he lived in Europe. In 1919 he sent a petition asking for Vietnamese independence to the Versailles Peace Conference and in 1920 he joined the **French Communist Party**. From 1922 to 1924 Ho worked in Moscow with the **Comintern**, where he pressed for acknowledgement and support of anti-colonial revolutionary movements. In 1925 he returned to Vietnam and in 1930 established the **Indochinese Communist Party**. He represented the Comintern in Hong Kong until he was arrested by British police in 1931 and imprisoned until 1933. After several years back in the **Soviet Union**, Ho returned to China as an adviser with the Chinese Communist military, before helping to create the Vietnamese independence movement that fought the Japanese occupying troops.

In 1945 he led the communists in the August **revolution** that allowed the communists to seize power and to create the Democratic Republic of **Vietnam** (DRV) with Ho as president. Fighting continued against the French (the colonial power in Vietnam before the Japanese invaded) until 1954 when the French were decisively beaten in the battle of Dien Bien Phu. An armistice was signed dividing the country into a communist north and non-communist south. After several years of peace, war resumed, this time against the south, which was supported by the **United States**. The conflict was a protracted one with the United States pouring in more and more resources but unable to defeat the DRV forces (the Vietminh). Eventually the United States' commitment weakened followed by the withdrawal of support from the south and subsequent victory for North Vietnam and the reunification of the country in 1975.

Ho was in many respects pragmatic rather than ideological, and sought to combine nationalism and internationalism in his patriotic communism. He favored strong links with the Comintern and other anti-colonial movements, and at the same time endeavored to adapt communism to Vietnamese conditions.

HORKHEIMER, MAX (1895–1973). Horkheimer's contribution to **Marxism** consists in his role in creating the **Frankfurt School** and developing the "critical theory" that emerged from the school. Born in Stuttgart, Germany, Horkheimer was educated at the universities of Munich, Freiburg and Frankfurt, graduating from the last of these with a PhD in philosophy in 1923. He became Director of the Frankfurt Institute for Social Research in 1930, and used his position to appoint academics of a **humanist Marxist** bent that would come to be known as the "Frankfurt School." Most notable among these appointments were **Herbert Marcuse** and **Theodor Adorno**. Horkheimer emigrated to the **United States** in 1933 where he was able to reestablish the Institute as an affiliate of Columbia University in New York, and where it continued until a return to Frankfurt was made possible in the 1950s.

Horkheimer's own thought underwent a series of changes, but was most notable for a critique of positivism, empiricism and rationalism generally, and **determinist**, scientistic interpretations of Marxism in particular. 1947 saw the publication of *Dialectic of Enlightenment* written by Horkheimer and Adorno. This key work was strongly influenced by the background against which it was written, namely World War II and the barbarism of the Nazis. Horkheimer and Adorno linked the atrocities of the Nazis with the rational instrumentality embodied in Enlightenment thinking. The ideas and values of the Enlightenment had helped to progress humanity, but now in a **dialectical** shift these same ideas were serving to tyrannize humanity by destroying or degrading everything that was intangible or could not be quantified. A cold scientific logic was obliterating individuality, spirituality, and culture as everything was turned into a commodity for sale and purchase, a thing to be manipulated and controlled. Empiricism, rationalism, instrumentalism and positivism—the heirs of the Enlightenment—denied the existence and significance of what could not be observed or deduced or controlled.

While continuing to adhere to some Marxist tenets, such as the commitment to **materialism** and a historical approach, Horkheimer moved away from embracing the notion of the centrality of **class** struggle, and his critical view of science and technology also served to distance him from Marxism. His humanistic approach has provided a useful counterweight to the overly scientistic schools of Marxism, and his tendency to pessimism is a useful corrective to the undue optimism of some Marxists.

HOXHA, ENVER (1908–1985). Hoxha was the avowedly ultra orthodox **Marxist–Leninist** dictator of **Albania** from 1946 until his death. Having first served as prime minister from 1944 to 1954 and in tandem minister of foreign affairs from 1946 to 1953, as president he championed Albanian isolationism and never wavered in his support for **Stalinism**. Hoxha was head of the **Albanian Party of Labor** (originally the Albanian Communist Party [ACP]) from its inception in 1941, and used his position as first secretary of the party's Central Committee to retain effective control over the party and thus the country for over 40 years.

While at the University of Montpellier, Hoxha attended meetings of the Association of Workers, organized by the **French Communist Party,** and contributed articles on Albania to *Humanité* magazine, before dropping out of his degree course. He then worked in the Albanian consulate in Brussels, furthering his knowledge of Marxism–Leninism while studying law at the university in the city. Hoxha returned home to Albania in 1936 to become a teacher in Korçe. With the Italian invasion in 1939, Hoxha was banished from his teaching post for refusing to join the Albanian Fascist Party. He then moved to Tiranë to open a retail tobacco store. Here Hoxha and a small underground faction of **communists** often met, and in 1941 with Yugoslav aid they founded the ACP with Hoxha as leader. At the same time they plotted the resistance movement, culminating in the birth of the National Front of Liberation, a group aimed at attaining a united front between all parties, and its military wing the National Liberation Army. The group eventually brought about Albanian liberation in November 1944, with Hoxha, as the elected president of the National Anti-fascist Committee of Liberation, the first head of the new Albania.

Under Hoxha's tutelage, Albania was transformed from a country of semi-**feudalism** still caught in the era of the Ottoman Empire, into an industrialized, if totalitarian, **state**. Hoxha oversaw industrialization, the development of agriculture through the introduction of cooperatives, and a program for the development of education and culture. His regime brought almost full self-sufficiency in food crops, electricity to rural areas and improved literacy rates. With this, however, came an erosion of human rights and a clampdown on political opponents, many of whom ended up in prison camps at best. The dictator was deeply committed to Stalinism, embracing the Soviet model, and severing ties with his former comrades from **Yugoslavia** after their ideological break with Moscow in 1948. Hoxha's foreign policy decisions reflected his devotion to Stalinism again in 1961 when Albania broke with **Nikita Khrushchev** and the **Soviet Union**, and forged links with **Mao Zedong**'s **China**. This association itself was ended in 1978 following the death of Mao and China's increasing friendliness with the West. Hoxha resolved that Albania would adopt an isolationist stand and strive to become a model **socialist** republic alone, employing an anti-revisionist stance to criticize Moscow and Beijing. Hoxha formed alliances with whichever state suited Albania at a given juncture in time, and disengaged relations when Albanian sovereignty was threatened. He was as much a nationalist as he was a Stalinist.

Hoxha's brand of **Marxism** sat outside that of the Soviet Union, China and, for that matter, Yugoslavia, as he sought to guard Albanian Marxism and independence. Among his more distinctive acts was to declare Albania the world's first atheist state in 1967, destroying thousands of synagogues and mosques along the way.

HUMANIST MARXISM. *See* MARXIST HUMANISM.

HUNGARIAN SOCIALIST WORKERS PARTY. *See* HUNGARIAN WORKERS PARTY.

HUNGARIAN UPRISING (1956). The Hungarian uprising was a 12-day-long rebellion by students, workers and eventually soldiers against **communist** rule in **Hungary** that was mercilessly crushed by **Soviet** forces. Resentment toward the Soviet-dominated one-party system that had developed in Hungary following World War II had been mounting for some time, and when **Nikita Khrushchev** denounced **Josef Stalin** at the 20th Congress of the **Communist Party of the Soviet Union** in February 1956, Hungarians felt confident enough to adopt the denouncement as their own. In the atmosphere of increased de-Stalinization that Khrushchev's speech and the 1956 **Polish Uprising** propagated, the people of Hungary, already agitated by the continual presence of Soviet troops in their country and the repressive nature of the governments of Mátyás Rákosi and Erno Gerö, felt strong enough to rebel. Intellectual criticism of the Soviet regime in the aftermath of the 20th Congress soon turned to rebellion in Hungary among students and workers, as protestors destroyed statues of Stalin, demanded an end to the leadership of the country by any associates of the Rákosi-Gerö regimes, and called for immediate radical political reform.

These demonstrations developed into all-out revolt when on 23 October Hungarian forces loyal to the communist regime began to fire on protestors in Budapest. The arrival of Soviet tanks to quash the upheaval served only to exacerbate tensions, so much so that Hungarian soldiers joined the revolt, and Moscow ordered the withdrawal of its forces. The Hungarian government, sensing the need of reform to preserve, instigated a reshuffle that saw Imre Nagy take the reins as prime minister (Nagy had introduced reforms in his initial term of office from 1953 to 1955), and János Kádár become head of the **Hungarian Workers Party**. With the communist regime progressively undermined by the reemergence of political parties banned following World War II and the restoration of the church's role in society, Nagy propounded plans to form a coalition government that would create a mixed market economy, withdraw from the **Warsaw Pact** in order to attain neutral status for Hungary, and bring about a multi-party system.

Unsurprisingly, Moscow reacted angrily to these intentions, and began to work with party leader Kádár, also determined that the regime should strenuously avoid any reform, to form a counter-government to be placed in power by Soviet might. On 4 November Soviet forces invaded Hungary with the aim of crushing the rebellion and supplanting Prime Minister Nagy with Kádár's Moscow satellite government. Resistance was rapidly overcome and Soviet victory assured by November 14th, at which point the counter-revolutionary Kádár government took charge of party and state under the banner of the renamed **Hungarian Socialist Workers Party**. Some 190,000 Hungarians immediately fled, while Nagy and his fellow reformers were fooled by the Russian promise of safe conduct, taken to **Romania** and secretly executed in 1958.

The murdered leaders of the revolution were finally rehabilitated in 1989 by a communist regime on the verge of collapse, while surviving activists from the uprising formed a key component of postcommunist Hungary.

HUNGARIAN WORKERS PARTY. Created by **Josef Stalin** to rule over the **People's Republic of Hungary**, the Hungarian Workers Party (Magyar Mankáspórt) sought to transform the country according to the **Marxism–Leninism** disseminated from the **Soviet Union**. Following the events of the 1956 **Hungarian Uprising**, the party became the Hungarian Socialist Workers Party (HSWP, Magyar Szocialista Mankáspórt), led by the Soviet loyalist János Kádár. Despite the weighty influence of Moscow, the HSWP did garner a degree of ideological autonomy unheard of in other Soviet Bloc countries, paving the way for liberalizing economic measures in the 1970s and 1980s. With the **collapse of the Soviet Union**, the HSWP ceased to exist as a **Marxist** party, transforming itself in 1989 into the moderate Hungarian Socialist Party.

HUNGARY, PEOPLE'S REPUBLIC OF. In the years subsequent to the conclusion of World War II, Hungary was transformed into a **communist** state under the yoke of the **Soviet Union**. There were deviations from orthodox Soviet **ideology**, but on the whole the country followed the same doctrine of "official" **Marxism–Leninism** as the rest of the satellite region, and accordingly the regime collapsed in 1989/90.

The country was ruled by the **Hungarian Workers Party** (HWP, later **Hungarian Socialist Workers Party**, or HSWP) under General Secretaries Mátyás Rákosi between 1948 and 1956, and János Kádár between 1956 and 1988, at which point successor Károly Grósz oversaw the gradual folding of party and regime. The communist rise to power had begun in 1947 with the removal of anti-communist politicians from the scene under the watchful eye of **Josef Stalin**. In June 1948, aware of the Hungarian Communist Party's relative lack of influence or support, Stalin forced the Social Democratic Party into a merger that saw the creation of the HWP, and the election of Rákosi as general secretary. By the 1949 election, with all opposition smothered, the takeover was complete, and **Stalinist**-style purges began in order to consolidate the HWP's grip on the country. A new constitution modeled along Soviet lines was adopted, **state** organs and organizations such as trade unions were subordinated to party interests, and a mass resettlement of "enemies" occurred with 700,000 urban middle-**class** dwellers relocated to countryside labor camps. Such Sovietization suppressed Hungary's heavily nationalistic inclinations and sought to bring about a strong, centralized political dictatorship. Hungary rapidly assumed the characteristics of an orthodox Marxist–Leninist country, reorganizing along Stalin-approved lines that resulted in a heavy industrialization program and a reduction in the production of consumer items. A Stakhanovite system of rewards for reaching centrally planned targets rather than material gains was put into action, as was the **collectivization** of rural land.

This brisk transition to a Soviet, or more exactly Stalin-inspired, Hungary was slowed only with the death of the Moscow leader in 1953, as the heavily Stalinist Rákosi was forced to share power with the more liberal prime minister Imre Nagy whose "New Course" of reforms promised considerable change. The events of the 1956 **Hungarian Uprising**, however, culminated only in a return to orthodox Moscow-influenced rule under Soviet puppet leader Kádár's newly renamed HSWP. Kádár immediately set about consolidating the orthodox regime by ensuring party unity, chiefly through offering slight concessions to those baying for reform, for example in his "alliance policy" which sought to relax political and social discrimination. As time progressed there was also amnesty for a number of political prisoners, and the most tyrannical elements of Stalinism dissipated. The collectivization of land was successfully completed in the 1960s, largely because of liberalizing measures such as the adoption of economic rewards for workers' efforts and an element of free enterprise.

The 1968 New Economic Mechanism, similar to **Vladimir Ilich Lenin**'s New Economic Plan, was implemented by Kádár to rectify mounting fiscal problems in the country. The scheme promised and delivered reduced central planning and interference, and an increased role for the free market in Hungary's economic landscape. At the same time, concerned for its legitimacy in the eyes of its people, the Hungarian regime attempted policies of increased tolerance culturally, produced multiple-candidacy lists for parliamentary elections and strove to create full educational and employment opportunities for **women**, so that by the end of the 1960s a fairly developed welfare state had been fashioned. However, the **Leonid Brezhnev**–led government in Moscow, along with conservative figures in the Hungarian administration, were successful in halting the pace of reform by the mid-1970s. At the same time, cracks were appearing in the Hungarian economy, with the 1973 oil crisis causing a rise in the country's trade deficit and increasing its foreign debt to $8 billion. This economic downturn eventually contributed to the downfall of the Hungarian communist regime.

As the pendulum swung back toward reform in Hungary with a raft of decentralizing measures at the start of the 1980s, and, given that popular disgruntlement with the economic situation was already widespread, dissent among Hungarians grew dramatically. The country became increasingly liberalized economically, and socially as state censorship gave way to self-censorship and a "samizdat" oppositional press thrived. This "Goulash communism," akin to the "socialism with a human face" of **Alexander Dubcek** during the 1968 **Prague Spring**, when combined with **Mikhail Gorbachev**'s *glasnost* and *perestroika* reform agenda, whet the insatiable desire of Hungarian dissenters for change, and the communist regime's tenure looked unsteady. As Soviet dominance in Eastern Europe gradually receded, the Hungarian communists were rendered unable to count on any support to quell unrest as they had been in 1956, and a quiet revolution in May 1988 saw Kádár forced to resign.

The new HSWP leadership, under General Secretary Grósz, forwarded an agenda for the creation of a multi-party democracy and a market-oriented economy. At the same time, the solidarity that had once existed between states in the Eastern Bloc was imploding, as the Hungarian willingness to permit those fleeing the **German Democratic Republic** to pass through Hungary indicated. With a number of new political parties springing up in Hungary as the course of reform snowballed, the HSWP were forced into self-liquidation in October 1989, and out of its ashes arose the social democratic Hungarian Socialist Party. In May 1990, the communist era officially came to a close, and an amended constitution guaranteeing individual and civil rights, and the holding of free elections was announced. Hungary's first post-communist government, named the Democratic Forum, immediately set about a program of privatization and other reforms that sought to extirpate any last vestige of Marxism–Leninism from Hungarian life.

Hungarian Marxism, while predominantly sticking to the Soviet Leninist template until its demise in 1989–90, did break away from Moscow on a number of occasions, notably in the liberalizing eras of the early 1970s and 1980s. Additionally, events in 1956 represented a strong rebuking of Stalinist excesses and a concerted call for national autonomy. Though the uprising was eventually crushed, its occurrence paved the way for later reforms, and influenced Khrushchev into recognizing the validity of the concept of separate roads to socialism for Eastern European states. There also developed a separate philosophical stream in Hungary, chiefly in the guise of the Petofi Circle, which campaigned against the **deterministic** nature of Marxism–Leninism and called for a return to a **humanist** analysis of socialism. Influential intellectual notables such as Ferenc Fehar and

George Konrad were able to advance lengthy critiques of Soviet societies, and in the short period between Stalin's death and the suppression of the uprising, **revisionist**, anti-orthodox ideas infiltrated party, government and society in Hungary. However, such freedoms were gradually curtailed following the quelling of the uprising, but the Hungarian administration was unable to entirely ignore the reformers' agenda. Communist Hungary, while retaining the key elements of Marxist–Leninist orthodoxy, did offer slight deviations on the Soviet theme.

HYNDMAN, HENRY MAYERS (1842–1921). Hyndman was an early proponent and propagator of **Marxism** in Great Britain. He founded the **Social Democratic Federation** (SDF) in 1883, which up to World War I was the most influential and significant advocate of Marxist ideas in Britain. He combined Marxism with a belief in patriotism and in the progressive role of the British Empire. A firm belief in the correctness of his own views and intolerance of dissent contributed to splits in and defections from the SDF. He also neglected the trade unions and other labor organizations and supported the war effort in 1914, both views losing him and his party support on the left. In 1909 Hyndman formed the **British Socialist Party** in an unsuccessful attempt to create an alliance of Marxists and other **socialists**. His writings included *Socialism Made Plain* (1883) and *The Historical Basis of Socialism* (1883).

HYPPOLITE, JEAN (1907–1968). A significant scholar and philosopher in the 20th century, Hyppolite contributed to the Hegelian Marxist and **Western Marxist** traditions by highlighting the influence of **Georg Wilhelm Friedrich Hegel** on **Karl Marx** and the theoretical links between them. This he did in his teaching (his pupils included Michel Foucault, Gilles Deleuze and Jacques Derrida) and his writing, most notably his *Studies on Marx and Hegel* (1955). Hyppolite drew attention to the themes of the realization of reason in history, the goal of freedom, and **alienation** and dehumanization in society that connected Marx with Hegel.

Born in Jonzac, France, Hyppolite was educated at the École Normale Supérieure, and went on to teach at various provincial lycées throughout France.

He took up a position at the University of Strasbourg after World War II, and in 1949 was appointed chair at the Sorbonne where he taught until 1954 when he became director of the École Normale Supérieure. In 1963 he was appointed to the Collège de France. His teachings and writings provided support for and helped to direct attention toward the theories of such Hegel-inspired **Marxists** as **Georgii Lukács, Karl Korsch** and **Antonio Gramsci**.

– I –

IDEALISM. Friedrich Engels asserted that the great divide in philosophy is between the schools of idealism and **materialism**, that is those who regard mind as having primacy over nature, and those who regard nature as having primacy over mind. According to philosophical idealists the only things that fully exist are minds and their contents, and the material world does not exist independently of minds. For example, one idealist argument is that to be is to be perceived or to be a perceiver. Idealist philosophy, and that of **Georg Wilhelm Friedrich Hegel** in particular, dominated German philosophical thinking for much of the 19th century, and had a profound effect on **Karl Marx**. Marx counted himself a disciple of Hegel while at university, and much of his early writing, such as *Critique of Hegel's Philosophy of Right* (1843), *Critique of Hegel's Philosophy of Right: Introduction* (1844), *Economic and Philosophical Manuscripts* (1844), *The Holy Family* (1844), *Theses on Feuerbach* (1845), *The German Ideology* (1846) and *The Poverty of Philosophy* (1847) contained a critique of idealism and a working out of his own position in relation to idealism.

To give an example of Marx's divergence from Hegel, the latter understands history as the development of the idea of freedom, with ideas, thought, consciousness or, as Hegel often puts it, *Geist*, giving history meaning, purpose and direction. For Hegel it is *Geist* or mind, the ideal realm, that is the source of the creative impulse or driving force in the world. According to Marx, this approach is fundamentally wrong and ends up imposing abstract concepts and categories on the world. The starting point is the material world and in particular human activity from which ideas and consciousness are derived.

Influenced by the critique of Hegelianism provided by Ludwig Feuerbach, Marx sees Hegel as having mystified reality by inverting the real relations between things, for example portraying man as the creation of God, when in fact, according to Feuerbach and Marx, God is the creation of man. On history, Marx develops his theory of **historical materialism**, or as he referred to it, his materialist conception of history, emphasizing material factors in the development of history, particularly human activity and production.

IDEOLOGY. In the *Communist Manifesto* (1848) **Karl Marx** writes, "The ideas of the **ruling class** are in every epoch the ruling ideas," and this is a key aspect of his theory of ideology. For Marx ideology is both a distorted view of reality and a view that serves the interests of the ruling **class**. Marx's theory of ideology developed throughout his writings remaining consistent in the notions that ideology involved an inverted view of reality, but an inversion that was ultimately rooted in reality itself. For example, Marx's critique of religion follows Ludwig Feuerbach's view that the religious consciousness inverts reality when it claims that God made man, because in reality God and religion are human constructs. However, Marx goes beyond Feuerbach in seeking the root cause of religious consciousness which he locates in a world where people are unhappy, unfulfilled and oppressed, and who seek comfort in religion. So the problem is not just false ideas that can be countered by true ones, but a deficient reality that generates false ideas, and therefore the reality must be changed in order to change the false ideas.

Marx, with his **dialectical** perspective, identifies contradictions in reality, in the economic system for example, that are concealed by distorted ideas, and such ideological distortions, which in general serve the interests of the ruling class, cannot be eliminated by mere counter-arguments, but can only be ended by resolving the real contradictions in the world that give rise to them. In his later writings on **capitalism** Marx discusses how the market gives the appearance of a free and equal system, with workers free to sell their labor and all men and women equal. **Bourgeois** ideology with its stress on liberty, rights, and property reflects this distorted appearance. Beneath the surface of the exchange system though lies the truth of unfreedom and inequality, where **surplus value** is generated through the labor power of workers who are **exploited** by their capitalist employers and denied access to the **means of production**. For Marx ideology is a term employed critically and negatively. Later Marxists developed a more neutral view of ideology as a term for the totality of forms of social consciousness. In other words, ideology came to be seen by such Marxists as **Georgii Plekhanov** as part of the **superstructure**, ideas reflecting material conditions in the economic base. **Eduard Bernstein** took the step of describing **Marxism** itself as an ideology without in any way intending this to be a critical or negative comment, and **Vladimir Ilich Lenin** developed the view of ideology as meaning the political consciousness of classes, so that there is a **proletarian** ideology standing in opposition to bourgeois ideology. **Georgii Lukács** followed Lenin's line and described Marxism as "the ideological expression of the proletariat," also viewing ideology as a key arena of struggle between the bourgeoisie and the proletariat. **Antonio Gramsci** developed the theory of ideology further linking it to his notion of **hegemony** and the overall struggle for domination between classes. For Gramsci the rule of the dominant class is achieved as much by ideology as by force, and ideology is an entire conception of the world that permeates all aspects of life. This view affords a much more significant role to intellectuals and to ideological institutions such as churches and schools. Gramsci specifically identified four levels of ideology: philosophy; religion; common sense; and folklore. **Louis Althusser** distinguished between a theory of ideology in general which concerns ideology as a cohesive force in society, and a theory of particular ideologies which concerns ideology as a means of achieving domination for a single class. Ideology he views as a relatively autonomous level of society, a part of the superstructure, reflecting social and economic factors and interests. He contrasts ideology with science, the latter being an autonomous practice that solely pursues truth and knowledge, and Marxism he divides into Marx's earlier ideological writings and later scientific writings, with what he terms an "epistemological break" separating the two.

IMPERIALISM. Three of the most significant contributors to the **Marxist** theory of imperialism are **Nikolai Bukharin**, **Karl Kautsky** and **Vladimir Ilich Lenin**. Bukharin in *Imperialism and the World Economy* (1918) developed **Karl Marx**'s model of **capitalism** into a model of the world economic system dominated by capitalism. He identified a tendency for the **state** to grow as capitalism developed leading to state capitalism at the national level. This allowed for greater central planning, organization and regulation of the economy within countries and the virtual elimination of internal **crises**, but competition, conflict and crisis he saw as continuing at the international level where the struggle was between "state capitalist trusts." This economic struggle led to military struggle and war.

Kautsky viewed imperialism as the relationship between powerful, advanced capitalist countries and weak, underdeveloped, precapitalist countries which are exploited and oppressed by the former. He thought that capitalism had entered a new stage of monopoly or ultra-imperialism, where the cartels developed in the advanced capitalist countries would unite to form a single world trust, that would end competition within and between the advanced capitalist countries, leaving a struggle between colonists and colonized. From this perspective World War I was something of an aberration, and not as Bukharin and Lenin suggested the consequence of imperialism. The "dependency theory" school of thought that developed after World War II, in seeking to investigate and explain economic development and underdevelopment in the world, followed Kautsky's line of argument.

Lenin, most famously and influentially of the three, argued in his *Imperialism: The Highest Stage of Capitalism* (1916) that capitalism had entered a new period of "monopoly capitalism" in which monopoly replaced competition within countries, production had become concentrated in trusts and cartels, finance and industrial capital had merged with the former having the upper hand, and export of capital had replaced export of goods. The cartels, dominated by the banks, looked to underdeveloped countries to invest (export) their capital in the pursuit of ever greater profits. The competition between cartels brought the capitalist powers into conflict as they divided, and tried to re-divide, the world into spheres of influence. This ultimately led to war such as World War I, capital accumulation being the root cause as it developed on a global scale.

INDEPENDENT GERMAN SOCIALIST PARTY (OR GERMAN INDEPENDENT SOCIALIST PARTY). *See* GERMAN SOCIAL DEMOCRATIC PARTY; SPARTACUS LEAGUE.

INDEPENDENT LABOUR PARTY (ILP). Formed in 1893 at the Bradford Conference, the Independent Labour Party was originally composed of 120 representatives of local **socialist** and labor organizations from throughout Great Britain. Its formation was the result of Keir Hardie's calls for a united labor party, and it followed a socialist policy "to secure the collective ownership of the means of production, distribution and exchange. Its social program was progressive with demands for reforms such as the abolition of child labor and an eight-hour working day, and from its earliest days **women** were able to stand for positions on the same terms as men. The ILP was influenced by **Marxist** ideas and members from it became founder members of the **British Socialist Party** which later merged with various other left-wing groups to become the **Communist Party of Great Britain**. However, the ILP was more significant in the creation of the British Labour Party and as a radical pressure group within it. It dissolved in 1975.

INDOCHINESE COMMUNIST PARTY (ICP). Founded in 1930 by **Ho Chi Minh**, the Indochinese Communist Party was largely Vietnamese in composition. It suffered from repression by the French colonial administration in **Vietnam** until in 1936 a new Popular Front government in France gave greater political freedom and allowed the ICP to organize, propagandize and participate in elections. This ended with the collapse of the Popular Front government and the ICP returned to clandestine activities in 1939. Supported by the **Soviet Union** the ICP followed the **Comintern** line of condemning World War II when it broke out in Europe, and then switching to the antifascist united front line in keeping with the Comintern lead. During the war the ICP moved to a strategy of prioritizing national liberation and to this end created a broad front called the League for the Independence of Vietnam (Viet Nam Doc Lap Dong Minh), or Vietminh for short. When the Japanese took over rule of Vietnam the Vietminh engaged in a struggle with them, and with the defeat of Japan abroad by the Allied forces, the Vietminh seized power with Ho Chi Minh declaring the independent Democratic Republic of Vietnam (DRV) on 2 September 1945. Membership of the party rapidly rose from around 5,000 just before the creation of the DRV to 20,000 the following year, and 700,000 by 1950. In 1951 the ICP was renamed the

Vietnam Workers' Party (VWP), and after the division of Vietnam in 1954 the branch of the party in the south renamed itself the People's Revolutionary Party. After a protracted war the victorious DRV named the newly unified Vietnam the **Socialist Republic of Vietnam**, and the VWP became the Vietnamese Communist Party (Dang Cong San Viet Nam).

INTERNATIONAL ALLIANCE OF SOCIALIST DEMOCRACY (IASD). Inaugurated in Geneva in 1868, the short-lived International Alliance of Socialist Democracy brought together **First International** members under Michael Bakunin to offer an alternative to the association's application of **Marxism**. Dubbed "an International within the International" by an outraged **Karl Marx**, schisms within the IASD led to its termination in 1872.

INTERNATIONAL WORKERS OF THE WORLD (IWW). Founded in Chicago in 1905, the International Workers of the World was an anarcho-**syndicalist** organization though influenced by **Marxism**. **Eugene Debs** and **Daniel De Leon** were involved in the founding of the IWW, and their parties, the **Socialist Party of America** and the Socialist Labor Party, were linked to the IWW, although the anarcho-syndicalism of the IWW led to it breaking with Debs, De Leon and their parties. The IWW dissolved in 1925.

INTERNATIONAL WORKING MEN'S ASSOCIATION. *See* FIRST INTERNATIONAL.

INTERNATIONAL WORKING UNION OF SOCIALIST PARTIES (IWUSP). The International Working Union of Socialist Parties, also known as the Vienna Union and by **Vladimir Ilich Lenin** as the "two-and-half International," was an organization founded in 1921 to facilitate the cooperation of socialist groups. Under secretary **Max Adler,** the union brought together, among others, the **Austrian Social Democratic Party**, the **French Socialist Party** and the **German Social Democratic Party** to offer an alternative to orthodox **Marxism**. In May 1923, with disputes rife, many union members split to form the Labor and Socialist International along with former affiliates of the **Second International**. Battered by the onslaught of fascism and the heavy influence on the left of the **Third Interna-**

tional, the IWUSP gradually became obsolete and was succeeded with the 1951 creation of the Socialist International.

INTERNATIONALISM. The notion of internationalism was strongly embraced by **Karl Marx** and **Friedrich Engels**, and is expressed in the slogan of the **Communist League** "Proletarians of All Countries, Unite!" Marx and Engels saw **class** identity, interests and struggle as crossing national frontiers, and they sought to promote internationalism as much as possible, for example, through the creation of the **First International**. However, this did not prevent them from also supporting nationalist movements, for example in Poland and Ireland, since they believed that the struggle of the proletariat and **bourgeoisie** first takes a national form. National proletarian **revolutions**, though, could not succeed if they did not rapidly spread to other countries to become truly international revolutions.

Vladimir Ilich Lenin continued to advocate internationalism while also allowing for national self-determination, but under **Josef Stalin** the **Soviet Union**, while ostensibly supporting international **communism** through the **Communist International**, grew more nationalistic pursuing its own interests through the Communist International and denying self-determination to other nationalities. Support for anti-colonial independence movements around the world by the Soviet Union and **China** might be seen as evidence of a commitment to internationalism, but the rivalry and outright conflict between different Marxist countries points to a continuing tension between nationalism and internationalism within Marxism.

ITALIAN COMMUNIST PARTY. The Italian Communist Party (*Partito Comunista Italiano*—PCI) emerged in 1921 when advocates of **Leninism** broke away from the **Italian Socialist Party**. The PCI was declared illegal by Italian premier Benito Mussolini in 1926, though under the direction of **Antonio Gramsci** and after his imprisonment **Palmiro Togliatti** it continued as an underground organization. Having been re-legalized in 1944, the PCI was a constituent of coalition governments until 1947, though it suffered defeat in the general election a year later. Though never formally taking office, the PCI lent its support to left-wing governments in Italy from this time onwards. Under **Luigi Longo**, the party moved closer to the **Soviet Union**

and received generous aid from **Leonid Brezhnev**'s administration. However, the emergence of **Enrico Berlinguer** as PCI leader saw the party cast aside its **Marxism–Leninism** and promulgate **eurocommunism**. After Moscow refused to condemn Czechoslovakian support for the terrorist **Red Brigades**, in 1979 the PCI severed all ties with the Soviet Union. In the 1980s, it shed its Marxist ideals entirely and transformed into a social democratic party, before disbanding in 1991 to form the moderate Democratic Party of the Left (*Partito Democratico della Sinistra* — PDS).

ITALIAN SOCIALIST PARTY. Founded in 1892, the Italian Socialist Party (*Partito Socialista Italiano* — PSI) traditionally struggled to gain a foothold in Italy, largely because of the strength of the other group on the left, the **Italian Communist Party**. The PSI joined the **Third International** in 1919, though hopes of progression were stunted first by the departure of left-wing party members who broke away to form the Communist Party, and then by repression at the hands of Benito Mussolini's "Blackshirt" forces. Having been banned by Mussolini in 1926, the PSI continued to meet in Paris, and in 1934 signed a Unity of Action agreement aimed at mutual cooperation in labor affairs with the Italian Communist Party that was to last until the middle of the 1950s.

However, from that period onwards the two parties begin to pursue different courses, and in 1978 moderate leader Bettino Craxi dropped all mentions of **Marxism** from the PSI constitution, re-fashioning the party into a social democratic organization. In 1983 Craxi's PSI became Italy's first socialist government, serving until 1987 and then again as a coalition partner from 1989 to 1994. However, the PSI came to a spectacular if inauspicious end in that final year of governance as Craxi and a host of party luminaries were convicted of fraud. Disgraced, the PSI was liquidated by its own members, and re-formed as the low-profile Italian Socialists (*Socialisti Italiani* — SI). Following the 2001 general election, a number of former PSI affiliates tasted power once more, as their Socialist Party–New PSI (*Partito Socialista–Nuovo PSI* — PS-NPSI) became part of Silvio Berlusconi's right-wing House of Freedoms Coalition. That they did so indicated just how comprehensively Marxism has been discarded by much of the Italian left.

– J –

JAMES, CYRIL LIONEL ROBERT (1901–1989). A **Marxist** historian, novelist, critic, philosopher and lecturer, C.L.R. James, among many other accomplishments, wrote one of the finest history books of the 20th century, *The Black Jacobins: Toussaint L'Ouverture and the San Domingo Revolution* (1938). Born in Trinidad to a comfortable middle-**class** family, James developed an early interest in both literature and cricket as well as demonstrating outstanding academic ability. In the 1920s he was editor of *Trinidad*, a literary review, as well as contributing pieces to the London *Saturday Review* and writing a novel, *Minty Alley*. In 1932 he moved to Great Britain where he became a cricket correspondent for *The Manchester Guardian* and embraced revolutionary **socialism**. His lifelong passion for cricket found its most brilliant expression in his partly biographical book *Beyond a Boundary* (1963), in which he discussed not just cricket, but also its social context. He moved to the **United States** in 1939 from which he was expelled in 1953 for his political activities when McCarthyism held sway. Back in Trinidad he became editor of the Trinidad People's National Movement (PNM) journal *The Nation* in 1958, spent time as secretary of the West Indian Federal Labour Party, and in 1965 co-founded the radical Workers' and Farmers' Party. After 1966 he lived abroad in the United States and Britain.

James' revolutionary political outlook developed from **Trotskyism** to an independent libertarian Marxism. He opposed the bureaucratic centralism of **Stalinism** and any notions of a **vanguard party** or of statist **socialism**. Philosophically his Marxism was influenced by **Georg Wilhelm Friedrich Hegel** and he sought always to emphasize the importance of culture and national identity while retaining the radical spirit of Marxism and not losing sight of the goal of universal human emancipation. He was seen as a forerunner of both Pan-Africanism and "new left" politics.

JAPANESE COMMUNIST PARTY (JCP). The JCP (*Nihon Kyosanto*) was formed from the Japanese branch of the **Communist International** in 1922 but was deemed to be illegal. It was forced to dissolve briefly in 1924 but reorganized in 1926. It was particularly the subject of police repression due to advocacy of the abolition of the emperor as part of a **bourgeois** democratic **revolution** to precede a **socialist** revolution in a second stage. The party engaged in underground activity and was active in labor unions and other groups. However, arrests or exile of the top leadership and frequent forced conversions of **communists** meant that the party was in tatters for most of its early existence.

The JCP gained legal status in 1945 at the end of the Pacific War under the Allied Occupation of Japan. It leaders were released from jail or returned from exile. In the first postwar election, it obtained five seats and its first representation in the Japanese parliament. Moreover, its tendency to encourage illegal anti-government action caused its relationship with the Allied Occupation authorities to deteriorate and it was subject to a "Red Purge" with its members or suspected members losing their jobs in government and private industry. Intervention from Moscow also increased in this period and the party split into several smaller factions. The dominant faction organized sporadic guerrilla actions in rural areas but this was soon put down by the Japanese police.

From 1955 Kenji Miyamoto emerged as the leader and proceeded to rebuild the JCP. Internationally, the party took the Chinese side in the Sino–Soviet split but both nations attempted to actively intervene in the party to gain influence. At the same time, the party toned down its ideological propaganda and became active in issues of everyday livelihood in both rural and urban Japan. It was particularly successful in urban areas such as Osaka, Kyoto and Tokyo. It worked with the **Japanese Socialist Party** in the 1970s to elect progressive mayors and governors to a number of major urban areas. By 1979 it had 41 seats in parliament. However, this was only a little over 10 percent of the seats and the JCP was still mistrusted by the other opposition parties.

The party welcomed the fall of the **Soviet Union** and took advantage of the collapse of the Japan Socialist Party in 1996 to regain electoral strength that it had lost during the 1980s. However, this revival was short-lived. By the 2004 upper house election, it had even lost all of its seats in its stronghold of Kyoto. Nonetheless, reform of the party program has proceeded. In 2000, it eliminated the term **vanguard party** from its platform, and in 2004 accepted Japan was a **capitalist** nation but advocated democratic control of the economy and opposition to militarism. In addition, it emphasized its commitment to freedom and democracy. It even now accepts the current constitutional position of the emperor but opposes the use of the Imperial House for political purposes. *See also* KATAYAMA, SEN; KOZA FACTION.

JAPANESE MARXISM. Marxism has failed to gain significant support in Japan despite the country having had a large urban working class and having been at the forefront of technological development since World War II. The Japanese Communist Party (JCP; *Nihon Kyosanto*) was formed in 1922 and delegates from it attended **Second International** meetings. It was a tiny, illegal organization and suffered from government repression until 1945. Allowed to participate in the 1946 elections it gained over two million votes and won five seats in the lower house. The Korean War saw the suppression of the party, but after the mid-1950s it was made legal once more and participated in elections and mainstream politics. Under Kenji Miyamoto the JCP pursued a gradualist, electoralist approach and gained a degree of success. The JCP is the largest Marxist organization in Japan, gaining 29 lower house seats in 1980 and with as many as 465,000 members in 1985, but electoral support has not exceeded the 11 percent reached in 1972. The party has in part based its appeal on a nationalism that has included an anti-Americanism and that has stressed the party's independence from both **Soviet** and **Chinese communism**.

Marxist theory has had a major impact in Japan from the 1920s, and Marxist debates in Japan were conducted at a sophisticated level drawing on the German linguistic capabilities of its thinkers, their overseas experience and the position of Japan as the first major non-Western capitalist nation. Marxism was the dominant influence on postwar Japanese economics and history, and early postwar government economic policies were developed by Marxist economists. At present, Japanese Marxist economics is divided into four groups: the **Koza faction**, the **Rono faction**, the Civil Society faction (regulation theory), and Marxian quantitative theory group. Marxism continues to be a strong influence in Japanese academic circles.

JAPANESE SOCIALIST PARTY. Formed immediately after the end of the Pacific War in 1945, the Japanese Socialist Party combined the various non-**communist** groups of the prewar Japanese left into one party. The name in Japanese was the Japan Socialist Party (*Nihon Shakai To*) but in English it sometimes referred to itself as the Social Democratic Party of Japan (SDJP) reflecting doctrinal disputes whereby the left of the party rejected social democracy as reformist. At first the party was primarily led by Christian **socialists** with the **Marxist** left wing playing a major role as activists, both in the party and in the labor and tenant farmer movements. It became the largest party in parliament in the 1947 General Election and its leader, the Christian socialist Tetsu Katayama, was prime minister of Japan from May 1947 to February 1948. The party participated in another coalition cabinet from February 1948 to November 1948. From that point forward, the party was out of power until the mid-1990s.

At the Fourth Party Congress in 1949 a fierce debate over the direction of the party occurred regarding whether the party was to be a national party or a **class** party, and was resolved in the compromise concept of a "class-based mass" party. However, during the ratification of the San Francisco Peace Treaty, the party split over the issue of a comprehensive peace (i.e., to demand that the treaty also include the **Soviet Union** and the **People's Republic of China**). Though the party divided into Left Socialist and Right Socialist parties, both declared themselves to be the Japan Socialist Party and the two wings merged again in 1955. After reunification, the party rose to 166 seats in the all-important lower house of the Japanese parliament in 1958, the peak of its strength, but with the unification of the center-right parties into the Liberal Democratic Party (LDP), the JSP only held one-third of the seats in parliament with no prospect of another coalition government. In 1959, moreover, it lost all of its seats in Tokyo in an upper house election. Debate raged in the party over how to overcome the barriers to further electoral growth. In 1959, the right and left wings fell out over the Miike Mine dispute, which the left propelled into a cause célèbre against monopoly **capitalism**. Many right socialist MPs defected to the newly formed Democratic Socialist Party backed by moderate unions.

The party appeared to gain strength and support when it strongly opposed the ratification of the revised Mutual Security Treaty with the United States in 1960, but in the 1960 lower house election, the party's number of seats fell to 145 while the Liberal Democratic Party grew in strength. The JSP made an attempt at "structural reform" in the early 1960s in order to transform itself into a more "realistic" party in the wake of the failure of the Security Treaty and Miike Mine protests but the influence of the left wing of the party quashed all attempts at reform. By 1969 the number of lower house seats held by the JSP fell to 90. Even though the party saw a slight revival in the 1970s, and it helped to elect candidates to local office jointly with the **Japan Communist Party**, it now became just one of a number of smaller parties. Strongly pacifistic in orientation, the party took the Soviet side as the Cold War reignited in the 1980s.

As a result of another devastating defeat in the 1986 General Election and the reorganization of the Japanese union movement, the party slowly moved toward reform. In 1989, under the leadership of its first female leader, Takako Doi, the party suddenly saw an electoral spurt in its favor. In the upper house election of 1989, the LDP only gained 36 seats against 46 for the JSP. However, the party was in the spotlight in the 1990 lower house election and it soon became clear that the party of committed Marxists had merely rebranded itself but could not produce distinctive or realistic policies. The party briefly returned to power in 1993 when the LDP was finally forced from office temporarily, but to the surprise of many, it then entered a coalition with the LDP in 1994 in order to stay in power. The party effectively collapsed in the 1996 lower house election with most of its key MPs defecting to the newly formed center-left Democratic Party and the small rump transforming itself into the small Social Democratic Party. *See also* KATAYAMA, SEN.

JAURÈS, JEAN (1854–1914). A leading **socialist** before World War I, Jaurès acknowledged the value of **Marxism** but without committing himself to Marxism as such. He embraced **class** struggle and the goal of socialism, seeking to combine **historical materialism** with Hegelian **idealism**. Born in Castres, France, he was both a politician and a scholar. As the former he represented his native region, the Tarn, in the Chamber of Deputies from 1885 to 1887, 1893 to 1898 and 1902 to his murder by a nationalist fanatic aggrieved by his anti-war position in 1914. Jaurès was active in the **Second International** and in the political grouping that became the **French Socialist Party**. He founded *L'Humanité*, which later became the organ of the **French Communist Party**. As a scholar he produced several books, most notably a history of socialism, *Histoire Socialiste*, 1789–1900 (1908).

JIANG ZEMIN (1926–). Veteran Chinese communist leader who unexpectedly rose to power in the **People's Republic of China** after the fall of **Zhao Ziyang** and crushing of the pro-democracy movement in June 1989. Jiang trained as an electrical engineer and worked in the machine building industry for 26 years. He kept a low profile during the **Cultural Revolution**, his political career only becoming noteworthy in the 1980s. With his background he became vice chairman of the State Council's commissions on imports, exports and foreign investments in 1980 and from 1982 to 1985 he served as electronic industry minister. In 1985 he became mayor of Shanghai and during this time he defused student protests without resort to the military. After the outbreak of the Tiananmen Square protests in 1989 Jiang was the first provincial leader to indicate his support for martial law in Beijing, and he was brought to the capital by **Deng Xiaoping** after the Tiananmen Square massacre and made a member of the Politburo Standing Committee and the party Secretariat. In November 1989 he succeeded Deng Xiaoping, becoming president of the People's Republic of China and general secretary of the **Chinese Communist Party**. Jiang has overseen gradual economic reforms in China, although favoring a much more conservative approach to change in the political sphere.

JUSTO, JUAN BAUTISTA (1865–1928). Justo was one of the early thinkers and activists who tried to create a Latin American **Marxism**. His brand of Marxism was most notable for its strong evolutionary character. An Argentinean physician and professor, Justo studied in Europe, returning to Argentina where he founded the **socialist** journal *La Vanguardia* in 1894, and where he helped found the Socialist Party of Argentina in 1895. In the same year he completed the first Spanish translation of **Karl Marx**'s *Capital*. In 1912 he was elected as a socialist deputy to the Argentine Congress.

In his thought Justo was most strongly influenced by the French socialist thinker **Jean Jaurès**, the German "**revisionist**" socialist **Eduard Bernstein**, and above all by the evolutionary liberal thinker Herbert Spencer. Like Spencer he linked the notion of human biological struggle to political theory, and stressed evolutionary progress in society. While embracing Marx's general vision of history as expressing evolutionary ideas, he rejected Marxist ideas of imperialism and even advocated the encouragement of foreign investment in Argentina in order to speed up economic and social development and, hence, accelerate the evolutionary process toward full socialization of the **means of production**. He also revised the Marxist view of **class** with its emphasis on the **proletariat** to take account of the class composition in Argentina where there was a very small, underdeveloped working class. Justo sought to mobilize middle class and rural wage earners in addition to the traditionally defined proletariat. In adapting Marxism to Latin American conditions Justo contributed to the overcoming of Marxism's Eurocentrism.

– K –

KAISON PHOMVIHAN (1920–1992). A Laotian nationalist and **communist**, Kaison led the Pathet Lao (communist party army), and was prime minister of the **People's Democratic Republic of Laos** and general secretary of the **Lao People's Revolutionary Party**. Born in Savannakhet province and educated at Hanoi University Kaison fought in the wars of independence against the French first in **Vietnam** and then in Laos. He fought with the Pathet Lao in the Laotian civil war after the ousting of the French, and in 1975 became the first prime minister of the newly formed People's Democratic Republic of Laos and president from 1991 to 1992. He pursued a radical policy of nationalizing industry and **collectivizing** agriculture, although this was moderated over time.

KAMPUCHEA, DEMOCRATIC. The 1975 attainment of power by **Pol Pot's Khmer Rouge** movement in modern-day Cambodia led to a tyrannical reign of power cut short only by the **Vietnamese** capture of the capital Phnom Penh in 1979. Espousing a distorted form of **Marxism–Leninism** that owed more to the worst excesses of **Stalinism** than genuine Marxian analysis, the Khmer Rouge was responsible for about a million fatalities within Kampuchea's borders.

Having held considerable sway in the left-leaning government of King Norodom Sihanouk that had come to power in 1970, the thinly veiled **communists** of the Khmer Rouge attained outright power for themselves in April 1975. They renamed the country Democratic Kampuchea, and built an impenetrable power bloc by placing senior party officials in lofty **state** positions. Though the Khmer Rouge only outwardly professed their adherence to Marxism–Leninism for the first time in September 1976, right from the beginning of their reign they implemented their interpretation of the **ideology**. The primary strand of this Kampuchean Marxism was the relocation of urban dwellers to the countryside, where they were to partake in forced labor on newly **collectivized** farms, but more commonly perished in the alien territory of rural surroundings. This radical program was buttressed by a brutal system of state terror, as Pol Pot ordered the mass execution of "counter revolutionary" groups from teachers, intellectuals and civil servants to police and army officers. Religious groups faced persecution too, as the Khmer Rouge sought to wipe out organized faith in anything but the party line. Reflecting the coziness between Phnom Penh and Beijing that emerged after **Deng Xiaoping**'s 1976 succeeding of **Mao Zedong**, the Kampuchean dictator initiated a cull of educational influence similar to that witnessed in the Chinese **Cultural Revolution**, as the major goal of learning became the installment of revolutionary values among the young.

There was one discernible departure from orthodox **Maoism**, however, in the form of the Kampuchean regime's fanatical pursuit of economic self-sufficiency. To that end, currency was liquidated, a barter system introduced, and foreign trade almost completely eradicated, though limited dealings with **China** and France among others began again in 1977. Claiming that the country was free from the shackles of foreign economic hegemony for the first time in two millennia, and having mobilized the populace into military-like work brigades, Pol Pot was able to announce the achievement of full (albeit forced) employment.

From the very opening of the Khmer Rouge epoch, hostilities with neighboring Vietnam rarely abated. Border skirmishes, mutual military encroachment into one another's territory, and clandestine Vietnamese support for anti-Pol Pot forces such as the United Front for the National Salvation of Kampuchea (UFNSK) constantly undermined the Khmer Rouge's hold on power. Hanoi finally lost patience with Kampuchea's rampant bellicosity in late 1978, sending into the country a force of 120,000 soldiers to overthrow the government. Phnom Penh fell in early 1979; the dictatorship of Pol Pot and the Khmer Rouge soon crumbled with it. The Vietnamese established rule in the country, though they faced constant insecurity and insurrectionary threats throughout the 1980s and beyond from Pol Pot and his loyal henchmen who had fled into the jungle and then into hiding in Thailand. The resultant state of civil war finally ceased with the staging of a United Nations–supervised election in 1993 that saw King Sihanouk reclaim his throne. Five years later, Pol Pot was dead and his remaining supporters had surrendered.

In the 1976 Constitution of Democratic Kampuchea, the Khmer Rouge claimed to be the only Marxist–Leninist state on earth to have eradicated **class** distinctions between **peasants**, workers, the **bourgeoisie**, industrialists and **feudalists**, chiefly by literally eradicating many of the constituents of those groups. Pol Pot claimed the country had become a three-tier society of workers, peasants and "all other Kampuchean working people," in which measures such as the relocation of urban dwellers and the devastation of the education system had eliminated industrialists and the bourgeoisie respectively. Kampuchean Marxism–Leninism entirely negated the doctrines of stage theory and aimed to leap straight to an almost primeval form of communism, leaping over any obstructive intermediate steps such as the "new democracy" phase adopted in **China**. The denouement of this haphazard approach to Marxist analysis, though, was the destruction of an entire people and land.

KARDELJ, EDVARD (1910–1979). A leading politician and theoretician in communist **Yugoslavia**, Kardelj cooperated closely with **Milovan Djilas** and **Josef Tito**. He worked as a schoolteacher and was imprisoned as a communist during the dictatorship of Alexander I. For a while he lived in the **Soviet Union** before returning to fight against the fascists during World War II. He was vice president of the anti-fascist council (AVNOJ) from 1945 to 1953 and was minister of foreign affairs during Tito's regime. He was a leading figure in drawing up the Yugoslavian federal constitution and a significant contributor to the Yugoslavian school of **Marxism** that developed as an alternative to **Stalinist** Marxism.

KATAYAMA, SEN (1859–1933). Born as Sugataro Yabuki into a family which for many generations had been a leading family of his village, Sen Katayama spent one year at what is now the Education Department of Okayama University then traveling to the **United States** in 1884 where he washed dishes while attending university and later graduate school where he obtained degrees in sociology and theology.

He became a Christian and put his efforts into the labor movement, playing a major role in the establishment of Japan's first labor union. In 1901 he participated in the formation of Japan's first **socialist** party, the Social Democratic Party of Japan, which was immediately banned. In 1906 he joined in the formation of the **Japanese Socialist Party** but he was soon in conflict with his fellow founding members. As a result of his leadership of the 1911 Tokyo City electric strike, he was arrested and jailed.

In 1914 after being released from prison Sen Katayama went into exile in the United States where he became a Marxist as a result of the Russian revolution in 1917 and put his energies into the establishment of the American and the Mexican Communist Parties. In 1921 he traveled to the **Soviet Union** to become a top official in the **Communist International**. From there, he directed the formation of the **Japanese Communist Party**. He died in Moscow on 5 November 1933 where his funeral on 9 November was attended by 150,000 people. His coffin was carried by 14 people including **Josef Stalin** and Sanzo Nosaka, future leader of the Japanese Communist Party. He was buried within the Kremlin.

KAUTSKY, KARL (1854–1938). Karl Kautsky was for many years the leading theorist of the **German Social Democratic Party** (SPD) and of the **Second International**. He advocated an orthodox interpretation of **Marxism** that emphasized the scientific, **materialist** and **deterministic** character of **Karl Marx**'s thought. Kautsky was born in Prague in 1854, studied history, economics and philosophy at the University of Vienna, and began his active involvement in organized politics in 1875 when he joined the **Austrian Social Democratic Party**. After dealings with various leading European Marxists, most notably **Eduard Bernstein**, and founding and editing the influential journal *Die Neue Zeit*, Kautsky moved to London where he worked with **Friedrich Engels**. Moving back to Germany when restrictions on socialist parties were lifted in 1890 he became active in the SPD. He wrote the crucial theory section of the party's Erfurt Program in 1891, which was virtually the bible of the SPD and a major influence on other European socialist organizations. He briefly left in 1917 to join the German Independent Social Democratic Party (USPD) because of his opposition to the increasing collaboration of the SPD in the war effort, but rejoined in 1922. By the 1930s his influence and involvement in politics was dwindling and he died in Amsterdam in 1938.

Kautsky's view of Marxism dominated the European Marxist movement for the best part of two decades. It centered on the notion that Marxism was a science that had identified the laws of history. These laws showed that the collapse of **capitalism** was inevitable, as was its replacement by **socialism**. Influenced by Darwinian evolution theory, Kautsky saw human history as evolving, and Marxism allowed an objective scientific analysis of the material conditions of society, which showed the inexorable progress toward worker self-emancipation and self-government. The implications of this deterministic view were that history could not be hurried and that politically workers and workers' parties must wait for the material economic conditions to be ripe before the revolutionary transformation of society could take place. This saw the SPD adopt a gradualist approach, taking advantage of the **bourgeois** parliamentary democracy to improve workers' lives until capitalism was brought down by its objective internal contradictions.

Kautsky's position led him into disputes with other leading Marxists. He battled with Eduard Bernstein, who favored a more ethically based and openly reformist approach, with **Rosa Luxemburg**, who advocated worker spontancity and a mass strike, and with **Vladimir Ilich Lenin**, who Kautsky believed had initiated the **revolution** in Russia prematurely and who was leading the country toward tyranny.

KAWAKAMI, HAJIME (1879–1946). After graduating from the Law Department (politics section) of Tokyo Imperial University in 1902, Hajime Kawakami lectured in agriculture and wrote newspaper articles on economics for a major daily newspaper. He became a lecturer at Kyoto University in 1908 and traveled for two years in Europe (1914–15). In 1916 he was made a professor but quit his position in 1928 in order to become a full-time activist. With Kunio Oyama he formed the Labor-Farmers Party (*Rodo Nomin To*) but split with the party after moving to Tokyo in 1930. He joined the underground **Japanese Communist Party** in 1932 but was questioned by the police in the following year and briefly imprisoned. He quit politics, began writing Chinese poetry and retired to Kyoto. During his academic and political career he published several famous works on wealth and poverty, but is best known for introducing **Marxist**

economics into Japanese including translating **Karl Marx**'s *Das Kapital* (*Capital*).

KEREKOU, MATHIEU (1933–). Born in northwest **Benin** (formerly the French colony of Dahomey), Africa, Kerekou became president of Dahomey and oversaw its transformation into the avowedly **Marxist–Leninist** People's Republic of Benin. Kerekou had joined the French colonial army, transferred to the newly formed Dahomean army in 1961 and rose to become lieutenant colonel. He seized power in a coup on 26 October 1972 but only after two years was Benin declared a People's Republic and committed to Marxism–Leninism. The key ideological tenets of the regime as outlined by Kerekou were national economic independence through the placing of the **means of production** in the hands of the **state**, the transformation of society into a harmonious alliance of workers and **peasants**, realignment of foreign policy to side with **communist** countries, and a political structure based on **democratic centralism**. In 1975 the country's name was changed to Benin and the People's Revolutionary Party (*Parti de la Révolution Populaire*) of Benin was created. In 1977 the fundamental law of Benin was issued describing the organization of the state and the evolutionary stages through which it was passing on the way to the final socialist **revolution**. More pragmatic nationalist than ideologically socialist, more rhetoric than reality and more authoritarian than democratic, Kerekou's regime showed itself to be increasingly incompetent and corrupt. Eventually, in 1990, Kerekou was stripped of his powers and a civilian government installed.

KHMER ROUGE. The guerrilla army of the Kampuchean Communist Party that gained victory over the Cambodian government of Lon Nol, and involved in the murderous policies of **Pol Pot** and his **Democratic Kampuchea** regime.

KHRUSHCHEV, NIKITA SERGEVICH (1894–1971). Khrushchev was the preeminent leader of the **Soviet Union** for a decade after the death of **Josef Stalin**. He is chiefly remembered for his denunciation of Stalin, the initiation of "de-Stalinization" of both the Soviet Union and the **Communist Party of the Soviet Union** (CPSU), and for his advocacy of "peaceful coexistence" with the **capitalist** world and the **United States** in particular.

Khrushchev was a miner when he joined the **Bolsheviks** in 1918. He fought in the Russian Civil War, and as a loyal **Stalinist** rose through the ranks of the CPSU to become a member of the Central Committee in 1934 and of the Politburo in 1939. The death of Stalin in 1953 saw a power struggle from which Khrushchev emerged victorious, rapidly establishing a new identity as an anti-Stalinist. In 1956 at the 20th Party Congress he made his famous "secret speech" in which he denounced Stalin, accusing him of crimes against the people and the party, and of creating a cult of personality. Rehabilitation of victims of Stalinism, a relaxation in censorship, curbs on the arbitrary use of power ("socialist legality") and greater involvement of the people in implementing policies all followed. The party retained a monopoly of power and maintained strict control over the country. Internationally the Khrushchev era was characterized by the continuation of the Cold War, with incidents such as the shooting down of the United States' spy plane in 1960 and the Cuban missile crisis in 1963. The space race was another notable feature, along with the growing split with the **People's Republic of China**. Ideologically, in spite of the Cold War, Khrushchev supported "peaceful coexistence" with the capitalist world, and the nuclear test ban treaty of 1963 was one significant achievement of this doctrine. There was, though, no softening of policy toward the Eastern Bloc countries which remained firmly under the control of the Soviet Union as the crushing of the 1956 **Hungarian Uprising** showed.

Failures of policy, notably in agriculture, and conflicts with colleagues led to Khrushchev being deposed in 1964. Forced to resign he rapidly became a "non-person" taking no further part in politics or public life, and his death in 1971 was barely marked in the Soviet Union.

KIM IL SUNG (KIM SUNG CHU) (1912–1994). **Communist** leader of the **Democratic People's Republic of Korea** from 1946 until his death in 1994, Kim Il Sung created a dictatorial regime based around his own personality cult. Born near Pyongyang the son of a **peasant**, he was active in the communist party youth in the late 1920s, and by 1932 was organizing guerrilla activity against the Japanese. He received training in the **Soviet Union** in the early 1940s, and in 1945 he became head of the Korean Communist Party northern branch. He headed the Interim People's Committee in 1946 (the North Korean provisional government), and became premier of the Democratic People's Republic of Korea at its founding in 1948. A new constitution in 1972 gave Kim the new title of president, a position to which he was reelected in 1982, 1986 and 1990.

Kim's leadership of North Korea was characterized by the development of a police state that quashed all dissent, the propagation of a massive cult of personality, a **Stalinist** political–economic system, and an isolationist and hostile attitude toward most other countries combined with a veil of secrecy that strictly limited contact with the outside world and the outside world's knowledge of events inside North Korea. Kim also initiated the Korean War (1950–1953) with a surprise attack by North Korean forces on South Korea and pursued a Cold War subsequently. He was succeeded by his son, **Kim Jong Il**, who in 1998 oversaw changes to the constitution that abolished the position of president and the proclaiming of his father "Eternal President."

KIM JONG IL (1942–). Eldest son and political heir of **Kim Il Sung**, Kim Jong Il was born in the **Soviet Union** where his mother was taking refuge during the struggle against Japan. He loyally supported his father, helping in the development of the cult of personality and holding a number of political posts in his father's regime. On the death of his father he took over as leader of the **Democratic People's Republic of Korea**, but only after an official three-year mourning period had elapsed did he became official leader of the **Korean Workers' Party**. With the abolition of the position of president in 1998, the post of chairman of the National Defense Commission, held by Kim Jong Il since 1993, became the highest and most powerful office of state. There are indications that North Korea under Kim Jong Il is becoming marginally less secretive and isolationist.

KOLLANTAI, ALEXANDRA (1872–1952). Alexandra Kollantai was the leading **Marxist** feminist of her generation, and is significant for efforts to make female emancipation a central issue on the Marxist revolutionary agenda. Born in St. Petersburg, Russia into a liberal aristocratic family, she turned to revolutionary politics in 1899 when she joined the Marxist **Russian Social Democratic Labor Party** (RSDLP). Her interest in **women**'s emancipation soon became apparent and in 1908 she wrote *The Social Bases of the Woman Question* in which she outlined a Marxist approach to the issue. Also in this year, in danger of arrest, she fled to Western Europe, where she remained, lecturing and writing, until returning to Russia in 1917. Back in Russia she was elected to the RSDLP's Central Committee, and after the **revolution** she was appointed commissar of social welfare. In this post she worked to establish public funding of maternity care and to introduce laws allowing civil marriage and divorce, and also laws to protect women at work.

In 1920 Kollantai was appointed director of the Party's *Zhenotdel* (Women's Department). Here she worked to develop in Russia maternity hospitals, child-care facilities such as nurseries and day-care centers, and even restaurants to ease women's domestic work. She also tried to get women included in decision-making bodies in party, government and unions, and endeavored to publicize women's rights and to stop male abuse of women.

Kollantai's relationship with the party leadership was strained first by her opposition to the Treaty of Brest-Litovsk in 1918, and then by her involvement in the Workers' Opposition group in 1921, which criticized the bureaucratization, elitism, lack of democracy and the New Economic Policy. This, along with criticisms of her feminism, led to her dismissal from the *Zhenotdel* in 1922. She took no further part in activities relating to the "Woman Question," instead becoming a diplomat for the **Soviet Union**. She rose to become ambassador to Sweden before retiring in 1945. She died in Moscow in 1952.

In her writing on women's emancipation Kollantai criticized the **bourgeois** family and morality, and argued for their abolition. In their place she advocated what she called "winged eros," a pure monogamous love between women and men freed from the distortions created by male domination and the **capitalist** economic system. This notion included being freed from the burden of child-care, a task she believed should be undertaken communally. Her perspective on women's issues was in keeping with the orthodox Marxist view insofar as she believed the economic revolution including the abolition of private **property** had to come before women could be emancipated. For Kollantai **class** had primacy over gender, and women were divided by class in the same way as men were, and did not have an identity that transcended class as bourgeois feminists believed.

KOREA, DEMOCRATIC PEOPLE'S REPUBLIC OF. In 1948 the **Korean Workers' Party** (KWP) announced the creation of the

Democratic People's Republic of Korea (DPRK) in the northern section of the Korean peninsula, an area that had fallen into the hands of the **Soviet Union** in the chaos of the post–World War II period. The DPRK, led by revolutionary **socialist** and future "Great Leader" of the nation Kim Il Sung, initially espoused **Marxism**. The transition to Marxism of then North Korea began in 1945 when Moscow ceded the area in post-conflict negotiations, staffing the ruling Executive Committee of the Korean People with Soviet-trained Korean **communists**. In September 1948 the KWP pronounced the end of Soviet occupation and the start of the DPRK under President Kim Il Sung. When in 1950 the **United States–**held south of Korea declared itself autonomous from the DPRK, Kim Il Sung ordered a June invasion aimed at reunifying the country under the banner of Marxism. What resulted was a three-year civil war which cost over two million lives, caused economic devastation, and in the DPRK and Democratic Republic of Korea (DRK) created two ideologically irreconcilable countries that came to define the battle lines of the Cold War. An armistice signed in July 1953 ended the Korean War, and the KWP, its expansive urges contained by the arrangement, was able to concentrate on implementing its own creed of Marxism in the DPRK. A series of three, five, seven and ten-year Soviet-style industrialization plans was undertaken over the course of the next two decades, and, owing a great deal to the assistance of Moscow and the **People's Republic of China** (PRC), economic growth was rapid at first. Agriculture went through a period of sustained **collectivization**, and the DPRK declared itself as officially atheist.

While Marxism remained a key tenet of KWP thought, its ideological hegemony over the DPRK was gradually sidelined by the government's adherence to "Juche." Translating as "self-reliance," Juche was originally formulated as a means with which to reassert the DPRK's independence from those states seeking to bear influence on its course, chiefly the PRC and the Soviet Union. Routed in Kim Il Sung's interpretation of **Stalinism**, Juche initially consisted of the twin assertions that the **revolution** belonged to the people, and that that people required guidance from a single strong leader. This definition was later transformed into an elongated physiological metaphor, as Kim Il Sung declared himself, the leader, as the brain that allowed the body, the masses, to function. Communication between brain and body was provided by the nervous system, handily the KWP. In reality, such verbose posturing was merely a method by which power could be massively centralized, allowing Kim Il Sung to create a classically Stalinist totalitarian system. Juche crossed into the economic sphere, too, decreeing that the DPRK become stringently self-sufficient, and demanding a reduction of reliance on foreign aid. Juche was, and remains, seminal to the North Korean concept of national solipsism, the idea that the entire world looks upon the DPRK as the center of the universe and the guiding light for the salvation of humanity. Juche came to dominate life in the DPRK, and Marxism inevitably played second fiddle as the 1970s progressed. Formal recognition of this came in 1977 when the constitution was amended to make Juche the official **ideology** of the **state**.

Kim Il Sung remained in power until his death in 1994, having constructed a cult of personality rivaled previously only by that of **Joseph Stalin**. His son, **Kim Jong Il**, replaced him as leader, nepotism ensuring that the tight grasp on power of a minute clique has remained a constancy. The first decade of Kim Jong Il's tenure has been characterized by tentative improvements in relations with the DRK, alleged human rights abuses, confusion as to the scale of the country's nuclear weapons program, and inclusion in President George W. Bush's much-vaunted "Axis of Evil." The Soviet-style collectivization of agriculture now plays second fiddle to military investment, with current spending at 23 percent of GDP. Though the vast majority of industry remains in the hands of the state, professed commitment to Marxism has been all but eliminated.

In its preference for a strongly centralist and anti-pluralist system guiding the masses toward a series of shared and nonmalleable goals, North Korean Marxism, where it exists and has existed, bears greatest resemblance to the corporatist model. Yet in the struggle between orthodox Marxism and the Korean nationalism of Juche, the latter won out convincingly, highlighting that early commitment to the former was merely rhetorical. Though KWP rule remains essentially Stalinist, this owes more to Juche than **Marxism–Leninism**, such have local conditions diluted the ideological orthodoxy that existed in 1948.

KOREAN MARXISM. The origins of Korean **Marxism** can be found in the Korean community living in Russia at the beginning of the 20th century. Immigrants and refugees had moved to Siberia and

Manchuria in significant numbers to the extent that in 1919 there were some 200,000 Koreans in the former and some 430,000 in the latter. With a common enemy in the Japanese, Russian **communists** linked up with Koreans introducing them to Marxist ideas. In 1918 the Korean People's Socialist Party (KPSP) was established in Siberia with **Bolshevik** support and guidance, and many Koreans joined the Bolsheviks, some fighting in the civil war, at this time. In 1919 the Communist Party of All Koreans in Russia was formed and took over from the KPSP. In Korea itself, after various small and semi-communist groups had emerged, the first official Korean Communist Party (KCP) was established in 1925. Plagued by factionalism and undermined by repeated infiltration and arrests the KCP struggled to maintain its existence and in 1928 it was in effect dissolved, leading Korean communists to base themselves abroad, often joining the Soviet, Chinese or Japanese communists. It was not until 1945 and the defeat of Japan and the end of World War II that the Korean communist movement in Korea itself was revitalized. Reestablished in 1945 the KCP soon merged with the New Democratic Party to become the North Korean Workers' Party, and in 1949 merged with the South Korean Workers' Party to become the **Korean Workers' Party** (KWP). **Kim Il Sung** was one of the foremost leaders of the KCP and became leader of the KWP, and with the founding of the **Democratic People's Republic of Korea** (DPRK) in 1948 he became premier and subsequently president.

While Korean Marxism has been shaped by both **Soviet** and **Chinese Marxism**, it is Kim Il Sung's outlook that has given it its own distinctive character. Soviet-style five-year plans and agricultural **collectivization**, and imitation of the Chinese Great Leap Forward and mass line indicate something of the influence of the Soviets and Chinese on the Koreans, but the Koreans departed from policies and approach of their larger communist neighbors on various occasions, and as early as 1955 Kim Il Sung began to outline a more distinctive Korean approach called "juche." This notion refers to a policy of self-reliance, and in practice has seen the DPRK adopt a nationalistic and isolationist approach.

KOREAN WORKERS' PARTY (KWP). The North Korean Workers' Party (NKWP) was formed in 1946 from a merger of the North Korean Communist Party and the New Democratic Party, and the

NKWP's subsequent merger with the South Korean Workers' Party produced the Korean Workers' Party (*Chosen Nodong-Tang*). The Korean Workers' Party has been the ruling party of the **Democratic People's Republic of Korea** (DPRK) since the Republic was created and as such has represented **Korean Marxism** since 1948. It has been dominated by **Kim Il Sung** and after his death by his son **Kim Jong Il**.

KORSCH, KARL (1886–1961). One of the most significant **Marxist** thinkers of the 20th century, Karl Korsch emphasized the Hegelian aspects of **Karl Marx**'s thought and put forward a strong critique of orthodox Marxism and **Stalinism**. His book *Marxism and Philosophy* (1923) stands as one of the key texts in the Marxist canon.

Korsch was born in Todstedt, Germany, and he studied law, economics and philosophy at the Universities of Munich, Berlin, Geneva and Jena, gaining his doctorate from the last of these in 1910. Despite opposing the war he served in the German army during World War I and was twice awarded the Iron Cross. In 1919 he became a lecturer at Jena University, a post he held until the Nazis came to power and he left the country for Denmark before moving on to the **United States** in 1936. Here he lived until his death in 1961, spending the years 1945–1950 working at the International Institute of Social Research (**Frankfurt School**). Although an academic, Korsch was also politically active. He joined the Fabians in 1912 while staying in London, became a member of the anti-war independent German Socialist Party (USPD) in 1917, and was a founding member of the **German Communist Party** (KPD) in 1921. He also supported the **Spartacists**' uprising in Berlin in 1919 and the attempt to set up a Soviet Republic in Munich in the same year. In 1923 he was elected to the Thuringian Parliament and became minister of justice in the short-lived revolutionary government of Thuringia. The following year he was a delegate to the Fifth World Congress of the **Comintern** where he was criticized for his unorthodox Marxism. In 1926 he was expelled from the KPD for his continuing dissent from the party line and his anti-Stalinism.

In terms of his political thought Korsch emphasized the **dialectical** category of "totality," i.e., the idea that everything is interconnected and forms an indissoluble whole. In particular, Korsch highlighted the unity of theory and practice in Marxism, a unity neglected by the orthodox Marxism of the **Second International** and prominent Marxists such as **Karl Kautsky**. Kautsky and his followers stressed the objective, **deterministic** side of Marxism and neglected the subjective, activist dimension, taking refuge instead in a theory separated from practice. In his *Marxism and Philosophy* Korsch analyzed Marxism itself on the basis of Marxist principles, and suggested it had evolved through three distinct stages, each corresponding to phases of development of the workers' movement and consciousness. The first stage, 1843–1848, was expressed in the early writings of Marx and reflected the beginnings of the **class** struggle. It was dominated by philosophy and a stress on the subjective. The second stage, 1848–1900, saw Marxism develop theoretically, though separated into economics, politics and ideology, and now dominated by a stress on science and the objective. This phase saw a tendency toward "vulgar Marxism" that propounded crude laws of history and lost touch with the class struggle and the revolutionary essence of Marxism. The third phase, from 1900 onwards, saw a shift from economic determinism to class struggle again, a reassertion of the unity of theory and practice. For Korsch, Kautsky, and for that matter **Vladimir Ilich Lenin**, fell into the one-sidedness of the second stage of Marxism, separating subject and object, theory and practice, by their treatment of Marxism as pure science rather than as a reflection of the class consciousness of the workers. He even came to view **Leninism** as linked to the despotism characteristic of the **Soviet Union**, and he saw the Soviet state as closer to the totalitarian states of fascism than to Marxism.

By the time of his *Why I Am A Marxist* (1935) and *Karl Marx* (1938) Korsch had become increasingly critical of orthodox Marxism, and he sought to outline a revised Marxism stating its most important principles "in the light of recent historical events and of the new theoretical needs which have arisen." The key elements he identified were Marxism's historical specificity—it was a specific analysis of a specific historical period, not a set of general laws or tenets—and its critical and practical character.

KOZA FACTION. The Koza faction is one position in a fierce debate, which began in the period 1927–1937 between Japanese **Marxist** economists and historians regarding the nature of Japanese **capitalism** and the modern Japanese **state**. The Koza faction emphasized a two-stage **revolutionary** process because of the importance it placed on the continuing existence of remnants from Japanese **feudalism**, which made Japan a special hybrid case. According to the Koza faction, Japan required a **bourgeois** democratic revolution as the process by which the country had developed capitalism had distorted its civil society. The Meiji Restoration (1868) that marked the beginning of the modern Japanese state merely reorganized landownership but perpetuated the continuation of feudal and semi-feudal relations. On some readings, this meant that Koza Marxism reflected the concepts of "national community" and "family state" influential in the development of Japanese social science.

The Koza faction position was based on the 1927 and 1932 theses communicated to the **Japan Communist Party** (JCP) by the **Communist International**. According to these theses, Japan was expected to have a bourgeois democratic revolution similar to Russia prior to its own **socialist** revolution. This became the official position of the JCP. However, the influence of the Koza faction has extended beyond the Communist Party. Political and historical analysis of the "Emperor system" (*tennosei*) in Japan and numerous historical novels which have emphasized the feudal elements in Japanese society all reflect the Koza faction influence.

KUN, BELA (1886–1939). Bela Kun was a Hungarian **communist** leader who was active in the **Bolshevik** Party before becoming a victim of **Josef Stalin**'s purges. Born in Transylvania in 1886 Kun's career in radical politics began as a journalist for a radical newspaper in 1906. He joined the Workers Insurance Bureau in Kolozsvar in 1910, becoming its managing director, and in 1913 was a delegate to the Hungarian Social Democratic Party Congress. In World War I he served in the Hungarian army on the Russian front where he was captured in 1916. As a Russian prisoner he converted to Bolshevism, becoming first leader of the Hungarian section of the Bolshevik Party, and then in 1918 head of the new Bolshevik-supported Hungarian Communist Party.

In 1918 Kun launched a coup against the Hungarian government that failed and led to his imprisonment. However, the government rapidly collapsed and Kun was invited to join a coalition government. He soon took over leadership of the coalition and set about ousting anyone who was not a **socialist** or communist. He then attempted to create a Soviet Republic in Hungary, nationalizing land and industry, but after a mere 133 days the Republic collapsed. Kun went into exile in Austria before traveling to Russia to fight for the Bolsheviks in the civil war. As chairman of the Crimean Soviet he ordered the execution of nearly 20,000 White Russian officers. In 1921 he became an official of the **Communist International** and supported the disastrous attempted coup in Germany that year.

Kun was a dogmatic **Marxist–Leninist** and a loyal **Stalinist** until his failures, foreignness and Jewishness made him a target of Stalin's purges. He was arrested by the Soviet secret police (NKVD) in 1937, and suffered torture before being executed in 1939. His prominence stems from his activism rather than any theoretical contribution, but he did influence Soviet policy toward acceptance of a nationalist element in Central European **proletarian** revolutions and inclusion of nationalist petty **bourgeois** revolutionaries in the initial stages of such **revolutions**.

– L –

LABOR THEORY OF VALUE. This theory, elaborated by classical economists, most notably David Ricardo in 1817, who had preceded **Karl Marx**, is the starting point for Marx's own theory of **surplus value** or **exploitation**. According to the labor theory of value the value of any object (or to be more precise any **commodity**) is to be measured in terms of the amount of labor embodied in it. In other words, the value of a commodity is determined by the labor time required to produce it. So if it takes one day to produce a chair and two days to produce a table, then the value of the table is twice that of the chair. Different people will take different amounts of time to make a given commodity, so the labor theory of value takes an average, the "socially necessary labor time." The value of any given commodity is based on the socially necessary labor time to produce it, that is, the time required to produce the commodity under average conditions of production, with average degree of skill and intensity of labor.

LABRIOLA, ANTONIO (1843–1904). Labriola is noteworthy as the first "professorial **Marxist**" or academic Marxist, who made a significant contribution to Marxist theory, and influenced the Italian **socialist** movement, directing it away from **syndicalism** and toward

Marxism. Labriola was for much of his career professor of moral philosophy and pedagogy at the University of Rome. While here he wrote his very influential *Essay on the Materialist Conception of History* (1895/6). His influence is indicated by the links he had with the leading socialists of his time including **Friedrich Engels**, **Karl Kautsky**, **Karl Liebknecht**, **Max Adler**, **August Bebel**, **Paul Lafargue**, Fillipo Turato, and **Georges Sorel**. He engaged in theoretical polemics with these figures defending **historical materialism** against **revisionism** and philosophical **idealism**. He himself was influenced by **Georg Wilhelm Friedrich Hegel**'s ideas.

Labriola's interpretation of Marxism was open and pragmatic with a significant empirical element. He saw historical materialism as unifying social science, but remaining sufficiently flexible to avoid descending into a rigid, deductive, mechanical model. Within this interpretation social psychology played a key part linking human beings and their social circumstances. This is reflected in his notion of **praxis** that focused on human activity, particularly productive activity, in the development of history.

LACLAU, ERNESTO (1935–). Noted for his work with Chantal Mouffe in formulating a "post-**Marxism**," Ernesto Laclau has been a leading figure in attempts to revise Marxism in the light of contemporary conditions and to integrate new theoretical insights into Marxist thought. Laclau was born and educated in Buenos Aires, Argentina, and worked in various Argentinean universities before moving to Great Britain and lecturing at Essex University. His key works include *Hegemony and Socialist Strategy: Towards a radical democratic politics* (1985, with Chantal Mouffe), *Post-Marxism without apologies* (*New Left Review*, 166, 1987), and *The Making of Political Identities* (1994). He made the distinction between "*Post*-Marxism" and "Post-*Marxism*." The former, according to Laclau, refers to viewpoints of ex-Marxists who have rejected Marxism, and the latter to approaches by Marxists who seek to reexamine all aspects of Marxism, rejecting those aspects no longer relevant or valid and incorporating new theoretical developments into the Marxist framework.

Laclau sees Marxism as in crisis and in danger of ossifying, with "evident truths" of classical Marxism, such as notions of a universal **class** and historical inevitability, called into question, and change or revision an imperative. The kind of change to Marxism Laclau envisages involves going beyond Marxism, via **Antonio Gramsci**'s notion of **hegemony** to a new form of **socialist** politics based on "radical democracy." The key elements of radical democracy are indeterminacy and pluralism: an approach that embraces diversity, encourages and celebrates the actions and protests of the range of new social movements (feminism, environmentalism, anti-racism, etc.), and that seeks to deepen and expand liberal democracy rather than reject it. Mainstream Marxists have criticized Laclau for demolishing rather than deconstructing Marxism, and see his perspective as ex- rather than neo-Marxist.

LAFARGUE, PAUL (1841–1911). Described by **Vladimir Ilich Lenin** as "one of the most important and profound propagators of Marxist ideas." He also has a place in the history of **Marxism** as husband of **Karl Marx**'s second daughter Laura. Lafargue was born in **Cuba** but moved to France where he studied medicine and became actively involved in radical politics, including membership of the Bordeaux Commune and the **First International**. In 1882 he helped form the Marxist *Parti Ouvrier Français*, and from 1891 to 1898 he was parliamentary deputy for Lille. He ended his life in 1911 by committing suicide with his wife, both fearing the onset of senility. His Marxism was theoretically unsophisticated and marked by its mechanical **materialism**. He was an ardent rationalist and anti-cleric, rejecting all notions of free will and religion. His writings and activities show an interest in **women**'s rights, economics, **imperialism** and anthropology.

LANGE, OSKAR RYSARD (1904–1965). Oskar Lange was a noted economist and social theorist who made a significant contribution to **socialist** economic theory. Born in **Poland** he became an academic teaching at universities in both Poland and the **United States**. He was actively involved in politics, becoming ambassador of the Polish People's Republic in Washington. He was also Polish representative to the United Nations Security Council in 1945, chaired the Economic Council for the Polish People's Republic from 1957 to 1962, chaired the European Economic Council from 1957 to 1959, and provided economic planning advice to the governments of India, Ceylon and Iraq.

Lange's contributions to economic theory included the elaboration of a model of market socialism. He saw the dangers of economic centralization and bureaucratization and tried to create an alternative that involved democratic planning, decentralized decision-making and a role for the market. He endeavored to synthesize neo-classical, Keynesian and **Marxist** economic theories, and placed emphasis on what he called "praxeology," the theory of efficient and rational economic decision-making. In his later years he took a keen interest in cybernetics and its parallels and connections with **dialectical materialism.**

LAO PEOPLE'S DEMOCRATIC REPUBLIC (LPDR). Following in the wake of newly created **Marxist** governments in **Vietnam** and **Kampuchea,** the 1975 overthrow of the royalist Laotian government of King Savangatthana saw the **communist** Pathet Lao movement take power and pronounce the birth of the Lao People's Democratic Republic. It remains, if only in name, one of the few existing communist states on earth. On gaining control, the Pathet Lao transformed themselves into the **Lao People's Revolutionary Party** (LPRP) under the guidance of General Secretary and Prime Minister **Kaison Phomvihan**, and the inaugural president, **Suphanouvong**. They constructed a system of government akin to that of the **Soviet Union**, with a dominant nine-member Politburo, chosen by a Central Committee, determining party and accordingly government policy. The initial direction the LPRP took borrowed heavily from **Stalinist** Soviet politics too, with overbearing party cadres enforcing strict bureaucratic control, limited travel for nationals, state scrutiny of individual conduct, and a propaganda onslaught that included the staging of political education seminars. The LPRP maintained a solid friendship with neighboring Vietnam, as codified in the 1977 25-year Treaty of Friendship between the two. The LPRP borrowed many characteristics of the **Vietnamese Communist Party**, which in turn was able to exercise considerable authority over the course of Laotian party, military and economic affairs.

By 1979 the LPRP government, driven by a chronic food shortage and the flight to Thailand of thousands of Laotians, diluted its orthodox **Marxist–Leninist** standpoint in favor of a more liberal approach. Private enterprise in agriculture was legalized and encouraged, and social policies were reformed. The 1980s saw further departures from orthodoxy: economic restrictions were loosened further and market solutions were introduced, state control over nationalized industry relaxed and **collectivization** abandoned entirely. However, the LPRP leadership refused steadfastly to embrace **Mikhail Gorbachev**'s *glasnost* program, determined that their unyielding grip on politics and society should remain intact and free from the threats posed by a free press and political pluralism. By the end of 1991, the **collapse of the Soviet Union** and Vietnam's increasingly inward looking status allowed the Laotian administration the opportunity to further relinquish their commitment to Marxism. Under the guidance of Nuhak Phumsavan and then Khamtai Siphandon, economic Marxism was jettisoned and free market **capitalism** encouraged. Siphandon, elected to serve a third term as president and party leader in 2001, has continued and accentuated this policy with the courting of International Monetary Fund and World Bank loans. The chief legacy of Marxism in the LPDR has been the sole-party status achieved by the resolutely unshakeable LPRP, whose tight control of dissent has continued long after that of the communist parties of the Soviet Bloc withered.

The LPRP hold on power has been historically justified by their dedication to **democratic centralism**. This was first professed as part of the revolutionary Marxism they espoused when they assumed power in 1975, a Marxism that sought to create a "new socialist society and socialist man" through a fervent allegiance to orthodox **ideology**. Yet by the 1980s this adherence to orthodoxy was waning, and the Marxist–Leninist rhetoric emanating from the ranks of the LPRP did little to disguise their move toward a liberal capitalist approach to the economy. This was justified, the party hierarchy stressed, by the necessity to pass through a stage of "state capitalism." The LPRP similarly vindicated their implementation of *perestroika* by suggesting it was as a means of adhering to **Vladimir Ilich Lenin**'s New Economic Policy. By the 1990s, though, there was little disguising the fact that the regime had turned its back on Marxism almost entirely, with the retention of exclusive power by the LPRP the only tenet of the ideological militancy of the 1970s remaining.

LAO PEOPLE'S REVOLUTIONARY PARTY (LPRP). The successor to the Lao People's Party (*Phak Paxaxon Lao*) formed in 1955, the Lao People's Revolutionary Party (*Phak Paxaxon Pativat Lao*) was linked to the **Vietnamese Communist Party** and its predecessor the **Indochinese Communist Party**. It became the ruling party of the **Lao People's Democratic Republic** when it was formed in 1975, and its leaders have included **Suphanouvong** and **Kaison Phomvihan**.

LASSALLE, FERDINAND (1825–1864). An important early German **socialist** who founded the first German workers' party, the German Workers' Union (*Allgemeiner Deutscher Arbeiterverein*) in 1863, which was a forerunner of the **German Social Democratic Party** (SPD). Although associated with **Karl Marx** and **Friedrich Engels** in the political propagandizing and agitating at the time of the 1848 **Revolution** in Germany, his socialism was soon seen to differ significantly from theirs. He based his socialism partly on an economic analysis of **capitalism** that included the positing of an "iron law of wages" that stated that workers' wages could never rise above subsistence level in capitalism. Industry had to be reorganized to place ownership in the hands of the workers, and this was to be carried out by the government of the day, pressured by the labor movement. This solution, looking to the **state** of the day, highlighted his Hegelianism, that saw the state as representing the common good above the self-interest of individuals. Ultimately, Lassalle's socialism represented a form of state socialism, and a rival to Marx's socialism. He died when wounded in a duel relating to a love affair.

LATIN AMERICAN SOLIDARITY ORGANIZATION. Initiated by **Cuba** in 1967, the Latin American Solidarity Organization (*Organización de Latinamericana Solidaridad*—OLAS) sought, according to its official dogma, to "coordinate and foment the fight against North American imperialism." Made up of **Marxist** agitators from throughout Latin America, the group attempted through terrorist means to topple the **capitalist** governments of the western hemisphere. For its own region, OLAS decreed that the way to socialist **revolution** was through the building up of armed guerrilla forces in rural areas.

LEAGUE OF COMMUNISTS. Founded in Paris in 1836 the League of Communists (also known as the Communist League) was an organization of German émigré workers largely based in London. **Karl Marx** and **Friedrich Engels** joined it in 1847, became its leading theoreticians, and were commissioned by the League to write the

Communist Manifesto (1848). Coming out of the League of the Just, the League of Communists was a small revolutionary **socialist** group that dissolved in 1850, and is chiefly remembered because of its association with Marx and the *Communist Manifesto*.

LEAGUE OF COMMUNISTS OF YUGOSLAVIA. Until 1952 the **Communist Party of Yugoslavia**, the League of Communists of Yugoslavia (*Savez Komunista Jugoslavije*—SKJ) ruled in the **People's Republic of Yugoslavia** (PRY) from its inception in 1945 to its implosion in 1989–90. The SKJ's history was dominated by **Josip Tito**, who became leader of the then outlawed party in 1937, 18 years after its inception. The communists played a key role in driving out the occupying German Nazis during World War II, emerging from the conflict as the outright leaders of the newly unified Yugoslavia. Until 1948, the party embraced **Stalinism**, but its independence tested Moscow's resolve to the extent that the PRY was expelled from the **Cominform** in that year. For the next four decades, the SKJ led the PRY according to its own brand of communism, or "Titoism." This included deviations from orthodox **Marxism–Leninism** such as decentralization of power, and worker self-management of an economy that contained market elements, as espoused by party reformists such as **Milovan Djilas**. Despite this, it remained nominally committed to **democratic centralism**. When Tito died in 1980, the collective leadership that replaced him was unable to halt the breakup of both the PRY and the SKJ, and at its 14th party congress in 1991, the party was effectively disbanded. The SKJ units in the federal states that had comprised the PRY each became individual social democratic parties contesting multi-party elections with varying degrees of success.

LEFEBVRE, HENRI (1901–1991). A noted French **Marxist** academic, who contributed to the schools of Hegelian and **humanist Marxism**, Henri Lefebvre was born in the Landes department of France and studied philosophy at the Sorbonne in Paris. In 1928 he joined the **French Communist Party** (PCF) and was involved with the Marxist theoretical journal *La Revue Marxiste*. In the 1930s he helped to translate and publish the first selections in French of **Karl Marx's** *Economic and Philosophical Manuscripts* (EPM) and **Vladimir Ilich Lenin's** *Philosophical Notebooks*. The *EPM* was a particularly important source for interpretations of Marxism that focused on the theme of **alienation**. In 1939 Lefebvre's *Dialectical Materialism* was published, and in its stress on the influence of **Georg Wilhelm Friedrich Hegel** and the importance of Marx's early works it conflicted with the **Stalinist** (and PCF) viewpoint. His growing anti-Stalinism eventually led to his expulsion from the party in 1956 (he re-joined a freer, less rigid PCF in 1978). During World War II Lefebvre fought in the French Resistance and afterwards took up a job in broadcasting whilst continuing his writing. In his academic career he held posts at the *Centre National de la Recherche Scientifique*, the University of Strasbourg, the University of Paris at Nanterre and the *École Practique des Hautes Études* in Paris.

Lefebvre's political and philosophical views caused him to launch attacks on **Jean-Paul Sartre**'s existentialism and **Louis Althusser**'s **structuralist Marxism**. He opposed dogmatism and attempts at systematization of Marxism claiming these led to the hypostatization of theory. A prolific writer, his key works include *Dialectical Materialism* (1939), *Critique of Everyday Life* (1947), *Les Problèmes actuels du marxisme* (1958), *Métaphilosophie* (1965), *The Explosion: Marxism and the French Upheaval* (1968), and *The Production of Space* (1974). Typically these explored themes of alienation, **praxis**, culture and everyday life, with emphasis on a humanist, **dialectical materialist** approach.

LEGAL MARXISM. An interpretation of **Marxism** developed by Russian scholars at the end of the 19th century. P.B. Struve, M.I. Tugan-Baranovsky, N.A. Berdyaev, S.N. Bulgakov and S.L. Frank were as critical of Marxism as they were sympathetic to it, many of their criticisms paralleling those of **Eduard Bernstein** with regard to the empirical shortcomings of Marxism and its need of an ethical theory. They also contributed to Marxist economic theory, but their increasingly critical view of Marxism and lack of involvement with Marxist or workers' political organizations soon saw the group and its ideas disappear. The chief significance of legal Marxism probably lies in its propagation of Marxist ideas in Russia contributing to the displacement of the then dominant radical ideas of populism by Marxism.

LENIN, VLADIMIR ILICH ULYANOV (1870–1924). Lenin was the alias used by Vladimir Ilich Ulyanov. He is the most influential **Marxist** political leader and theorist bar none. As a political leader he led the **Bolsheviks** in their seizure of power in October 1917, and was head of the first-ever **communist** state. Although his greatest achievements are as a political activist and leader, Lenin also made important contributions to Marxist theory, particularly on the themes of **class**, party, **imperialism** and **revolution**.

He was born in 1870 to a middle-class family, and his parents were politically moderate liberals. His older brother Alexander became involved in revolutionary politics and, when Lenin was 17, was executed for his involvement in a plot to assassinate the Tsar. Lenin went to Kazan University from which he was expelled for his involvement in a student protest meeting. In 1895 he was arrested, imprisoned and then exiled to Siberia. After his term of exile he left the country in 1900 to go to Geneva where he met with Russian Marxist exiles including the great thinker and activist **Georgii Plekhanov**. Continuing his political activities Lenin remained in Switzerland until the **Russian Revolution** of 1905 prompted his return. The failure to convert the revolution into lasting radical change and the reassertion of order and government control led to Lenin, now in danger of arrest and imprisonment, returning to Western Europe. Here he remained, still as politically active as ever, until World War I saw the collapse of Tsarsism in Russia. The German government, hoping to hasten the defeat of the Russian army, assisted Lenin in returning to Russia via Germany in April 1917. In October of that year Lenin led the Bolsheviks in a seizure of power. He immediately had to deal with civil war, foreign intervention, famine, and an army and infrastructure in a state of collapse. Surviving these he showed his flexibility and pragmatism in instituting in 1921 the New Economic Policy (NEP), which allowed significant amounts of free trade and private enterprise. In 1922 Lenin suffered two strokes and his day-to-day involvement in politics ceased. In 1924 he died, and, against his wishes, was buried with great ceremony in Red Square, Moscow.

Lenin endeavored to apply Marxism to Russian conditions, modifying it where necessary. He argued as early as 1899 in *The Development of Capitalism in Russia*, that Russia was already becoming **capitalist**, that capitalism was penetrating the countryside, and, in his words, causing the "proletarianization of the **peasantry**." Although Russia was a largely agrarian society, Russian agriculture was becoming capitalist in character and the peasants were becoming agricultural wage workers. The emancipation of the serfs in 1861 had, according to Lenin, helped turn the peasantry from serfs into agricultural workers with greater freedom to move and to sell their labor. The gradual development of capitalism in both the towns and the countryside was inevitable Lenin claimed. It could not be halted, nor should it be. Lenin, like **Karl Marx**, saw capitalism as progressive. For all its faults capitalism brought with it great advances in science, technology and economic production. Only on the basis of capitalism's achievements could socialism be achieved.

However, Lenin did not simply impose on Russia a Marxist model of society based on the western advanced capitalist countries. Lenin noted the differences between Russia and the advanced capitalist countries of Western Europe, and the political implications of those differences. He noted that in Russia, unlike Western Europe, the main class conflict was between the peasantry and the aristocracy. The peasantry, as well as being the largest class, also had revolutionary potential. Like the **proletariat** it was an exploited class, and it shared an interest with the proletariat in overthrowing the existing order. In Western Europe, Marxists tended to view the peasantry as a conservative, reactionary force. Lenin also noted that in the countries of Western Europe the bourgeois and proletarian classes were well developed and strong. In Russia the proletariat was still at an embryonic stage and the **bourgeoisie** was small and weak. Industrial development in Russia was not greatly advanced, and such as it was, it was the result of collaboration between the Russian feudal aristocracy and foreign capitalists. As a result, the Russian bourgeoisie was underdeveloped and lacked the strength and will to push through a bourgeois political revolution.

The political significance of this was that the bourgeoisie would not overthrow the Tsarist autocracy if left to do so on its own. The bourgeois would always, according to Lenin, recoil from revolution, too afraid of the consequences, too afraid of its own weakness, too afraid of the proletariat. The proletariat, aided by the peasantry, must take the initiative and push the bourgeoisie into revolution. As soon as the bourgeois revolution was achieved, Lenin argued that the proletariat in alliance with the peasantry should start working toward a further revolution, the proletarian revolution. The struggle for the bourgeois and proletarian revolutions should, according to Lenin, constitute a single "uninterrupted revolution."

Lenin's theory of the party and his view of **class consciousness** is found in his book *What Is to Be Done?* (1902). Marx's belief in the spontaneous emergence of a revolutionary class consciousness was rejected by Lenin. Lenin believed that it was impossible for the workers to develop a revolutionary class consciousness spontaneously, on their own. It could only be brought to the workers from outside, by the party. Left to themselves the workers will only develop what Lenin called "trade union consciousness," that is to say, workers would become aware of the antagonism between themselves and their bosses in their own workplace, but not of the wider class conflict. Left to themselves the consciousness of workers would only rise to the level of trade union-type demands for better pay and conditions. Without the introduction of Marxist theory by a Marxist party, the workers' consciousness would remain limited to the narrow economic struggle and not be widened to the general political struggle. Trade union consciousness, according to Lenin, ultimately hinders the proletarian revolution and helps to perpetuate capitalism, because it operates within capitalism without challenging it.

The role of the party, according to Lenin, is to bring Marxist theory to the masses, to combat spontaneity and trade union consciousness, and to foster instead a revolutionary socialist consciousness. For Lenin, the party must take a leading role, it must be a **vanguard party**. The party must consist of fully trained, full-time revolutionaries, an elite of dedicated professional revolutionaries. There should be a distinction between the mass of workers and the party, so party membership should be limited to an elite and dedicated few. Lenin also advocated a centralized, hierarchical party organization, characterized by strict secrecy and discipline. He rejected the idea of internal party democracy as utopian under the then existing conditions where the communist party in Russia was an illegal organization operating in an autocratic state with a secret political police. As circumstances in Russia changed, Lenin's views adapted, and following the 1905 revolution the Bolsheviks opened up party membership and gained large numbers of new members. At the 1906 party congress, Lenin put forward the principle of **democratic centralism**. In essence, democratic centralism meant that decisions within the party should be taken democratically, but once made they should be centrally imposed. Democratic centralism allowed completely free discussion before decision-making, and required absolute conformity and discipline afterwards; in Lenin's words, "freedom of discussion, unity of action." The democratic aspect in practice took second place to the centralist aspect of the principle. The reassertion of state oppression after 1905 made internal party democracy impossible again, and even after the 1917 revolution that brought the Bolsheviks to power, the emphasis was on centralism rather than democracy. In 1921 Lenin oversaw the banning of factions within the party. Centralized unity was achieved at the expense democracy.

In 1916 Lenin published a hugely influential booklet called *Imperialism: The Highest Stage of Capitalism*. According to Lenin, imperialism, the building of empires by powerful countries, resulted from a change in the character of capitalism. At the beginning of the 20th century, Lenin claimed, there was a shift from competitive capitalism to monopoly capitalism. Production and capital had become more and more concentrated in the hands of a few cartels or trusts. These cartels effectively operated as monopolies, eliminating free competition. In addition, Lenin identified a trend toward greater integration of industrial and finance capital with finance capital becoming dominant over industrial capital. In other words, the banks and industry were becoming more integrated, and the banks were exercising ever greater control over industry. The institutions of finance capital, such as the banks, were controlled by the cartels. In the search for ever greater profits the finance institutions controlled by the cartels looked to the economically backward countries to invest their capital in. Lenin described these finance institutions as exporting capital rather than exporting **commodities**. In the less developed countries the price of land, labor and raw materials was low, so allowing high profits to be made.

According to Lenin, it was this drive to reap profits from the export of capital to less developed countries, the drive to divide up the world between the international cartels, that produced imperialism. The cartels struggled against each other to gain spheres of influence in the world, where they could control investment and gain high profits. The competition between the cartels led to the advanced capitalist countries seeking to gain territories abroad in the form of colonies, resulting in war. Lenin noted that imperialism brings economic benefits to the advanced capitalist countries, to the imperialist countries, in the form of high profits. These can, in part, be used by the ruling capitalist class to buy off the workers in their own countries, to bribe the workers with extra pay and benefits. The ruling class in the advanced capitalist countries can afford to pass on some of the economic benefits of imperialism to the working class, and in so doing buy the loyalty and acquiescence of the workers. This is one reason, according to Lenin, why a revolution had not occurred in the advanced capitalist countries yet: imperialism allowed the **ruling class** to corrupt the working class by sharing the economic benefits.

In addition, imperialism makes the class struggle international according to Lenin. It globalizes the class struggle and makes it possible for a truly international revolution to take place. It also means that Marxists should not necessarily look to the advanced capitalist countries for a proletarian revolution to happen first, because developed countries can buy off their workers. Instead, according to Lenin, Marxists should look for the "weakest link" in the chain of capitalism: a country (or countries) where capitalism has sufficiently developed to create a proletarian class, but where the bourgeoisie is not so developed that it can acquire colonies, and, with the benefits it receives from colonization, buy off the workers. Imperialism, Lenin argued, means that revolution is more likely to happen in a relatively backward country such as Russia, than in an advanced capitalist country like Germany. Russia, in Lenin's view, was the "weakest link" in the chain.

In 1917, at a crucial time of political change and social unrest, a time when one might expect Lenin to be taken up with revolutionary activity rather than writing, he wrote another important text, *State and Revolution*. Even more remarkable is the utopian character of the book, unlike any of Lenin's other works. In *State and Revolution* Lenin outlines what appears to be a utopian vision of the future socialist state and society. However, as with all his writings, Lenin had a very specific reason for producing this book at this time. Lenin had two targets in mind when he wrote it: first, the **German Social Democratic Party** (SPD), and **Karl Kautsky** in particular; and second, the anarchists. *State and Revolution* is an attempt to counter the arguments of these two groups. The SPD was becoming increasingly reformist in practice and, according to Lenin, had replaced the idea of class struggle with the idea of class harmony. For Lenin, the SPD was guilty of misunderstanding the nature of the **state**. According to Lenin a state is "an organization of violence for the suppression of some class." In other words, the state is, by its very nature a repressive organization and cannot be used by the workers or their representatives to create a socialist society. So, against the German SPD, Lenin argued that the state was an organization of violence for the suppression of the proletariat, and that it had to be completely destroyed

Lenin was equally concerned to distance himself from the anarchists. He rejected the anarchist view that there would be no state at all after the revolution. While Lenin believed the bourgeois state should be smashed, he also thought that a form of workers' state would initially be necessary after the revolution. The error of the anarchists was not that they believed that the state should be abolished, but that they believed it could be abolished overnight, that there would be no transitional stage. Lenin argued that in place of the bourgeois state there would have to be a state of armed workers, the **dictatorship of the proletariat**. This he described as a semi-state, which would begin to wither away almost as soon as it came into existence. The dictatorship of the proletariat, according to Lenin, would be temporary, a transitional period between the end of capitalism and full communism. The dictatorship of the proletariat was necessary in order to crush the resistance of the old exploiting class, the bourgeoisie, and to lead the masses in the construction of the socialist society. Under capitalism the state is a machine for the suppression of the majority by the exploiting minority; the dictatorship of the proletariat is the suppression of the minority exploiter class by the overwhelming majority. Only when communism is achieved will the state completely disappear. With its repressive functions gone all that will remain of previous state functions will be simple administration, which the people themselves will be able to perform. The fundamental rules of social behavior will, according to Lenin, become a matter of habit, and not require the state to enforce them.

It is ironic given Lenin's pragmatism, the views he expresses in *State and Revolution*, and his dislike of personal praise and hero worship, that **Leninism** should have become such a dogma, the Soviet State should have become a Behemoth, and Lenin himself should have become a venerated figure, treated as hero/god by his party, the Soviet state, and innumerable followers. *See also* COMMUNIST PARTY OF THE SOVIET UNION.

LENINISM. The term "Leninism" is in effect a shortened version of "**Marxism–Leninism**" since Leninists view Leninism as simply the development of **Marxism** and its application to Russian conditions. Leninists view **Vladimir Ilich Lenin** as the true heir of **Karl Marx** and as true to Marx's theories. In particular Leninism emphasizes Marx's belief in a **dialectical** and **materialist** philosophical approach, his scientific method and discovery of scientific laws relating to history and society, and his **class** analysis and commitment to class struggle. What Leninism adds to Marxism is a development of a theory of **imperialism**, a theory of the party, and a class analysis adapted to Russian conditions. Lenin's theory of imperialism directed attention to the potential of Russia and other relatively backward countries (in terms of economic and class development) as locations for **revolution**. The "weakest link" of **capitalism**, according to his theory, lies in these underdeveloped countries. This view ties up with the Leninist view of the **peasantry**, the predominant class in underdeveloped countries, as having revolutionary potential. Leninism gives greater weight to the peasantry in such phrases as "revolutionary toilers" referring to the peasantry as well as the **proletariat**. The Leninist theory of the party argues for a "**vanguard party**" of dedicated, professional revolutionaries who will lead the masses, guiding and educating them. Most subsequent Marxists have claimed a link to Lenin, most notably **Stalinists**, **Trotskyists** and **Maoists**.

LIEBKNECHT, KARL (1871–1919). A significant figure in the **German Social Democratic Party** (SPD), Liebknecht was also a leader of the ultra-left **Spartacist** movement along with **Rosa Luxemburg**. The son of **Wilhelm Liebknecht**, he was born in Leipzig, where he also attended university studying law and political economy. In 1907 he was imprisoned because of his critical writings on German militarism (*Militarism and Anti-Militarism*, 1907), and in 1908 he was elected to the Prussian House of Deputies. Elected to the Reichstag in 1912 he vehemently opposed German involvement in World War I and called for a **revolution**. In 1916 he was expelled from the SPD for his views and was again imprisoned for leading an anti-war demonstration. Released in 1918 he led the Spartacists' attempted revolution against the Social Democratic government of Friedrich Ebert in January 1918. The revolt was defeated and he was arrested and murdered.

LIEBKNECKT, WILHELM (1826–1900). A founder of the **German Social Democratic Party** (SPD) and an important figure in the **Sec-**

ond International, Wilhelm Liebknecht was also a close associate of **Friedrich Engels** and **August Bebel**. Liebknecht participated in the 1848 **revolution** in Germany, was imprisoned and spent 12 years in exile in London where he met **Karl Marx**. He returned to Germany in 1862 where he worked with **Ferdinand Lassalle** in Berlin until arguments with the Lassalleans led to him moving to Saxony. Here he teamed up with August Bebel to create the League of Working Men Association (LWMA) and the Social Democratic Workers Party (*Sozial Demokratische Arbeiterpartei*—SDA). At the Gotha Congress of 1875 he helped to unite the SDA and the General Association of German Workers to form a party that in 1891 took the name the **German Social Democratic Party** (*Sozial Demokratische Partei Deutschlands*—SPD). In 1889 he helped in the creation of the **Second International** of which he was an important member for the next decade. Liebknecht put great stress on the importance of democracy, gradual reform, and an open and democratic party rather than an elitist party or dictatorship of the **proletariat**. He was largely responsible for writing the draft Gotha program for the SPD in 1875 which denounced **capitalism** and advocated common ownership, international solidarity and proletarian self-reliance, although it was also heavily criticized by Karl Marx.

LI PENG (1928–). Chinese **communist** political leader who was appointed prime minister in 1987. Born in Chengdu in the Sichuan province of China, Li was educated in Yan'an and in Moscow. At the age of 11 he was taken under the wing of **Zhou Enlai** when his father was executed for his participation in the communist rebellion of 1930. Trained as an engineer he worked in the Ministry of the Electric Power Industry and became vice minister of power in 1979 and minister in 1981. In 1982 he became a member of the **Chinese Communist Party** Central Committee, and in 1985 was appointed to the Politiburo. As prime minister he supported **Deng Xiaoping**'s violent, hard-line response to the Chinese student-led demonstrations of 1989, and has been viewed as on the conservative wing of Chinese communism.

LIN BIAO (1907–1971). Lin Biao was a leading **communist** military commander during the **Chinese Revolution**, and a key figure in the country's leadership from 1959 until his death. Born in Hubei province, Lin was above all a military man, attending the Whampoa Military Academy, and serving in the Kuomintang (KMT) army before joining the communist **Red Army**. He commanded the First Red Army during the **Long March**, and after World War II led the communist Northeast Liberation Army to victory over the nationalist KMT forces. He became minister of national defense and head of the People's Liberation Army in 1959. His political appointments included vice chairman of the party in 1958, and he was viewed as the second-ranking member of the **Chinese Communist Party** from 1966 until his death, and the officially designated successor to **Mao Zedong**. For most his political career Lin was close and loyal to Mao, and he sought to educate first the military and then society at large in the thought of Mao. He was responsible for the (in)famous "Little Red Book," the book of maxims from Mao's thought that was widely issued in the **People's Republic of China** and beyond. Lin not only inculcated the army with Mao's **ideology**, but also contributed to militarizing Chinese Marxist ideology. He espoused the notion of a "people's war," which painted the world as a battlefield between rural and urban societies (such as China and the **United States** respectively), and which encouraged guerrilla warfare in people's wars around the globe. Lin gradually became a rival to Mao, opposing both the policies and direction of Mao after the **Cultural Revolution**. He died in an airplane crash in 1971 when apparently trying to flee to the **Soviet Union** after the failure of an attempted coup against Mao.

LIU SHAOQI (1898–1969). A senior figure in the **Chinese Communist Party** (CCP) leadership under **Mao Zedong**, Liu Shaoqi was president of the **People's Republic of China** from 1959 to 1968, and for a period was second only to Mao in the party hierarchy. Born in Hunan province, Liu joined the Socialist Youth League in Shanghai, went to Moscow to study in 1920, and returned the following year when he joined the CCP and became involved in union organizing. In 1928 he was made chair of the CCP Labor Department and in 1931 he became chair of the All-China Labor Federation in Shanghai. When the Japanese invaded in 1936 Liu became a leading organizer of the Chinese communist underground movement behind Japanese lines. He also helped to organize the **Red Army** and took part in the **Long March**. By 1945 he was second in command to Mao and was named as heir apparent in 1959. During the **Cultural Revolution**, he clashed with Mao and was denounced as a "capitalist roader." Expelled from the party and dismissed from his state posts in 1968, he died in prison in 1969.

Liu's contributions to Chinese communism were largely in the realm of organization and organizational theory. He wrote *How to Be a Good Communist* and *On Inner Party Struggle* in which he combined **Marxism–Leninism** with Chinese (Confucian) themes. Largely an orthodox Marxist–Leninist he did adopt a less dogmatic approach in economics, which provided evidence for Mao's accusations of "revisionist" deviations. In 1980 he was rehabilitated by the party, which now portrayed him as ideologically orthodox and economically pragmatic.

LONG MARCH (1934–1935). Defeat by the Chinese nationalists, the Kuomintang (KMT), forced the Chinese **communists** to retreat from Jiangxi to the communists' base in Shanxi. Traversing a distance of some 5,000 kilometers and attacked by nationalist troops along the way, the 100,000 communists that took part in the Long March were reduced to an estimated 50,000 by the end of it. **Mao Zedong** was one of the main leaders of the communists on the march and the part he played in saving the communists from annihilation at the hands of the nationalists helped him to attain his position as supreme leader. The Long March has acquired legendary status in Chinese communist history as a demonstration of the discipline and commitment of the Chinese communists and in particular of party members.

LONGO, LUIGI (1900–1980). An important figure in the European **communist** movement, Longo helped to found the **Italian Communist Party** in 1921 and was party leader from 1964 to 1972. He fought in the Spanish Civil War with the international brigades, and led partisan units against the fascists in northern Italy in World War II. After the war he was deputy to **Palmiro Togliatti** in the Italian Communist Party until becoming its leader, and as leader he helped to take the party in a direction away from Soviet communism and influence and toward **Eurocommunism**.

LUKÁCS, GEORGII (1885–1971). One of the foremost **Marxist** intellectuals of the 20th century and one of the most important and influential contributors to Marxist theory. Lukács interpreted **Karl**

Marx from a Hegelian perspective, emphasizing the influence of **Georg Wilhelm Friedrich Hegel** on Marx and drawing out the humanism of Marx's thought. Of particular note is his advancement of a political theory of **alienation** and **reification**, a sociological theory of **class consciousness**, a theory of aesthetics and significant contributions to the development of Marxist literary criticism. Lukács is one of the giants of **Western Marxism** and a key influence on the **Frankfurt School**.

Born in Budapest, **Hungary**, Lukács studied in Berlin, Budapest, Heidelberg and Moscow, gaining three doctorates in the course of his studies. In 1918 he joined the Hungarian Communist Party and in 1919 he became people's commissar for education and culture in the short-lived communist Hungarian Republic of Councils. After its collapse he fled the country, a death sentence being passed on him in his absence. He then lived in Austria and Germany before emigrating to Moscow in 1933 after the Nazis came to power in Germany. During his years of exile he wrote prolifically, including his brilliant theoretical work *History and Class Consciousness* in 1923. Condemned at the time by the **Comintern**, it has subsequently become acknowledged as an outstanding piece of political theory and a classic of Marxist writing. A further notable work from this period was his *Lenin: A Study on the Unity of His Thought* (1924).

Lukács returned to Hungary in 1945 where he again wrote extensively and was very active in the fields of culture and politics, founding the cultural journal *Forum*. Vehemently attacked by the politically dominant Hungarian **Stalinists**, Lukács retreated into philosophical studies until the 1956 uprising and brief government of **Imre Nagy** under whom Lukács served as minister of culture. The defeat of Nagy's government by the intervention of Soviet troops saw Lukács deported to Rumania. He was allowed to return in 1957 and his most significant achievements in the final period of his life were major works on aesthetics, *The Specific Nature of the Aesthetic* (1962), and on social ontology, *Towards an Ontology of Social Being* (1971). He died in Budapest in 1971.

Lukács' intellectual contributions include the significant concept of reification. By this Lukács means the process of dehumanization where human beings become mere "things" subject to social forces beyond their control. We become governed by a system composed of things we created that become independent of us, and this system is centered around the **commodity**, the characteristic feature of **capitalism**. According to Lukács, the whole of capitalist society is permeated by reification, with human beings losing their essential humanity as the logic of the system, its seemingly unalterable laws, strips us of our imagination, creativity and spirituality. Efficiency, rationality and profit govern both the system of production and the social system as a whole, making the masses passive and less than fully human. However, influenced by Hegel Lukács adopts an optimistic teleological view of the future, putting his faith in the **proletariat** as the agent of **revolution** and seeing history as moving toward **communism**, directed by an inner logic.

As well as the notion of teleology and historical progress, Lukács also drew from Hegel the notion of "totality." All parts of reality are interconnected in a whole and the parts can only be understood in relation to this whole, this totality. We must grasp this totality (this is the point of Marx's method of analysis), and in understanding the totality we will change reality as part of a single process. Theory and practice constitute a unity; we understand as we act upon the world and our understanding directs our actions. The proletariat stands at the end of a long process of **dialectical** development, uniquely placed to grasp the totality, and Marxism represents the truth or meaning of the totality, the key to understanding history. Proletarian class consciousness, that only exists as potential in capitalism, will develop to express the same essential truth found in Marxism.

LUMPENPROLETARIAT. A term used by **Karl Marx** in *The 18th Brumaire of Louis Bonaparte* (1852) to describe the "scum, offal, refuse of all classes" that gave support to Louis Bonaparte, and which was composed of "ruined and adventurous off-shoots of the bourgeoisie, vagabonds, discharged soldiers, discharged jailbirds...pickpockets, brothel keepers, rag-pickers, beggars." Otto Bauer writing while fascists were in power in Germany and Italy suggested the fascists derived support from the lumpenproletariat, and in general the term is viewed by **Marxists** as referring to a rag-bag social group formed in conditions of crisis and susceptible to reactionary movements and **ideologies**.

LUXEMBURG, ROSA (1871–1919). One of the leading **Marxists** of the 20th century, Rosa Luxemburg exerted great influence within the

socialist movement during her life, and her ideas and political actions have continued to inspire Marxists and shape **Marxism** long after her death. Born in Zamosc, **Poland**, in 1871, Luxemburg was brought up in a well-off middle-class Jewish family. Physically frail with a twisted body and limp she demonstrated from an early age an outstanding intellect, graduating top of her class from her school in Warsaw. Luxemburg also became involved in radical politics at an early age and had to flee to Switzerland at the age of 18 to avoid arrest. She attended Zurich University where she studied mathematics, natural science and political economy, and wrote a doctoral dissertation on Poland's industrial development. She worked with Russian exiles in Switzerland, including **Vladimir Ilich Lenin, Georgii Plekhanov,** and **Paul Axelrod,** and helped to establish the Social Democracy of the Kingdom of Poland, the Polish Marxist party, in 1894.

In 1898 Luxemburg moved to Germany where she married a German, Gustav Luebeck, in order to gain German citizenship. She was active in the **German Social Democratic Party** (SPD) and rapidly became a leading figure in the party. Her activities included contributing to the party's theoretical journal, *Neue Zeit*, editing various radical provincial journals and the SPD newspaper *Vorwärts*, and teaching Marxist economics at the party's training school. Her political activism brought her spells in prison in 1905 and during World War I. At the outbreak of World War I she formed the **Spartacus League** with **Karl Liebknecht,** and in 1919 took part in an unsuccessful uprising after which she was arrested and murdered by German army officers.

Among Luxemburg's key interventions in socialist debates of the time is her booklet *Social Reform or Revolution* (1899), a response to **Eduard Bernstein's** *Evolutionary Socialism* (1899) in which he argued for a reformist approach to achieving socialism. In this seminal work she argued that reform alone could never lead to socialism; only the revolutionary overthrow of **capitalism** could result in socialism. She did not reject reforms as such, but argued that their success depended on the revolutionary threat behind them, and that ultimately any gain could be clawed back unless a **revolution** followed.

Luxemburg entered into dispute with **Vladimir Ilich Lenin** on the role of the party and the spontaneity of the masses. As early as 1904 she saw the **Bolsheviks** as too controlling of the working class and she criticized the notion of the **vanguard party**, i.e., a professional, elite party guiding the workers. For her the party should help to foster a collective revolutionary consciousness and would then become redundant after the revolution. She was strongly in favor of spontaneous political action by the workers, and in particular she believed in the potency of the weapon of the mass strike. The mass strike she saw as the supreme form of revolutionary action: it links the political and economic struggles; its effects are immediate and dramatic; it embodies worker spontaneity and it overcomes the bureaucratic inertia to which political parties are prone. In her analyses of the **Russian Revolution** she criticized the controlling and dictatorial character of Lenin and the Bolsheviks after the revolution, while still applauding their attempt to bring about a socialist revolution. She also disagreed with Lenin on the issue of nationalism, rejecting the ideas of national self-determination, and particularly independence for Poland, that Lenin favored.

Luxemburg's other significant contribution to socialist thought is found in her book *The Accumulation of Capital* (1913) in which she discussed capitalism's inherent tendency to collapse and the causes of **imperialism**. For Luxemburg imperialism is the struggle between capitalist countries to control noncapitalist areas of the world. Without access to these noncapitalist areas the capitalist countries would themselves collapse as a result of their inherent contradictions. Ultimately, once capitalism had spread to all areas of the world through imperialism, it would self-destruct. The choice then would be "socialism or barbarism."

LYSENKOISM. Trofim Denisovich Lysenko (1898–1976) was elevated to a position of considerable power and influence in Soviet agriculture on the basis of his theory of inheritance of acquired characteristics in plants and his claims that the seasonal patterns and yields of crops could be dramatically changed on the basis of his theory. His views went completely against the emerging science of plant genetics, but backed by **Josef Stalin** and **Nikita Khrushchev** his **proletarian** science held sway in the **Soviet Union** over the "**capitalist**" science of genetics. As president of the Soviet Academy of Agricultural Sciences (1938–1956 and 1961–1962) he promoted his approach and theory and purged the Soviet scientific community of those who supported genetics, even to the extent of their being imprisoned or shot. Lysenkoism as science was completely wrong and contributed to the failures of Soviet agriculture. Lysenkoism also serves as a term to denote a policy of ideological and state intervention in science and the dangers of such an approach.

– M –

MACHEL, SAMORA MOISES (1933–1986). Machel led the **Front for the Liberation of Mozambique** (FRELIMO) and was the first president of the **People's Republic of Mozambique**. Born in Gaza province, southern Mozambique (then a Portuguese colony), Machel worked as a medical assistant before joining FRELIMO in 1962. He went to Algeria in 1963 to receive military training, returning the following year as a guerrilla fighter. He became commander in chief of the military wing of FRELIMO, the People's Forces for the Liberation of Mozambique, and in 1970 the FRELIMO Central Committee formally made Machel party president. In 1974 Machel led the FRELIMO delegation in peace talks with the Portuguese who had finally conceded that they were losing the protracted war against the independence movement. In June 1975 he was invested as president of the newly formed and avowedly **Marxist** People's Republic of Mozambique. He died on 19 October 1986 in an air crash.

MACLEAN, JOHN (1879–1923). A popular agitator and an inspirational orator, MacLean sought to bring about an independent Scottish workers' republic as part of a **socialist** international, chiefly through a **Marxist** reeducation of the working **class** and the use of mass organized action. He is regarded by present-day Scottish socialists as the founding father of republican socialism in Scotland, and one of the first to call for a parliament independent of Westminster. MacLean had the value of education instilled in him from an early age, and to this end attended the Free Church Training School in order to become a teacher. While here he became a strong advocate of Marxian socialism, studied political economy at Glasgow University, and graduated with an M.A. in 1903 transfixed with the idea of raising the educational levels of those within the labor movement. The Scot began his political life as a member of the Progressive Union, and in 1903 joined the **Social Democratic Federation**, but split from the group in 1911 as a response to its pro-war position and joined the **British Socialist Party** (BSP).

MacLean was also the driving force behind a number of other workers' groups. These included the revolutionary Clyde Workers Committee, arguably the earliest ever shop stewards' combine, and the Scottish Labor College and Labor College Committee, establishments that aimed to educate workers in Marxist principles as a foundation for **revolution**. MacLean was also instrumental in the formation of the Tramp Trust Unlimited, a band of Marxist agitators spreading the gospel of Scottish revolutionary politics at outdoor gatherings across the land. He was recognized by illustrious Marxists from abroad including **Karl Liebknecht**, **Rosa Luxemburg**, and **Vladimir Ilich Lenin**, who appointed MacLean honorary president of the First All-Russian Congress of Soviets, and **Bolshevik** Consul for Scotland.

MacLean was forced out of the BSP in 1920, and disillusioned with that group and others on the left he founded the Scottish Workers' Republican Party (SWRP) two years later. The party aimed to bring about a "Scottish Workers Republic," on the basis that Scottish workers (as opposed to their English counterparts, tainted by the trappings of Empire) made the most vehement Marxists. MacLean believed a **communist** organization based in Scotland would stand the greatest chance of attaining a workers' revolution, and subsequently assisting its spread through Great Britain. For MacLean, the de-construction of the British state and its supplanting with a Scottish workers' republic represented the swiftest route to world revolution. With national independence would come social independence, a seminal part of MacLean's democratic socialism.

Throughout this time MacLean was a pivotal figure in strike action and agitation. His teachings and influence were central in the 1911 Clydebank Singer Strike, and in the subsequent miners strike MacLean helped set up the South Wales Miners Reform Committee. In 1915 MacLean addressed a rally of 10,000 people calling for a general strike should rent increases threatened by landlords be implemented. This action formed part of wider rent strikes across Glasgow, and together with ferment elsewhere, forced the government into passing the Rent Restriction Act, a victory for MacLean and the labor movement. MacLean was a central character in the emergence of "Red Clydeside," a hugely militant pocket of Glasgow so often on the brink of revolutionary change. MacLean was imprisoned five times between 1914 and 1923 on various sedition charges, chiefly under the Defence of the Realm Act.

In conjunction with his unstinting political campaign work, MacLean remained committed to educating workers and the unemployed in Marxian economics and industrial history, and did so in hugely popular night schools. MacLean was a fierce advocate of the **Russian Revolution** and Irish independence, and a stern opponent of World War I. He gained notoriety for traveling through Great Britain giving rousing anti-war and anti-militarism sermons on street corners and at factory gates. MacLean was dismayed to find that left-wing parties throughout Europe (including the BSP) had backed their governments in the decision to enter the conflict, and argued that the war would benefit only the ruling **imperialists** at the cost of working class lives.

More an activist than a theorist, MacLean's main contributions to the cause of Marxism were practical ones, as his ethos of "educate, agitate and organize" infused Clydeside and beyond. MacLean endeavored to explain complex Marxian concepts in a manner the uneducated working class could follow, and inspired it into political action. In terms of adding to Marxist theory, affected by Marx's acknowledgement of the Highland Clearances, he propounded that as "Celtic communism" had been the organizational structure in Scottish clans, the emergence of an independent Scotland would be a return to this natural state, and coined the phrase "back to communism and forward to communism." MacLean died in 1923 of double pneumonia after collapsing while addressing a rally. Tens of thousands lined the streets at his funeral, marking his popularity and the effect he had in bringing Marxism to the workers of Glasgow.

MANDEL, ERNEST (1923–1995). An influential **Marxist** economist, theorist and activist, Mandel was prominent in the **Trotskyist Fourth International** and wrote two major texts in the Marxist canon, *Marxist Economic Theory* (1962) and *Late Capitalism* (1975). Of Belgian origin, he grew up in Antwerp where he joined a Belgian affiliate of the Fourth International when just 17 years old. He was active in the anti-Nazi resistance during World War II for which he was arrested and sent to a prison camp in 1944. After the war he studied in Paris and Brussels, and he later earned a doctorate in political economy from the Free University of Berlin. A loyal Trotskyist (he was a member of the Fourth International's Central Committee from 1941 until his death), Mandel subscribed to the view that **Vladimir Ilich Lenin**

and **Leon Trotsky** had helped to lay the foundations of a socialist **state**, but that **Josef Stalin**'s actions had turned the **Soviet Union** into a "degenerated workers' state" and had created "deformed workers' states" in the Eastern Bloc. Mandel's greater contribution to Marxism lay in his economic theorizing, particularly his analysis of late **capitalism**. In *Late Capitalism* he applied Marx's theory outlined in *Capital* to contemporary capitalism. Modern capitalism, while different in key respects from the capitalism of Marx's time, for example, in the development of the dominance of multinational corporations and in the greater role of the state in the national and international economy, remained fundamentally the same in terms of its crisis-prone and contradictory nature. Capitalism is characterized by periodic **crises** of under-consumption when workers cannot afford to buy the goods they have produced and by an overall decline in the rate of profit, ultimately leading to capitalism's collapse. Capitalism, according to Mandel, went through different stages of development—national competition, international competition/**imperialism**, and late capitalism—and these saw "long waves" of development in which the rate of profit rises and falls, and prosperity along with it. These waves might last 50 years between economic crises. The message in brief according to Mandel was that capitalism cannot be regulated or be used to create social justice, and that Marx's basic analysis of capitalism was correct: it is crisis-prone and liable to collapse.

MAOISM. The unofficial term for **Maothought** or the ideas and politics of **Mao Zedong**. The principal themes are an emphasis on voluntarism, **dialectical** philosophy especially the theme of contradictions, a class analysis that focuses on the attitudinal aspect of **class** identity and on the revolutionary role of the **peasantry**, a revolutionary theory incorporating the notions of guerrilla warfare and "encirclement," and a commitment to **democratic centralism** and the "mass line." Maoism has been popular among Third World Marxists, for example the **Shining Path**.

MAOTHOUGHT. Within Chinese **communism Marxism** is considered to be the basic theory set down by **Karl Marx**, the unchanging and universally true principles, while Maothought is the application of those principles to the specific circumstances of **China**.

Marxism is the pure theory and Maothought is the applied theory or practical **ideology**. Maothought represents the thought of **Mao Zedong** and has been described as the "Sinification" of Marxism, or, since Mao's knowledge of Marxism was largely derived from Russian sources, as the Sinification of the "Russification" of Marxism. Questions have been raised regarding the validity of Maothought as a variant of Marxism given its significant departures from Marx's ideas.

MAO ZEDONG (1893–1976). Chinese **Marxism** is dominated by the figure of Mao Zedong who was its foremost political leader and theoretician during his lifetime, and remains hugely influential. Born into a **peasant** family in Hunan province, he was politically active from an early age and was present at the meeting in Shanghai in 1921 that established the **Chinese Communist Party** (CCP). During the mid-1920s Mao was prominent in the United Front when the Communist Party allied with the nationalist Kuomintang (KMT). An early advocate of peasant involvement in **revolution**, he was head of the peasant institute in Guangzhou in 1925 and active in the "Autumn Harvest" peasant uprising in 1927. When war broke out between the communists and the Kuomintang Mao became chairman (head of state) of the newly formed Chinese Soviet Republic. When the republic was defeated by the KMT in 1934 (despite some success for the communists with their guerrilla warfare tactics), Mao led the communists to safety by undertaking the 5,000-kilometer "**Long March**." The Japanese invasion of China led to the renewal of the communist–KMT alliance in 1937 to fight the common enemy. During the war the communists grew in strength, achieving great successes against the Japanese, while the nationalists, undermined by corruption and economic problems in the area they controlled, were gradually pushed to the most southwestern part of China. By 1949 the KMT was defeated and the **People's Republic of China** declared with Mao at its head. Made party leader in 1935, he became chair of the party Politburo and Central Committee Secretariat in 1943, state president from 1949 to 1959, and supreme commander of China in 1970. Mao died in Beijing in 1976 at the age of 83, having ruled China for nearly 30 years.

Mao's leadership was marked by several distinct periods, policies and upheavals. The first of these was the "New Democracy" period from 1949 to 1953. Viewing China as essentially a semi-colonial and semi-feudal society, the Chinese communists believed there would have to be a period of transition to bring China to the same point as the modern, industrial **capitalist** countries before a **socialist** society could be created. New Democracy represented this period of **bourgeois**-democratic revolution before the socialist revolution. During this New Democracy period private enterprise was encouraged, industrial development prioritized and noncommunist parties permitted. The communists claimed the support of a four-**class** alliance between **workers**, peasants, the petty bourgeoisie and the national bourgeoisie during this period. The liberal and democratic elements were limited though with the state taking the lead role in the economy and the CCP taking the leading political role. Economically, the New Democracy period gave way to the first five-year plan in 1953. Modeled on the **Soviet Union**'s economic plans, the first Chinese five-year plan focused on heavy industry for development and set strict targets for production output. In 1958 another economic initiative marked a further distinct period in post-revolutionary China's history, namely the "Great Leap Forward." This was an attempt to rapidly increase production while moving away from the Soviet five-year plan model. It involved decentralization of economic decision-making, more emphasis on light industry and agriculture, and the creation of communes and small-scale local units of production. An example of this was the attempt to set up backyard furnaces throughout China in place of huge industrial ones. The Great Leap Forward was not a success. It failed to produce sustained increases in production, often saw the quality of goods produced decline and required coercion to implement. It was abandoned in the early 1960s.

In political and ideological terms the New Democracy period was followed first by the "One Hundred Flowers" period. This campaign began in 1956 after Mao made a speech in which he said, "let a hundred flowers bloom, a hundred schools of thought contend." Mao wanted to encourage the expression of diverse and even divergent points of view. He encouraged criticism of the Communist Party and greater freedom of expression. After some initial hesitation, a trickle of criticism turned into a torrent critical of the communist regime provoking unrest throughout the country. Mao responded with a speech in which he said that the "poisonous weeds" had to be distinguished from "fragrant flowers," and the poisonous weeds were subsequently discouraged by labor camps and other coercive measures. Within a year the One Hundred Flowers campaign was over. The most (in)famous ideological campaign followed some 10 years later and was titled the "Great Proletarian **Cultural Revolution**." Begun in 1966 it was ostensibly an attempt to revitalize the CCP, and it involved the mobilization of revolutionary zealots in the form of the **Red Guard**. The Red Guard was mostly composed of students and its mission was to counter bureaucratic and bourgeois tendencies and to ensure loyalty to Mao. The Red Guard acquired notoriety for its violent and disruptive attacks on anyone or anything it deemed to be bourgeois or bureaucratic, even turning on some party officials (Mao was happy to see those in the party establishment who were against him attacked by the Red Guard). The Red Guard's excesses provoked rioting and almost wrecked the CCP. Mao and the CCP reasserted control using the army and disbanded the Red Guard. By 1969 the Cultural Revolution was over in all but name.

As well as dominating communist political practice in China, Mao also dominated communist political theory. The term **Maoism** is widely used to refer to the adaptation of Marxist theory to Chinese conditions, although in China the official term "**Maothought**" is used to refer to the application of Marx's universal principles to the specific circumstances of China; Marxism is the pure theory, Maothought the applied theory. Mao's thought found expression in his writings such as *New Democracy* (1940) and *The Thoughts of Chairman Mao* (the "little red book").

Five principal themes of Maothought can be discerned. The first of these concerns Mao's non-**determinist** interpretation of **historical materialism**. Maothought rejects the notion that the economic **base** of society always determines the **superstructure**, and instead takes a voluntarist viewpoint that emphasizes consciousness, ideas, moral and political attitudes rather than economic conditions. Contrary to orthodox Marxism Maothought allows for ideas to bring about revolution and largely sees politics as taking precedence over economics, hence the Chinese Marxist slogan "Politics in Command" and the emphasis on ideological campaigns such as the Cultural Revolution.

The second key feature of Maothought is a new class analysis that incorporates the idea of class as a state of mind, rather than simply being determined by a person's relationship to the **means of production**. Class origins—the class background of your parents and immediate family predecessors—may lead to the persistence of class-based attitudes even making a person a traitor to the revolution. The class analysis in Maothought also gave a central role and importance to the peasantry, and in practice a leading role over the proletariat.

The third main theme of Maothought is the view of revolution which gives a key role to the peasantry and to the tactic of guerrilla warfare. In Maothought the countryside encircles the towns and is the starting point for a revolution which will spread to the urban areas. In similar fashion world revolution will begin in the less developed countries that encircle the developed countries, eventually carrying the revolution into the most advanced countries. Maothought also stresses the importance of political, ideological and continual revolution.

A fourth principal feature of Maothought is the notion of democracy and the "Mass Line," a notion that builds on the **Leninist** idea of **democratic centralism**. The mass line insists on the masses being consulted by the party, with the party line being derived from the idea of the masses. The party turns the scattered and unsystematic ideas of the masses into a coherent doctrine which is then taken back to the masses and the dialogue continued. In practice the mass line tended to mean the party line and dissent from it by the masses was not tolerated.

The final key characteristic of Maothought is the theory of contradictions inspired by **dialectical** philosophy. Mao identified two particular types of contradiction: principal and secondary; and antagonistic and nonantagonistic. Antagonistic contradictions are those that threaten the socialist revolution and can only be resolved by crushing one side of the contradiction. They include the contradiction between the Chinese and the Japanese imperialists, between the people and the oppressor classes, and between the people and class enemies. Nonantagonistic contradictions are those that exist among the people themselves, but which do not threaten the revolution and can be resolved by peaceful means, for example the contradiction between town and countryside. The notion of principal and secondary contradictions refers to the idea that at any given time there may be several contradictions operating, but one will be more important and need resolving first. For example, the contradiction between the Chinese and Japanese invaders took precedence over the contradiction between the people and the oppressor classes.

There is some debate as to the legitimacy of Mao's Marxism given his departures from orthodox Marxism and central ideas of Marx. The issue hinges on the extent to which Marxism may be stretched in its application to Chinese conditions. Some commentators argue that Maoism constitutes a separate ideology from Marxism, and others have characterized it as the Sinification of the Russification of Marxism.

MARCUSE, HERBERT (1898–1979). The "guru" of the New Left in Europe in the 1960s, Marcuse was one of the most significant of **Marxist** thinkers in the 20th century. His writings inspired much of the student protest movement of the 1960s and he developed Marxism in new ways, incorporating other theories such as Freudianism. Born in Berlin Marcuse served in a reserve unit of the German army in World War I. He went to university first in Berlin and then in Freiberg where he obtained a doctorate studying literature, philosophy and political economy. For a while he worked as an assistant to the philosopher Martin Heidigger before he became a member of the Institute for Social Research (**Frankfurt School**). In 1934 he emigrated to the **United States** in response to the Nazis coming to power in Germany. He continued his association with the Institute for Social Research in New York, and then worked for the United States government between 1942 and 1950, first for the Office of Strategic Services and then for the State Department. Research fellowships and professorships followed at Brandeis, Columbia, Harvard, Yale and San Diego universities in the United States, and the École Practique des Hautes Études and University of Berlin in Europe.

Marcuse's most notable works are *Reason and Revolution* (1949), *Eros and Civilization* (1955), *Soviet Marxism* (1958), and, perhaps most influential of all, *One-Dimensional Man* (1964). In these works Marcuse pursued typical Frankfurt School themes such as a critique of science and technology from a humanist perspective, and he drew on the ideas of a range of non-Marxist thinkers, notably **Georg Wilhelm Friedrich Hegel** and Sigmund Freud, in developing his own critical social theory. His use of Freud to develop a "metapsychology" linking the individual and society is one of Marcuse's most distinctive contributions. Specifically, Marcuse took from Freud the idea that human history is the history of human repression, with human instincts repressed in the course of the development of civilization. Unlike Freud, though, Marcuse saw the repression of the instinctive "pleasure principle" as characteristic of a society where there was scarcity, rather than an inevitable and universal occurrence. In other words, for Marcuse repression of essential human features was historically or culturally specific, restricted to those societies based on scarcity. In *Eros and Civilization* Marcuse argued that with technological advance came the possibility of overcoming scarcity, and with the overcoming of scarcity would come an end to repression and the freeing of "Eros" or the "pleasure principle" to use Freud's terminology.

In his later work *One-Dimensional Man* Marcuse elaborated his critique of technology arguing that it provided the basis for "pleasant" forms of social control that would draw the sting from revolutionary movements and attempts to liberate society. By helping to create affluence and meeting many material desires, technology pacifies the masses leading them to acquiesce to social control by the existing **ruling class** and to become integrated into the **capitalist** system. Consumerism shapes our ideas and personalities, creating a false consciousness and a system of false needs that we pursue at the expense of liberation. Furthermore, a mindset dominated by the rationality of science and technology denies or fails to see the importance or value of the intangible; all that matters is what can be observed, measured and manipulated, and human beings themselves become but "things" to be observed, measured and manipulated in accordance with creating the most "efficient" and "rational" society. In his *Soviet Marxism* Marcuse noted that repression and a lack of freedom characterized the bureaucratic Soviet system as much as it did capitalism.

Marcuse arguably both invigorated and undermined Marxism. He, like other members of the Frankfurt School, tended toward a pessimistic view of the prospects for **revolution** and doubted the revolutionary potential of the **proletariat**. But he also introduced new elements to Marxist theory (e.g., Freudianism), and opened up the atrophying orthodox Marxism to critical examination and reconstruction in the light of the new conditions of capitalism in the mid-20th century. He also helped to draw attention to the importance of Marx's early works and the influence of Hegel on Marx's thought.

MARIATEGUI, JOSÉ CARLOS (1894–1930). Mariategui was a Peruvian **socialist** thinker and leader, who was dubbed "Latin America's Gramsci." Born into a poor family in the small Peruvian town of Moquegua, he became a journalist and political activist. His political activities and involvement in the working class movement attracted the attention of the authorities forcing him to flee to Europe in 1919, where he stayed until 1923. Here he was particularly influenced by **Bendeto Croce**, **Georges Sorel** and **Antonio Gramsci**. Returning to Peru he engaged in revolutionary political activity to the detriment of his health. He spoke at numerous meetings of workers and peasants, wrote numerous articles, edited the influential journal *Amauta*, was involved in the formation of the General Confederation of Peruvian Workers (established 1929), and was the first secretary general of the Peruvian Marxist–Leninist Party. Among his most important works are *Internationalism and Nationalism* and *Seven Interpretive Essays on Peruvian Reality* (1928).

Mariategui's thinking is characterized by its open, fluid and undogmatic character. While embracing **Marxism** he rejected **deterministic** Marxism and came into conflict with the orthodox Marxists in the **Communist International**. The 1929 Conference of Latin American Communist Parties censured him for describing his party as "socialist" instead of "**communist**," and for being "populist." His significance and originality stem from his view that Marxism is not some universal truth to be applied to Peru, but, rather, that Marxism must become a true expression of Peruvian social reality. Marxism, for Mariategui, had to be flexible enough to adapt to Peruvian circumstances. In particular, he believed in an "indigenous renaissance" that would create an Indo–American society in Peru based on the communal values of the Incas. He was also one of the earliest Third World Marxists to appreciate the importance of the **peasantry** and its revolutionary potential given the absence of a large **proletariat**. As well as his "national Marxism" Mariategui was a keen **internationalist** and promoted solidarity with the Cuban and Nicaraguan revolutionary movements as well as with the new communist government of Russia.

MARTOV, YULI (1873–1923). Initially a close colleague of **Vladimir Ilich Lenin**, Martov broke with him in 1903 over the issue of the role and organization of the **Russian Social Democratic Party**. Martov's faction became known as the **Mensheviks**, and Martov was forced to flee Russia in 1920 when his party was outlawed by Lenin's **Bolshevik** government.

MARX, ELEANOR (1855–1898). The youngest of **Karl Marx**'s three daughters who survived to adulthood, Eleanor Marx was actively involved in the **socialist** movement throughout her life. She was involved in the **Socialist Democratic Federation**, **Socialist League**, **Independent Labour Party**, and **Second International**, but was especially active working for militant trade unions in the late 1880s and 1890s, particularly as a committee member for the Gasworkers' Union and as an activist helping to mobilize women strikers. She had an unhappy personal life, and eventually committed suicide by taking prussic acid aided by her husband **Edward Bibbins Aveling**.

MARX, KARL HEINRICH (1818–1883). The founder of **Marxism** through his extensive writings and his political activism, Karl Marx is one of the most influential political thinkers of all time. He was born in Trier, Germany, to a comfortably off middle-**class** family that had converted from Judaism to Protestantism in order for his father Heinrich Marx to keep his post in the Prussian civil service. He was educated at the universities of Bonn, Berlin and Jena, receiving his doctorate in philosophy from the last of these. While at Berlin Marx came under the influence of the "Young Hegelians," disciples of **Georg Wilhelm Friedrich Hegel**, who had taught for many years there. The radical political and atheistic views of Marx and his academic mentor, Bruno Bauer, prevented him from gaining an academic post and he turned to journalism, working for the liberal Cologne paper *Rheinische Zeitung* from 1842 until its suppression by the government the following year. In June 1843 he married Jenny von Westphalen with whom he had six children, Guido, Franziska, Edgar, Jenny, Laura and **Eleanor**, though only the latter three lived beyond childhood. In the same year that he married Jenny von Westphalen he made his intellectual divorce from Hegel writing *Critique of Hegel's Philosophy of Right* in which he developed his views on political philosophy through a fierce critique of Hegel's ideas. He continued his critique of Hegel and Hegelianism in his *Critique of Hegel's Philosophy of Right: Introduction* written in 1844 and in *The German Ideology* written in 1846, although the influence of Hegel on Marx's thought is evident in later works such as the *Grundrisse* (written 1857/8), *Theories of Surplus Value* (written 1862/3) and the introduction to *Capital* volume I (1867).

In 1844 Marx met **Friedrich Engels** in Paris who was to become his lifelong friend and collaborator. They had briefly met two years earlier but did not establish a friendship at the time. However, from 1844 onwards they were extremely close personally, politically and in their working relationship. Engels directed Marx toward a study of economics, which was crucial in his intellectual and political development, and provided financial, psychological and intellectual support to Marx throughout his life. As well as jointly writing *The Holy Family* (1845), *The German Ideology* (1845/46) and the *Communist Manifesto* (1848), Marx and Engels discussed all the major concepts of Marxism as they developed, and exchanged some 1,350 letters in the course of their collaboration. 1844 also saw Marx write *Economic and Philosophical Manuscripts*, in which he discussed **alienation** and put forward a **humanist** conception of **communism**. At the time he was strongly influenced by the **materialist** and atheist philosophy of Ludwig Feuerbach, an influence he was to outgrow the following year when he wrote his *Theses on Feuerbach*. This work saw him move beyond Feuerbach as well as Hegel and was the first writing in which Marx outlined the foundation of the materialist conception of history (**historical materialism**), albeit in a very terse and schematic form. Historical materialism along with his analysis of **capitalism** contained in the three volumes of *Capital* represent Marx's greatest intellectual achievement.

Forced to move from Paris because of his **revolutionary** views and activities, Marx went to Brussels where he was involved with a network of revolutionary groups, most notably the League of the Just, which became the **Communist League** in 1847. In 1848 Marx and Engels, at the behest of the Communist League, wrote the *Communist Manifesto*. The *Manifesto* expressed key ideas of Marx as well as a call for revolution in a straightforward manner. For example, it begins with the words, "The history of all hitherto existing society is the history of class struggles," which conveys the heart of Marx's approach to history. Elsewhere the *Manifesto* describes the relation between the development of capitalism and the advent of communism, the former creating the preconditions for the latter, and the relation between socio-economic conditions and the development of ideas ("What else does the history of ideas prove, than that intellectual production changes its character in proportion as material production is changed? The ruling ideas of each age have ever been the ideas of its ruling class."). The *Manifesto* ends with a call for revolution: "The Communists disdain to conceal their views and aims. They openly declare that their ends can be attained only by the forcible overthrow of all existing social conditions. Let the ruling classes tremble at a Communistic revolution. The Proletarians have nothing to lose but their chains. They have a world to win. WORKING MEN OF ALL COUNTRIES UNITE!"

Unsuccessful revolutions in various places across Europe, most notably Paris and Berlin, did follow the publication of the *Manifesto*, but the *Manifesto* itself was not responsible for these and only achieved its fame/notoriety and huge influence subsequently. The revolutionary unrest elsewhere led the Belgian authorities to expel Marx and he moved to Paris and then Cologne. In Cologne Marx worked to establish a new radical periodical the *Neue Rheinische Zeitung*, which he edited and for which he wrote some 80 articles until he was arrested and tried on a charge of inciting armed insurrection. He was acquitted but expelled from Germany and the *Neue Rheinische Zeitung* closed in 1849. Marx then moved to London via Paris, and continued to live in England for the rest of his life. In London during the 1850s Marx and his family lived for much of the time in poverty, and relied on the generosity of Engels for an income, supplemented with earnings from articles written for the New York *Daily Tribune*.

During his time in England he wrote his major historical studies, *The Class Struggles in France* (1850), *The Eighteenth Brumaire of Louis Bonaparte* (1852) and *The Civil War in France* (1871), as well as his major economic works, the three volumes of *Capital* (written 1861–1879). In the former works he applied his theory of historical materialism and developed aspects of his theories of the **state**, class and revolution. In his economic works he elaborated his theory of **exploitation** and introduced his key notions of the **commodity** and **surplus value**. Marx's political activities also continued in England. The Communist League dissolved in 1852, but Marx remained in contact with radicals and revolutionaries throughout Europe and in 1864 he helped to found the **First International**, a loose association of socialist and workers' political parties and trade unions. Marx served on the International's General Council and was active in the preparations for the annual Congresses. He also devoted considerable time and energy to fighting against the influence of the anarchists in the International led by Michael Bakunin.

In his later years Marx began to withdraw from his political activities, spending more time with his family. Persistent health problems contributed to this withdrawal, hindering his work in the final decade of his life and worsening his already marked tendency to procrastinate and leave work incomplete. Nevertheless, he still contributed to debates on contemporary politics, most notably his intervention in the affairs of the German labor movement in the form of his *Critique of the Gotha Program* (1875). In this he criticized the state socialism of **Ferdinand Lassalle** and elaborated various points about equality, communism and the state. In 1881 Marx's wife Jenny died, and this was followed by the death of his eldest daughter Jenny in January 1883. Marx only lived two months after his daughter's death and was buried in Highgate cemetery on 17 March 1883.

MARXISM. The term "Marxism" first appeared in the 1880s, achieving widespread use by the turn of the century. In 1894 **Georgii Plekhanov** described Marxism as "a whole world view," but **Karl Marx** himself viewed his thought as primarily a **revolutionary class**–based critique of **capitalism** and a **materialist** conception of history focusing particularly on economic production. With the divergent interpretations of Marxism came the development of "hyphenated Marxisms" such as **Marxism–Leninism, Austro-Marxism** and **Afro-Marxism.** As an ideology and a movement Marxism can be said to have had as profound an effect on the world as any of its political rivals.

MARXISM–LENINISM. *See* LENINISM.

MARXIST FEMINISM. From the writings of **Karl Marx** and **Friedrich Engels** onwards, the **Marxist** tradition has engaged with the issue of **women**'s oppression and with feminist ideas. Engels' *The Origins of the Family, Private Property and the State* (1884), **August Bebel**'s *Woman Under Socialism* (1878), and the work and ideas of **Clara Zetkin** and **Alexandra Kollantai** were all significant contributions by early Marxists to the development of a Marxist feminism. Heidi Hartmann, Lise Vogel, Mariarosa Dalla Costa, Juliet Mitchell and Michelle Barrett represent a more recent wave of Marxist feminists who have extended and developed Marxism in a more radical way to address the issue of women's oppression.

The orthodox Marxist view of women's oppression stemming from Engels' writing accredits biology as a factor, but one without any significance in itself, only becoming important with the advent of **class** society. The key to women's emancipation lies in their participation in the labor force and the subsequent overthrow of **capitalism**. This orthodox view in effect accords women's oppression a secondary status with class conflict having primary status. Hartmann represents an approach that seeks to "marry" Marxism and feminism, each complementing the other and each focusing on a different structure of oppression. According to this viewpoint, where Marxism focuses on the economic laws of development, feminism examines relations between men and women; Marxism analyses and explains capital, and feminism does the same for patriarchy. For Hartmann and others adopting this approach, women's oppression cannot be reduced to a by-product of class oppression.

Vogel and Dalla Costa are examples of a Marxist feminism that endeavors to apply Marxist analytical tools and concepts to areas relating to women that have previously been ignored. For example, the role of domestic labor, largely performed by women, in the process of the production of **surplus value** is highlighted by this strand of Marxist feminism along with the way in which the family is functional for capitalism with women serving to reproduce labor by meeting the needs of their husbands and producing and rearing children. Mitchell and Barrett represent revisionists who look to modify Marxism where it fails to provide an adequate account of women's oppression. For example, Mitchell draws on developments in Freudian psychoanalysis, and both Mitchell and Barrett pinpoint the realm of **ideology** as a key sphere in which women's oppression is constructed and reproduced. From this viewpoint the focus of attention is turned away from relations of economic appropriation and **exploitation** and more toward the previously neglected area of ideology, although the basic historical and **materialist** approach of Marxism is retained.

MARXIST HUMANISM. An interpretation of Marxism that stresses the humanist themes found in Marx's early writings, Marxist humanism is most closely associated with the Yugoslav **Praxis School**, and can also be traced in the work of the **Frankfurt School** and **Jean-Paul Sartre**. In Marxist humanism attention is given to developing

Marx's theory of human nature and **alienation**, and Marxism itself is viewed as a philosophy rather than as a science.

MARXIST STRUCTURALISM. This school of thought is primarily associated with the French Marxist thinker **Louis Althusser** and with **Nicos Poulantzas**. The chief characteristic of Marxist structuralism is a focus on the structural analysis of social totalities, that is, Marxism is understood to be concerned with social structures or practices rather than with human beings as subjects. Marxist structuralism stands in direct opposition to **Marxist humanism**, asserting a structural determinism to be operating in society and denying the role of human consciousness in shaping the social world.

MATERIALISM. As the principal terms and labels for **Karl Marx**'s central theory and approach suggest ("the materialist conception of history," "**historical materialism**," "**dialectical materialism**"), materialism lies at the heart of **Marxism**. Marx developed his materialist approach in opposition to philosophical **idealism**, and in particular to the idealism of **Georg Wilhelm Friedrich Hegel** and his followers. There is much debate among Marxists as to the exact nature of Marx's materialism, but six main materialist theses can be discerned in his thought.

First, there is the thesis that there exists a world independent of our perception of it, that material objects exist separately and independently of thought/mind/spirit. Secondly, Marx embraces a primacy of matter thesis which holds that matter is primary in that it can exist without mind, and it is primary in that mind emerges from matter. Thirdly, Marx espouses a naturalism thesis, meaning the natural world constitutes the entirety of reality, and nature is not derived from or dependent upon any supernatural entity. These first three theses may be described as Marx's philosophical materialism. The fourth thesis to which Marx subscribes is embodied in his historical materialism and in essence states that social production determines or conditions the existence of human beings and of society in general. It ascribes causal primacy to the **mode of production** over ideas/the **ideological** sphere in social life. Fifthly, there is what may be termed the **praxis** thesis which asserts the constitutive role of human practice in changing nature, society, social being, and social consciousness, and also asserts the unity of theory and practice. Finally, there is what may be called the materialist methodology thesis which consists in a method of inquiry that takes as its starting point concrete determinate forms of life, the empirical rather than abstractions or *a priori* categories. These last three theses represent the more distinctive aspects of Marx's materialism and convey the differences between his materialism and what he saw as the reductionist, abstract, passive, contemplative and nondialectical old materialism that preceded his innovations.

Friedrich Engels in *Anti-Dühring* (1878) and *Ludwig Feuerbach and the End of Classical German Philosophy* (1886) explored materialism as a cosmology, ontology and philosophical world outlook and was enormously influential on theorists of the **Second International**, such as **Eduard Bernstein**, **Karl Kautsky** and **Georgii Plekhanov**, and on **Soviet Marxism**. Engels' materialism formed the basis for what became known as **dialectical materialism**, a comprehensive though rather dogmatic and narrow philosophical outlook espoused particularly by Soviet ideologists. **Vladimir Ilich Lenin** also wrote about materialism in his *Materialism and the Empirico-Criticism* (1908), again asserting its centrality to Marxism, although focusing more on epistemology rather than ontology. Other Marxists have stressed materialism much less, **Antonio Gramsci**, for example, suggesting that the emphasis should be put on "historical" in historical materialism rather than on "materialism," and **Jean-Paul Sartre** arguing that "no materialism of any kind can ever explain [freedom]."

MEANS OF PRODUCTION. For **Karl Marx** the means of production and who owns them are crucial factors in determining the nature, **class** configuration and distribution of power in any given society. The means of production are those things necessary in order to produce, for example, machinery, land and money. According to Marx, the means of production are part of the **forces of production**, and whichever class owns and controls them is the dominant class in society. The capitalists' ownership and control of the means of production in capitalist society makes them the **ruling class**, giving them both economic and political power.

MEDVEDEV, ROY ALEXANDROVICH (1925–). Born in Tbilisi, the capital of the Soviet republic of Georgia, Medvedev has contributed to the documenting and analyzing of **Stalinism**, most notably in his landmark work, *Let History Judge: The Origins and Consequences of Stalinism* (1971). He studied philosophy and education at Leningrad University and became a member of the Institute of Professional Education at the Academy of Pedagogical Sciences. His attention turned to Soviet history and Stalinism in particular following the denunciation of **Josef Stalin** by **Nikita Khrushchev** in 1956. His first attempts to get *Let History Judge* published resulted in his expulsion from the communist party in 1969, and from the 1970s on he was active in the Soviet dissident movement. He has been often published in Europe and the **United States**, and aside from *Let History Judge*, his key works are *A Question of Madness* (1971, co-authored with his brother Zhores), *On Socialist Democracy* (1975), *The October Revolution* (1979), and *Leninism and Western Socialism* (1981).

Medvedev approached the issue of Stalinism from a **Marxist** perspective, but an undogmatic one that left room for the role of subjective factors in history as well as objective ones, and allowed for the significance of the individual and of culture in shaping society and historical development. For example, Stalin's cunning personality and the undeveloped culture of the masses leaving them open to manipulation are key factors in the development of Stalinism according to Medvedev. He was more sympathetic to **Leninism**, but still viewed **Vladimir Ilich Lenin** and the **Bolsheviks'** attempts to achieve various **socialist** goals as premature given the existing objective social and economic conditions. He increasingly focused on the importance of democracy and the kind of democratic procedures and structures found in **bourgeois** countries, for example, freedom of speech, rule of law and protection of minorities. The **Soviet Union** desperately needed democratization in his view, and without it there was increasing intellectual, economic and cultural stagnation. Medvedev during the life of the Soviet Union also advocated the development of a universal ethics and a crucial role for intellectuals in promoting social progress.

MEHRING, FRANZ (1846–1919). Notable as the author of the first major biography of **Karl Marx**, Franz Mehring was a member of the **German Social Democratic Party** (SPD) and then the Independent Social Democratic Party (USPD). Aside from *Karl Marx* (1918), he also wrote *History of German Social Democracy* (1897–1898) in which he outlined the growth of **socialism** in the context of German political, social and intellectual developments. He converted to socialism in 1890 and soon allied himself with **Rosa Luxemburg** and **Karl Liebknecht** on the left of the party. He attacked the official SPD position of cooperation with the German government during World War I, joining the anti-war USPD in 1917, and helping to create the extreme left **Spartacist League** with Luxemburg.

MELLA, JULIO ANTONIO (1903–1929). A significant figure in the development of Cuban revolutionary **socialism**, Mella was above all a political activist. In 1922 he organized the Cuban Federation of University Students and then moved on to help form the José Marti Popular University (named after the Cuban revolutionary nationalist), which integrated students, workers and professors. The university also took up the cause of Cuban workers and their appalling working conditions and protested against **United States** imperialism, before the government closed it down. Mella then founded an Anti-Clerical League, considering the church to be reactionary and an obstacle to socialism and scientific thinking. He also helped start the Cuban section of the Anti-Imperialist League of the Americas, which campaigned against the undemocratic regimes in the region and the sway international **capital** held over them. He embraced **Vladimir Ilich Lenin**'s theory of **imperialism**, and in 1925 he helped organize the Constitutional Congress of the **Communist Party of Cuba**. He was assassinated in Mexico in 1929 by agents of the Cuban government.

MENGISTU, HAILE MARIAM (1937?–). Ethiopian head of state from 1977 until forced to flee to Zimbabwe in the face of rebellion in 1991. Having led a military coup that deposed Emperor Haile Selassie in 1974, he triumphed in a struggle for power, and subsequently oversaw the transition of **Ethiopia** into a "socialist" state based on **Marxist** ideology. Born in Addis Ababa he began his military career at the age of 17 as a cadet in the Ethiopian army and by 1974 had attained the rank of lieutenant colonel. He took part in a failed coup against Haile Selassie in 1960, but was pardoned. After the 1974 coup he liquidated his rivals and gained the support of the **Soviet Union** and **Cuba**. As early as 1974 the newly formed Provisional Military Administrative Council (Dergue) called for the creation of a socialist Ethiopia, and the Marxist direction of Ethiopia under Mengistu was signaled by the creation of the Union of Ethiopian **Marxist–Leninist** Organizations as the sole legal party in 1977. In 1984 the Workers' Party of Ethiopia, committed to Marxism–Leninism, was formed with Mengistu at its head.

Mengistu's Marxism consisted of a concentration of power in the hands of the **state**, to be exercised on behalf of the people without the need for democratic structures or procedures. Agricultural land was nationalized and efforts were made to end poverty, with the grander aim of leaping from **feudalism** to **communism**. However, Mengistu's regime was unable to prevent near economic collapse and famine, let alone bring about the communist ideal. At no time did the regime enjoy peace from either civil unrest or external conflict, with wars involving Somalia and the region of Eritrea throughout much of Mengistu's rule. Civil war eventually led to Mengistu's flight to Zimbabwe in 1991.

MENSHEVIKS. The term Mensheviks refers to the faction of the **Russian Social Democratic Labor Party** led by **Yuri Martov** and **Paul Axelrod** that opposed **Vladimir Ilich Lenin** at the second party congress in 1903. At the congress the main point of difference between Lenin's followers (the **Bolsheviks**) and the Mensheviks was the latter's advocacy of a broad party membership in opposition to the former's position favoring a narrower, tightly organized and disciplined active membership. The Bolsheviks (from the Russian for majoritarians) gained a majority on the party's Central Committee which gave the Mensheviks their name from the Russian word *men'shinstvo* meaning the minority. Menshevism also came to be associated with the view that a **bourgeois** democratic **revolution** would have to take place in Russia and a period of **capitalism** would have to occur before the conditions were ripe for the **socialist** revolution.

In 1912 the Bolsheviks formally broke with the Mensheviks, and the Mensheviks themselves experienced splits over their attitude to World War I and the provisional government. Taking part in the elections to the Constituent Assembly in 1917 the Mensheviks achieved less than 3 percent of the votes compared with the 24 percent received by the Bolsheviks. They denounced the October Revolution by the Bolsheviks as a coup d'état and, after broadly supporting the Bolshevik government in the civil war that followed the 1917 **Rus-**

sian **Revolution**, they continued their critical stance toward the Bolsheviks by their support for the Kronstadt uprising in 1921. Suppressed by the government after the Kronstadt revolt they continued to have a voice in the émigré journal *Sotsialisticheskivy Vestnik* (Socialist Courier) until 1965.

MILIBAND, RALPH (BORN ADOLPHE) (1924–1994). A notable **Marxist** academic, Miliband wrote the influential *The State in Capitalist Society* (1969), and was also noteworthy as the co-editor of perhaps the foremost English-language Marxist journal, *The Socialist Register*. Born in Brussels into a Polish–Jewish family, he fled with his father to Great Britain when the Nazis invaded Belgium. Here he became a politics student at the London School of Economics in 1941 before moving on to further study at Cambridge University. In 1949 he became a lecturer at the London School of Economics, where he stayed until 1972 when he was appointed professor of politics at Leeds University, taking up a final academic post at Brandeis University in the **United States** in 1978. Miliband's political involvement in Britain began with membership of the Labour Party in 1951. However, critical of the moderate, cautious approach of the Labour Party and skeptical of its capacity to be a vehicle for **socialism**, but equally hostile to the authoritarianism of the **Soviet Union**, he aligned himself with the British "New Left," along with such figures as **E.P. Thompson**, Raymond Williams and Stuart Hall.

Miliband embraced Marxism, but would not join the British communist party, and concerned himself with a wide range of issues that included nuclear weapons, popular culture and **imperialism** as well as **class** struggle. In terms of Marxist theory he contributed particularly to the Marxist theory of the **state**, and was involved in a notable debate with **Nicos Poulantzas** on the issue. Miliband viewed the state as an instrument for realizing the interests of the **ruling class**, but he qualified this by an acknowledgement of the role of human agency, the complex relation between class power and state power, and the "relative autonomy" of the state from the ruling class.

MODE OF PRODUCTION. This term is ambiguous in **Karl Marx**'s writings, but can be defined as the way in which surplus is created, extracted and controlled, and acts as the basis for social and political arrangements. Incorporating the **forces** and **relations of production**, the mode of production can be seen as a model of economic organization, and over history different modes of production have developed. Five different modes can be discerned in Marx's writings: **Asiatic** (a primitive communal form of production), ancient (based on slavery); **feudal** (based on serfdom), **capitalist** (based on wage labor), and **communist** (based on communal ownership of the **means of production**). In discussing these different modes Marx, while focusing on the economic form, also comments on the corresponding social and political forms including the **classes** and nature of the **state**. Marxists have debated the extent to which modes of production can be used to periodize history and whether or not all societies must pass through the different modes of production or if they can skip stages. Marx in looking at real societies used the term "socio-economic formations" which he suggested could contain elements of more than one mode of production. For example, 19th-century Great Britain while essentially capitalist also contained significant elements of feudalism.

MONGOLIAN PEOPLE'S REPUBLIC (MPR—BÜGD NAYRAMDAH MÒNGOL ARD ULS). Heavily backed by the Soviet **Red Army**, Mongolian revolutionaries were able to grasp control of their country in 1921, and three years later declare the existence of the **Marxist–Leninist** Mongolian People's Republic. Led by the domineering Mongolian People's Revolutionary Party (MPRP—*Mongol Ardyn Khuv'sgalt Nam*), for the next 70 years the country wholeheartedly embraced Soviet orthodoxy and became one of Moscow's most dependable satellite states. Having succeeded in repelling both previous occupiers, **China** and the anti-**Bolshevik** White Army, the Soviet Red Army assisted in the 1921 elevation to power of a self-styled "people's government" encompassing a broad array of left-wing individuals banded together in the Mongolian People's Party. Mongolian acquiescence with Soviet will was formalized soon after with the signing between the two of an Agreement on Mutual Recognition and Friendly Relations.

It was this alliance that enabled pro-Soviet elements within the Mongolian government to sideline those looking to curtail Muscovite intervention and in May 1924 declare the existence of the MPR. The word "Revolutionary" was shoehorned into the party's title, and an organizational structure paralleling that of the **Communist Party of**

the Soviet Union (CPSU) established. In November, the pronouncement of a radical constitution entirely sculpted from the same material as that of the Soviet Union signaled that the MPR intended to embark upon Sovietization with zeal. In following the Soviet economic model, **feudal** properties were confiscated prior to the **collectivization** of animal husbandry, and currency was nationalized through the creation of the Mongolian National Bank. Additionally, the government gave formal approval to a Soviet trade monopoly that provided, alongside the burgeoning cooperative movement, support for the transformation to a centrally planned economy.

The formative years of MPRP rule were characterized too by further factional infighting between staunch pro-Soviets and their more cautious, "rightist" counterparts. With decisive backing from the CPSU, the former prevailed as the 1920s drew to a close and quickly instigated a series of purges against their counterparts. Prominent in this action was Horloogiyn Choybalsan, an ultra-orthodox **Marxist–Leninist**, who used the conflict to lever himself into the highest echelons of government and party (effectively the same thing). Choybalsan, widely referred to in retrospectives as "Mongolia's Stalin," hastened the pace of repression against the "rightists" as well as other sections of Mongolian society. In the early years of Choybalsan's administration, confiscation of monastic **property** and widespread brutality toward religious figures, subjugation of those resistant to **collectivization**, as well as a ferociously enforced outright ban on private industry were all commonplace. The latter two of these helped bring about famine in the MPR, and precipitated an unlikely response from the Soviet Union: 1932 saw an edict from Moscow demanding an end to Mongolian extremism and a move to "gradualism." The result was a raft of "New Turn Policy" reforms that denounced the government's recent undertakings as "leftist deviations," dropped the collectivization and worker cooperative programs, and made allowances for the ownership of private property.

Despite this, a fresh constitution in 1940 reaffirmed both the necessity of overall state planning and Mongolian commitment to **Vladimir Ilich Lenin**'s "road to socialism bypassing capitalism." It was perhaps this underlying adherence to orthodoxy that led the MPR to become a noncombative Eastern buffer zone for the Soviets in World War II, and in August 1945 to send 80,000 troops by way of assistance to an offensive against Japanese troops in Inner Mongolia.

Their loyalty was rewarded following Allied victory with a number of fresh friendship agreements with Moscow, and in addition with the newborn **communist** states of the Eastern Bloc. It was in this climate that the MPRP felt confident enough to abandon gradualism and embrace orthodox Marxism–Leninism once more. 1947 witnessed the outlawing of all private enterprise as a policy of absolute communization took hold, and the ratification of a Soviet-financed five-year economic plan aimed at "**socialist** construction." The 1952 death of Choybalsan allowed Yumjaagiyn Tsedenbal to assume overall control of the government. Tsedenbal's denunciation of the "personality cult" built up around his predecessor proved to be the first of many occasions on which his actions mirrored those of his opposite number in Moscow, **Nikita Khrushchev**, who was issuing a rebuke for his own former superior, **Josef Stalin**, at around the same time. The two relatively moderate leaders, and indeed Khrushchev's successor **Leonid Brezhnev**, worked to accelerate the program of socialist construction in the MPR throughout the 1950s and 1960s, attempting to induce modernization through a series of economic and social plans aimed at speeding the country toward socialism. In return, the MPR became a vital military shield for the Soviet Union as tensions between Moscow and Beijing reached their apogee.

However, the majority of Mongolians remained part of an illiterate, nonindustrial and certainly nonrevolutionary peasant class, and with an acute lack of natural resources inhibiting any semblance of modernization biting hard in tandem, socialist construction stagnated. The MPRP acted decisively, relieving the long-serving Tsedenbal of his duties as he undertook a state visit to Moscow in August 1984. Tsedenbal's replacement as overall leader came in the shape of Jambyn Batmonh, a committed reformist whose ideas chimed with those of **Mikhail Gorbachev** just as Tsedenbal's had with Khrushchev's, and Choybalsan's with Stalin's. Embracing a Mongolian *perestroika*, for the first time since 1921 an oppositional group, the Mongolian Democratic Union, was formally recognized by the **state**, and anti-government street demonstrations broke out. It was this mood of unrest that forced the ruling MPRP Politburo to tender its resignation in March 1990, and two months later induce the endorsement of a new constitution that legalized all opposition parties and paved the way for multi-party free elections. The MPRP reneged on its commitment to Marxism, and re-branded itself as a dimly left-wing social democratic organization, a move that garnered a victory in newly renamed Mongolia's first plural elections. The MPRP government made scant contribution to the development of Marxist thought and analysis, instead aping Soviet policy at its every turn. The one difference was presented by the natural habitat the regime inherited when it took power, that of a pre-agrarian society light years behind the Russia of the October 1917 **Revolution**. Any notion of "bypassing" capitalism was fanciful, and the Mongolians were obliged to slowly build up organized agriculture before they could even consider replicating the Soviet push to industrialization, with all its stage-hopping implications, they so idolized.

MOZAMBIQUE, PEOPLE'S REPUBLIC OF. When the Portuguese "Carnation **Revolution**" of 1974 saw the colonialist dictatorship in Lisbon jettisoned from power, the southeast African colony of Mozambique was able to declare independence. From 1977 until 1989 the country's **Front for the Liberation of Mozambique** (*Frente de Libertação de Moçambique*—FRELIMO) government practiced **Marxism–Leninism** as official state **ideology**. Radical nationalists in FRELIMO had taken up arms in 1964 in a bid to bring a halt to Portuguese rule. FRELIMO was led following the 1969 assassination of its founder Eduardo Mondlane by guerrilla fighter **Samora Machel**. Having overseen the move to independence in 1975, Machel became the inaugural president of a one-party **state**.

Early in its tenure the FRELIMO government displayed its radical tendencies by implementing inherently **socialist** policies, with widespread **collectivization** of rural areas and nationalization of the industrial economy. In this context, the official state adoption of Marxism–Leninism in 1977 was hardly revelatory. A mass "villagization" campaign was launched to curb the influence of religion on Mozambicans and replace it instead with the teachings of **Karl Marx**. FRELIMO converted into a Leninist **vanguard party**, and efforts were made to encourage support and aid from **communist** companion countries such as the **Soviet Union** and the **German Democratic Republic**. In turn, Machel and his administration lent their own assistance to black revolutionary movements in neighboring Southern Rhodesia (now Zimbabwe) and South Africa.

However, when the governments of these two countries reacted by sponsoring the formation of the anti-communist National Resistance

Movement (*Resistência Nacional Moçambicana*—RENAMO), the decision to back such factions inadvertently plunged Mozambique into a 16-year-long civil war. From 1977 until after Marxism–Leninism had all but disappeared from the Mozambican political terrain, fighting between the FRELIMO administration's troops and RENAMO guerrilla soldiers resulted in up to one million fatalities. Many of these deaths resulted from a crippling famine that had arisen owing to the draining of the economy and decimation of the country's fertile land by the conflict.

In this context, by 1984 the continuation of Marxist–Leninist rule looked uncertain. Under the influence of Western states, Machel began to move the government away from an orthodox position, for instance through the introduction of a mixed economy, and attempted to make peace with South Africa under the auspices of the Nkomati Accord. When Machel, after all the architect of the **revolution**, perished in an air crash in 1986 to be replaced by the reformist Joachim Chissano, the end of the ideological stranglehold of Marxism–Leninism over Mozambique appeared imminent. Thus, between the conclusion of 1989 and the commencement of 1990, the government renounced adherence to the doctrine, and implemented a new constitution that promised and delivered multi-party elections.

Owing to the underdeveloped nature of the country, attempts to apply Marxism to Mozambique necessitated a malleable approach to the ideology. On the one hand, there was the 1983 "Operation Production" program that sought to relocate over 20,000 urban dwellers to rural areas, perhaps in recognition of the country's lack of the "advanced" conditions required for the transition to actually existing **socialism** (such eschewing of orthodox Muscovite edicts no doubt influenced the decision not to allow Mozambique entry into Comecon in that same year). On the other, the Marxism frequently espoused by FRELIMO was rooted in abstract theory provided by foreign thinkers of a very different context and era. It was perhaps the inherent contradictions of such malleability, alongside a protracted civil war, that led to the abject failure of Mozambican Marxism.

– N –

NEGATION OF THE NEGATION. Originally a concept of **Georg Wilhelm Friedrich Hegel**, the negation of the negation is a movement of the triadic **dialectic** whereby conflict between opposites is resolved. Although **Karl Marx** makes use of the Hegelian terminology, he differs in both the loci of the methodology and the conception of the negation of the negation. The concept appears, either explicitly or tacitly, in all of Marx's major works and is notably given a lengthy treatment in **Friedrich Engels'** *Anti-Dühring* (1878).

The negation of the negation is the confrontation between the negation of the original, positive thesis and a negativity which seeks to restore the positivity of what was first negated, thus resolving the contradiction between thesis and antithesis, yet at the same time canceling those moments and preserving them in a movement Hegel calls "Aufhebung," or "sublation." Engels states that in this "one law of motion" the material is in a perpetual dialectical process and there can be no regression but only further negation.

In Marx's **materialist** paradigm, the first negation is that of the individual property of the laborer by **capital.** The narrow **mode of production** in which the laborer works for himself creates the material conditions for the annihilation of that epoch in the conflict between the **forces** and **relations of production.** Individual production is negated by socialization of production in a mode of production based upon the private ownership of the **means of production** in which the **capitalist** extracts **surplus value** from labor. As the thesis begets the contradiction, so the negation supposes the expropriation of private **property.** Individual property, which fetters production, and private property, which both fetters production and negates the human being, are sublated by a classless society in which property is both social and individual.

"**Communism** is the negation of the negation," a necessary phase in human emancipation when man no longer loses himself to his product, thereby negating **exploitation,** thus Marx's negation of the negation is intrinsic to his theory of **revolution.** The negation of the negation is a resolution to the contradictions of **bourgeois** society, nevertheless, the existence of contradiction is elementary to dialectical logic, and contradiction in production is fundamental to materialism implying that communism itself must be negated.

NEGRI, ANTONIO (1933–). A writer and political activist, the Italian Antonio Negri published prolifically in the 1970s, although his most notable work is *Empire* written with Michael Hardt. His earlier publications include *Crisi dello Stato-piano* (1974), *Proletari e Stato*

(1976), *La forma Stato* (1977), *Il dominio e il Sabotaggio* (1978), *Dall'operaio Mass all'operaio Sociale* (1979), and *Marx oltre Marx, quaderno di lavaro sui Grundrisse* (1980). As an activist he was involved in the founding of Potere Operaio (Worker Power) for the Veneto-Emiliano region in 1966. He then helped to found the Autonomia Operaio (Worker Autonomy Movement) and worked on the radical *Rosso* newspaper. In 1979 he was arrested on charges of involvement with a plot to create an armed insurrection against the **state**, the formation of an armed gang and the kidnap and murder of Aldo Moro, the president of the Christian Democratic Party. In 1983 while in prison during his prolonged court case, he was elected to the Italian parliament as a representative of the Radical Party. This gave him immunity from prosecution and saw him released from prison. After the Italian Chamber of Deputies then voted to have him re-arrested Negri fled to Paris and was sentenced in his absence to 30 years' imprisonment. Returning to Italy in 1997 he was arrested and sent to serve his sentence.

Negri's intellectual contribution lies in his efforts to produce a new **Marxist** analysis of **capitalism** taking into account changes in the nature of capitalist society, particularly in relation to the role of the state. In his influential work *Empire* he argues that globalization and mercerization of the world since the late 1960s represents an unprecedented historical development, and he explores issues relating to the information society, network economy and globalization.

NETO, AGOSTINHO (1922–1979). Political leader of the **Movimento Popular de Libertação de Angola** (MPLA), and first president of independent **Angola**, Neto was a leading African **Marxist**. Born in a village near Luanda, Angola, he was one of the fortunate few to receive an education in Angola, which was then a Portuguese colony. He went on to work for the Luanda colonial health service before in 1947 going to Portugal as a recipient of a Methodist scholarship to train as a doctor. In Portugal he joined an anti-Salazar youth movement (the MUD-J), and his political activities led to his arrest in 1951, 1952 and 1955, the last of these resulting in a two-year jail term. He qualified as a doctor in 1958 and returned to Luanda in 1959, where he opened a medical practice and worked secretly for the MPLA. He was again arrested in 1960 and sent to **Cape Verde**, where he was rearrested in 1961 and sent to prison in Portugal. On his release he escaped from Portugal where he was still subject to residence restrictions and police surveillance, ending up in Kinshasa where he was formally elected president of the MPLA at its first national conference. From 1961 until he died of cancer in 1979, Neto led the MPLA.

Neto and the MPLA, while on the one hand clearly nationalist in character, were also Marxist. Neto's Marxism began to develop while a student in Portugal, and although he was careful not to proclaim it while involved in the struggle for independence, his commitment to Marxist **socialism** became clear with the establishment of the People's Republic of Angola in 1975. Doctrines of **scientific socialism** and **Marxism–Leninism** became explicit, and the MPLA became the MPLA Workers' Party based on Marxist–Leninist notions of the **vanguard party** and **democratic centralism**.

NORTH KOREA. See KOREA, DEMOCRATIC PEOPLE'S REPUBLIC OF.

NORTH VIETNAM. See VIETNAM, SOCIALIST REPUBLIC OF.

– P –

PANNEKOEK, ANTONIE (1873–1960). A key theorist of council communism, Antonie Pannekoek was also a leading European **Marxist** in the early 20th century and helped to introduce Marxist ideas to his native country, the Netherlands. Having studied mathematics at the University of Leyden Pannekoek turned to the subject that became his career, astronomy. He received a doctorate in astronomy in 1902 and then worked at Leyden Observatory, later becoming a lecturer and in 1932 a professor of astronomy at the University of Amsterdam. His political activities began in 1902 when he joined the Dutch Social Democratic Party. He was expelled in 1909 because of his opposition to the **revisionist** line of the leadership, and joined the Marxist Social Democratic Party, which in 1919 became the Dutch Communist Party. Much of his political activity took place in Germany where he was involved with the **German Social Democratic Party** (SPD), teaching at its school in Berlin and contributing to its newspaper *Die Neue Zeit*. On the left wing of the SPD, he opposed the party's support for fighting in World War I, and he also became a strong critic of the **Bolsheviks** and broke with the **Comintern** in 1920. He helped to found the anti-Bolshevik Communist Workers' Party in both the Netherlands and Germany, and was a leading figure in the Dutch Group of International Communists.

Pannekoek's council communism involved a rejection of any attempt to establish a party or leadership that was above the workers or sought to act on behalf of the workers. He believed that only action and organizations that emerged from the workers were authentic and legitimate. Pannekoek had great faith in the spontaneity of the masses and their ability to organize themselves, and he favored workers' councils as a form of political organization over parties and unions. A prolific writer, his key works are *Marxism and Darwinism* (1909/12), *Ethics and Socialism* (1906) and *Workers' Councils* (1946).

PARIS COMMUNE (1871). A short-lived rebel government in power in the French capital from 18 March until 28 May 1871, at which point it was violently put down by Adolphe Thiers' Government of National Defense. When the provisional government in France signed a humiliating peace with Bismarck following the conclusion of the Franco–Prussian War in 1871, the republican and **socialist** majority in the city of Paris reacted with disgust. Napoleon III had agreed to relinquish Alsace-Lorraine to Bismarck, and allow the Prussian army to occupy Paris. Horrified at such concessions, Parisians demanded a continuation of the war, and a return to the principles of the First Republic. As rebellion against the government appeared impending, the Bordeaux-based National Assembly further infuriated the public by ending the legal ban on wages owed to the National Guard, thus robbing the impoverished population of many of the public funds they had been surviving on. The balance finally tipped when it was decreed that all artillery in Paris be surrendered.

Government troops sent to seize canons were violently resisted with two generals hanged. Parisians demanded independence from the national government, and open revolt broke out. On 18 March, the Paris Commune was hastily assembled to organize the rebellion and take up the governance of Paris. The National Guard, having defended Paris during the five-month Prussian siege, held elections 10 days later to select a 92-member body to run the Commune. A

229,000 strong electorate put into power a collection of moderates and radicals, who in turn formed a Central Committee including neo-Jacobins, Blanquists, socialists from across the spectrum, anarchists, and members of the **First International** from all walks of Parisian life. The group favored a federal approach to governance, both in terms of a system for their central executive, and the way in which their program would be adopted by a federation of autonomous self-governing communes throughout France. Indeed, they divided Paris itself into 48 sections. The name Paris Commune was chosen not because of its relation to the word "communism" (though this connotation was enough to galvanize frenzied **bourgeois** opposition), but to pay homage to a movement of the same name in 1792 that had done much to radicalize the **French Revolution** in the turmoil of that time.

The Paris Commune's defying of Thiers' bourgeois republic caused indignation in the National Assembly, which sat initially in Bordeaux before fleeing to the Palace of Versailles. The monarchist National Assembly refused to recognize the authority of the Paris Commune, and with neither party contemplating compromise, Thiers demanded that the revolt be ruthlessly crushed. The communards, rather than being able to concentrate on implementing their raft of radical reforms to hand control to workers, pursue anti-clerical measures, and execute the Franco–Prussian war, were instead forced to prepare themselves for invasion. The Versailles army, led by General Gallifet, slowly progressed, avenue by avenue, toward the center of Paris. Having seen in April their initial offensive on the forts of Mont Valerian repelled by the communards, the Assembly troops made steady gains, blockaded themselves in, and in the final days of May prepared for a final assault. On 21 May, the Versailles troops began a week of bloody fighting which would see some 25,000 people killed. The besieged communards burned down a number of public buildings such as the Hôtel de Ville, and executed a number of their prisoners including the Archbishop of Paris. Their resistance was brutally put down by Thiers' men, and any last vestige of hope they may have possessed was extinguished by the summary execution of the remaining communard leadership at the cemetery of Pére Lachaise, a site which was to become a shrine for socialists and **Marxists** everywhere. Following the demise of the Commune, the National Assembly undertook a series of fierce reprisals, imprisoning or executing 13,000 suspected Commune supporters, and deporting 7,500 to New

Caledonia. National Guard troops who had fought on the side of the Commune were arrested or executed, as the reactionary **classes** attempted to teach working class socialists and radicals a painful lesson. The inadvertent legacy of this was a widening of class divisions in France, as mutual hatred and bitterness reached new heights on all sides.

The Paris Commune was of immense importance to Marxists throughout Europe, if only through the legendary status it assumed among radicals as the first ever **proletarian** revolt. The violence that the Commune was met with, while slowing the march of revolutionary socialism in France, instilled in Marxian thinkers an awareness that radical revolution would be met with reprisals from conservative elements. **Karl Marx** himself claimed that the Paris Commune had represented the first step to full communist revolution, and in *The Civil War in France* (1871) he provided a description of events relating to the Commune that was later used by **Vladimir Ilich Lenin** to justify the **dictatorship of the proletariat** in Russia.

PARIS RISING (1848). When the newly established Second Republic failed to meet the political, social and economic demands of Paris' restless working classes, and furthermore curtailed much of what workers had gained in the years since the 1789 **French Revolution**, violence broke out in the French capital as radicals looked to bring about a further **revolution**. Turmoil never seemed far away between the February Revolution that created the Second Republic and the outbreak of violence in June. Elections at the end of April saw a reactionary government, bolstered by **peasant** votes, returned with a mandate to restore discipline and quash the **socialist** threat. The catalyst for disorder came on 21 June when the government announced plans to close down the National Workshops that guaranteed a safety net for the vulnerable of Paris. The Workshops, a working class gain of the February Revolution, supported a third of the adult population in Paris, but the new government saw them as an expensive **communist** experiment and decreed on 23 June to disband them inside three days, offering members the choice of army service, forced labor or dismissal instead. Confrontation had already been stirring between government and workers, with a vociferous demonstration on 15 May culminating in the appointment of the hard-line General Eugène Cavaignac to mobilize the National Guard for the defense of Paris.

Cavaignac was granted dictatorial powers to halt the street confrontations and restore stability. Restive Parisians continued to agitate against the government throughout June, and toward the end of the month erected hundreds of barricades in preparation for a showdown with Cavaignac's government troops. Following the National Assembly's diktat against the National Workshops, tensions snapped and on 23 June a vicious battle broke out. Cavaignac ordered three columns to march into Paris and destroy the barricades, making gradual progress in the north of the city. A day later on 24 June, aided by "red" hating National Guard soldiers drafted in from the provinces, his troops laid heavy siege on the Lamorcière region. By 26 June the Parisian rebels were surrounded by governmental troops in an ever-shrinking area to the east of the city, and Cavaignac's men pressed on for a final assault. With many of the rebels untrained and crippled by a lack of communication with their fellow units, resistance capitulated fairly swiftly, and on 27 June the rebellion was resolutely defeated with the indiscriminate shooting of 3,000 prisoners by the National Guard. In all, up to 10,000 insurgents and 6,000 National Guards perished in the fighting, and 4,000 Parisian workers were deported.

The immediate political beneficiaries of the rising were conservatives and monarchists, who had seen the radical threat diminished and the socialist experiment of the National Workshops condemned to history. Cavaignac himself relinquished his dictatorial powers on 28 June, but such was his popularity inside the reactionary National Assembly that he was subsequently named prime minister. However, it was Prince Louis-Napoléon Bonaparte who benefited most from the return to order, as a shell-shocked **bourgeoisie** and **peasantry** joined his Catholic and monarchist supporters to elect him president in 1851. The repression that had met the protests of the Parisian workers had social repercussions too, as French class relations were influenced and embittered for many years to come.

For **Karl Marx**, positive lessons could be drawn from the experience. He stressed that the 1848 Paris Rising had taught revolutionaries that the bourgeoisie could no longer be expected to play a progressive role as it had in France in 1789, as its fear of the working class outweighed its desire for reform and democratic rights. Instead, Marx proposed, the working class had now become the key dynamic for opposition and change in modern society.

PARTY OF DEMOCRATIC SOCIALISM. The Party of Democratic Socialism (*Partei des Demokratischen Sozialismus*—PDS) is the successor to the **East German Communist Party** (SED) that ruled in the **German Democratic Republic** until 1989. The PDS was founded by reformist elements of the SED who gradually moved the party away from its advocacy of **Marxism–Leninism** and toward moderate socialism. As of 2005, the PDS entered into an alliance named the Party of the Left (*Die Linkspartei*) with the Labor and Social Justice Party to bolster its insignificant support in the former Federal Republic of Germany.

PARTY OF LABOR OF ALBANIA. *See* ALBANIAN PARTY OF LABOR.

PASHUKANIS, YEVGENI BRONISLAVICH (1891–c.1937). A Russian legal theorist and one of the most significant contributors to **Marxist** theory of law, Pashukanis served as people's commissar for justice in 1936, before a change in Soviet legal theory toward "socialist legality" and away from Pashukanis' notion of the "withering away of law" led to his disappearance and presumed murder at the hands of **Josef Stalin's** henchmen. In his most notable work, *Law and Marxism* (1924), he argued that law is a historical form of regulation that occurs in societies based on **commodity** exchange, and is inappropriate for **communism**. He therefore argued for the "dejuridification" of the **Soviet Union** as part of the "withering away of law," with laws to be replaced by "technical regulation."

PEASANTRY. **Karl Marx** did not accord the same significance to the peasantry as he did to the **proletariat**. The former he saw as essentially a doomed **class** that would be swept aside by **capitalism**, while the proletariat represented the agent of **revolution** that would usher in **socialism**. Nevertheless, Marx did pay attention to the role of the peasantry in his various historical analyses, most notably in *The Eighteenth Brumaire of Louis Bonaparte* (1852), where he described the small-holding peasants as the class that provided crucial support for Louis Bonaparte and in whose interests he largely ruled. He also saw at least some radical potential in the peasantry, potential realized in the support given to bourgeois revolutions and, under proletarian leadership, in possible participation in a socialist revolution. The persistence of the peasantry as a class in capitalism led Marx to advocate nationalism of the land as a final means of eliminating this outdated class.

Subsequent Marxists such as **Vladimir Ilich Lenin, Mao Zedong** and **Frantz Fanon** gave greater attention and accorded more significance to the peasantry, which constituted the majority of the population in their respective countries. For Lenin the peasantry represented a truly revolutionary class, that hand in hand with the workers would overthrow the existing order allowing for a proletarian revolution to then take place. He saw the emancipation of the serfs in 1861 as having led to the creation of landless peasants working as wage laborers, akin to the proletariat in the urban areas. Ultimately, the leading role would still be fulfilled by the proletariat though. For Mao the peasantry was the leading revolutionary class in practice, and Fanon saw the peasantry as having the necessary qualities of collectivism, spontaneity and violent potential, along with a consciousness relatively untainted by the colonists' ideological outlook to enable them to be the key revolutionary class in colonized Third World countries.

PEOPLE'S REPUBLIC OF. *See* under individual country names, e.g., CHINA, PEOPLE'S REPUBLIC OF.

PERESTROIKA. Meaning "restructuring" this slogan was used in the **Soviet Union** during **Mikhail Gorbachev**'s period in office to refer to the changes in the economy and society with particular emphasis on greater private ownership of economic enterprises, a more market-oriented economy, and a general lessening and decentralizing of economic planning. Hand in hand with *glasnost*, *perestroika* was part of an overall attempt to democratize the Soviet Union, and eliminate corruption and economic inefficiencies. Gorbachev lost power and the Soviet Union broke up before the reforms could be completed.

PERUVIAN MARXISM. Arguably the most influential group in the history of Peruvian **Marxism** is *Sendero Luminoso* (Shining Path). A nominally **Maoist** collection of guerrilla fighters, the organization sought, largely through violent means, to bring about the destruction of Peruvian **state** institutions and their replacement with a peasant **communist** revolutionary regime. Taking their name from a slogan of the organization they defected from, the Peruvian Communist

Party ("follow the shining path of [**José Carlos**] **Mariategui**"), the group was formed in the late 1960s by a committed Maoist, Abimael Guzmán, later referred to as "Presidente Gonzalo." It was not until 1980 that they took up their armed struggle for power, a decision that led to the deaths of tens of thousands of Peruvians, including scores of fellow **Marxists**. By the middle of the 1980s, membership of Sendero Luminoso had reached its 10,000-plus peak, and the group controlled large stretches of rural territory. Here they were able to implement their own version of communism, banning **capitalist** ventures, enforcing prohibition, redistributing land, setting production targets and organizing an educational system. However, their reactionary policy of indiscriminate and callous violence toward their own people proved to be their downfall, as the **peasantry** largely rejected their rule, and the Peruvian government more tellingly enforced a phase of Martial Law that saw the 1992 arrest of the influential Guzmán and other Sendero Luminoso commanders.

The group subsequently dwindled in size, and exists today as a splinter faction, capable only of sporadic action and committed more to wrestling control of Peru's coca forests than pursuing their own vision of Marxism. Guzmán, a former university professor and the chief ideologue behind Sendero Luminoso, grandiosely declared his group's "Marxism–Leninism–Maoism and Gonzalo Thought" as the "new, third and higher stage of Marxism." In reality, the movement's contribution to Marxist thought amounted to little, as Guzmán championed revolutionary violence, emphasized the centrality of the **class** struggle and the **dictatorship of the proletariat,** and railed against **revisionism** in a manner witnessed on countless occasions since **Vladimir Ilich Lenin** came to prominence. The only difference was that all of this was meted out alongside a reactionary approach to violence that chimed more with the Marxism of **Josef Stalin**.

Elsewhere in Peru, a number of parties have at various times claimed to be the chief proponents of communistic ideas. The group *Sendero Luminoso* derived from the Peruvian Communist Party (*Partido Comunista Peruano-unidad*—PCP) claim to be the oldest Marxist party in the country, while the Communist Party of Peru–Red Fatherland (*Partido Comunista del Peru–Patria Roja*—PCP-PR) has also figured prominently. Additionally, the **Unified Mariateguista Party** (*Partido Unificado Mariateguista*—PUM) has presented itself as a **vanguard** revolutionary party which advocates a brand of market socialism similar to that practiced by the **Chinese Communist Party** as of 1978. In the 1980s the PUM joined other Marxist groups in the broad United Left (*Izquierda Unidad*—IU) coalition that unsuccessfully contested Peruvian general elections. However, the dominant left-wing organization in the country today is the Peruvian Communist Party–Red Flag (*Partido Comunista Peruano–Bandero Roja*—PCP-BR), a Maoist group containing former members of *Sendero Luminoso*.

PETROVIC, GAJO (1927–). A major **Marxist** theorist of the 20th century, Petrovic was a leading member of the Yugoslav "**Praxis**" school of Marxism. He studied at the University of Zagreb receiving a PhD in philosophy from there in 1956, and he worked as a lecturer and then professor at Zagreb throughout his career. He has written numerous books and articles, his most famous book being *Marx in the Mid-Twentieth Century* (1967), and he edited the influential journal *Praxis* for many years. Petrovic's Marxism is **humanist** in character and emphasizes Marx's theory of **alienation**. For Petrovic human beings are essentially conscious, creative, and free, an essence which is not expressed or developed in the course of their labor in **capitalist** society. The notion of praxis embodies the view that human beings create and change both the world they live in and themselves through their self-creative activity, and this distinguishes us from other animals. Marxist **revolution**, according to Petrovic, aims to abolish self-alienation through praxis, and to create a truly human society characterized by the free creative activity of human beings.

PETTY BOURGEOISIE. A term used by **Karl Marx** to refer to the middle **classes** lying between the **bourgeoisie** and the **proletariat** and typified by shopkeepers owning their own small businesses. The label class is used of the petty bourgeoisie in a loose sense as they constitute a social group or stratum rather than a fully fledged class in the **Marxist** sense. They have little political significance compared to the bourgeoisie and proletariat, although **Leon Trotsky** identified them as a key element of support for the fascists.

PLEKHANOV, GEORGII VALENTINOVICH (1856–1918). Known as the "father of Russian **Marxism**," Plekhanov was a hugely influential figure among Russian radicals including **Vladimir Ilich**

Lenin. Born into the Russian gentry he became part of the movement to the people by radical intellectuals. He joined the Narodnist Populist movement while still a student at military school, and soon became a leader of the populists' organization Land and Liberty. During this early phase of his political career he was arrested twice and in 1880 he was forced to flee abroad. Living in exile in Geneva he became a convert to Marxism, and in 1883 he helped to found the first Russian Marxist group, the **Emancipation of Labor Group**. In 1882 he published the first Russian translation of the *Communist Manifesto* and between 1889 and 1904 he was the Russian delegate to the **Second International**. In 1900 he co-edited the Marxist journal *Iskra* (The Spark) with Lenin, but his influence gradually declined after failing to embrace the 1905 **Russian Revolution**. Plekhanov sided with the **Mensheviks** against the **Bolsheviks**, and became increasingly critical of Lenin and his party for their "unprincipled" activities and for having attempted a **revolution** in 1917 in "violation of all the laws of history."

Plekhanov wrote a great many works of which *The Role of the Individual in History* (1908), *Fundamental Problems of Marxism* (1908) and *Development of the Monist View of History* (1895) remain as significant entries in the Marxist canon. For many years the source of Russian Marxist orthodoxy, he rejected what he saw as departures from Marx, notably **Eduard Bernstein**'s **revisionism** and Lenin's voluntarist deviation from the stages of historical development. He essentially put forward an economic **determinist** interpretation of Marxism that took the economic **base** of society to be all-determining. For Plekhanov Marxism was an all-encompassing worldview from which he derived an epistemology as well as a theory of history and political doctrines.

POLAND, PEOPLE'S REPUBLIC OF. Following the success of the Polish resistance to the Third Reich in World War II, a **Soviet Union**–sponsored **communist** regime emerged in Poland and ruled for over 40 years. Though predominantly following the orthodox **Marxism–Leninism** espoused from Moscow, there were a number of departures, and dissent remained, as expressed in the 1956 **Polish Uprising** and later the Solidarity movement. January 1947 saw Poland's first postwar parliamentary elections, heavily under Soviet influence, return a Democratic Bloc government with 384 of 444 seats going to the communist Polish Workers Party (*Polska Partia Robotnicza*—PPR). Eight months later Wladyslaw Gomulka, who also held the position of general secretary of the PPR, became prime minister, and set about merging his party with the Polish Socialist (Social Democratic) party. This was achieved in mid-December, signaling the foundation of the **Polish United Workers Party** (*Polska Zjednoczona Partia Robotnicza*—PZPR), and at the same time the subordination of the only other party pursuing a socialist agenda and the working class vote to the **Marxist** program of the former PZPR.

The monopoly of political power accomplished, the PZPR immediately set about implementing **Stalinist** measures. Industry was speedily nationalized, a **collectivization** plan launched, and police terror initiated to quash perceived oppositional activity. **Josef Stalin**, seeking to tighten the Soviet grip on its satellite states, instigated a purge of leading party, "opposition" and military members, the foremost casualty of which was Gomulka, replaced as general secretary in 1948 by Bolesław Bierut, and then arrested in 1951. This rush toward Stalinism also saw Poland become a founding member of the Council of Mutual Economic Assistance (Comecon), and in 1955 came adherence to the **Warsaw Pact**. In 1952 the Polish parliament, the Sejm, adopted a new, Stalinist, constitution. This was identical to that the Soviet Union had embraced in 1936, and in its renaming of the country as the People's Republic of Poland formally placed it alongside the other Soviet satellite states of the Eastern Bloc. The "People's Republic" moniker, decreed Marxism–Leninism, applied to those countries placed in between the historical stages of **capitalism** and **socialism**. The constitution called for the industrialized working class to act as the guiding light of the revolutionary movement, and work in unison with the **peasantry** to achieve the goal of communism.

However, the regime was soon to move away from rigid Stalinist policies. Alongside growing domestic unrest, primarily at the government's sudden decision to impose price increases, the death of Stalin in 1953 and his subsequent denunciation by **Nikita Khrushchev** resulted in the 1956 **Polish Uprising**. The outcome of this turmoil was the reappointment of Gomulka, released from prison in April 1956, as general secretary of the PZPR following the death of Bierut. Gomulka immediately proceeded with efforts to calm Polish unrest by rescinding the price increases. He then condemned the extremes of Stalinism, axed a number of orthodox Soviet leaders of the Polish government and military, allowed the reversal of collectivization and relaxed censorship on media and academia alike. Despite this early reformist agenda, by the beginning of 1960 Gomulka was gravitating more and more toward Marxist–Leninist orthodoxy. Relations between church and state hit a fresh nadir after the 1959 banning of religious instructions in schools, intellectuals faced repressive cultural policies that prompted the infamous 1964 "Letter of 34" censuring governmental interference in the arts, and in 1966 the PZPR attempted to limit the influential Catholic church's Millennial Celebration with the state-sponsored propagandistic Millennium Celebrations. There was, too, a 1968 pogrom of Jewish party members following the Arab–Israeli war, called for by Gomulka after Polish intellectuals had delighted in Israeli victory, thus, held the leader, making them part of a Zionist conspiracy. Such repression, as in 1956, was followed by rioting, chiefly among students demanding an end to intrusive party censorship. Having successfully put down these stirrings, the Gomulka government further indicated its support of Soviet orthodoxy by assisting the Warsaw Pact invasion of **Czechoslovaki**a that sought to halt the reformist 1968 **Prague Spring** and avowing its approval of the **Brezhnev Doctrine**. Yet, Gomulka's position was by no means secure, and when in December 1970 a wave of government price hikes was announced, protests emanating from the militant Gdańsk shipyards spread and brought an end to his leadership.

His replacement was Edward Gierek, whose first task on taking up the role of general secretary was to remove troops Gomulka had sent in to repress demonstrations. Having achieved this, like his predecessor had in 1956, Gierek reversed the price increases, and consented to a pay increase for industrial workers. The new leader also promoted initiatives to breed openness within the PZPR, and embraced a consumer-oriented approach to economics that saw trade with the West increase and the acceptance of aid from the **United States** and West Germany. It was these links to the western economy that resulted in a harsh economic downturn in Poland, though, as the 1973 oil crisis prompted a fall in Polish prices. As ever, in 1976 the government responded to economic decline with price rises that, true to form, were reversed following mass demonstrations, chiefly in Radom. There followed a surge in rebellion and opposition to the regime over the coming years. In September 1976 the anti-government Workers' Defense Committee (*Komitet Obrong Robotników*—KOR) was founded, and various intellectual groups calling for the government to adhere to the human rights pledges undertaken in its 1975 signing of the Helsinki Accords surfaced. This revolt was accompanied by a resurgence in power of the Catholic church that culminated in the rapturous visit to Poland of the first Polish pope, John Paul II. The most prominent oppositional movement, though, was still to come.

The Solidarity trade union, led by the charismatic Lech Walesa, was born out of the August 1980 strikes that had occurred in reaction to the Gierek government's demands for an increase in consumer production. Such was the magnitude of worker support for Solidarity that, in a firm break from orthodox Soviet policy, the government was forced to officially recognize and legalize independent trade unions in the Gdańsk Agreement of 31 August. Among other pledges, this document guaranteed the right of workers to take strike action, and loosened PZPR press and religious censorship. Gierek resigned in September, reputedly because of ill health, to be replaced as general secretary by Stanislaw Kania. Meanwhile, Solidarity gained prestige, power and huge popularity. It forced the government to announce a maximum working week of 41.5 hours, helped construct an agricultural trade union, Rural Solidarity, and gained such widespread support that at its first national congress in September 1981 it was able to announce that nine million Polish workers had joined their union, many having defected from the PZPR. Furthermore, governmental censorship of the media fell to its lowest level yet in the communist era, and elements of self-management, like those employed in **Josip Tito**'s **Yugoslavia**, entered much of Polish life.

In Moscow, alarm bells began to ring as the enormous influence of Solidarity in brokering these changes became clear. At the end of 1980, Soviet troops were deployed adjacent to the Polish border, their maneuvers sending out a clear threat that further departures from the orthodox Marxist–Leninist program could lead to military intervention. A continuous state of tension prevailed through 1981, with government repression of principal Solidarity figures and further exercises inside Poland from Warsaw Pact forces. In October, General Secretary Kania was replaced by Wojciech Jaruzelski. With the Soviet Union baying for the PZPR to stifle the rapidly budding Solidarity, one of Jaruzelski's first acts was to place Poland under a state of

Martial Law. Thousands of Solidarity organizers were immediately arrested, the group made illegal, and government troops sent into industrial workplaces to quell any resistance. The period also saw the PZPR-led banning and destruction of all organized trade union groups. Martial Law was proclaimed officially over in December 1982, but with pivotal individuals such as Walesa free once more to spread ferment, and the spirit of Solidarity merely dampened rather than drowned, the threat to communist hegemony in Poland remained real. As the decade progressed, reformers inside Poland attracted increasing support, and in 1986 Jaruzelski was forced to begin a program to banish Muscovite hardliners from the PZPR. Two years later the government made a tectonic plate-shifting announcement ushering in reforms to move Poland from a planned, subsidized economy toward the free market. The PZPR administration had come under scrutiny and criticism throughout the decade, as economic measures had resulted only in price increases and deteriorating living standards. Alongside this unrest, with **Mikhail Gorbachev**'s *glasnost* and *perestroika* initiatives in full swing the Polish government had little option other than taking such radical action in order to attempt to retain power. Concurrently with economic reforms, the government allowed an independent cultural and intellectual scene to flourish, and for the first time since the conclusion of World War II genuine freedom of speech existed.

In such an atmosphere of flux, encouraged by the still illegal Solidarity, mass strikes erupted across Poland in the summer of 1988, and the government, apparently at breaking point, consented to negotiations with Walesa. After the initial talks in August 1988 broke down, the historic "Round Table Talks" between Solidarity and the government proceeded in February 1989. The PZPR, grappling to hold onto office, offered Walesa and his union the chance to join the government. Having rejected the invitation, the upper hand was with Solidarity, and it seized the opportunity to the extent that by April an agreement had been thrashed out that granted political pluralism, freedom of speech, and most importantly free elections. These elections, held in June, returned an overwhelming Solidarity victory, and in August Tadeusz Mazowiecki was made prime minister of Poland's first noncommunist government for over 40 years. In January 1990 the PZPR was formally dissolved and replaced by the Social Democracy of the Polish Republic, and as elsewhere in the Eastern Bloc, the reign of Marxism–Leninism was categorically over.

The Marxism–Leninism practiced during the communist era in Poland was not always entirely in line with the orthodox doctrine emanating from the Soviet Union. Unlike in other Soviet satellite states, collectivization was never undertaken with any particular gusto, and at a number of junctures some relative intellectual autonomy appeared. There were repeated periods of unrest and protest that often led to the gaining of concessions from the government, and a vibrant youth culture emerged that was later to inform and encourage the movement to bring an end to communist rule. Opposition groups such as the KOR and Solidarity existed and often thrived, and along with the influence of the Catholic church ensured that the PZPR failed to attain political monopoly on the scale of other communist parties in the region. By the 1980s, with the collective Polish psyche deeply distrustful of Marxism–Leninism, the PZPR adopted a more pragmatic, opportunistic approach to governance that was more in line with western conservatism than communism. Polish Marxism, while in the main carrying out most Soviet diktats, did retain some independence, perhaps chiefly because of the country's historical tradition of dissent and opposition. It remained until its demise inside the Soviet umbrella, but not without distortions.

POLISH UNITED WORKERS PARTY. The Polish United Workers Party (*Polska Zjednoczona Partia Robotnicza*—PZPR) presided over the **People's Republic of Poland** from its foundation in 1948 until its collapse in 1989. Formed by virtue of a **Soviet Union**–stimulated monopolizing merger between the Polish Workers Party and the Polish Socialist (Social Democratic) Party, the PZPR initially embraced **Stalinism**. This gave way following the turmoil of the 1956 **Polish Uprising**, at which point the party repudiated much of its Stalinist past and committed itself to a more moderate form of **Marxism–Leninism.** Despite the PZPR's devotion to Moscow, there remained scope for limited ideological independence, allowing oppositional groups to remain relatively prominent. This helped pave the way for the events of the 1980s when the Solidarity trade union rocked the PZPR to its core, and forced it first into reforms and then out of existence. By January 1990, the PZPR's Marxism had gone the way of its grip on power, and it remolded itself into the Social Democracy of the Polish Republic (*Socjaldemokracja Rzeczpospolitej*

Polskiej—SdKP), in which guise it became a principal member of the Alliance of the Democratic Left.

POLISH UPRISING (1956). A series of revolts and rebellions that led to a number of liberalizing reforms in **Poland**. Disillusionment with **Stalinist** rule in Poland had been developing for some time, and the appetite for change was whetted following reforms enacted by the Polish government after the 1953 death of **Josef Stalin** that freed 100,000 political prisoners and abolished the detested Ministry of the Interior. Economic changes were also made, with alterations that would allow the system to take heed of consumer demand. The Stalinist system had come under increased criticism by Poles as a consequence of pressures from within Poland and proceedings in the **Soviet Union**. Writers and intellectuals expressed their resentment at the influence of Stalinism in popular culture, Polish Communist Party members grew fatigued at the subordination of their interests to those of Moscow, and economists urged the creation of a more flexible economic system in tune with Polish rather than Soviet needs. **Nikita Khrushchev**'s endeavors to gain a rapprochement in 1955 with **Yugoslavia** appeared to offer hope to those in Poland who believed in the validity of "separate roads to **socialism**," while the Soviet leader's denunciation of Stalin at the 20th Congress of the **Communist Party of the Soviet Union** in February 1956 seemed to legitimize calls for a break with Stalinism. Further hope that reform was imminent came when the Stalinist leader of Poland, Boleslaw Bierut, passed away, an event that allowed for election of the liberal Edward Ochab as first secretary of the party.

With indifference toward the Soviet regime rife, and glimmers of optimism that reform was possible frequent, revolt looked likely. In June 1956 industrial workers in Poznan began to strike against desperate economic conditions that had led to widespread hunger. The revolt was contagious, and soon a general strike began amid an atmosphere of constant protest and riot, with demands no longer merely economic but also political. What ensued was a massacre led by Soviet Deputy Minister of Defense Konstantin Rokossovsky, with 53 demonstrators left dead and hundreds more injured as the government clamped down on dissent. Nevertheless, the reformists' demands had achieved the support of both the majority of the population and important figures within the party. Aware that such will for change could not simply be swept under the carpet, the Polish communist regime looked for a leader who could achieve reform moderate enough not to cause concern for hard-liners, and yet far-reaching enough to appease reformists. Accordingly, Wladyslaw Gomulka was identified and duly elected as first secretary of the party at the end of October and, in spite of Soviet objections, he went about installing a new, liberal Politburo. Gomulka's masterstroke was to persuade Moscow of his ability to keep change to a minimum and curtail disturbance to the regime, therefore avoiding Russian invasion, the cruel fate that had met the 1956 **Hungarian Uprising**. In reality this amounted to discarding the liberal program that the reformists of 1956 had fought to implement, and by the conclusion of the next decade, Gomulka had developed into an orthodox communist leader firmly in the pocket of Moscow.

Following the lead of the **German Democratic Republic**, Poland was the second Eastern European country to strive for a release from at least some of the shackles of Soviet rule, and subsequently prompted similar attempts in **Hungary**. Such rebellions served as early warnings to the Soviet Marxist regime that it was far from infallible.

POL POT (1925–1998). Born as Saloth Sar, Pol Pot was prime minister and dictator of Cambodia between 1976 and 1979. He renamed the country **Democratic Kampuchea**, and instigated a repressive campaign to remodel the nation according to his own **communist** design. It is estimated that under his rule a million people died as a direct result of the actions of his regime, particularly in the notorious "killing fields."

Pol Pot became embroiled in **Marxist** ideology while on a scholarship to study radio electronics at the École du Livre in Paris. Here he became active in the Association of Khmer students, in particular the "Marxist Circle" of the group under the leadership of Ieng Sary. However, owing to poor results, Pol Pot's scholarship was withdrawn (a factor some have put behind his later persecution of intellectuals), and he was forced to return to Cambodia where he became a teacher. Having received his grounding in Marxism in France, Pol Pot was central to the inception of the Kampuchean People's Revolutionary Party (KPRP) in 1960, and became a member of its original Politburo. In 1962 he became KPRP general secretary, and the following year oversaw the transition of the party to an underground guerrilla campaign group that later became the **Khmer Rouge**. The group unsettled the governments of Prince Sihanouk and General Lon Nol, and by 1975 had utilized its strength in the countryside and taken power, heralding the birth of Democratic Kampuchea. Pol Pot, using that moniker for the first time, became prime minister of the Khmer Rouge regime in April 1976.

It took until September 1977 for Pol Pot to announce in a statement that the Democratic Kampuchea of the Khmer Rouge regime amounted to a front for **Marxist–Leninist** groups, chiefly the previously unacknowledged KPRP. The leader asserted that as relations with neighboring **Vietnam** were fractious, an increased emphasis on building and developing resources inside Democratic Kampuchea was imperative. In order to facilitate this, Pol Pot had set about bringing into fruition his vision of a **peasant**-dominated, fully agrarian society free from the shackles of the urban **proletariat** and **bourgeoisie**. However, the result of this was not the achieving of a revolutionary dream, but the death of hundreds of thousands of citizens, as Pol Pot initiated the forced migration of residents from the capital Phnom Penh to the countryside, with many executed on the way. Pol Pot had been correct to sense the depth of friction with Vietnam, as toward the end of 1978 the Vietnamese army invaded Democratic Kampuchea. The invasion was successful as Khmer Rouge troops fled into the jungles on either side of the border with Thailand, causing countless fatalities on their way. Pol Pot's regime had been deposed and Democratic Kampuchea had ceased to exist. The former dictator only officially resigned the leadership in 1985, and many suspected he was still pulling strings from his place of hiding in Thailand throughout the guerrilla-ridden occupied Cambodia of the 1980s. These fears were finally allayed when a United Nations–brokered peace occurred in 1991 between warring factions within Cambodia, establishing a coalition government following the withdrawal of Vietnamese troops two years previously.

Pol Pot's Democratic Kampuchea was the first socialist country to declare that contradictions between urban and rural dwellers, and physical workers and intellectuals, had been eradicated. This erasing of the metropolitan remnants of Western **imperialism** had been achieved by measures to eliminate the industrialized and the bourgeoisie, for instance through the abolition of a formal education system and mass-enforced migration to rural areas. The reality, however, was something far removed from a peaceful return to modest bucolic life. Pol Pot was captured in 1997, escaped the following year and was recaptured in April 1998, dying shortly afterwards.

POPULAR MOVEMENT FOR THE LIBERATION OF ANGOLA. The Popular Movement for the Liberation of Angola (*Movimento Popular de Libertação de Angola*—MPLA) was inaugurated in 1956 to work for Angolan independence from Portugal. That aim achieved in 1975, the MPLA set up the **People's Republic of Angola**, and under the leadership of **Agostinho Neto** pledged itself to "scientific" **Marxism–Leninism**. The MPLA had won control of post-independence Angola with aid from **Cuba** and the **Soviet Union**, and this proximity to the two communist states led to the organization's 1977 transformation from a movement of national liberation into a **vanguard party**. But its commitment to orthodox Marxism–Leninism was always undermined by the practical realities facing Angola, with its proximity to the anti-communist South Africa and a civil war–burdened economy which meant that private enterprise continued to exist and foreign companies retained considerable economic influence. In this context, Neto's 1979 replacement as party leader and president, the moderate José Eduardo dos Santos, began moving the MPLA toward reform. This renewal was hastened by the **collapse of the Soviet Union**, and by the 1990s, the MPLA had abandoned Marxism altogether, reemerging as a social democratic party with consistent electoral success.

POSADISM. An eccentric and marginal **Trotskyite** sect characterized by a belief in UFOs. Founded by Juan R. Posada (born Homero Cristalli 1912; died 1981), an Argentinian Trotskyite, the Posadists espoused an unorthodox form of Trotskyism that included advocating nuclear war to hasten the collapse of **capitalism** and a belief that UFOs were evidence of **socialist** aliens. In keeping with **deterministic** interpretations of **historical materialism**, the Posadists reasoned that since advances in technology bring about advances in society, then UFOs representing a more advanced technology than that of capitalism must be from a post-capitalist society, i.e., a socialist society. Aliens have never stayed for any length of time on Earth because human society is at a primitive pre-socialist level and therefore of no interest to them. Posadas himself wrote about flying saucers and socialism in his book *Les soucoupes volantes* (1968), and, while following the death of Posada in 1981 Posadism has itself become virtually extinct, Paul Schulz in Germany has been publishing Posada-inspired work into the 21st century.

POULANTZAS, NICOS (1936–1979). The most influential of **Louis Althusser**'s disciples, Nicos Poulantzas developed Althusser's **structuralist** approach applying it in the elaboration of a Marxist theory of the **state**. He also contributed to Marxist analyses of **classes** and fascism. Born in Greece, Poulantzas attended the University of Athens, followed by further study at the University of Heidelberg and then the University of Paris, where he was a student of Althusser. He held various academic posts in Paris, and politically he was active in the Greek Democratic Alliance, the Greek Communist Party and Greek Communist Party of the Interior, and also served as an advisor on education for the new democratic government of Greece after the collapse of the military dictatorship.

Poulantzas' chief contribution to **Marxism** lies in the field of political theory, particularly the area of state theory. While accepting the Marxist starting point that the state served the interests of the **ruling class**, he sought to elaborate a more sophisticated theoretical framework on this basic insight. According to Poulantzas the **capitalist** state did not automatically represent the dominant classes' economic interests, but rather represented their political interests. He also followed Althusser in distinguishing between the state's repressive state apparatus and **ideological** state apparatus. The former consisting of the army, police, judiciary and so on did not, as some orthodox Marxists believed, capture the entire nature of the state. The latter, consisting of schools, the media, churches and so on, was a vital part of the state and crucial in maintaining the dominance of the ruling class. Poulantzas also followed Althusser in stressing the relative autonomy of the state, the fact that it was a complex and contradictory sphere that could not be connected to the economic **base** of society in a simple, linear **deterministic** way.

He also contributed to the Marxist analysis of fascism arguing that earlier Marxist approaches, such as that of the **Third International**, had adopted an overly deterministic or economistic view of the relation between base and **superstructure**. The Third International view had been that fascism (or, as the Third International labeled it, "social fascism") was a product of economic backwardness. Poulantzas discussed fascism with reference to the notion of the "exceptional capitalist state," a form of state that includes **Bonapartism** and some military dictatorships. While the fascist states saw the continued "dictatorship of **capital**" they were also relatively autonomous. The military dictatorships of Spain, Portugal and Greece he also saw as "exceptional states" dependent on international capital and representing conflicting capitalist interests and classes.

Poulantzas' publications include *Political Power and Social Classes* (1968), *Fascism and Dictatorship* (1970), *Classes in Contemporary Capitalism* (1974), *The Crisis of the Dictatorships* (1975) and *State, Power and Socialism* (1978). He committed suicide in Paris in 1979.

PRAGUE SPRING (1968). Attempts in communist **Czechoslovakia** to implement liberal reforms and bring about Czech leader **Alexander Dubcek**'s vision of "**socialism** with a human face" were brought to an abrupt halt by the invasion of **Soviet** troops. The popular movement for reform was a reaction to economic and political disharmony throughout Czechoslovakia. Economic performance had been in decline throughout the decade, and this led many to believe that decentralization and increased free market involvement were necessary. Though this desire was acknowledged in the introduction of the "New Economic System" in 1967, for economic reformers such as Ota Sik the changes simply did not go far enough. Sik and his fellow agitators for economic change duly elected to join forces with the creative intelligentsia to call for political alteration. Together with schisms inside the **Communist Party of Czechoslovakia**, campaigning by this group and other discontented factions led to the replacement of Antonin Novotny as party first secretary with the reformist Alexander Dubcek in January 1968. In April Dubcek set about putting into service his "Action Program" to decentralize planning and management, and bring about competition using a market mechanism. The program was a giant nod to Sik's new economic model and set Czechoslovakia on the road to reform of economy and polity alike. Before *perestroika* these proposals were the most far-reaching and significant **communist** party-led blueprints aimed at bringing about a pluralist, democratic socialism anywhere in the Eastern Bloc.

What Dubcek termed "socialism with a human face" began to emerge, with human rights now assured, the introduction of an independent judiciary heralded, public participation in politics encouraged and the system increasingly democratized. The Czech system was undergoing a complete makeover, with enormous public support for the democratic reconstruction of the federal Czechoslovakian **state**. In June Ludvik Vaculik's *Manifesto of 2000 Words* embodied the spirit of the newly liberalized Prague, inspiring vast scholarly and creative outpourings and guaranteeing support for the government's reforms among the intelligentsia. Public debate blossomed as the Czech people embraced new levels of freedom of opinion and speech, and the communist party itself became a forum for discussions between hard-liners and reformers. The creation of a westernized civil society appeared imminent.

However, though reforms were enacted speedily, Dubcek still faced the opposition of conservative elements within the party attempting to bring a halt to reforms and a return to Soviet-style communism. In addition to resistance from inside, Dubcek's reforms attracted the angry attention of Moscow, and the Czech leader faced repeated calls from **Leonid Brezhnev** to halt a slide toward democracy that threatened the existence of the "socialist camp" in Eastern and Central Europe. In August the **Soviet Union** finally lost patience with Czechoslovakia and instructed **Warsaw Pact** troops to invade. The forces brutally repressed the liberalized Czech people, and the Soviet occupation began.

In April 1969 Dubcek was replaced as party leader by Gustav Husák, and with him went all the reformist gains of the Prague Spring. Husák's "normalization" policy saw half a million Czechs flee abroad, brought about two decades of corruption, and extinguished any hope of party-led reform in the country. The region had lost its best chance yet for reform. The deepest irony for those who had campaigned so vehemently for change in 1968 came when Soviet leader **Mikhail Gorbachev** announced a policy of *perestroika* that contained many of the reforms they had initiated as part of the Prague Spring prior to the **Red Army**'s invasion. By the time the Czechoslovakian regime finally collapsed in 1989, such was the extent of disgruntlement with the communist system that the ethos of the Prague Spring was largely eschewed by a public deeply skeptical toward the idea of reformist **Marxism**.

PRAXIS. The term praxis means practice or activity, but its use is intended within **Marxism** to denote something more than this. For **Karl Marx**, in the first place it denotes the activity by which human beings distinguish themselves from other creatures, a practice informed by consciousness and purpose. This is in contrast to much philosophy that identifies the distinctiveness of human beings in terms of abstract human reason or consciousness. Secondly, it denotes practical **materialism** as opposed to passive or abstract materialism. The latter conceives material reality as an object of observation or contemplation, as something essentially passive and separate from thought (which is active). The notion of praxis makes the point that human activity is part of the material world. Thirdly, praxis denies the existence of thought separate from thinking matter, i.e., the premise of **idealism**. The unit of theory and practice is a rejection of the abstractions of idealism as well as of contemplative materialism. Fourthly, it denotes practical philosophy, both in terms of the practical application of philosophy to reality, and in terms of the resolution of theoretical problems through and in practice. Finally, it denotes the role of human practice in constituting both society and human beings themselves.

Friedrich Engels, Georgii Plekhanov, Vladimir Ilich Lenin and **Josef Stalin** all gave attention to the notion of praxis, but conceived it largely in a narrow epistemological sense as a criterion of truth. **Mao Zedong** in his *On Praxis* (1937) stressed the unity of theory and action aspect, and **Antonio Labriola** and **Antonio Gramsci** both suggested the centrality of praxis in their descriptions of Marxism as the "philosophy of praxis." **Georgii Lukács, Karl Korsch, Herbert Marcuse** and the **Frankfurt School** generally contributed to the development of the theory of praxis, but the term and theory came to be most closely associated with what became known as the **Praxis School**, composed of a number of Yugoslav Marxist philosophers in the 1950s and 1960s, most notably **Gajo Petrovic** and Mihailo Markovic.

PRAXIS SCHOOL. This school of thought was named after the theoretical journal to which many of its proponents contributed and also after the central concept in their writings. Based in **Yugoslavia** the leading figures of the Praxis School include **Gajo Petrovic** and Mihailo Markovic. The Praxis School emphasizes the **humanist** character of **Marxism**. The notion of praxis embodies the view that human beings create and change both the world they live in and themselves through their self-creative activity, and this distinguishes us from other animals.

PREOBRAZHENSKY, EVGENY ALEXEYEVICH (1886–1937). Preobrazhensky was a significant figure in the **Bolshevik** party and in the newly formed Soviet state. He also made an important and lasting contribution to **Marxist** economic theory. Born in Russia Preobrazhensky joined the **Russian Social Democratic Party** (RSDP) in 1903, and in 1920 he was made a party secretary and member of the Central Committee. He was committed to industrialization and democratization of the **Soviet Union** and to international **revolution**. He opposed **Josef Stalin**'s bureaucratization and centralization of the party and advocacy of "**Socialism in One Country**." This led him to become a leader of the Left Opposition and to become linked to **Leon Trotsky** in the 1920s, a position that resulted in Stalin engineering his expulsion from the party. When Stalin embraced rapid industrialization as a key aim Preobrazhensky moved away from Trotsky and the Left Opposition and was allowed back into the party. However, Stalin did not forget his previous opposition and he was arrested in 1935 and shot in 1937 under Stalin's orders.

Preobrazhensky's main innovation in Marxist economic theory was his law of "primitive socialist accumulation." This was part of his theory of how to achieve the transition from **capitalism** to **socialism**, and in particular how to achieve the necessary industrialization in a backward agricultural economy such as Russia's. Without foreign investment or the possibility of self-development, industry had to be generated by squeezing agriculture, according to Preobrazhensky. He advocated establishing state trading monopolies to buy agricultural goods directly from **peasant** farmers at low prices instead of using the market. Industrial goods would be sold at high prices back to the agricultural sector, and this unequal exchange would make possible the financing of the expansion of industrial capacity. It would also have the advantage of reducing profits of rich peasants and preventing the development of capitalism in the countryside.

PROLETARIAT. This is the term used by **Karl Marx** to refer to the working **class**, and it is defined as the class within **capitalism** that does not own the **means of production**, the class that owns nothing other than its labor power. The proletariat is locked in struggle with the **bourgeoisie** which owns and controls the means of production, and by extension controls the **state**. Gradually developing in size, organization, and **class consciousness** the proletariat, Marx believes, will bring about **revolutionary** change, overthrowing capitalism and instituting **communism** after a transitional phase of the **dictatorship of the proletariat**. With the advent of communism and the abolition of private **property** the proletariat along with all other classes will disappear.

There are a number of significant problems with Marx's notion of the proletariat. First, Marx nowhere develops a theory of class and fails to offer more than a terse definition of the proletariat. This means that it is very difficult to determine exactly who falls into the category of proletarian. For example, managers, professionals, intellectuals and housewives/husbands are all propertyless, but it is not clear if they should be included in the proletariat since they do not create value and in the case of managers and professionals in particular they may earn vastly more than and see themselves very differently from a more typical member of the proletariat such as a factory worker. Also, there is the problem of the lack of a revolutionary consciousness emerging in the proletariat, which has led to some Marxists, such as **Vladimir Ilich Lenin**, arguing for a **vanguard party** to import revolutionary consciousness into the proletariat, and others, for example the members of the **Frankfurt School**, taking a more pessimistic view of the possibility of the proletariat being an agent of revolution at all.

PROPERTY. For **Marxists** property is a term with a specific meaning that excludes personal possessions. Property in Marxist terminology refers to the **means of production**, that is to say, the machinery, land, **capital** and so on required to engage in production. Property ownership is crucial in determining the **relations of production** and distribution, and different forms of property are the chief characterizing feature of different **modes of production** or stages of history. Private property or private ownership of the means of production is characteristic of **capitalism** and inimical to **socialism**.

– R –

RATIONAL CHOICE MARXISM. A term often used as a synonym for **analytical Marxism**, but while all rational choice Marxists are analytical Marxists, not all analytical Marxists are rational choice

Marxists. Rational choice Marxism differs from the broader school of analytical Marxism in its specific commitment to methodological individualism (the doctrine that all social phenomena can only be explained in terms of the actions, beliefs, etc. of individual subjects) and the use of rational choice theory in interpreting, developing and reconstructing Marxist theory. Analytical Marxism allows for methodological collectivism, for example, as found in the writings of the main founder of analytical Marxism, Gerry Cohen.

RECABARREN, LUIS EMILIO (1876–1924). Chilean theorist, activist and politician Luis Emilio Recabarren left an indelible mark on the Latin American workers' movement. Having joined the Partido Democrático in 1894, he set about radicalizing the impoverished **peasantry** of his homeland through education, chiefly via his editorship of the newspaper *El Trabajador*, and of the periodicals *El Proletario*, *La Vanguardia* and *El Grito Popular*. A conviction that **Marxist** literature comprised a crucial apparatus for the spread of **socialism** underpinned Recabarren's writing and editorial work.

Recabarren was elected to Congress for the *Partido Democrático* to represent the mining district of Antofagasta in 1906, but his refusal to take an oath of office that contained a pledge of allegiance to God saw him denied his seat. Having split with the Partido Democrático, in 1912 he founded the more explicitly socialist *Partido Obrero Socialista* (POS). Having unsuccessfully stood as presidential candidate for the party in 1920, Recabarren was elected to Congress in 1921, the same year in which he negotiated the dissolution of the POS and its supplanting with the *Partido Communista* (PC). He subsequently served in Congress under the banner of the PC. He also presided over a number of practical accomplishments in the trade union arena, organizing many of Chile's poor into unions for the first time, and playing a determining role in the creation of a **Marxist** labor movement centered around the Chilean nitrate mining region. This movement was the first of its kind in the region, and signaled Recabarren's success in putting Marxist theory into practice. Recabarren propounded an unparalleled system of worker control for Chile, with trade unions central at every point. His three-tier governmental system would consist firstly of industrial assemblies containing workers, secondly of municipalities run by delegates from these assemblies, and finally of a national assembly made up of delegates from the largest municipal territories and led by committees.

RED ARMY. The term Red Army refers to both the Soviet and Chinese armies. Under the guidance of **Leon Trotsky**, the Red Army of Workers and Peasants was founded during the course of the Russian Civil War, and, having superseded the **Red Guard**, became the established army of the new **Soviet Union** following the completion of the 1917 **Russian Revolution**. The actions of the Red Army were determined by the **Communist Party of the Soviet Union**, which installed in every unit a political commissar to overrule military officers should their commands run counter to official **Marxism–Leninism**. The Red Army existed as an enforcer of Soviet Moscow's will.

Following the German invasion in 1941, the Red Army initially suffered devastating territorial and human losses, its ill preparedness for attack obvious. Despite the loss of over seven million lives, however, it was able to turn its fortunes around with a series of masterful tactical displays, and declare victory in what the Soviet regime termed "The Great Patriotic War." In 1946 the Red Army was renamed the Soviet Army to mark the fact that it was no longer the enforcer of the **revolution** but the legal army of an established independent country. The army played a critical role in establishing the Soviet satellite buffer states of the Eastern Bloc. In the Cold War period, with a staff of up to five million, the Soviet Army was the largest operating force in the world, and used its might to crush the 1956 **Hungarian Uprising** and 1968 **Prague Spring**. Though the Cold War never heated up, the army saw action from 1979 in **Afghanistan**, where it helped install a **communist** government before entering into combat with militant Islamic, tribal, and nationalist forces who opposed the new regime. The war proved to be economically unviable, and new Soviet leader **Mikhail Gorbachev** called for a downsizing of operations in Afghanistan and elsewhere, in order to lessen the financial burden military spending had become. As part of this, Gorbachev reneged on the **Warsaw Pact**, demanding nation states resolve their own difficulties. The tide had already turned, though, and with democracy gradually taking hold in Eastern Bloc countries, the **collapse of the Soviet Union** left the Soviet Army with no country to protect. It was subsequently disbanded, its components distributed between the new sovereign states that developed out of the old Soviet Union.

The Chinese Red Army originated in 1927 and was created by Zhu De at **Mao Zedong**'s Jiangxi **soviet**. It was a key element in the Chinese communists success in defeating the nationalists and coming to power, and grew from around 22,000 in 1936 (after the **Long March**) to some 900,000 in 1945 and to a peak of four million in the 1970s. It was renamed the People's Liberation Army in 1946 and as such fought in Tibet, Korea and Vietnam among others, as well as being involved in the **Cultural Revolution** and the Tiananmen Square massacre.

RED ARMY FACTION. The Red Army Faction (*Rote Armee Fraktion*—RAF) was a left-wing terrorist group in Germany which carried out a series of high profile kidnappings and murders from the 1970s until 1998. The RAF, also known as the Baader-Meinhof Group, sought to bring about the collapse of the "**imperialist**" German system and supplant it with governance based on **Marxism**.

RED BRIGADE. Founded between 1969 and 1970, the Red Brigade (*Brigate Rosse*—BR) is a **Marxist–Leninist** terrorist organization in Italy, though by the 21st century its activities have largely ceased. Influenced by the writings of **Antonio Negri**, the BR advocated violence as a means of **class** warfare with which to force the disintegration of the Italian state and its replacement with a revolutionary Marxist system. To this end, its members kidnapped and assassinated state figures, most infamously in 1978 the former prime minister Aldo Moro. Following a spate of similar actions between 1984 and 1988, a police clampdown on the BR led to the arrests of several of its key leaders, and the group's activities subsequently dwindled. By 1989 the BR had all but disbanded, though it was connected with killings as recently as 2003.

RED GUARDS. The term refers to both the **Bolshevik** fighters established at the time of the 1917 **Russian Revolution** and also to the young, radical activists in the **People's Republic of China** (PRC) who zealously carried out the **Cultural Revolution**. In the Soviet Union the Red Guard was supplanted by the permanent **Red Army**, and in the PRC, after initially endorsing the Red Guards and their actions, **Mao Zedong** ordered their disintegration in 1969 when their extremism and violence spiraled out of control.

REIFICATION. The term reification is linked to the notions of **alienation** and **commodity fetishism**. It refers to the idea that human qualities, relations, actions and even human beings themselves are transformed in the course of **capitalist** production into things, and these things come to have power over human beings. **Karl Marx** implicitly discusses the phenomenon of reification in the *Economic and Philosophical Manuscripts* (1844), and explicitly analyses it in the *Grundrisse* (1857/58) and *Capital* (volume I, 1867; volume II, 1885; volume III, 1894). According to Marx, all the key elements of capitalist production, for example, the **commodity**, money, **capital**, profit, and wages, involve this process of reification. Social relations between individuals become thing-like relations between persons and social relations between things; social actions take the form of the action of things. Human creations become independent of their creators and human beings become subject to their own creations; human beings are governed by the system of commodity production that they created. The social origin of these economic creations, of wealth and value, becomes obscured, and **bourgeois** economists compound this mystification by presenting the attributes of these elements of capitalism as natural properties.

The notion of reification was given prominence in **Marxist** thinking by **Georgii Lukács** in his *History and Class Consciousness* (1923) in which the main chapter was devoted to "Reification and the Consciousness of the **Proletariat**." According to Lukács, commodity production entailed the key problem of fetishism, giving a relation between people the character of a thing and obscuring its origins. Reification gradually seeps into the inner life of society, even into the consciousness of human beings. Bourgeois society is in thrall to rationalism and rationalization, to the calculable and the measurable, and in the grip of a false consciousness that does not allow the social origins of capitalist relations to be perceived. The proletariat, its members treated as objects, as commodities, when it develops its class consciousness will actively rebel against reification and end it by ending capitalism. The place of reification in Marxist theory and its relation to other aspects remains a point of debate. For some it is a form or aspect of either alienation or commodity fetishism, while others see it as replacing the immature concept of alienation which was still rooted in philosophical **idealism**. In general, it has not received the same attention or been accorded the same importance as alienation and commodity fetishism.

RELATIONS OF PRODUCTION. This is a key term in **Karl Marx**'s theory of **historical materialism**. Relations of production, or production relations, consist of relations involved in actual production and relations which arise because production creates a need for them. To put it another way, they are the relations which exist between people, or between people and things, in the productive process. For example, the relation of a supervisor in a factory to the workers he supervises, the relation between a manager and his staff, the relations between employer and employee, between slave and master, between serf and lord, or worker and **capitalist** are all relations of production. Examples of relations of production between people and things involved in the productive process include ownership relations or **property** relations, such as the ownership of land or factories, or any **means of production**. Along with the forces of production, the relations of production constitute the economic **base** of society which shapes the character of the rest of society. A change in the forces of production leads to a contradiction between them and the relations of production, with the latter frustrating the development of the former. This produces a **crisis** in the mode of production which is reflected in the social and political spheres, and ultimately leads to **revolutionary** change.

RENNER, KARL (1870–1950). Moderate **socialist** Karl Renner was an Austrian social democratic theorist, a pioneer in the **Marxist** study of law, and twice chancellor of his home nation. Having joined the **Austrian Social Democratic Party** (SPÖ) in 1896, Renner represented it in parliament from 1907. In 1918 he became the first chancellor of the fledgling Austrian republic, a position he held until 1920, and following the end of German occupation in April 1945, the first chancellor of the second Austrian republic. Renner had also served as president of the Austrian parliament between 1930 and 1933. In December 1945 he was elected president of Austria by the parliament, a position he occupied for five years until his death in 1950. Renner led the right wing of the SPÖ, espousing a more reformist agenda than that of Otto Bauer, the leader of the dominant left of the party. In 1916 Renner's *Probleme des Marxismus* collection of essays was published. Here he attempted to modify the Marxist theory of **state** and of **class**, wishing to emphasize the impact of huge state intervention in the economy, and the rise of the new "service class" within the middle classes. His 1904 work, *The Institutions of*

Private Law and their Social Functions, offered a groundbreaking insight into the social functions of law from a Marxist perspective.

REVISIONISM. In one sense **Marxism** embraces revisionism based as it is on a constant **dialectic** between theory and practice, and with an emphasis on change and development. **Vladimir Ilich Lenin, Leon Trotsky, Rosa Luxemburg, Mao Zedong, Frantz Fanon—** the list could go on—all revised Marxism in light of the circumstances in which they found themselves. However, it is with **Eduard Bernstein** that the term revisionism has become most closely associated after he challenged the prevailing Marxist orthodoxy embodied in the writings and words of **Karl Kautsky**, the so-called Pope of Marxism. In the 1890s and early 1900s the **German Social Democratic Party**, of which Bernstein and Kautsky were leading figures, was the largest Marxist party in the world and espoused a very **deterministic** interpretation of Marxism with a belief in the inevitable collapse of **capitalism** and its replacement by **communism**. Bernstein highlighted the growing disparity between the **revolutionary** theory of the party and the reformist practice, and argued that the empirical evidence accumulated since the death of **Karl Marx** showed that many of his central predictions were false: the middle **class** was not disappearing as classes polarized into **proletariat** and **bourgeoisie**; immiserization of the workers was not growing; capitalism was not lurching from crisis to crisis and the collapse of capitalism seemed further off than ever. Bernstein's proposed revisions in the direction of a more open reformism and an ethical basis for Marxism were vehemently opposed not just by Kautsky, but also by **Rosa Luxemburg** who saw his evolutionary socialism as leading to a different goal from that of revolutionary socialism. Since this dispute revisionism has been used as a term of abuse with the intention of discrediting a viewpoint, the **Soviet Union**, for example, condemning **Josip Tito's Yugoslavia** and **Eurocommunism** as revisionist because of their challenge to the Soviet orthodoxy.

REVOLUTION. Karl Marx's theory of revolution is rooted in his **materialist** conception of history (**historical materialism**). In very schematic terms Marx sees the origins of revolutionary change beginning in the economic base of society where technological developments lead to changes in the **relations of production** and these in turn see the **superstructure** of society transformed. In other words, new **forces of production** will come into conflict with old institutions and social organization, newer, rising **classes** will come into conflict with old **ruling classes**, new ideas will conflict with established ones, and the result will be epochal change. There are certain material preconditions for **revolution** to occur, and without these no agitation or political slogans will make it happen. Marx's theory of revolution is concerned with the revolutionary leaps between different **modes of production**, for example from **feudalism** to **capitalism**. The next such revolution predicted by Marx is the **proletarian** revolution that will bring about a **socialist** society. Previous revolutions may have involved a transition from one mode of production to another, but they have still all been carried out by or on behalf of minority classes. The proletarian revolution will be the first carried out by and on behalf of the immense majority, and it will also be the first truly comprehensive social revolution bringing about the conditions for social as well as political emancipation. The proletarian revolution, instead of swapping the rule of one **property**-owning class for another, will do away with property altogether, and in so doing will bring about the abolition of all classes.

According to Marx's theory, the proletarian revolution would take place in the conditions of an advanced capitalist economy, where technology is advanced and a developed and organized working class in place. England met all the material conditions in terms of its development but lacked "revolutionary spirit." However, Marx was prepared to be flexible with regard to material economic conditions if other circumstances were favorable to revolution. For example, he allowed for the outbreak of revolution in less developed countries such as Russia where the **state** and ruling class were very weak, provided that the revolution quickly spread to the advanced industrial countries of Western Europe. He also suggested that in Germany, which was also relatively backward, a **bourgeois** revolution might take place immediately followed by a proletarian revolution forced through by the communists, who would create what he termed a "permanent revolution." In addition, Marx, while in the main advocating and foreseeing violent revolution, seems to have allowed for the possibility of peaceful change in countries such as England where democracy was sufficiently developed to allow the possibility of a proletarian party being elected to power.

Later Marxists developed and disputed Marx's theory of revolution. **Eduard Bernstein** in the **revisionist** dispute argued for a peaceful, parliamentary road to socialism against the militant revolutionary line of **Rosa Luxemburg**. **Leon Trotsky** meanwhile, picked up the notion of "permanent revolution" to argue that bourgeois and proletarian revolutions could be telescoped together without having to wait for bourgeois social relations to fully develop before instigating the **communist** revolution. Trotsky's view came to be one side of the dispute with **Josef Stalin** in the struggle for power after the death of **Vladimir Ilich Lenin**. Stalin, while not abandoning the goal of world revolution was less optimistic about the prospects of imminent revolution in Europe and so supported a more inward-looking doctrine of "Socialism in one country," that country being Russia. Lenin had followed Trotsky's argument in pre-revolutionary Russia, and supported by his own theory of **imperialism** and the **vanguard party** pushed through the **Bolshevik** revolution of 1917. **Antonio Gramsci**, seeing the failure of revolutionary attempts in Europe after the Bolshevik revolution, theorized a distinction between active and passive revolutions, with the former taking the form of violent uprisings and the latter referring to slow, patient "molecular change." **Eurocommunism** moved further towards gradualism and reformism, pursuing a democratic parliamentary road to socialism, while **China**, particularly under **Mao Zedong**, zealously promoted revolution around the world.

REVOLUTIONARY LEAGUE FOR THE INDEPENDENCE OF VIETNAM. *See* VIETMINH.

REVOLUTIONS (1848). A sequence of uprisings across Western and Central Europe sparked by the February **revolution** in France the revolutions of 1848 were characterized by radical economic and political demands, and in some cases a desire for national independence. The areas most afflicted by the unrest were France, Germany, Austria, Italy and **Hungary**, as the population of each of those countries reacted against autocratic rule, economic hardship and the failure of governments to suitably extend the franchise.

In France, the revolution in February resulted in the abdication of the reactionary King Louis-Phillipe and the end of the July Monarchy, the foundation of the Second Republic, the creation of the socialistic National Workshop scheme and the establishment of a provisional government. The French people, deeply afflicted by rising unemployment and a distaste for the king and his chief minister, François Guizot, had begun to riot against the authorities on 23 February 1848, sparked into doing so chiefly by the banning of an antigovernment banquet a day previously. The revolution was galvanized fully on 24 February as government troops began firing on demonstrators. Violent clashes followed, and by the end of the day both the king and Guizot had fled, and the Second Republic had been proclaimed. A provisional government comprising moderates and Louis Blanc's **socialists** was formed, and having recognized "the right to work," on 26 February they created the National Workshops, and on 2 March granted full male suffrage. Such rapid change coupled with constant agitation from workers on the streets of Paris backfired on the radicals, as a fear of **communist** revolution resulted in the April election of a reactionary government. However, though the revolution had been started primarily by a **bourgeoisie** yearning for political change, the working classes had become politicized and made revolutionary fervor their own, as later witnessed in the 1848 **Paris Rising** and the 1871 **Paris Commune**.

Invigorated by events in France, in Germany and Austria people began to demand change, and by the end of March 1849, monarchs in Prussia, some German states and Austria had consented to the formation of liberal dominated constituent assemblies. Rebellion began in Berlin in March 1848 when citizens constructed barricades and temporarily drove the ruling king, Frederick William IV, and his army from the city to the nearby garrison town of Potsdam. At the same time, an uprising in Vienna saw the avowedly conservative Prime Minister Klemens Metternich take flight, followed by the abdication in December of King Ferdinand and his replacement with nephew Francis Joseph I, who was now to preside over a new constituent assembly. Emboldened by events in Berlin and Vienna, in Frankfurt-am-Main a congress was convened by reformists to draft a liberal constitution that would unite confederate Germany. After much deliberation, the Frankfurt congress members elected to offer the crown of their newly united Germany to King Frederick William IV. However, the only consequence of the offer was a swift and unsuccessful conclusion to the revolution, as King Frederick refused the offer, counter-revolution in Prussia succeeded, and non-German minorities rebelled against the Frankfurt directive, the architects of which were paralyzed without the support of the monarchist Prussian army. The king's refusal meant unification was delayed for a further 23 years, and when it did occur it was to be led by military force rather than liberal reform. In the meantime, December saw King Frederick order the Prussian army to crush any remaining rebels in Berlin and then the rest of western Germany, something that they achieved with consummate ease, dousing the flames of revolution in Germany. While events were playing themselves out in Germany, the Austrian establishment was similarly attempting to crush the liberal rebellion. Metternich's replacement was Prince Felix Zu Schwarzenberg who, crucially, had control of the Austrian army and was accordingly able to quash rebellion throughout the country, and in September enter Vienna. The rebellion in the Austrian capital, like that in France, was becoming increasingly radicalized and the radical baton was passing from middle to working class. Fearful of the situation, the Austrian army violently put down the revolt, massacring workers to eventually restore order. Despite the return to order by the turn of the year, in both Austria and a number of German states liberal constitutions had been installed, and a radical spirit amongst the working classes of both countries had become inherent.

In Italy upheaval was also widespread. Republican rebellion had begun in Sicily, even before events in France, and antipathy towards Austrian rule in the Kingdom of Lombardy-Venetia had seen liberal Italian nationalists rouse the population into protest. The pressure applied led a number of rulers to grant concessions that only served to further heighten reformist demands and the level of protest, and for a fleeting time constitutional republican rule, under the tutelage of Giuseppe Mazzini, dominated in much of the country. In addition, Pope Pius IX was forced out of office, and large numbers of Austrians were expelled. However, ideological and regional schisms between reformist groups, the ever-present fear of radical change from within the Italian establishment, and the reinstallation of conservative administrations in Vienna and Paris left republican Italy extremely volatile. Sensing this fragility, Napoleon resolved to send forces into the country to restore the old order to power, and with the rebellion trampled into the ground, papal government was soon reinstated.

In Hungary, events in France, Italy and Vienna inspired Lajos Kossuth's "Springtime of Nations," as protestors took to the streets to demand the emancipation of **peasants**, wide-reaching civil rights, and independence from Austrian rule. Kossuth led the revolt, advocating an anti-Habsburg stance, and in April 1849 announcing a liberal constitution that would see Hungary become a republic under his charge. The new president set about instructing his forces to drive the Austrians from Hungarian territory in order to secure full independence. However, Kossuth's agenda did not fit with the desires of the various nationalities within Hungary's borders, and minority groups, chiefly the Croats, began to rebel. Austria, enraged by Kossuth's actions, called for Russian assistance to conquer the new Hungarian republic and return it to monarchical rule, and the Russian imperial army duly obliged. Independence for Hungary and the adoption of demands that came out of the revolution would have been plausible events had the upheavals elsewhere, and especially in Austria, not been crushed. Nevertheless, the Hungarian movement for reform and independence was alive, and its essence patently tangible during the 1956 **Hungarian Uprising**.

Meanwhile, in **Czechoslovakia** too, demonstrations for independence took place in Prague and the Pan-Slav Congress demanded autonomy within a federal Austria. In Great Britain, the Chartist movement led mass stirrings and demands for emancipation and civil rights.

The revolutions of 1848 stood apart from the uprisings that were to follow in the next century. Where events in the former were led by a bourgeoisie hungry for liberal reform that in turn led to mass working class demonstration and activity, revolutions such as those in **Russia** in 1905 and 1917 were led by political parties and organizations. Though each insurrection was ultimately subdued by counter-revolutionary forces and the old order restored, the origins of modern Europe had appeared, with the concepts of monarchy and **feudal** rule thrown into doubt, and the ideals of reform and liberal constitution commonplace.

Events across Europe in 1848 were important for the development of **Marxist** doctrine, and **Karl Marx** himself was quick to assert that like the 1789 **French Revolution**, those in Germany, Austria, Italy, Hungary and elsewhere were essentially bourgeois-led. A true socialist revolution leading to communism and the adaptation of Marxist **ideology** was impossible where **capitalism** was still under-developed, as was the case in each of these areas. Without an abundant, robust working class, created only in a fully developed capitalist society, revolutionary activity would be left to artisans and the peasantry who simply did not possess the progressive zeal of an industrialized mass **proletariat**. The revolutions of 1848 were important though in the development of the process to bring about that class, as only through liberal reform could capitalism and democracy thrive. Once they did so, an economic foundation and an institutional framework in which a radical working class could grow would be duly created. Still, 1848 did provide liberal reform and to some extent democracy, in so doing laying the groundwork from which a socialist proletariat would later emerge.

ROMANIA, SOCIALIST REPUBLIC OF. In accordance with the regional pattern, following the close of World War II Romania found itself embracing **Marxism–Leninism** as espoused by the **Soviet Union**. At the behest of Moscow, a **communist** government was installed in Budapest in March of 1945. The Soviets immediately set about pillaging Romania's natural resources, with the creation of the SOVROM agency in July to manage the expropriation of land and redistribution to the Soviet Union of foodstuffs. Despite the lack of ground support for the communists, such was the influence of the Soviet Union that by February 1948 the Romanian monarchy had been abolished and the **Romanian Communist Party** (RCP, then the Romanian Workers' Party) had assumed absolute control of the country's congress. The RCP embarked on a period of concerted Sovietization, nationalizing industry and financial institutions, beginning a mass **collectivization** program and creating a rigid, centralized economic system governed by target-led five-year plans. A constitution mirroring that of the Soviet Union was adopted in April 1948, and a **Stalinist** wave of elimination and terror, signaled by the creation of the Securitate secret police, took hold of society. The education system, the arts, culture and religion became mere mouthpieces of the righteousness of Marxist–Leninist ideals. The army was expanded and reformed into a force identical to the Soviet **Red Army**, and a commissarial structure of governance implemented, making the **state** subordinate to the RCP and the RCP to its general secretary. By the start of the 1950s, Romania had developed into a fully fledged satellite state of the Soviet Union, a status confirmed by Budapest's signing of the **Warsaw Pact** in 1955.

Romanian devotion to the orthodox Stalinist line was emphasized from 1956, the year in which the new Soviet leader **Nikita Khrushchev** heavily criticized the regime of his predecessor **Josef Stalin**. Where other Soviet satellite states used the denunciation to undergo a number of liberalizing and anti-Stalinist reforms, then General Secretary Georghe Gheorghiu-Dej and his RCP perceived no need for change, fearing it would undermine their reign. While they did bend slightly (for example, state terror was decelerated), the economy remained firmly command-based and centralized, and Romanian nationalism was employed to reassert any legitimacy lost through Khrushchev's potentially damaging words. There was to be no concerted effort to de-Stalinize as elsewhere, with the RCP using the opportunity to reaffirm both its grip on power, and the sway of Marxist–Leninist ideals in Romania. In adhering to the politics of the pre-Khrushchev Soviet Union, Romanian relations with Moscow began to worsen. This was further compounded in 1964 when Gheorghiu-Dej, who died the following year, signed an April Declaration that avowed individual nation's right to pursue their own domestic routes to communism free from Soviet interference.

On inheriting Gheorghiu-Dej's position as general secretary, Nicolae Ceauşescu began to further distance Romania from the Soviet Union, and steered the country towards a form of communist nationalism. The detachment developed into a rift towards the end of the 1960s, with Ceauşescu's scathing attack on Soviet intervention in the 1968 **Prague Spring**. The final push for the RCP to pursue an independent, nationalist route to communism came following a demand from the Soviet Union and other Eastern Bloc countries for Romania to halt its rapid industrialization program and concentrate on becoming the agricultural backbone of the region. This notion was abhorred by the defiantly Marxist–Leninist RCP, which in line with that **ideology** saw the creation of a militant urban **proletariat** as the route to communism. Its loyalty to the Stalinist mantra of breakneck industrialization to create this proletariat meant the chances of it consenting to the diktat were finite. Ceauşescu ordered instead an increase in industrial production, and began to utilize the ideas of separatist intellectuals to ideologically underpin the move towards independence, and to promote Romanian nationalist communism, or rather Stalinism.

Despite the RCP consistently pursuing an orthodox Marxist–Leninist line throughout its existence, in his early years Ceauşescu was to an extent a liberalizing force, presiding over cultural, economic and diplomatic reforms that led to visits from **United States** presidents including Richard Nixon. Such recognition from the West gave credence to one of the underpinning notions of Ceauşescu's nationalist Stalinism, that it would lead Romania to a more prestigious world position. However, from 1971 the emphasis was replaced on intense Stalinism and all the trappings of intolerance that entailed. Internal control deepened, and any acknowledgement of private enterprise that had occurred in the formative years of Ceauşescu's reign was discarded. The general secretary used RCP and state organs to build up a cult of personality around him and his wife Elena, instigating a brief "**cultural revolution**" in November 1971, and three years later obligating the Romanian Grand National Assembly to elect him the first ever president of Romania. Despite such clear devotion to Stalinism, Ceauşescu continued to forward his country's world position, and in 1975 Romania became the first communist country ever to gain most-favored-nation trade status with the United States. The nationalist element of Ceauşescu's doctrine had clearly not been sidelined but merely forgotten behind a cloud of Stalinist repression, and this was further underlined when he introduced special birth control measures to facilitate a rapid population surge.

As the 1980s began Romania faced a looming economic **crisis** caused by its ever-increasing foreign debt. Ceauşescu responded with a series of austerity measures designed to hasten repayment, the chief effect of which was a dramatic fall in living standards and the introduction of a rationing system for all basic goods. The impoverished Romanian people grew restless and impatient with Ceauşescu and his government. The leader responded in an insular manner, turning to his most ardent cronies and family, and attempting to re-legitimize his rule through the use of crass nationalism. He attempted to refresh the cult of personality he and his wife had previously constructed, undertaking a number of measures towards deification aimed at preserving his rule, including an infamous palace construction program in Bucharest that saw 10,000 residents displaced into slums. Such measures were aimed at strengthening Ceauşescu's nationalist Stalinism in the face of the emergence of the reformist **Mikhail Gorbachev** in the Soviet Union. A program of "systemization" was announced to stifle any last vestiges of an independent **peasantry**, further harsh economic demands were made, and popular revolts that occurred in response were heavily crushed by the armed forces and secret police. Yet with pressure rising and the inexorable atmosphere of ferment throughout the rest of the Eastern Bloc and the Soviet Union, Ceauşescu's days were numbered. Having called a demonstration for 21 December 1989 to condemn anti-government forces and reassert the validity of nationalist Stalinism, Ceauşescu took the podium only to be rendered inaudible by the screams of the baying crowd. The next few days saw further demonstrations, before both Nicolae and Elena Ceauşescu were arrested, summarily tried and found guilty of genocide and the destruction of the Romanian economy, then on 25 December 1989 dramatically executed. The successor government announced liberalizing reforms, and in May 1990 a free general election was won by the National Salvation Front, a group that contained many ex-members of the now outlawed RCP. Romania, in tandem with the rest of the Eastern Bloc, immediately set out on the road to democratization.

The Marxism promulgated by the RCP was consistently Stalinist in nature, and from the late 1960s the Romanian regime coupled Stalinism with nationalism in order to tread for Romania an individual path towards communism. Nationalist Stalinism and its chief proponent Nicolae Ceauşescu consistently ignored the will of Moscow once Stalin had passed away, but could not ignore the tide of change in the Eastern Bloc and the Soviet Union in 1989.

ROMANIAN COMMUNIST PARTY. The Romanian Communist Party (*Partidul Comunist Român*—PCR) was founded in 1921, though until after World War II it existed as a relatively minor organization. Having assisted in removing Romania's German Nazi occupiers, the PCR grew in strength to the extent that by 1947 it was in full control of the newly proclaimed **People's Republic of Romania**. The party quickly reconstituted itself as a clone of the **Communist Party of the Soviet Union**, firmly committing itself to **Marxism–Leninism**, installing a Central Committee and an all-powerful Permanent Bureau, as well as banning opposition parties. Under General Secretary Gheorge Gheorgiu-Dej, who in 1948 forced the Romanian Social Democratic Party into a merger and temporarily renamed the PCR the Romanian Workers' Party, the party embraced **Stalinism**, advocating **democratic centralism**, enacting the forceful **collectivization** of agriculture, and presiding over violent purges of perceived opponents. Gheorgiu-Dej's party scrupulously shunned **Nikita Khruschev**'s denunciations of Stalinist excess, moving Romania away from the **Soviet Union** and towards a nationalist form of **communism** that amounted to Stalinism in all but name.

His replacement as PCR leader in 1965 was Nicolae Ceauşescu, who further emphasized the split with Moscow by declaring Romania a "Socialist" rather than a "People's" Republic, and changing the party's name back to the PCR. Ceauşescu assembled a cult of personality around himself, meaning his hold over the PCR, state and society was seemingly impregnable, and from 1971 he moved further towards Stalinism, increasing societal repression and becoming an archetypal dictator. Thus, in the 1980s the PCR moved from its ideological position as the nominal **vanguard party** of the **proletariat** into a bureaucratic and monarchical juggernaut. This angered Romanians and by 1989 popular unrest had reached unprecedented levels. Ceauşescu and the PCR were toppled, and Romania became a multi-party democracy. Former PCR members formed the moderate and distinctly un-Marxist Romanian Party of Social Democracy, victorious in the 1992 elections but defeated four years later.

RONO FACTION. The Rono Faction constituted one position in a fierce debate, which began in the period 1927–37, between Japanese **Marxist** economists and historians regarding the nature of Japanese **capitalism** and the modern Japanese **state**. The Rono faction argued that the development of Japanese capitalism since the emergence of the modern Japanese state in 1868 meant that a movement toward an immediate **socialist** revolution was possible, the so-called one-stage **revolution** theory as opposed to the two-stage revolution proposed by their opponents in the **Koza faction**. They asserted that the Meiji Restoration in 1868 was a **bourgeois** revolution. For them, the high payments made by tenant farmers to landlords were not **feudalistic** transactions but reflected economic competition in a **commodity** economy between tenant farmers. It also viewed Japan as one of a number of **imperialist** finance capitalist nations. As such, the Rono faction has been seen as more universalistic than the Koza faction. The Rono faction strongly influenced the non-communist left parties of the prewar period and was the dominant influence on the left-wing of the Japan Socialist Party (1945–1996).

ROY, MANABENDRA NATH (1887–1954). One of the first Indian **communists**, Roy was notable for his involvement in the **Communist International** and his contribution to **Marxist** thought on colonialism. Born in Bengal, India, Roy was initially a nationalist **revolutionary** working to oust the British from his homeland. He spent some time in the **United States** where he discovered **Marxism**, and, also influenced by the 1917 **Russian Revolution**, he switched from nationalist to communist. By this time he was living in Mexico and he became general secretary of the Mexican Socialist Party in 1918 and was then invited to the Second Congress of the Communist International in Moscow. Staying in the **Soviet Union** he was sent to Tashkent to organize a training center for Indian revolutionaries, and he also contributed to the drafting of **Vladimir Ilich Lenin**'s *Theses on the National and Colonial Question*. In 1924 Roy was made a full voting member of the executive committee of the Communist International, and in 1927 he headed a Communist International delegation to **China**. The lack of success of this mission and increasing disagreements over policy led to his expulsion from the Communist International in 1929.

Roy returned to India in 1930 where he was soon jailed for six years for communist conspiracy. On his release he joined the Indian National Congress (INC) and formed the League of Radical Congressmen. He disagreed with what he saw as the conservatism of the leadership of the Congress and its Gandhian **ideology**, but he had faith in the revolutionary potential of the rank and file members. He supported the British government in World War II against fascism, and in 1940 left the INC to form the Radical Democratic Party. Roy hoped to unite workers, **peasants** and the **petty bourgeois** in a fight against feudalism, **capitalism** and **imperialism**, but the party had very little impact and was dissolved in 1948. At this point he made his final break with communism when he founded a new radical, humanist movement.

RULING CLASS. For **Marxists** the ruling **class** is the economically dominant class, and the economically dominant class is the class that owns and controls the **means of production**. With economic power comes political power, and **Karl Marx** saw the ruling class as controlling the **state**. Furthermore, the ruling class is intellectually dominant, which Marx expressed as, "The ideas of the ruling class are, in every age, the ruling ideas." The notion of a ruling class can obscure or oversimplify complexities of class rule. For example, as Marx himself notes in discussing various actual historical examples, the ruling class may be split into different sections, or may be difficult to determine, and the **Soviet Union** raised the question of whether or not its leadership constituted a new ruling class not defined in terms of its **property** ownership. The state itself may develop its own autonomy and interests separate from those of the dominant economic class, a complicating factor explored by **Nico Poulantzas** and **Ralph Miliband**. The issue of the ruling class's ideas being the ruling ideas is a further issue of debate within Marxism, with **Antonio Gramsci**'s notion of **hegemony**, and the **Frankfurt School**'s focus on **ideology** raising the question of the extent to which ideology is instrumental in maintaining class rule.

RUSSIAN COMMUNIST PARTY. *See* RUSSIAN SOCIAL DEMO-CRATIC LABOR PARTY.

RUSSIAN REVOLUTION (1905). The year-long agitation by peasants, industrial workers and sections of the armed forces against Tsarist rule that occurred in 1905 stood as a precursor to the successful 1917 **Russian Revolution**, and established a constitutional monarchy in Russia. The **peasantry**, suffering abject poverty, had become increasingly aggrieved by harsh repression from their landlords and the willingness of the reactionary Tsar Nicholas II to prop up a system that maintained **feudal** relations. With no legal outlet for their objections, the peasants were forced into the arms of socialist **revolutionaries**, and driven to direct action. Discontent over the losses of the disastrous Russo–Japanese War and harsh tax rises added to disillusionment, and brought urban dwellers in on the struggle. Industrial workers were hit hard by a recession that began in 1899 following a period of rapid growth and industrialization, and the resultant mass unemployment had bred a desire for wholesale change. Opposition to the Tsarist regime was led by an intelligentsia busily founding illegal, underground political movements and parties, for example the Union of Liberation, which came about in 1903 in Switzerland and united a number of liberal and **Marxist** figures in the name of demanding political reform in Russia.

The catalyst for direct action occurred on 9 January 1905 (22 January in the Gregorian calendar), a day subsequently referred to in Russia as "Bloody Sunday."

The day began with a peaceful procession of Russian workers, headed by Father Georges Gapone and brandishing little more than hymn sheets and models of religious icons, to the Tsar's Winter Palace in St. Petersburg. Here they presented a petition calling for economic and social reform, and then began to protest outside the palace gates. Having refused to disperse, the peaceful crowd was fired on by guards, and a day of violent clashes between the army and citizens of the city ensued, with up to 800 dead by nightfall. The events of Bloody Sunday had a cataclysmic effect on Russian society, as widespread demonstrations and strikes occurred all over the country, and an atmosphere of revolution was galvanized by the brutal repression of the Tsar's troops. The peasants' militancy increased and in July they formed the Peasants Union to organize rural protest, the October rail strike turned into a general strike, and sailors on the *Potemkin* battleship undertook a famous mutiny. Striking urban workers established committees to debate the course of action and other social matters affecting their class. The influence of revolutionary political parties, in particular the **Mensheviks**, escalated in the wake of such events, and **Leon Trotsky** was able to found his seminal St. Petersburg Soviet of Workers' Deputies, while the rise in trade unionism led to the formation of the Union of Unions. The overall aim of both the agitation and the reformist, negotiation-based tactics of the Union of Liberation was to attain a democratic, representative constitution and government, something that they attained, to an extent, in October 1905.

The "October Manifesto" consisted of a pledge from the tsar to create a representative "Duma" (Russian parliament) that would consider governmental legislation, and proclaimed the cessation of press censorship, the right to associate freely with any organization (including trade unions), and a widening of the franchise. The constitution, drafted and offered in the final two weeks of October by the government of Count Sergius Witte, was anathema for Tsar Nicholas II who desired a military dictatorship to facilitate a return to order, but was forced into political reform when a suitable candidate for dictator failed to materialize. However, even the concessions in the manifesto were not enough to bring an end to the violence and turmoil across the country, as revolutionaries and others on the left rallied against the fact that they were still bereft of a constituent assembly. In addition, strong nationalist elements came to the fore across the Russian empire, and, encouraged by reactionary groups such as the Russian Monarchist Party, instigated a series of violent attacks on intellectuals, revolutionaries, and the Jews, against whom the worst pogrom for 150 years was carried out. Following the announcement of the manifesto, the movement for constitutional reform fragmented into the conservative Octobrist and liberal Kadet factions, and the left imploded into those moderate liberals content with the reforms offered, and those, chiefly the **soviets**, unhappy at anything short of a full overthrow of the Tsarist regime.

The revolutionary movement of 1905, save for a brief **Bolshevik** uprising in Moscow in December and an attempted armed uprising on the Ekaterinin railroad, slowly fizzled out in the face of harsh government repression, and as most of the armed forces remained loyal to the tsar following their return from conflict at the end of the Russo–Japanese War in August, any chance of the peasantry and workers taking power by force dwindled. Trotsky's St. Petersburg Soviet was dispersed and banned by the police, and activities like that at Ekaterinin met with bloody reprisals from Tsarist troops. In July 1906 P.A. Stolypin, minister of the interior from February until that point, was made prime minister and soon went about firmly restoring autocratic monarchical rule, and a large Anglo–French loan was secured to restore Russian solvency. With such stability reached, the Duma was able to water down the October Manifesto and withdraw many of the concessions it had granted. Though the gains of 1905 were ultimately negligible in the view of revolutionaries such as Trotsky and **Vladimir Ilich Lenin**, the seed of revolution had been sown among the Russian people so that 12 years later it was to be an altogether different story.

RUSSIAN REVOLUTION (1917). In 1917 Russia underwent a seismic regime shift from the three-century old Tsarist dynasty to the birth of the **Soviet Union**, a transformation achieved through a year of reform and **revolution**, chiefly with the middle-class liberal, political revolution of March, and then the workers' Soviet revolution of November.

Twelve years on from the 1905 **Russian Revolution**, political liberals had grown frustrated at the lack of fruits that that initial action had borne them. Tsar Nicholas Romanoff II had become distanced from his nation, with the role of Rasputin causing widespread consternation amongst the Russian people, a people entirely dismayed by their lack of input into state policy. As Russia began participation in World War I, society was polarizing at an alarming rate for the Tsarist regime, with Nicholas II and his tiny clique of followers pitted against the revolutionary will of vast swarms of the Russian people. Russian involvement in the conflict became an unmitigated disaster, with technological and productive backwardness resulting in heavy losses, including some six million dead and wounded soldiers. As the beleaguered Russian troops struggled to get supplies of food and fuel to their country, the revolutionary climate threatened to boil over. On 7 March workers at St Petersburg's principal industrial plant, the Putilov factory, began to strike for better pay and working conditions, at which point they were ejected from the premises by their employers.

The following day, the now redundant workers joined with protestors attending an International Women's Day rally against food shortages and lack of fuel. The group began to agitate outside factories all across St Petersburg, so much so that by 9 March their numbers had swollen and 200,000 people, half of the city's industrial workers, were on strike. This increase in numbers was accompanied by flourishing radicalism amongst the strikers, who were in turn suppressed by heightened police violence. Yet the revolutionary tide proved difficult to stem, and when army troops began to lose faith in the Tsarist regime (including those Cossacks of the St. Petersburg garrison who refused to shoot down protestors on March 12th), the collapse of the regime appeared imminent. Unlike in 1905, those calling for change had large sections of the armed forces on their side. Inside the Duma, liberals demanded a government accountable to parliament, while professional revolutionaries capitalized on the disillusionment outside the corridors of power, with a rise in support for the **Bolsheviks** and their allies, such as **Leon Trotsky** and those in the **soviet** movement, throughout Russia. At the same time, a group of **socialist** leaders formed a temporary executive to recreate the St. Petersburg Soviet of Workers' Deputies that had been a catalyst for radical action in 1905.

In response to these tumultuous events, a newly formed provisional committee inside the no-longer meek Duma requested that in order to attain stability, Tsar Nicholas II should abdicate with immediate effect. On 15 March, in the face of a crippling lack of backing from the generals of the Supreme Command of the Russian Imperial Army, the tsar did so, and also passed over the right to rule of his haemophiliac son Alexei. Nicholas hoped that his brother the Grand Duke Michael Alexandrovich Romanoff would take the reins, but when he declined the offer of power, a Provisional Government was installed to guide the revolution along moderate lines, and maintain Russia's war effort against Germany. The Provisional Government was formed by the committee that had called for Nicholas' renunciation of power in consultation with the Soviet group, and ruled by the progressive liberal Constitutional Democratic Party (Kadets) and the conservative Octobrists. The prime minister was the reform-minded Prince Georgi Lvov, and he presided over an offer to members of the Soviet to join the government, an offer declined by the group which, alongside other radical **Marxist** factions, thought it best to remain in opposition at that particular juncture. While this period of "dual power" vested formal authority in the Provisional Government, the Soviets possessed the backing of a large majority of the population and, crucially, the military garrison. Inevitably, tensions between the Provisional Government and the Soviet were never far from the surface. The former held constitutional power, benefited from fear of the rebelliousness of the masses, and represented middle and even upper-**class** views, while the latter embodied physical power, championed further revolution, and commanded the support of the army and workers. Growing discontent with increased economic hardship and constant wartime defeat swayed many ordinary Russians towards support for the radical Marxist program of the Soviets.

The time bomb of friction between the two groups finally exploded in May over the issue of war aims. The primary goal of the first Provisional Government was victory in World War I and the imperial gains it would bring, and all other matters were to be deliberately neglected until this had been secured. Conversely, the Soviet demanded cessation of conflict to be followed by a democratic peace that featured no annexations or indemnities on any side. On 1 May Provisional Government Foreign Minister Professor Pavel Milyukov presented a note announcing that Russia had entered into an Entente agreement to continue the conflict until victory had been assured, and then strip Germany of much of its financial and natural wealth. When this became public, demonstrations of soldiers and workers broke out on the streets; the desires of the Soviets and their many supporters had been completely ignored, and the Russian people were outraged. The popular pressure was too much for a government living in fear of a restless workers' revolutionary movement, and Milyukov, along with Octobrist leader Alexander Guchkov, was forced to resign. Lvov remained as prime minister, and appointed the socialist Alexander Kerensky minister for war, while Soviet representatives were included in a new coalition cabinet which included **Menshevik**, Tradovik, Popular Socialist and Socialist Revolutionary party representatives. The Bolsheviks, however, remained outside of the coalition and continued to call for a fully Soviet Bolshevik government comprising only the working classes, as outlined in **Vladimir Ilich Lenin**'s April Theses (Lenin had returned to Russia in that month, with Trotsky following him in May).

Support for the Soviet movement was gathering pace, and as radicalization spread further amongst the population, in June the first all-Russian Congress of Soviets convened in the city, with 400 representatives of Soviets from all over Russia present. Disenchantment with the Provisional Government intensified yet again in July, when news of Kerensky's disastrous campaign against the Germans at Galicia reached home. The offensive, despite early gains, was crushed by the Germans, and with it so too was the will of the army. In Russia people began to question the wisdom and capability of the Provisional Government, and Lenin's Bolsheviks seized the opportunity to court military and worker support for their campaign to hand **state** power to the Soviets. Spontaneous demonstrations, later known as the "July Days," once again erupted on the streets of St. Petersburg, with an angry populous demanding that the Provisional Government be replaced with the All-Russian Central Executive Committee of the Soviets, and calling for Russia's withdrawal from World War I. However, after two days of violent siege, as a consequence of a lack of direction within the movement and a number of troops remaining loyal to the government, on 18 July the July Days came to a halt with hundreds dead and no Soviet power secured. The failure of the insurrection led Lenin to believe more than ever in the importance of a **vanguard party** to direct and lead revolution.

However, the July Days did succeed in forcing Prime Minister Lvov to resign. His replacement, Kerensky, announced in early August the formation of a coalition government containing 10 socialist members and seven non-socialists. Yet this did not represent a swing towards allowing Soviet power, as Kerensky instigated a period of repression against Bolsheviks and other revolutionary figures that saw Lenin flee to Finland. Kerensky's new cabinet was enough, though, to cause grave concern for the political right in Russia. Alarmed too by the leftwards sway of public opinion, Russian reactionaries and centrists transformed the new prime minister's Moscow state conference into a rallying cry for bringing about a return to authoritarian rule and crushing revolutionary fervor. It was thus decided that General Lavr Kornilov, commander-in-chief of the Russian armed forces, was the "strong man" required for the job. At the end of August, Kornilov sent troops towards St. Petersburg. Their aim was to displace and arrest Kerensky and his ministers, put down any revolutionary uprisings, and install the General as the head of a military dictatorship. This attempted coup ended only in disaster for Kornilov, as socialist railwaymen refused to move his troops, and Soviet activists in St. Petersburg persuaded his men there not to fire on "their brothers." Instead, Kornilov's men joined in the mobilization to defend the city, and the attempt ended only in acrimony and arrest in September for Kornilov. For the Bolsheviks, to an extent alienated following the failures of the July Days, the outcome was far more positive. They gained renewed legitimacy from the rest of the Soviet movement as a result of their willingness to fight tooth and nail for the cause, and from the ever-radicalizing public attained increased support that was fuelled by the popular rumor that Kerensky played a part in the Kornilov plot. It was in this more favorable atmosphere for the Bolsheviks that Lenin was able to return to Russia in October, and call for an armed uprising against a Provisional Government now led dictatorially by Kerensky, the four-man cabinet of which included two senior military figures.

All this made the second, this time worker-led, revolution of 1917 inevitable, and on 7 November, not merely by coincidence the day of the Second All-Russian Congress of Soviets, the Bolsheviks seized power from Kerensky, and the transformation of Russia from Tsarist autocracy to Soviet **dictatorship of the proletariat** began. Aside from taking root in the volatile political landscape of 1917, revolution also came about as a response to the desperate situation of a great number of Russians. Industrial production had plummeted, the transportation system hit stasis, and fuel and raw materials had grown ever more scarce. In the countryside widespread hunger looked set to turn to famine, prompting **peasant** revolt and seizure of land, and soldiers were deserting the army in great numbers in spite of continuing war with Germany. Thus, with political and social conditions perfect for a Bolshevik tilt at gaining power, and the party now the majority force in the Soviet Congress, Lenin launched the revolution on 6 November. Kerensky's Provisional Government were rapidly overthrown by the Bolshevik-led force of armed workers (or "**Red Guard**"), soldiers and sailors in a relatively bloodless coup organized by the Military Revolutionary Committee of the St. Petersburg Soviet. Lenin's timing was impeccable as he was able to exploit the Provisional Government's acute failure to offer any answers to Russia's multiple crises, and use the Bolshevik hold on the Soviets to call for and obtain the seizure of power in cities across the country. The Bolsheviks were well aware that the Russian people were fatigued with the Provisional Government's insistence on continuing World War I indefinitely, and Lenin promised, and in the shape of Brest-Litovsk delivered, peace. In doing so, he gained the vital backing of sizeable elements of the armed forces, a lesson perhaps learned from the failures of the July Days. It was left to Leon Trotsky to announce the dissolution and arrest of the Provisional Government, save for Kerensky who had already fled. In unison, soldiers and workers proclaimed the Bolsheviks the legitimate governors of the country at the All-Russian Congress of Soviets, and the Soviet of People's Commissars (Sovnarkom), with Lenin as chairman, was created as the new legitimate ruling body.

To ensure the continued backing of the extensive peasantry, the new government set about enacting radical land reforms and encouraged peasant seizure of land to bring about the elimination of aristocratic social and economic muscle. The major consequence of this was the Peasant Revolution of 1918, where mass land seizures and the expropriation of noble property greatly improved the lot of the rural poor and strengthened their support for the Bolsheviks. Urban support was maintained and cultivated by the Bolshevik pledge to put bread on the tables of Russian industrial workers and their families. In July 1918 the Soviet constitution was announced, and Lenin shifted governance from St. Petersburg to Moscow. Counter-revolutionary forces had begun resistance against the Bolshevik revolution immediately in its aftermath, and this soon sprouted into a fully fledged civil war between Trotsky's **Red Army**, and the anti-Soviet White Army. Lenin took Russia into a ruthless period of "war communism," with the chief casualties being the peasants, as their bread, meat and grain were commandeered for supply to the cities in the name of the war effort. Ultimately, the counter-revolutionary forces of the White Army suffered greatly from their inability to knit together and fight as one, and by 1921 Lenin was able to proclaim the existence of the Soviet Union. What developed next was the creation of the **Marxist–Leninist** dictatorship of the proletariat, in reality the creation of a boundless bureaucratic state that eventually paved the way for the authoritarian rule of **Josef Stalin**.

The character of the second revolution of 1917 was more in keeping with the idea of a Marxist workers' revolution. The March Revolution, though spontaneous and with the backing of the Russian proletariat, was essentially **bourgeois** and moderate in nature, and failed as it attained the support of only a minority of the armed forces. In contrast, the November Revolution was closer to the Marxist conception of a **proletarian** insurrection, a planned, precise operation led by a vanguard party (the Bolsheviks) swept into power with the backing of the proletariat, peasantry, and most of the armed forces to implement a radical program.

RUSSIAN SOCIAL DEMOCRATIC LABOR PARTY. Founded in 1898 in Minsk, Russia, the Russian Social Democratic Labor Party (Rossiiskaia Sotsial-demokraticheskaia Rabochaia Partiia—RSDRP) initially lacked rules, a program and much in the way of organization until its second congress in 1903. Here the party both established itself in terms of both doctrinal and organizational substance, and here it also split into two rival factions that became known as the **Bolsheviks** and the **Mensheviks**. The two factions were led by **Vladimir Ilich Lenin** and **Yuli Martov** respectively and they split over the issue of party organization with Lenin favoring a tighter, more active and committed party membership and Martov advocating a broader, looser and less participatory one. Lenin's faction gained control of the Central Committee and ultimately of the party. In 1917 the party changed its name to Russian Social Democratic Labor Party

(Bolsheviks), and again in 1918 to Russian Communist Party (Bolsheviks). In 1925 yet another name change saw the party labeled the All-Union Communist Party (Bolsheviks), and finally in 1952 the party became the **Communist Party of the Soviet Union**.

– S –

SAKISAKA, ITSURO (1897–1985). Born in Fukuoka prefecture, Japan, the son of a company employee, Itsuro Sakisaka attended the Economics Department of Tokyo Imperial University graduating in 1921, but staying on as a teaching assistant. In order to study German he read the works of **Karl Marx**. In 1922 he went to study in Germany and was able to amass a substantial collection of books on **Marxism**. After his return to Japan, he was hired as an assistant professor at Kyushu Imperial University rising to full professor in 1926. He contributed to the journal *Labor-Farmer*, but because of increasing police repression of the far left and pressure from inside his own university, Sakisaka was forced to resign his professorship in 1928. He then moved to Tokyo where he began a translation of the collected works of Marx and **Friedrich Engels**. In 1937 he was arrested as part of the First Peoples Front incident and briefly imprisoned, and even after his release his speaking and writing activity was prohibited so he lived as a farmer until the end of the Pacific War in 1945. After the war, he was restored to his post in Kyushu University.

In 1951 he joined with Hiroshi Yamakawa in the formation of the *Shakaishugi Kyokai*, which became the theoretical center of the left wing of the Japanese Socialist Party. With Kaoru Oita and Akira Iwai he criticized the reunification of the Socialist Party in 1955 after it had split into two separate parties in 1952. Upon Yamakawa's death in 1958, he became the key figure in the *Kyokai*. In addition to his university teaching and speaking activities, he gave lectures for socialist and labor activists in his home and held study groups to educate workers at locations throughout Japan. The intensity of and intellectual forment created by the infamous Miike Miner's Strike of 1960 in Fukuoka where he worked, lived, and was most active can be largely attributed to the educational activities of Sakisaka.

When the Japanese Socialist Party tried to transform itself into a more competitive political party in the early 1960s, however, Sakisaka attacked the reformers as "**revisionists**." *Kyokai* activists joined with the faction of *Kozo Sasaki* to defeat the movement toward change, and at the same time, increased Sakisaka's influence in the party. In 1967, the *Shakaishugi Kyokai* split into the Oita faction and Sakisaka faction but most delegates to the JSP party conferences remained Sakisaka supporters so his influence was undiminished.

The JSP, however, began a period of slow electoral decline in the late 1960s. By the 1970s, younger party activists were dissatisfied with the grip of the old left-wing leadership of the party, and Oita joined with reformer Saburo Eda to oppose Sakisaka's influence in the party. When Eda was verbally abused by *Kyokai* members at the 1977 JSP party conference, it became one of the causes of Eda's split to form his own party the following year. As other intellectuals became more interested in European-style social democracy, Sakisaka continued to be firmly to the left to the extent that he was elected a member of the Soviet Institute for **Marxism–Leninism**. After his death in 1985, his papers and extensive collection of books in Japanese and German were donated to the Ohara Institute at Hosei University in Tokyo.

SANDINISTAS. The Sandinista National Liberation Front (*Frente Sandinista de Liberación Nacional*—FSLN), more commonly known as Sandinistas, ruled Nicaragua from 1979 until 1990, attempting to transform the country along **Marxist**-influenced lines. The group formed in the early 1960s, and spent the first two decades of its existence engaged in a guerrilla campaign against the dictatorship of Anastasio Somoza, receiving backing from **Cuba** which remained a close ally when the Sandinistas took office. With popular revulsion towards Somoza rising, in 1978 the Sandinistas encouraged the Nicaraguan people to rise up against his regime. After a brief but bloody battle, in July 1979 the dictator was forced into exile, and the Sandinistas emerged victorious. With the country in a state of morass, they quickly convened a multi-interest five-person Junta of National Reconstruction to implement sweeping changes. The junta included rigid Marxist and long-serving Sandinista Daniel Ortega, and under his influence Somoza's vast array of **property** and land was confiscated and brought under public ownership. Additionally, mining, banking and a limited number of private enterprises were nationalized, sugar distribution was taken into state hands, and vast areas of rural land were expropriated and distributed among the **peasantry** as collective farms. There was also a highly successful literacy campaign, and the creation of neighborhood groups to place regional governance in the hands of workers.

Inevitably, these socialist undertakings got tangled up in the Cold War period **United States**, and in 1981 President Ronald Reagan began funding oppositional "Contra" groups which for the entire decade waged an economic and military guerrilla campaign against the Sandinista government. Despite this and in contrast to other **communist** states, the government fulfilled its commitment to political plurality, prompting the growth of opposition groups and parties banned under the previous administration. In keeping with this, an internationally recognized general election was held in 1984, returning Ortega as president and giving the Sandinistas 61 of 90 parliamentary seats. Yet, in the election of 1990, the now peaceful Contra's National Opposition Union emerged victorious, and Ortega's Sandinistas were relegated to the position of the second party in Nicaraguan politics, a status they retain today.

The Marxism of the Sandinistas offered an alternative to the **Marxism–Leninism** of the Soviet Bloc and elsewhere. This emanated from the fact that the group attempted to blend a Christian perspective on theories of liberation with a fervent devotion to both democracy and the Marxian concepts of **dialectical materialism**, worker rule and **proletariat**-led **revolution**. The result was an arguably fairly successful form of **socialism** cut short by regional factors.

SARTRE, JEAN-PAUL (1905–1980). The prolific, erudite Jean-Paul Sartre significantly influenced the spheres of 20th-century philosophy, politics and literature. The Parisian began his intellectual life at the select École Normale Supérieure, and in 1929 he graduated with a doctorate in philosophy. While serving as an army meteorologist in World War II, Sartre was captured by the Germans but released due to ill health in 1941. He was able to flee to Paris and become a key actor in the French Resistance, helping to found the ephemeral group *Socialisme et Liberté*. In the period following Allied victory, Sartre became increasingly politicized and by 1957 considered himself a **Marxist**. He was involved in the foundation of the *Rassemblement Démocratique Révolutionnaire*, a group which aimed to cross all political lines and appeal to the consciousness of every individual.

Sartre advocated **communism** but never joined the **French Communist Party** (PCF). Nevertheless, he stayed close to the organization until 1968, finally breaking with it in that year after having become disillusioned with its pro-**Soviet** stance on events in **Hungary** in 1956, its role in the Algerian war of liberation, and what he perceived to be its betrayal of the Paris May **Revolution** (Sartre felt the PCF had aided the restabilizing of the ruling establishment at a time when it was suffering an acute crisis).

Following this break Sartre associated with a number of minor **Maoist** "groupscules," and edited the government-banned *La Cause du Peuple* journal. Throughout this time, he was a committed human rights and peace activist, condemning Soviet concentration camps, in his 1952 work *The Communists and Peace* and protesting vehemently against the Rosenberg executions. He also signed a manifesto opposing the Cold War, and attended the 1954 World Council for Peace meeting in Berlin. Sartre was unflinching in his criticisms of Soviet foreign policy, attacking the invasions of Hungary and **Czechoslovakia**.

Sartre was concerned with marrying existentialist ideas of self-determinism with communist principles holding that socio-economic influences beyond individual control determine human existence, for example in his essay *Between Existentialism and Marxism* (1972). The existential theme of Sartre's *La Nausée* (1938), in placing a stress on the power of unconscious things over living beings, echoed **Karl Marx**'s concept of **commodity fetishism**, the criticism of the hold commodities exert on humans. Sartre used his *Search for a Method* (1963) and *Critique of Dialectical Reason* (1976) to promote a popular, politically activist existentialism and assert that only **dialectical**, and not analytical, reason can be used to understand the project of human history. Every member of a society, despite the contradictions and vicissitudes throughout the progress of history, has total responsibility for the rest of mankind, and so the course of that history is ultimately rational. It is questionable whether the key existential tenets of free will, individuality and the meaninglessness of life can be reconciled with the **determinism**, collectivism and teleological strands of Marxism. For some the *Critique of Dialectical Reason* represents a critique of Marxism itself, but Sartre saw himself as engaged in a Marxist theoretical project drawing on Marx rather than the vulgarized **ideology** of later Marxists.

SCIENTIFIC SOCIALISM. One of the preferred terms of **Karl Marx** and **Friedrich Engels** to describe the form of **socialism** they put forward. This term was particularly used to distinguish Marx's socialism from the unscientific, utopian socialism of Robert Owen, Charles Fourier and Henri Saint-Simon and their followers. Engels' *Socialism: Utopian and Scientific* (1880) set out this distinction, arguing that the earlier socialists had made the error of conjuring up a vision of socialism in their imaginations and believing that it could be achieved by a moral critique of existing society and an appeal to the good sense and reason of rulers and people without any recognition of the **class struggle** and the role of the **proletariat** in the **revolutionary** overthrow of **capitalism**. **Marxism**, according to Marx and Engels, involved a rigorous analysis of capitalism, identifying its inherent contradictions and necessary tendencies, from which its inevitable collapse and the possibility of socialism were derived. There is some tension between Marx the scientist and Marx the revolutionary, the critiques of the former seeming to fall into outraged moral condemnations and calls for revolution under the influence of the latter.

The scientific status of Marxism has been taken seriously by a great many Marxists including **Karl Kautsky, Eduard Bernstein, Georgii Plekhanov, Vladimir Ilich Lenin, Nicholai Bukharin, Josef Stalin, Leon Trotsky, Soviet Marxism, Austro-Marxism** and **Louis Althusser**. The exact nature of Marx's approach has been disputed, and other important Marxists have rejected the scientific label entirely, including **Georgii Lukács, Herbert Marcuse**, and **Jean-Paul Sartre**.

SECOND INTERNATIONAL. Founded at the International Workers' Congress in Paris in 1889, the Second International was a loose association of **socialist** and workers' political parties and trade unions. It was dominated by the very strong German social democratic movement, although it also included representatives from most of the major working-class organizations in Europe. The political parties affiliated to the Second International were supported by some 12 million voters in elections in their home countries, and had a total membership of around four million. Ideologically the Second International was dominated by **Marxism**, although other viewpoints were represented, most notably anarchism until the anarchists were expelled in 1896. The individuals whose interpretations of Marxism held sway were first and foremost **Friedrich Engels**, **Karl Kautsky** and **Georgii Plekhanov**, with the ideas of **Vladimir Illich Lenin** and **Rosa Luxemburg** also being influential. The Second International was primarily concerned with developing and coordinating strategy and tactics and with establishing common policies for its member organizations. Congress meetings were held every two to four years, and an International Socialist Bureau administered and coordinated the affairs of the International. Four notable issues dominated debates within the International. The first was the issues of the extent to which member organizations of the Second International should work with **bourgeois** governments, and the Paris Congress of 1900 decided that as a temporary expedient such cooperation was permissible. The second issue concerned modifications of Marx's ideas and in particular the questions of whether reform or **revolution** was the appropriate road to **communism**, and if a Marxist ethics should be developed. The Amsterdam Congress in 1904 condemned the leading **revisionist** thinker **Eduard Bernstein** who argued for a modified Marxism that embraced a Marxist ethical code and sought to achieve communism through a gradualist, electoralist strategy. Third was the issue of colonialism and whether or not there were circumstances when it was progressive as a civilizing force. The Stuttgart Congress in 1907 decided against colonialism ever being acceptable. Finally, the Second International policy on war was also decided at the 1907 Congress. The resolution was to try to prevent war between countries, but if it should break out, to exploit the situation to bring about the collapse of capitalism. The outbreak of World War I in 1914 tested this resolution and saw the major parties in the Second International all back the war efforts of their own countries. This departure from **internationalism** and descent into nationalism led to the collapse of the Second International.

SENDERO LUMINOSO. *See* PERUVIAN MARXISM.

SERGE, VICTOR (1890–1947). Born Victor Lvovich Khibalchich in Brussels to Russian émigré parents, Serge developed into a journalist, novelist and revolutionary activist. Initially he was a member of the *Jeunes Gardes* socialist faction, but grew intolerant of their commitment to reformism and began, while in Paris, to embrace libertarian anarchism. Having played a part in the unsuccessful Barcelona uprising of syndicalists, Serge moved on to the **Soviet Union** in 1919, joining the **Communist Party of the Soviet Union** (CPSU) on arrival in St. Petersburg, and using his editorial, linguistic and journalistic skills to gain employment with the **First International**. Having been instrumental, alongside **Grigori Zinoviev**, in the formation of the Comintern, in the autumn of 1923 Serge helped plan the aborted insurrection in Germany through his role as a representative of that body in Berlin and Vienna. Serge returned to the Soviet Union in 1926 and joined the Left Opposition to **Josef Stalin**. Accordingly, he was ejected from Stalin's CSPU in 1927, and in 1930 exiled to Central Asia, before being expelled from the Soviet Union altogether in 1936. In subsequent years Serge dedicated his life to using the power of literature to agitate against the Soviet Union, authoring novels exposing the purges, for example *The Case of Comrade Tulayev* (1950). Having initially moved to France, Serge fled to Mexico following the Nazi advance on Paris. He died there in 1947.

Serge's autobiography, *Memoirs of a Revolutionary 1901–1941* (1980), offers little in the way of theory, but does provide a meticulous insight into early 20th-century radicalism in Russia and Europe. Here, and elsewhere, Serge advanced a critique of **Soviet Marxism** for its apparent contempt of individual human rights, suggesting that the outcome of the **Bolshevik** revolution had merely been a reaffirmation of the necessity of democracy, and he became one of the earliest critics to label the Soviet Union totalitarian.

SLOVO, JOE (1926–1995). Slovo, born in Lithuania, was a principal figure in South African politics throughout the struggle to end apartheid, serving as general secretary and then chairman of the **South African Communist Party** (SACP), and as the first white member of the African National Congress (ANC) national executive. Having graduated in law at Witwatersrand University, Slovo was renowned as a defense lawyer in political trials. As a consequence of his SACP activities, from 1950 he lived under certain restrictions, having been black-listed under the Suppression of Communism Act. In 1956 he faced further repression due to his membership of the Congress of the People, as he and other Congress members were charged, and later acquitted, with treason. Following the Sharpeville shootings in 1960, Slovo was again detained, this time for four months as the South African government declared a state of emergency. Slovo was a member of the Central Committee of the SACP from 1969 until its dissolution in 1983, when he served on the revolutionary council of the ANC.

Slovo was chief of staff of the ANC's military wing, *Umkhonto we Sizwe* (UWS), almost from its inception up until 1987, and in 1963 he left South Africa to work externally for UWS. While away from South Africa, Slovo continued to work for the SACP, ANC and UWS, and was able to set up an operational center for the ANC in Maputo, before the **Mozambican** government entered into an accord with South Africa bringing a halt to these activities. In 1986 he became SACP general secretary, a post he held up until 1991 when he resigned owing to ill health, and was duly elected party chairman. Slovo occupied various governmental and party positions in the years leading up to his death, including a position at the Convention for a Democratic South Africa where he assisted in the drafting of the new constitution.

Slovo was the symbol of the guerrilla war against conservative Afrikanerdom, and as such a figure of much distaste to the right who perceived him to be the **Marxist** theoretician plotting the struggle. This hard-line reputation was enhanced by Slovo's unstinting support of the **Soviet Union** and in particular the much-maligned **Leonid Brezhnev**. However, Slovo did oversee the SACP's adoption of a 1989 program which accepted negotiation and compromise as a method to achieve **communism**, in opposition to the revolutionary dogma of its past. In addition, Slovo's 1989 booklet, *Has Socialism Failed?*, committed the SACP to multiparty democracy and individual liberty.

SOCIAL DEMOCRATIC FEDERATION (SDF). The Social Democratic Federation was the first political group in the United Kingdom to openly advocate **Marxism**. Founded in 1881 as the Democratic Federation and changing its name to the SDF three years later, under the guidance of **Henry Hyndman** the organization emphasized the centrality of **class struggle** to attaining a Marxist **revolution**. The SDF numbered in its ranks **Edward Aveling**, **Eleanor Marx**, William Morris and **John MacLean**, and was instrumental in organizing widespread demonstrations against low wages and unemployment in 1886–87. Through encouraging such protests to develop into a state of riot, the SDF sought to move Great Britain toward revolution, a doctrine that provoked strong condemnation from **Friedrich Engels** who stressed the ill preparedness of Britain for such tumult. In advocating violence, Hyndman alienated some SDF members, and even before the demonstrations of 1886–87 Aveling, Marx and Morris had left to found the **Socialist League**. In 1900, along with the **Independent Labour Party** and trade union leaders, the SDF affiliated to the Labour Representation Committee (LRC) to promote the cause of **socialism** within parliament. However, a year later the SDF broke away from the LRC, which eventually developed into the British Labour Party, as a result of its failure to force the group to recognize class struggle as the chief dynamic of societal change. In 1911 Hyndman founded the **British Socialist Party** to contest general elections on a mandate filled with SDF principles, though the party failed to win a single seat, and disbanded during World War I over Hyndman's steadfast support for the Allies in the conflict. The SDF continued as an independent organization until 1939, though it was eventually swallowed up by the British Labour Party.

SOCIALISM. There is a history of socialism that both pre-dates **Marxism** and has developed independently of Marxism. The word "socialist" was coined by followers of the Welsh reformer Robert Owen in a cooperative magazine in 1827. The word "socialism" was first used by followers of the French thinker Henri Saint-Simon in a publication called the *Globe* in 1832. By 1840 the term was in common usage throughout Europe where it meant, more or less, the doctrine that ownership and control of the **means of production** should be held by the community as a whole and administered in the interests of all.

But the appearance of the word at this date does not necessarily mean that socialism did not exist beforehand. Some socialists claim a heritage stretching back to the slave rebellions in the Roman Empire, with Spartacus, the leader of the most famous of the slave rebellions in 73 BC, in struggling for the freedom and equality of slaves embodying basic socialist aspirations. In England the forerunners of socialism can be tracked at least as far back as the 14th century and the Peasants' Revolt. The **peasants** sought an end to some of the harsher aspects of **feudal** life, and a greater degree of freedom, aspirations which again appear to be consistent with socialist sympathies.

Another example often cited is Sir Thomas More who in 1516 wrote his book *Utopia* in which he put forward a vision of a society where there is no private property and no exploitation of the poor by the rich. Moving forward to the 17th century, the Diggers movement stands out as an expression of socialistic sentiments in its challenging of the rich, and its championing of the poor and their right to land. "Gracchus" Babeuf and the Conspiracy of Equals at the time of the **French Revolution** was a notable example of socialism in the 18th century, and in the early 19th century Robert Owen, Charles Fourier, Henri Saint-Simon, and the English Chartists were the more immediate forerunners of **Karl Marx**.

The very broad range of thinkers and ideas collected under the heading socialism make it difficult to define with any precision. In general, attempts at characterizing socialism highlight notions of equality, liberty, community, and an economic view based on a critique of **capitalism** and embracing some alternative that emphasizes common ownership and planning. On this basis it is possible to subsume Marxism under the heading socialism.

Marx sought to distinguish his socialism from that of his predecessors and rivals by claiming for it a scientific status, and by rejecting the idea of socialism as an ideal to be strived for. Marx saw socialism as the outcome of a historical development, specifically the tendencies within capitalism that would see socialism emergence as the negation of capitalism. In describing their socialism, Marx and Friedrich Engels did not favor the word Marxism and used a variety of terms instead including **communism**, "critical **materialist** socialism," "critical and **revolutionary** socialism," and "**scientific socialism**."

Vladimir Ilich Lenin picked up on a distinction made by Marx in *The Critique of the Gotha Program* (1875) between the first phase of communist society when **classes**, a **state**, with distribution according to work done, and various aspects of the former capitalist society will still exist, and the higher stage, which will be communism proper and as such stateless, classless, with distribution according to need, and so on. Lenin in his *The State and Revolution* (1917) identified the first phase described by Marx as socialism, and subsequent Marxists have largely adopted this usage. Hence, communist parties such as the **Communist Party of the Soviet Union** have ruled countries they themselves describe as socialist (the Union of Soviet *Socialist* Republics). The leaders of countries such as the **Soviet Union** claimed they were in the socialist first phase while always moving toward full communism. **Leonid Brezhnev**, for example, described the Soviet Union during his leadership as a form of "developed socialism." Marxists for many years disputed the status of these "really existing socialism" countries, and whether or not they constituted socialism in the **Leninist** sense of a transitional, post-capitalist stage on the way to communism.

SOCIALISM IN ONE COUNTRY. A **Soviet** slogan summarizing **Josef Stalin**'s approach in opposition to that of his rival for power, **Leon Trotsky** who advocated "**permanent revolution.**" The slogan refers to the policy of building **socialism** within the borders of the **Soviet Union** rather than seeking to pursue the **revolution** immediately abroad. From one perspective the policy represented more of a difference in emphasis, with international revolution still a goal toward which resources were devoted through the **Third International**, but in another respect the policy represented a vastly different approach, a turning inward and toward nationalism. Without revolution in adjacent countries and in the industrialized countries of the world in particular, the nature of socialism in the Soviet Union inevitably took on a very different character from that envisaged by **Karl Marx**.

SOCIALISME OU BARBARISME. Formed by a faction defecting from the French wing of the **Fourth International**, *Socialisme ou Barbarisme* (Socialism or Barbarism) offered from 1948 to 1966 a **Marxist** analysis of society at odds with orthodox **Trotskyite** and **Leninist** ideas. Elucidating their doctrines through a journal of the same title, they amassed an influence quite disproportionate to their negligible size, chiefly as a result of the outstanding analytical prowess of their pivotal talisman, Cornelius Castoriadis.

Socialisme ou Barbarisme railed against the bureaucratic megalith the **Soviet Union** had become, and portrayed a bleak future in which the two expansionist Cold War superpowers led the globe into a third world war. The only alternative, they held, was their version of **socialism**, hence the name Socialism or Barbarism. This entailed the handing of power through a "radical-socialist **revolution**" to rank and file workers, thus superseding the pitfalls of bureaucracy plaguing both **communist** and **capitalist** societies. This would eradicate traditional hierarchical struggles plaguing civilizations run according to both doctrines. Naturally critical of **Stalinism**, *Socialisme ou Barbarisme* also condemned Trotskyism claiming that the ideology no longer possessed an "independent ideological basis for existence," as Trotskyite thought was forever confined to defining itself in terms of its opposition to Stalinism.

By the mid-1960s, Castoriadis had begun to criticize Marxist thought, in particular questioning the modern value of historical and economic **determinism**. With the chief doctrinaire losing belief in the doctrines, the 40th and final issue of the journal was published in mid-1965, and shortly afterwards the group disbanded.

SOCIALIST LEAGUE. Created in 1884 and an offshoot of the **Social Democratic Federation**, the Socialist League included in its ranks **Eleanor Marx**, **Edward Aveling**, William Morris and Belfort Bax, and promoted **Marxist** ideas until taken over by anarchists in the 1890s.

SOCIALIST PARTY OF AMERICA (SPA). Founded in 1901 from factions of the Social Democratic Party, the Socialist Labor Party, Christian Democrats and others, the Socialist Party of America was committed to peaceful, democratic reforms as a means of achieving **socialism**. By 1912 it had 118,000 members, 1,000 of whom were in public office, and its candidate for the American presidency, **Eugene Debs**, gained 900,672 votes. Opposition to **United States** involvement in World War I led to a number of its members, including Debs, being imprisoned. The 1917 **Russian Revolution** saw the party split with **Bolshevik** sympathizers forming their own **communist** party. Support for the party declined after this with various splits and mergers marking its history and no party of its name existing today, although the Social Democrats, United States of America, and the Socialist Party of the United States of America both have their roots in the SPA.

SOCIALIST REPUBLIC OF. *See* under individual country names, e.g., ROMANIA, SOCIALIST REPUBLIC OF.

SOCIALIST UNITY PARTY OF GERMANY. Created by a **Soviet Union**–induced merger of the **German Communist Party** and the

German Social Democratic Party, the Socialist Unity Party of Germany (*Sozialistische Einheitspartei Deutschlands*—SED) governed the **German Democratic Republic** for its entire existence. The SED inflexibly pursued a **Marxist–Leninist** course and party direction was perennially shaped by Moscow. Despite desperately attempting to avoid the process of *glasnost*, the SED ceased to exist as a Marxist organization soon after the toppling of the **Berlin Wall**. In 1990 it became the **Party of Democratic Socialism**, and in that guise has remained influential in both national and local politics.

SOMALIA, DEMOCRATIC REPUBLIC OF. Having gained power through a military coup in 1969, **Muhammad Siad Barré** and his **revolutionary** associates attempted to transform Somalia into a **Marxist** state. Barré became president of the Supreme Revolutionary Council on 15 October 1969 following the assassination by a police officer of President Dr. Abdirashid Ali Shermarke. Government leaders faced instant arrest as the new president's army abrogated the legislative and declared in 1970 the official state adoption of single-party **scientific socialism**. To usher in **socialism** a number of Marxist measures were hastily undertaken. A majority of the economy was nationalized, and rural land was commandeered by the state as part of a program to establish **collective** farming in the country. There was a far-reaching drive to increase literacy, legislation to bring about equal pay for **women**, and the introduction of regional assemblies to lend some credence to the idea that the country was becoming a genuine people's state. A popular army of "victory pioneers" was raised to proselytize the natives in the vagaries of Somali Marxism, and in 1976 a **vanguard party**, the Somali Revolutionary Socialist Party (SRSP), was inaugurated to engage the nation in the march toward utopia.

There was, however, much suspicion that the government was enacting such policies merely to obtain further economic and military aid from the **Soviet Union**, which had supported Barré's quest for power through the 1960s and beyond. Yet, a rupture in the amity between the two nations occurred when Moscow signaled its unstinting support for Somalia's Marxist neighbor, **Ethiopia**. Somali nationalists inside the government still wished to see their country regain the Ethiopian area of Ogaden, lost in a conflict at the start of the 20th century. The Soviet decision to throw its weight behind Ethiopia prompted Barré to call for an invasion of the region, and in 1977 Somali troops crossed the border to launch the offensive. Relations with the Soviet Union came to an abrupt halt, and Barré sought and attained aid instead from the **United States**. With Soviet and **Cuban** assistance decisive, the Ethiopians emerged victorious, and the SRSP government was left reliant on Western countries and institutions, chiefly the United States and the International Monetary Fund, for survival.

By the 1980s Somalia's economy was suffering as a consequence of widespread drought and the Ogaden misadventure, which had swallowed up substantial vital resources. Militant oppositional factions from the ever-influential and ancient clan groupings in the country began to dissent as the extent of Somalia's financial malaise surfaced. The Somali president's response was an attempt to incite and stoke rivalry between the various clan units, the unfortunate consequence of which was the further destabilization of his nation. Barré's military government tackled the situation in the only way it knew: a mass army recruitment drive in order to restore government authority. The second half of the 1980s was characterized by fighting between the **state** army and the rebel clan units, and by the inevitable bloodshed that ensued. Inside the government, it was apparent that the Barré regime was unable to eschew the liberalization process afflicting Marxist governments elsewhere in Africa and beyond, as moves to end the rule of the command economy and institute multiparty elections took place. With the current thus, and the announcement in August 1990 that the three most powerful, and more saliently pro-democracy, clan groupings had joined force, the end of the Barré administration was nigh. Having reneged on a pledge to introduce imminent free elections, Barré and his garrison regime were forced from power by the pro-democracy majority. Barré fled to Nigeria, and Somalia began taking steps toward democracy that were to spark a prolonged civil war.

In the absence of a developed **class** system as embodied in Marxist theory, the army assumed the vanguard role usually reserved for a revolutionary **proletariat** political party, as Barré sought to apply the principles of scientific socialism to the conditions of late 20th-century Somalia. Lacking the galvanizing dynamic provided by a **class struggle** because of this absence of landowner, **bourgeoisie** and proletariat, and owing also to the continuing prominence of traditional clan networks and to Somalia's pariah status as regards the rest of the **communist** world save **China**, the October Revolution of 1969 resulted ultimately in the development of military rather than genuinely Marxist rule.

SOREL, GEORGES (1847–1922). One of the most original and controversial thinkers linked to the **Marxist** tradition, Sorel was for a time the leading theoretician of **revolutionary** syndicalism. Born in Cherbourg, France and educated at the École Polytechnique in Paris, Sorel spent much of his life working as a government engineer. He was drawn to Marxism in 1893 after his retirement and gradually worked out his own revolutionary theory via a critique of Marxism. His most influential book is *Reflections on Violence* (1906) in which he put the case for the necessity and desirability of violence. Sorel viewed **capitalism** as a system damaging to the **proletarian** majority and in a state of decline. Parliamentary democracy he saw as a sham, and reformist **socialists** he described as traitors to the working **class**. Capitalism had to be overthrown in Sorel's view by the unleashing of proletarian violence and the weapon of the general strike. Marxism identified the vital truth of the **class struggle**, but this had become lost in the theoretical elaborations of Marxists with some Marxists turning away from revolution and toward reformism. The truth of Marxism, Sorel argued, should be seen as a "myth" in the sense that it expressed images that acted as an inspiration to the workers to violently and valiantly fight their class enemy. He took Marxism as the inspiration for his revolutionary syndicalism stressing the aspect of class war, giving it a voluntarist and moral character, and adding his own distinctive theories of violence and myth.

SOUTH AFRICAN COMMUNIST PARTY (SACP). Founded in 1921 as the Communist Party of South Africa (CPSA), the South African Communist Party played a central role in ending apartheid rule. The CPSA affiliated with the **Comintern** from its inception, with Moscow compelling the party to adopt the "Native Republic" thesis. This asserted that South Africa belonged exclusively to its black natives, and underpinned party action for the next three decades. The 1930s were characterized by the partial Stalinization of the CPSA, with purges of white party officials commonplace. In line with Comintern edicts, owing to the Nazi–Soviet Pact the party initially opposed conflict with Germany in World War II, but upon German invasion in 1941 rallied behind the **Soviet Union**. Under the terms of the Suppression of Communism Act, the CPSA was declared illegal in 1950 by the newly reelected National Party. Operating underground, it relaunched in 1953 as the SACP and, having dropped Native Republic theory six years previously, set about forging ties with the African National Congress (ANC) in order to work toward a South Africa underpinned by equality between all ethnic groups. Under the direction of **Joe Slovo**, the SACP worked with the ANC to form the Spear of the Nation (*Umkhonto we Sizwe*—UWS), a group dedicated via propaganda and economic sabotage to halting the apartheid administration. The alliance also led to the creation of the Freedom Charter, a blueprint for a nonracial South Africa governed democratically by all people. By 1963, however, the government had suppressed and forced into exile chief UWS figures such as Slovo, though the organization continued its activities from outside South African borders, largely through aid from **communist** states elsewhere.

Throughout this period, the SACP worked alongside the ANC in order to engender a two-stage **revolution** of political liberation followed by economic transformation along **Marxist–Leninist** lines. Despite its Marxism–Leninism, in the 1980s the SACP could not evade the deluge of reforms embodied in Soviet *glasnost* and *perestroika*, and by 1987 Slovo had affirmed the party's commitment to multiparty politics and a partially market-oriented economy. When the new, nonracial South Africa was created in 1994, by virtue of their membership in the Tripartite Alliance alongside the ANC and Congress of South African Trade Unions, SACP members occupied National Assembly seats and ministerial positions, and continue to do so into the 21st century.

Having been a **Stalinist** organization for much of its existence, and though still according to its constitution "guided by Marxism–Leninism," the SACP stands out from many other communist parties in its espousal of gaining power through purely democratic means. By educating, organizing and mobilizing the working class electorate into voting for it, the SACP aimed upon its election to create a communist society via an interim stage of **socialism**. The Marxism of the SACP remains subject to local conditions, meaning that running concurrent to the aim of bringing about communism is that of completing the democratic revolution of 1994 and the national liberation of all South Africans.

SOVIET MARXISM. A single character or set of tenets cannot be ascribed to Soviet Marxism as the term refers to the theory and practice of the **Communist Party of the Soviet Union** over a period of some 70 years incorporating figures including **Vladimir Ilich Lenin, Josef Stalin, Nikita Khrushchev, Leonid Brezhnev** and **Mikhail Gorbachev.** As such, Soviet Marxism covers **Leninism** and **Stalinism,** the transformation of a revolutionary **ideology** into an official doctrine aimed at rationalizing and justifying an oppressive regime, and the evolution of a dogmatic, monolithic belief system into an open, pluralistic school of thought that ultimately abandoned large parts of orthodox Marxist thought before collapsing as the **Soviet Union** itself collapsed. However, the term "Soviet Marxism" is most usually associated with the rigid, authoritarian theory and practice of the Stalin era, and the sterile, conservative form typified by the Brezhnev era. For many years Soviet Marxism dominated Marxism throughout the world imposing the Soviet model where it could (for example, Eastern Europe) and supporting Soviet-style and Soviet sympathizing movements and parties using such means as its control of the **Communist International.**

SOVIET UNION. The 1917 **Russian Revolution** signaled the dawn of over 70 years of **communist** rule through the creation of the Soviet Union, a vast collection of 15 republics underpinned ideologically by **Marxism–Leninism.** The Soviet Union finally fragmented toward the conclusion of the 1980s, with **Mikhail Gorbachev** presiding over sweeping reforms as part of the Soviet *glasnost* and *perestroika* programs. Instead of renewing Soviet communism, these stood only to herald the break-up of the union into individual republics.

Events in 1917 brought to an end Tsarist rule and, in spite of opposition from the **Menshevik** wing of the movement, enabled **Bolshevik** leader **Vladimir Ilich Lenin** to form a government concerned with consolidating power and directing the Soviet Union toward communism. **Leon Trotsky** and **Josef Stalin** were immediately handed important positions in the **Communist Party of the Soviet Union** (CPSU). Financial institutions were nationalized and worker control of factories began. In subsequent months, to combat counter-revolutionary elements, the Soviet government founded the Cheka, the forerunner of the KGB, sought to undermine the stronghold of the church on the population by seizing much of its **property**, and began a program to nationalize land. On 10 July 1918 a Soviet Constitution that was to have a marked effect on subsequent history came formally into being. The document stated that the government would be run by the Politburo and the Central Committee of the CPSU, now the sole legal political party in the country, with power filtering outwards via a hierarchical system of local, provincial and national **soviets**. Legislative power was entirely in the hands of the highest echelons of the party, and the subordination of the state to the CSPU was now legally enshrined. Meanwhile, as World War I staggered to its conclusion, between 1918 and 1922 the Bolsheviks' **Red Army** combated the anti-communist forces of the White Army during a long and bitter Civil War. Largely because of Trotsky's erudite direction, the communists eventually emerged victorious.

As dissatisfaction with the state of the Soviet economy and food shortages grew in tandem, Lenin proposed a New Economic Plan (NEP) to improve conditions. The implementation of the NEP in 1921 meant an end to war communism, and its replacement by a tax-based system that allowed limited market elements to exist within the heavily nationalized Soviet economy. On 21 January 1924 a scramble for the CPSU leadership was sparked by the death of Lenin, as Stalin, Trotsky and **Nikolai Bukharin** among others vied to become party chief against the wish of the perished ruler who had asserted his desire to be succeeded by a collective leadership. Stalin, who assumed the all-important role of general secretary in 1922, eventually emerged supreme in 1927 at the 15th All-Union Congress having outmaneuvered his political rivals. The elevation of the Georgian to the forefront of the CPSU dramatically altered the course of Soviet history, as Marxist–Leninist principles were distorted and twisted to establish "**socialism in one country**," construct a cult of personality around the leader, and push through rapid industrialization and **collectivization** of agricultural land, chiefly through a series of five-year plans that replaced the NEP from 1928 onwards. The **Stalinist** regime was also characterized by a series of purges in the 1930s that saw high-profile political figures sidelined, and millions of ordinary citizens sent to "Gulag" labor camps or exterminated in the cause of consolidating Stalin's grip on power and the progress of the Soviet

Union toward communism. The collectivization policy he pursued led to devastating famine in the rural areas of the Soviet Union, adding millions to a death toll already swelled by the continuing purges, and later to be astronomically inflated by Soviet involvement in World War II.

Stalin had shocked the globe in 1939 with his August Nonaggression Pact with Adolf Hitler's Germany, but in 1941, following Nazi invasion, the Soviet Union switched sides and fought with the Allies. Over 20 million Soviet fatalities occurred over the course of the conflict, and at its close Stalin's industrialization program had been dealt a severe blow. However, the Soviet Union emerged from the conflict with superpower status in the region, something that gradually gave rise to the Cold War. A substantial cordon of Soviet satellite territories sprang up between Western Europe and the Soviet Union to exacerbate already existing ideological tensions between East and West, and in the Far East Moscow sought to impose communist governments in areas such as **North Korea** and Manchuria. In March 1953 Stalin passed away, and **Nikita Khrushchev** gradually emerged as general secretary.

In 1955 the Soviet Union risked further hostility from the West by compelling its Soviet satellite countries to join the **Warsaw Pact** military assistance agreement, a measure aimed as a response to the creation of the North Atlantic Treaty Organization (NATO). The following year Khrushchev's "Secret Speech" at the 20th Party Conference of the CPSU had an acute effect on the course of Soviet history, as the general secretary denounced the excesses of Stalin's rule and called for measures across the communist world to "de-Stalinize." Liberalization in varying forms followed, with the immediate outcome being an increase in dissent among the citizens of communist countries that culminated in the **Polish** and **Hungarian Uprisings**. Khrushchev pursued a reformist agenda throughout his rule as general secretary, but it was his reform of agricultural policy, alongside the loss of Soviet prestige following the Cuban Missile Crisis and the split with the **People's Republic of China** in 1960, that eventually led to his departure from office in 1964.

He was replaced by **Leonid Brezhnev** who immediately set about slowing the pace of reform and the overt repudiation of all things Stalin in Soviet propaganda. Brezhnev's anti-liberalization standpoint was emphasized when he called on Warsaw Pact troops to ruthlessly crush the 1968 **Prague Spring** and restore orthodox order in **Czechoslovakia**, an action he justified in his proclamation of the **Brezhnev Doctrine**. However, his administration did consent to economic reforms domestically, with the adoption of a system in which individual firms were allowed to determine production levels according to prices and profits rather than government-set targets. Brezhnev also oversaw a thaw in the Cold War as relations with the **United States** were dramatically improved by Soviet acquiescence in a policy of international cooperation. Yet, this relaxation proved to be only temporary, as the Soviet invasion of **Afghanistan** in 1979 to back the communist government, and threatened repression against the Polish Solidarity movement in 1980, soured relations between the two superpowers.

Brezhnev died in November of 1982 to be replaced as general secretary by former KGB controller Yuri Andropov. However, neither Andropov nor his successor, Konstantin Chernenko, had any time to instigate any discernible alterations in Soviet life, the former falling fatally ill in 1984, and the latter a year later. As this unusually swift succession of party leaders played itself out, Mikhail Gorbachev began to establish himself as a key figure in the CPSU, and was the obvious choice to take the reins as general secretary in 1985. The Gorbachev era brought about the end of the 80-year-long adhesion to Marxism in the Soviet Union and subsequently its satellite states. The Soviet leader liberalized the country through his *glasnost* and *perestroika* programs, with the embracing of free market economics, an end to censorship, the opening up of government, and the promise of free elections. Gorbachev steered the Soviet Union toward peace with the West, chiefly by reaching disarmament agreements with the United States and renewing international cooperation.

As reforms led to a societal and political relaxation, debate inside the 15 Soviet republics over their individual role in the union took hold and national independence movements blossomed. Constitutional reforms in 1989 legalizing the birth of a multiparty system further emboldened the clamor for independence and the breakup of the Soviet empire, as national interest movements and parties prospered. In August 1991 communist hard-liners failed in a coup designed to oust Gorbachev's reformers from power, a definite indication that the reign of orthodox Marxism–Leninism in the Soviet Union was entering its final chapter. The Baltic states of Lithuania, Estonia and

Latvia asserted their independence, and in December 1991 the Soviet Union was formally dissolved. The short-lived Commonwealth of Independent States (CIS) that followed soon disintegrated, and the 15 republics of the Soviet Union, the world's largest sovereign state, once more formed individual nations.

The development of Marxism inside the Soviet Union went through a number of phases. What began prior to 1917 as a revolutionary doctrine full of fervent radical principles was altered to become an **ideology** designed to consolidate and maintain rule. "Official" Marxism–Leninism became the monopolistic belief system in the Soviet Union, and its significance meant that all other ideologies and ways of thinking were eradicated. There was to be a sole interpretation that would dictate the course the country took, with state organs conceiving, disseminating and controlling ideas. The official ideology sought both to legitimize the role and actions of the CPSU, and to provide stimulus and direction for the transition to communism. Intellectual pluralism, especially following the emergence of Stalin as party leader, was basically nonexistent as all ideas were subordinate to the long-term goals of Marxism–Leninism. That ideology, in its promotion of **democratic centralism**, was twisted to validate the role of a strong leader at the top of party and country and to establish and maintain ideological **hegemony**. This leader would be able therefore to ideologically justify the elimination of political opponents as they were distorting the true path to communism as embodied by the official line. For instance, as Stalin emerged as this one strong leader following the death of Lenin he sidelined Trotsky by affirming that his own concept of "socialism in one country," as opposed to the Red Army chief's notion of permanent revolution, was the true doctrine of Marxism–Leninism. In this way he was able to mold the ideology to suit his own political purposes. Accordingly, as Marxism–Leninism justified and necessitated "socialism in one country," the practical undertakings required to achieve communism in the Soviet Union under the auspices of this doctrine, namely mass industrialization and collectivization, were ideologically vindicated.

To this end, from the moment Stalin's dictatorship of the CPSU commenced, genuine theoretical discourse, interpretation and development of Marxism ended, and the leader went about enforcing massive change in the Soviet Union, applying loosely fitting Marxian concepts to his actions usually subsequent to their being taken. In its prioritization of domestic interests, the concept of "socialism in one country" also allowed the CPSU to fuse Marxism with elements of nationalism in order to placate the patriotic tendencies of the constituent member nations of the Soviet Union. Stalin's interpretation of Marxism–Leninism resulted in intense political control. He adopted and extended Lenin's aversion toward the "class enemy" (in reality political opponents), and suggested the struggle against this group would intensify as full communism approached. Thus, a system was installed to guarantee ideological monism through ever-increasing suppression of opposing ideas and persons. Stalin appointed obdurate "nomenklatura" administrators who blindly carried out every instruction issued from the CPSU party central to ensure the monopoly of Marxism–Leninism was maintained. This party apparatus was backed up by a highly censored mass media, regime-run public organizations instead of groups such as independent trade unions, and an all-powerful secret police. Stalin became deified through the cult of personality that was built up around him to make him and the ideological orthodoxy his party stood for unassailable.

By the late 1930s the party had fully expounded a strong line on education, culture, science and history that brought the domination of Marxism–Leninism in each of these spheres throughout the nation. The 1936 Constitution declared the establishment of fully fledged socialism in the Soviet Union, setting a blueprint later adopted by other nations pursuing a communist path (mainly the Soviet satellite states of the Eastern Bloc). In 1938 ideological orthodoxy in the Soviet Union was espoused in a new chapter added by Stalin to the *History of the CPSU (Short Course)* on "**Dialectical** and **Historical Materialism**." This liturgical piece borrowed ideas from **Friedrich Engels**, **Karl Marx**, Lenin and other key figures from the annals of the Marxist past in order to reaffirm the correctness of the direction in which the CPSU was taking the Soviet Union. Ideological orthodoxy in the country was challenged only with the death of Stalin in 1953, and even then only partially, with the relative autonomy that some Soviet intellects were granted reflected in the rise in liberalism throughout the region, especially in satellite states like **Poland** and Czechoslovakia.

While Stalin had been reluctant to provide a timetable of the stages of transition to full communism, his successor Khrushchev did so, stating that in the 1970s the material and technical base of communism would be created, and in the 1980s actual communism would finally be achieved. While Khrushchev's model would finally mean an end to the **dictatorship of the proletariat** era ushered in following 1917, it did not, however, represent a "withering away of the state" as certified in the classic Marxist model. Instead, while some state elements would be extinguished (for example, repression), a principal element of central power would have to remain in the final phase of communism until the people were able to self-govern. Khrushchev's replacement by Brezhnev meant he would never be able to see his own ideological model transpire, and the new leader was quick to emphasize his own map to transition. Brezhnev suggested that the stage of socialism was not merely a bridge between capitalism and communism but was in fact a prolonged stage in itself. He was not offering a rejection of Khrushchev's aim for a leap to communism, but stressing that the process would be more of a drawn-out affair bereft of a strict itinerary. Brezhnev reemphasized the pivotal role of the CPSU and the Soviet state in deciphering the course the country would take, and as a consequence by the early 1980s the sheer magnitude of the party and government's reach had multiplied. The party had become an all-consuming, Leviathan machine, one of the Soviet Union's major employers and landowners with a giant bureaucracy and far-reaching institutional framework. It was the embodiment of the Marxist–Leninist concept of a **vanguard party**, dominating all aspects of Soviet life.

As such, when Gorbachev assumed the post of general secretary in 1985 the end of the Soviet Union looked light years away. Criticism, though, had been mounting prior to his accession to power, and so when he began his program of *glasnost* and *perestroika* the Soviet people used the reforms those concepts entailed to air their grievances. Party and state officials lost their cozy jobs, nationalist movements gained strength and fundamental questions about the nature of the Soviet system were openly raised. Ever since the 1917 revolution the CPSU had aimed to accelerate social and economic development through Marxist–Leninist planning, but in contrast Gorbachev began to embrace market elements that ran entirely contrary to that ethos. Marxism–Leninism waned concurrently with the Soviet Union, as democratization laid the groundwork for a political pluralism that simply could not allow for one monopolistic political ideology and course of action. As the CPSU attempted to halt its own inexorable collapse by embracing a number of reforms, Marxist–Leninist ideas were quickly replaced, and orthodox "official" ideology disintegrated alongside the Soviet Union.

SOVIETS. The first Soviet was formed in St. Petersburg in 1905 and acted as a form of council for organizing the people in their struggle against the Tsarist regime, and they were important organizations in the 1917 **Russian Revolution**. The **Bolsheviks** and **Mensheviks** were both prominent in the Soviets as they emerged in different cities, and the Bolsheviks used the slogan (for a period) "All Power to the Soviets." Soviets were seen as a potential alternative to state power, and **Vladimir Ilich Lenin** justified the dissolution of the Constituent Assembly after the **revolution** on the grounds that the Soviets provided a more democratic, not to mention more **socialist**, form of organization. The significance of the Soviets is underlined by the new name of Russia following the revolution, namely the Union of Soviet Socialist Republics or **Soviet Union**. Outside of the Soviet Union **Antonio Gramsci**, **Karl Korsch**, **Karl Renner** and **Antonie Pannekoek** all contributed to the theory of Soviets or councils viewing them as revolutionary organizations, models of a future socialist state, or a form of industrial democracy.

SPANISH COMMUNIST PARTY. Founded in 1921, the Spanish Communist Party (*Partido Comunista de España*—PCE) initially championed **Leninism** and was a loyal **Comintern** member. During the Spanish Civil War (1936–1939) it was influential in the ultimately unsuccessful Republican struggle against General Francisco Franco's National Front forces, using its closeness to the **Soviet Union** to wield huge power within the leftist coalition. Despite consistent state persecution, throughout Franco's subsequent dictatorship it remained the most effective oppositional force in Spain, and within days of being legalized in 1977 boasted 200,000 members. In that decade, PCE General Secretary **Santiago Carrillo** began the process of distancing the party from its Leninist past, and toward **Eurocommunism**. His acceptance of a social democratic outlook caused unrest among Marxist–Leninists within the PCE, prompting in 1982 the curtailment of his stewardship. By 1986 Carrillo's former opponents within the PCE, many of whom had temporarily deserted the party to form hard-line splinter groups, took the party into the United Left (*Izquierda Unida*—IU) coalition which duly became Spain's third largest political group. Under General Secretary Francisco Frutos, at the 2004 election the IU polled 5 percent of the total vote.

SPARTACUS LEAGUE. Composed of left radicals in the **German Social Democratic Party** (SPD) during and immediately after World War I, the Spartacus League derived its name from the leader of the slave rebellion against the Romans. Its foremost members were **Rosa Luxemburg** and **Karl Liebknecht**, with the former giving expression to the Spartacist position of opposition to the war, and a commitment to internationalism and mass action, in her *Junius Pamphlet* and *Either-Or*. Expelled from the SPD the Spartacists joined the newly formed Independent German Socialist Party (USPD). An uprising in January 1919 was blamed, incorrectly, on the Spartacus League, which along with other extreme left groups was then subject to repression, and Luxemburg and Liebknecht were murdered. *See also* SOCIALISM.

STALIN, JOSEF (JOSEF VISSARIONOVICH DZHUGASHVILI) (1879–1953). Born in Gori, Georgia, Josef Stalin was a **Bolshevik** revolutionary, general secretary of the **Communist Party of the Soviet Union** (CPSU), and the second leader of the **Soviet Union**. His career spanned a tumultuous period in Russian and European history, and witnessed the rapid industrialization of the Soviet Union, ultimate victory in World War II, and the exile or elimination of millions of people deemed opponents.

Stalin's political career began in 1898 when he joined the **Russian Social Democratic Party**, a decision that hastened his exit one year later from the Gori seminary where he had been studying Russian Orthodox Christianity. By 1903 he had joined the Bolsheviks, and soon began carrying out underground work for the banned party, the consequence of which was several periods of imprisonment and exile between 1902 and 1917. In 1911 he helped found the Bolshevik Party's *Pravda* newspaper, and in 1912 he was co-opted to the party's Central Committee. Although he played only a minor part in the 1917 **Russian Revolution**, Stalin, serving as people's commissar for nationalities, was embroiled in military matters on a number of fronts in the Russian Civil War following the **revolution**, and subsequently made a member in 1919 of the inaugural Politburo. Having filled numerous bureaucratic party posts, with **Vladimir Ilich Lenin** ill,

Stalin was appointed general secretary of the ruling CPSU in 1922, and used the wide-ranging organizational powers this position granted him to grasp firm control of the party organs and consolidate his power. Stalin's hand was further strengthened in 1924 when he replaced Lenin as chairman of the Politburo, and suppressed the disclosure of the dead leader's testament expressing grave doubts over his (Stalin's) motives. Lenin ordered that, on his death, the presidency of the Soviet Union and the CPSU should pass to a collective leadership comprising key members of the party. However, the wily Stalin out-maneuvered those around him set to share power, with Lev Kamenev, **Grigori Zinoviev, Leon Trotsky, Nikolai Bukharin**, and Sergei Kirov all sidelined by exile or worse. By 1928 Stalin's position as sole leader of party and **state** was unassailable, and any doubts as to the security of his position were terminally extinguished with the advent of the purges in the latter half of the 1930s.

Having developed such a rigorous hold on the CPSU, Stalin set about creating a command economy to expand his control over the Soviet Union. The "New Economic Policy" of the revolution was supplanted in 1928 with the first of Stalin's "Five Year Plans." The Five Year Plans aimed to bring about rapid industrialization through state guidance and heralded the **collectivization** of agriculture, justified by the Marxian concept of putting an end to the primitive accumulation of wealth. One result of this policy was repression, with *kulaks* (rich **peasants**) often sent to labor camps for "resisting." Stalin constantly used repressive methods to sideline those he perceived as a threat to his position and program in this manner. He instigated the purges, using assassination, expulsion, and the infamous show trials of 1936–1938, in order to eliminate the bulk of the original Bolshevik Central Committee, and other governmental and military rivals. The leader molded **ideology** to justify such repression, suggesting in 1928 that maturing Soviet **communism**, in its intensification of the **class struggle**, had made party violence necessary, thus allowing the crushing of the Left Opposition and *kulak* peasants. Stalin created a cult of personality, bolstering his public image through intensive propaganda, and employing the Soviet secret police, in its various guises, to maintain dominance of party, state and country.

Stalin was stunned when, in 1941, Adolf Hitler violated the Nazi–Soviet Nonaggression Pact and ordered the invasion of the Soviet Union. He became commander-in-chief of the military following the invasion, marshal in 1943, and generalissimo in 1945, eventually leading the Soviet Union to victory over Germany on the eastern front. Following the cessation of hostilities, Stalin anticipated that the **United States** withdrawal from Europe would allow Soviet dominance to prevail. When this hegemony failed to materialize, Stalin was forced to make a tactical shift, and duly went about transforming former satellite states in Central Europe into "buffer states" under the influence of Moscow. The chief result of this was the Cold War.

Central to Stalin's policy was his doctrine of "**socialism in one country**," a belief that sat in direct opposition to the **internationalism** of Trotsky's "permanent revolution," and stressed that the construction of **socialism** was possible in the Soviet Union without socialist revolution elsewhere. The concept provided a theoretical justification for the collectivization of agriculture, the creation of a command economy, and state terror.

Stalin's contribution to the canon of **Marxist** theory is negligible. Absolute power rendered theory dispensable and ideas were only ever used to pursue personal goals. Where he did acknowledge ideology and theory, Stalin was guilty of a crass oversimplification of Marxian concepts, for example in *The History of the Communist Party of the Soviet Union (Bolshevik): Short Course* (1938), which reduced **Marxism–Leninism** to numbered, simply expressed points intended for memorizing. Elsewhere, he pursued the **Leninist** doctrine of a robust centralist party based on professional revolutionaries, and mixed appeals to Russian nationalism with a quasi-Marxist class analysis. He departed from Leninism in denying the crucial notion of an imminent "withering away" of the state. For Stalin, state power required enhancing not weakening, as the enemies of the Soviet Union would grow increasingly desperate as the battle for socialism intensified. A strong state was to be the only antidote to **capitalist** encirclement, and its "withering away" could only occur once all enemies had been safely eradicated.

Following **Nikita Khrushchev**'s denunciation of Stalin in 1956 at the 20th Congress of the CPSU, a period of de-Stalinization began. In 1961 his embalmed body was removed from Lenin's mausoleum and relocated in a plain grave adjacent to the walls of the Kremlin, and the long process of outing the truths of the Stalinist regime began.

STALINISM. The term "Stalinism" refers both to the nature of the **Soviet Union** under **Josef Stalin**'s rule and to the interpretation of **Marxism** sanctioned by Stalin and promulgated by the Soviet Union while he was in power. Never official terms, "Stalinism" and "Stalinist" gained currency only after Stalin's death and, particularly, after his denunciation by **Nikita Khrushchev** at the 20th Congress of the **Communist Party of the Soviet Union** in 1956. Both terms have tended to be used in a derogatory way to describe a repressive, dictatorial and totalitarian regime and a crude, dogmatic **ideology**.

One key aspect of Stalinism is the idea and practice of **revolution** from above, led by the party and with a large and central role played by the **state**. In agriculture the approach under Stalin was one of "**collectivization**" where **peasant** farmers were brought into large collective or state farms. In industry the policy was one of rapid centrally controlled industrialization with particular emphasis on heavy industry. Both policies required the extreme centralization of power, a massive increase in the size of the state, and the widespread use of coercion. Stalinism is viewed by many as fundamentally totalitarian in character. The use of arbitrary repression was one of the most distinctive aspects of Stalin's regime with what came to be known as the "Great Terror" seeing extensive use of arbitrary arrests, labor camps, and executions, along with more selective, but equally notorious, use of "show trials." In the show trials many prominent Bolsheviks, including **Nicholai Bukharin** and **Gregori Zinoviev**, were forced to confess to crimes they had not committed, before being executed.

Stalinism saw Marxist theory turned into an official state ideology with Stalin overseeing the creation of a dogmatic Marxist orthodoxy propounded in party documents such as *History of the Communist Party of the Soviet Union* (1938). In this a simplified, reductionist and schematic account of Marxist philosophy was expounded, presenting **dialectical materialism** as a set of propositions and laws representing the **Marxist–Leninist** world outlook, and characterizing Marxism as a science that had identified the laws of history. The Stalinist transformation of Marxism into an official belief system served to provide an ideological rationalization of the Soviet regime. In terms of specific content, the most significant tenet of Stalinist ideology was "**socialism in one country**." This was directed against **Leon Trotsky**'s **internationalist** position that insisted on the necessity of international revolution in order to achieve socialism.

For many Marxists and commentators on Marxism Stalinism represents a significant distortion of Marxism, but it is viewed by Stalinists and some opponents of Marxism as the fulfillment of Marxism and a logical progression from Leninism.

STATE. A central concept in **Marxism** is the state, although **Karl Marx** himself did not set out a systematic theory of it. Marx's basic view of the state is set out in the *Communist Manifesto* (1848) where he wrote, "The executive of the modern state is but a committee for managing the common affairs of the whole **bourgeoisie**." For Marx, the state is an instrument for defending and promoting the interests of the **ruling class**, which in the case of **capitalism** is the bourgeoisie. The dominant economic **class**, the class that owns and controls the **means of production**, becomes the dominant political class by seizing control of the state.

Marx's view of the state gradually developed with his earliest discussion of it occurring in his *Critique of Hegel's Philosophy of Right* (1843) in which Marx criticizes **Georg Wilhelm Friedrich Hegel**'s conception of the state as representing the universal interest and promoting the common good. For Marx this misrepresented the nature of the state, which, according to him, always represented and promoted particular interests, at that time the interests of **property**. Marx at this point believed an extensive democratization of the state could transform it, but his views became more radical as his theory of **historical materialism** developed and he established a link between class society and the state. Marx developed the view that the state only exists in class society, and that in primitive, pre-class societies and in the future **communist** society there is no state because there are no classes locked in struggle and producing and needing a coercive body to maintain order. So in a free society, communism, the state would disappear or be abolished, in **Friedrich Engels**' phrase, "wither away." Marx talks of "governmental functions" disappearing and being replaced by merely "administrative functions," though he does not make clear what these are. Before the complete disappearance of the state Marx says there will be a transitional state controlled by the proletariat, the **dictatorship of the proletariat**.

Marx's basic view of the state was modified in his examinations of specific societies, where circumstances are inevitably much more complicated. Marx, for example, notes the possibility of the state representing the interests of a section of the ruling class as happened in France when financiers within the capitalist class gained control. His analysis of France under the dictatorial rule of Napoleon III in *The Eighteenth Brumaire of Louis Bonaparte* (1852) pointed to the autonomy the state can develop. With no one class sufficiently dominant, no one class could seize control of the state, making it ripe for being taken over by a dictator. Under Louis Bonaparte's rule the state was to a significant extent independent of classes, although Marx noted it did not have complete independence and remained linked to the **peasantry**. Furthermore, the Bonapartist state had a considerable bureaucratic and military organization, a state machinery with its own interest. A similar departure from the state as an instrument of class rule argument is suggested by Marx in his analysis of oriental despotism and the **Asiatic mode of production**. Here there is no private property or ownership of land, so the despot's rule is independent and the despotic state is not the instrument of a class owning the means of production.

Vladimir Ilich Lenin followed the basic viewpoint of Marx and offered his own definition of the state as "an organization of violence for the suppression of some class." He was concerned to combat what he saw as reformist tendencies in the **German Social Democratic Party** which he believed was looking to achieve **proletarian** emancipation using the state. Against this he argued that the state is by its very nature a repressive organization and cannot be used by the workers or their representatives to create a socialist society. In *The State and Revolution* (1917), where he outlined this argument, Lenin concluded that the bourgeois state must be smashed. He also emphasized the importance of the dictatorship of the proletariat in a polemic against the anarchists. With the end goal of a stateless society shared by the anarchists it was important politically to stress where they differed. While Lenin stressed the coercive nature of the state, **Antonio Gramsci** highlighted the extent to which the state achieves its aims by consent using **ideological** means to create a hegemonic rule. **Louis Althusser** also gave attention to this point with his notion of the "ideological state apparatus" as playing a key role in class rule alongside methods of force.

The Soviet state has also prompted developments in the Marxist theory of the state. Professing to be Marxist and with common ownership of the means of production the nature of the Soviet state raised serious issues for Marxist theorists. **Josef Stalin** described it as a new type of state representing the interests of the whole people, and as such was not a class state. **Leon Trotsky** viewed it as a "deformed workers' state" controlled by a bureaucracy, and others have theorized the creation of a new class controlling the state.

STRUCTURALIST MARXISM. *See* MARXIST STRUCTURALISM.

SUPERSTRUCTURE. *See* BASE AND SUPERSTRUCTURE.

SUPHANOUVONG, PRINCE (1902–1995). President of the **Lao People's Democratic Republic** and founder of the **communist** Pathet Lao army, Suphanouvong was a major figure in the history of Laos. He trained as an engineer in Paris before joining the Laos nationalist movement on his return in 1938. In 1950 he founded the Pathet Lao to fight the French colonists and continued to serve as a leader of the army in the struggle against the right-wing regime of Lao Issara after the French departed. In 1974 he was made chairman of the National Political Consultative Council, and the following year he became president of the newly formed People's Democratic Republic of Laos, a post he retained until his retirement due to ill health in 1986.

SURPLUS VALUE, THEORY OF. Surplus value is a central notion in **Karl Marx**'s analysis of **capitalism** and his theory of **exploitation**. Marx bases his theory of surplus value on the **labor theory of value** which assumes the value of goods to be determined by the relative quantity of labor embodied in them. Marx seizes on this insight, but goes beyond it to explain the source of profit. He begins his account of the theory of surplus value by examining what he takes to be the cornerstone of capitalism, namely the **commodity**. A commodity is something that is produced for exchange rather than for direct use by its producer. A commodity combines two aspects: use value and exchange value, the former referring to the use for which a commodity is produced (the want satisfied by the commodity) and the latter being what the commodity can be exchanged for. Marx poses the question, "If commodities exchange according to the value of the amount of labor embodied in them, where does the profit come from?" In other words, if everything sells for its value, how can there be any increment of value or profit? According to Marx, the answer lies with the unique character of one particular commodity, labor power. The worker in capitalism has one commodity he can sell, labor power, his capacity to work, and this commodity, as with all others, has an exchange value equivalent to the amount of labor required to produce it. The value spent on producing labor is whatever is required to keep the worker alive and sufficiently skilled to perform his job, in other words subsistence and training. The "natural wage" is subsistence, varied by historical and moral norms in any given society. Surplus value arises because there is a difference between this value of labor power, the subsistence wage modified according to social norms and conditions, and the value which the worker creates with his labor power in the process of production. A worker might spend half of his working time producing the value of his labor power, and the rest spent producing additional or surplus value. This division of working time into necessary labor time and surplus labor time highlights the source of surplus value and ultimately of profit in the capitalist system. The extraction or appropriation of surplus value from the worker by the capitalist is called exploitation.

SWEEZY, PAUL MARLOUR (1910–2004). Sweezy was a prominent **Marxist** economist and the founder of *Monthly Review* magazine. Born in New York, he obtained a doctorate in economics from Harvard University in 1937 following a spell at the London School of Economics, where he embraced Marxian concepts for the first time. After teaching at Harvard up until 1942, in 1949 Sweezy, along with Leo Huberman, founded the **socialist** magazine *Monthly Review*, a controversial move in the atmosphere of the American "Red Scare." In 1956 Sweezy was subpoenaed by the New Hampshire attorney general, who investigated his beliefs as a consequence of his lectures on socialism at the University of New Hampshire. However, Sweezy, quoting the First Amendment right to freedom of speech and testifying that he had never been part of the **Communist Party of the United States of America**, refused to conform and was cited for contempt of court. This was duly overturned by the U.S. Supreme Court. Sweezy was a committed **Stalinist** for much of his life, though he did align with **Maoist China** and then **Kim Il Sung**'s **North Korea**

shortly after **Nikita Khrushchev**'s denunciation of **Josef Stalin** at the 1956 **Communist Party of the Soviet Union** conference. Sweezy was a key theoretician for the left. His 1942 *Theory of Capitalist Development* comprised a seminal modern introduction to the thought of **Karl Marx**, and offered, for the first time in English, a critique of complex Marxian problems. He elucidated an underconsumptionist analysis of the crisis in **capitalism**, suggesting that as increases in consumption were not matching increases in investment, unproductive uses of output became required, for example military spending. In 1966 Sweezy and Paul Baran's *Monopoly Capital* was published. This became a key theoretical work for the "New Left" of the time, and forwarded the concept of stagnation theory. The central predicament facing capitalism was its difficulty in selling the economic surpluses left by capital accrual. The result, in an attempt to ease the declining rate of profit as foreseen by Marx, would be increases in defense spending, marketing and debt. Each of these "quick fixes," however, was extremely limited. The only consequence could be that monopoly capital would tend, in its restriction of output and technological innovation in the interest of maintaining profit, toward economic stagnation.

SYNDICALISM. The syndicalist movement represented a form of **revolutionary** trade unionism. Strongly influenced by anarchism, but also by **Marxism**, syndicalism was a significant political presence in France (the *Fédération des Bourses du Travail* and the *Confédération Générale du Travail*), Spain (the *Confederación Nacional de Trabajo*) and Italy (the *Unione Sindicale*). In the **United States** the **Industrial Workers of the World** and **Daniel De Leon** were influenced by syndicalism, and the Irish Marxist **James Connolly** was sympathetic to syndicalist ideas. Emphasizing action over theory, spontaneity, the use of violence and strike action, and a rejection of parliamentary politics, syndicalism found its most famous proponent in **Georges Sorel**.

– T –

THIRD INTERNATIONAL. Founded in Moscow in 1919 by the **Bolsheviks** to replace the **Second International** which had disintegrated with the outbreak of World War I the Third International largely served as an instrument of **Josef Stalin** and the **Soviet Union**. Also known as the Communist International and Comintern, the Third International's official objective was to work for a "World Union of Socialist Soviet Republics" and initially it focused on supporting revolutionary activities in Europe, Germany in particular, that it hoped would lead to international **revolution**. In order to keep out social democratic groups strict conditions of affiliation were created, and rivalry with non-Marxist **socialists** and combating social democracy became themes of the International. The Third International was notable for its emphasis at its second congress in 1920 on anti-**imperialism** and national liberation following **Vladimir Ilich Lenin**'s *Theses on the National and Colonial Question*. During the 1920s it became the battleground for Soviet internal disputes such as the struggle between **Leon Trotsky** and Josef Stalin over the issue of **socialism in one country**, which ultimately saw Trotsky expelled from its Executive Committee in 1927.

From 1928 until 1933 the Comintern promoted a policy of noncooperation with social democratic parties against fascism, arguing that social democracy was itself a form of "social fascism." With the success of the Nazis in Germany this policy gave way to one of collaboration between **communists** and socialists and the development of "Popular Fronts" in the struggle against fascism. Through the 1930s the Third International was used in carrying out Stalin's purges, including the elimination of the **Polish Communist Party** in 1938. The German–Soviet Nonaggression Pact of 1939 saw the Third International adopt a line of condemning both sides in World War II as imperialist until the Germans attacked the Soviet Union in 1941 when it sided with the Allied forces and promoted the war against the Axis powers. In 1943 the Third International was dissolved.

THOMPSON, EDWARD PALMER (1924–1993). Social historian, **Marxist** theoretician and a key Campaign for Nuclear Disarmament (CND) activist, E.P. Thompson wrote the classic text *The Making of the English Working Class* (1963). The Englishman Thompson served in Africa and Italy during World War II, and in 1946 experienced popular **communism** in progress as a rail worker in **Yugoslavia** and **Bulgaria**. He returned to England, committed to **Marxism**, to graduate from Cambridge University with a history degree, and then teach at the universities of Leeds and Warwick. Thompson was a prominent figure in British and European anti-nuclear movements from the 1950s right through to the 1980s, contributing to debate on disarmament and the Cold War from his leadership positions within the CND and the Committee for European Nuclear Disarmament. He wrote a series of essays published in 1983 in *Beyond the Cold War*, declaring the European peace movement a **socialist** cause and advocating the removal of all nuclear weapons from Europe to bring about a cessation of tensions. Thompson also wrote that the source of the arms race was the clamor of Western industrial nations to produce weaponry to maintain face and sustain industry, and not a program to meet rational defense requirements.

From 1942 he was a member of the **Communist Party of Great Britain**, but left in 1956 due to his rejection of **Stalinism**, fueled, like much of his work, by a severe aversion to absolutism. Motivated by this Soviet-generated crisis on the left, Thompson assisted in the foundation of *The New Reasoner* journal, offering a voice for others dissenting from orthodox communism. In 1960 this merged with *The Universities and Left Review* to become *The New Left Review*, and Thompson sat on the journal's board until 1963, when he was dismissed over his opposition to theoretical criticism of English Marxist traditions among board members.

In 1963 the publication of Thompson's *The Making of the English Working Class* put him at the forefront of social history theory. He affirmed that the English working class came about through an amalgamation of objective conditions and subjective struggle. Social class was a process where individuals developed a shared **class consciousness** as moral actors, selecting their beliefs and conducting themselves in response to social circumstances thrust upon them. This sat in direct opposition to the **determinism** of **structuralist Marxism** which was influential at the time. Thompson continued his criticism of the structuralist school of thought espoused by **Louis Althusser**, most strongly in *The Poverty of Theory* (1978), where he condemned the structuralist trait of ignoring concrete historical events in explaining change. Instead structuralists put shifts in society down to abstract categories, for example social structures, implying humans are mere passive agents in history. From Thompson's perspective, while **historical materialism** suggests a group of propositions and categories (for example, class and **exploitation**), these are only substantiated by empirical historical examination, that is, these concepts only gain value when viewed in conjunction with real historical events. Thompson died in 1993 having contributed enormously to the **humanist Marxist** tradition of reason, and the rejection of theological, structuralist and orthodox Marxism.

THOREZ, MAURICE (1900–1964). Born in France, Maurice Thorez rose from childhood labor as a coal miner to become general secretary, and then chairman, of the **French Communist Party** (PCF). Joining in 1920, Thorez was a member of the PCF almost from its inception. Having been imprisoned on several occasions for his left-wing beliefs, Thorez diligently worked his way up the PCF, and by 1930 he had become general secretary of the party. Two years later he was elected to the Chamber of Deputies, leading French **communists** within the parliament. Thorez, along with Leon Blum and other left-wing political figures, took part in the creation of the Popular Front coalition in response to the threat posed to France by the Third Reich. The Popular Front was victorious in the 1936 parliamentary elections, with Blum becoming prime minister and the PCF forming part of the coalition government having won 15 percent of votes cast. However, the advent of the 1939 Nazi–Soviet Pact saw the PCF banned by the French government, the Popular Front having been defeated in the 1938 election. Thorez fled to the **Soviet Union** and in doing so avoided army service, gaining a prison sentence in absentia which was amnestied in 1944. Following World War II the PCF joined with the **French Socialist Party** to form the government, with Thorez becoming deputy prime minister between 1946 and 1947. Following this spell he reverted to opposition, and served as PCF chairman until his death in 1964. His most renowned works were *Son of the People* (1937) and *Politics of French Greatness* (1945).

TITO, JOSIP (1892–1980). Tito, born Josip Broz, was one of the most prominent **communist** leaders of the 20th century, and his **Yugoslavia** stood uniquely independent of the **Soviet Union** and **China**. His political activism started in 1910 when he joined the Social–Democratic Party of Croatia and Slavonia. Despite his vehement opposition to the conflict, Tito was sent to fight in World War I, though he eventually managed to desert and flee to Russia. Here, in November 1917 he joined the **Red Army** and applied a year later to join the **Communist Party of the Soviet Union**. Tito became a member of the underground **Communist Party of Yugoslavia** (CPY) in 1920, and used his position as a **Comintern** member to liaise with **Josef Stalin** over its activities. In 1934 he became a member of the Political Bureau and Central Committee of the CPY, and in 1937 general secretary. When in April 1941 the Axis powers invaded Yugoslavia, Tito was at the forefront of the resistance movement, becoming chief commander of the Yugoslav National Liberation Army (NLA). The guerrilla tactics of the NLA were ultimately successful as they liberated chunks of territory, earning Tito the title of marshal in 1943 and eventually forcing the fascists out.

At the end of World War II, Tito became prime minister and minister of foreign affairs of Yugoslavia as part of a fresh coalition government. Shortly afterwards, in 1953, he succeeded Ivan Ribar as president of the country under the new constitution, and a decade later Yugoslavia became the Socialist Federal Republic of Yugoslavia. In 1974 Tito was named "president for life" following five consecutive election victories, a position he occupied through to his death six years later.

Tito succeeded in keeping the deeply fractious Yugoslavia cemented together, chiefly by diluting nationalist sentiments with common Yugoslav goals. But the country was constantly wracked by tensions among its composite peoples and Tito did have to utilize force to maintain this status quo, particularly in the "Croatian spring" when the government suppressed public demonstrations and inner-Party dissent. Tito's Yugoslavia became the first European communist country to cut all ties with Stalin and exist without Soviet aid. As Stalin pursued full control of the "buffer states" in the Eastern Bloc, he offered his former ally Tito aid in return for obedience, but in 1948 the Yugoslavian chose personal political freedom and full independence for his country. This signified a rejection of the Soviet model of **communism**, and enabled the Yugoslavian government to pursue its own vision.

As such, Tito and his key aides set about fashioning a uniquely Yugoslavian **socialism**, internally encouraging market socialism and decentralized worker self-management, and externally steadfastly refusing to align with either side in the Cold War. This latter policy led to Yugoslavia's membership of the Non-Alignment Movement, which Tito founded, along with Egypt's Gamal Abdel Nasser and India's Jawaharlal Nehru, in 1961. Yugoslavia benefited economically from the Tito government's version of communism, as, unlike those states relying on the Soviet Union, the country was able to form trading relationships with Western economies. Yet, totalitarian elements did surface, and with Tito unwilling to tolerate collaborators shifting too far ideologically toward Stalinist or on the other hand Western democratic viewpoints, expulsions and purges were not uncommon. "Titoism" was in practice something of a halfway house between **Stalinism** and Western liberalism, and it soon ceased to exist following the death of the **ideology**'s chief exponent. The collective leadership that Tito left behind to take the reins following his death failed to halt the disintegration of Yugoslavia.

TOGLIATTI, PALMIRO (1893–1964). As secretary of the **Italian Communist Party** (PCI) from 1926 to 1964, Togliatti was committed to attaining power by democratic, constitutional means. A graduate of the University of Turin in law and philosophy, his political career began with his membership of the **Italian Socialist Party** (PSI) before the start of the World War I. Togliatti associated himself with **Antonio Gramsci** and Angelo Tasca's *L'Ordine Nuovo* newspaper, and it was with this group that he broke away in 1921 and formed the PCI. Following Gramsci's arrest in 1926, Togliatti was made secretary of the party. When the Italian fascists came to power, he was forced into exile, and for 18 years ran the PCI from abroad, chiefly in Moscow. While out of Italy, as a **Comintern** secretary, Togliatti was sent in 1936 to take charge of communist units in the Spanish Civil War. He returned to Italy in 1944 following Mussolini's fall from power, and sought the reorganization of the PCI, while serving in the Liberation and Christian Democrat governments, before communist expulsion in May 1947. Togliatti was instrumental in the "Salerno Turn," a seismic shift in policy, as the PCI renounced all violent and revolutionary practices and pledged to pursue power via parliamentary and reformist means. Togliatti built the PCI into one of the largest political parties in Italy, and the only one in the **capitalist** West to gain one-third of electoral votes.

Togliatti felt that **communism** was essentially polycentric, and different strategies for individual communist parties were necessary. Once the seed of **Marxism** was planted in a national culture, in order to reach socialist transformation it would have to be adapted to meet the particular conditions of that culture. For Togliatti's Italy, this would mean the creation, through structural reforms, of a democracy that merged components of liberalism and **socialism**. Togliatti lived out his final years in the **Soviet Union**, dying in Yalta in 1964. The Russian city of Stavropol, the birthplace of **Mikhail Gorbachev**, was renamed Togliatti in his honor.

TOURÉ, AHMED SÉKOU (1922–1984). Touré was the first president of independent **Guinea** and a committed trade unionist. Leaving school before reaching his teenage years, Touré developed a deep knowledge of **Marxism** through his interaction with trade unionists and French and African politicians, and studious reading. In 1941 he began work as a low-ranking civil servant in the post office, and within four years had organized its members into Guinea's first trade union. For 12 years between 1942 and 1954 Touré was leader of his local branch of the French *Confédération Générale du Travail* (CGT), and having been dismissed from his post office position attended its Paris Congress, which quickly confirmed for him the validity of his Marxist convictions.

In 1947 Touré was a key figure in the inception of the *Parti Démocratique de Guinée* (PDG), and in 1953 he emerged as a dominant voice on the Guinean left as a result of the 73-day general strike that successfully obtained the governmental adoption of a Labor Code. Touré, in 1955, was elected mayor of Conakry, and became a member of the French parliament in 1956. His charisma and political aptitude helped him strengthen his grip on the PDG in this period, and in 1958 he was at the forefront of the campaign to say no to Charles de Gaulle's referendum on colonial constitutional reforms. This allowed Touré to lead Guinea to independence from France, and to emerge as the uncontested leader of party and **state**.

The capricious nature of Touré's many theoretical standpoints makes assessing his brand of Marxism troublesome. Initially he took an orthodox Marxist approach, but in the youthful years of independence his rejection of the primacy of **class** forces was closer to "African Socialism," and chiefly grew from a desire to protect the unity of the burgeoning state. In 1964 he gravitated back toward an orthodox position, reintroducing the concept of the class enemy, and three years later demanded that the PDG be organized as a **vanguard party**. Touré on some occasions replicated **Stalinist** organization, and on others **Maoist**. Toward the end of his rule, references to Marxism were less audible, and Touré became increasingly dictatorial. His chief legacy to Marxism was the application of **Marxist–Leninist** concepts to an African framework, though he is best remembered as the inspiration behind Guinean independence, and yet the instigator of numerous disastrous economic programs, and the master of the political about face. *See also* AFRO-MARXISM.

TROTSKY, LEON (ORIGINALLY LEV DAVIDOVICH BRON-STEIN) (1879–1940). One of the central figures in the establishment of the **Soviet Union**, the Ukrainian Leon Trotsky was a leading figure in the **Russian Communist Party (Bolshevik)**, a major **Marxist** theoretician and historian, and an insightful military tactician. His writings and thought remain an inspiration to a major school of Marxism. Trotsky's political activism began when he joined a group of Populists in Mykolayiv in 1896, but he soon turned to Marxism, and in 1897 he helped found the South Russian Workers' Union and was duly exiled to Siberia for doing so. On escape he fled to London in order to join **Vladimir Ilich Lenin** in editing the **Russian Social Democratic Labor Party** newspaper, *Iskra*. Drifting toward the **Menshevik** line of thought, Trotsky was critical of the centralized revolutionary party Lenin's **Bolsheviks** were rapidly becoming. In 1905 he returned to Russia and led the St. Petersburg Soviet of Workers' Deputies in the failed **revolution** attempt that year. Exiled for this activity, Trotsky was once again banished to Siberia, and once again escaped. He then spent time in Austria, Switzerland, France and New York.

Trotsky returned to Russia following the March 1917 revolution. Joining the Petrograd Soviet he soon became a leading figure, and, despite his concerns about the increasing centralization of the party, accepted Lenin's invitation to become a member of the Bolsheviks. He was elected to the party's Central Committee and became chair of the Petrograd Soviet and also of the Bolshevik Revolutionary Committee that planned the October 1917 **Russian Revolution**. In the inaugural cabinet after the Bolsheviks came to power Trotsky was the peoples' commissar for foreign affairs, and then became peoples' commissar for war, and in this position founded and led the **Red Army** to an improbable victory in the Russian civil war waged to defend the young republic.

With Lenin's stroke in 1922 preventing him from taking a fully active role, leadership of both the party and the state increasingly shifted toward the "Troika" group of **Grigori Zinoviev**, Lev Kamenev and **Josef Stalin**. Trotsky opposed Stalin as part of the "Left Opposition" within the party, but he was outmaneuvered by the Troika and by Stalin in particular. He was removed from his post as commissar for war in 1925, expelled from the Politburo in 1926, and exiled to Alma Ata in Soviet Central Asia in 1927. Two years later, Trotsky was deported to Turkey, and for the rest of his life sought refuge in France, Norway and Mexico. In Mexico in 1938 he founded the **Fourth International** as an alternative to the Stalinist **Third International (Comintern)**. During exile Trotsky wrote extensively and polemically on the way in which Stalin had betrayed the 1917 Revolution. His criticisms did not go unnoticed in Moscow, and in 1940 a Stalinist agent, Ramón Mercarder, assassinated Trotsky at his home in Mexico with an icepick. Despite the process of *glasnost*, Trotsky never received formal rehabilitation from the Kremlin.

The Red Army leader's strong **internationalism** and advocacy of **"permanent revolution,"** the antithesis of Stalin's **"socialism in one country,"** put him at odds with many in the party, and was a motivational factor in his dismissal by Stalin. Trotsky's permanent revolution entailed two main tenets of thought. First, as world **capitalism** had developed so unevenly and in Russia created only a tiny **bourgeoisie**, a workers' government could be formed immediately following revolution, with no need for a period of middle-class rule. Secondly, a country as agrarian and undeveloped as Russia could not exist as a sole workers' state encircled by hostile **capitalist** states. As such, events in Russia would be a precursor for revolution elsewhere, inspiring **proletarian** insurgencies in more advanced Western nations, and relying upon their success for the continuance of the Soviet Union. In his latter years, Trotsky, most notably in *The Revolution Betrayed* (1937), was forced to account for the continued survival of the Soviet Union despite the absence of successful revolution in Western countries. He argued that, in order to avoid collapse as a consequence of its isolation, the Soviet state had gone through a period of degeneration, attempting to solve pre-socialist problems (e.g., low economic development, the effects of world and civil war) with socialist approaches (e.g., **collectivization**).

Trotsky's anti-Stalinism never abated, and he used a number of works such as *My Life* (1930) and *The History of the Russian Revolution* (1931–1933) to criticize the direction the Soviet Union had taken following the death of Lenin. Trotsky somewhat prophetically warned that the only consequence of a party that commanded the proletariat would be a ruthless, bureaucratic dictatorship, and with that borne out he called for a new, political revolution to return the Soviet Union to the ideals of socialist democracy behind 1917.

TROTSKYISM. A school of thought within **Marxism** inspired by the writings and politics of **Leon Trotsky**, Trotskyism claims to be the true heir of **Karl Marx** and **Vladimir Ilich Lenin**. It is particularly distinguished by the notion of **permanent revolution**. According to this theory, which Trotsky first developed in 1906 and modified and refined in 1928, the movement toward **socialism** is characterized by "combined and uneven development." That is to say, different countries are at different stages of economic, social and political development, but the more backward countries can speed through stages of development producing societies that combine the most advanced aspects of development with features of more backward stages. Russia, for example, could move from its semi-**feudal** state through a **bourgeois** stage and directly to socialism via a permanent **revolution** that telescoped together different stages of development. This theory also incorporated the key element of **internationalism**, meaning in this context the view that socialist revolution must be international or else not be socialist. Trotskyism is thus particularly opposed to the **Stalinist** notion of **"socialism in one country"** which proclaims the possibility (even the necessity) of Russia developing socialism within its own borders first. According to Trotskyist doctrine this is a contradiction in terms.

The other notable ideological feature of Trotskyism lies in its analysis of the **Soviet Union** and Stalinism. Trotsky characterized it as a "degenerate workers'state," in other words, a **state** that had undergone a **proletarian** revolution but which had subsequently degenerated, betrayed by the rule of the Stalinist bureaucracy.

As a movement Trotskyism has been particularly spread through the **Fourth International**, which Trotsky established in 1938. Numerous parties and organizations (for example, the **American Socialist**

Workers Party, the International Socialists of Canada, the British Socialist Workers Party and Workers Revolutionary Party, the Portuguese *Liga Communista Internacionale* to name but a few) have been established claiming the label Trotskyist, but they have frequently diverged from each other ideologically and politically, at times becoming fierce opponents. In part this is due to the fact that Trotsky himself, as with any thinker, developed and changed his views over his lifetime, and different Trotskyist groups have seized on different views that Trotsky expressed. For example, on the party Trotsky's views ranged from rigidly centralist to favoring a broad, loose party organization and the different views of different Trotskyist groups have reflected this. Overall, Trotskyism has been a significant Marxist movement offering a critical viewpoint on communist regimes, but it is yet to achieve the size and significance to contend for political power anywhere.

TUVA. Established in 1921 in the wake of the regional victory of the **Red Army**, the Tuvan People's Republic (occasionally referred to as Tannu-Tuva) was formed out of the respective territorial claims of Mongolia, **China** and Tsarist Russia, becoming the third independent state to adopt **Marxism-Leninism**. Its ideological foundations are outlined in its first constitution: "For the past few decades, a **revolutionary** movement against . . . oppression and **exploitation** from the **ruling classes** has been developing in every country. . . . The most heroic example in this struggle is the great October Revolution, which freed Russia's workers and **peasants** from the yoke of autocracy and domination by **bourgeoisie** and the land owners. The Tuvan People, subjugated and exploited for centuries by internal and external oppressors . . . established the power of the working people in the form of the national government in the year 1921."

Almost entirely feudal, nomadic, Buddhist and Shamanist, the state of 300,000 citizens was led by the Tuvan People's Revolutionary Party, which sought "completion of the anti-**feudal** revolution, the actualisation of all democratic conversions and passage to the **socialist** stage of non-capitalistic development." Always under the hegemony of the **Soviet Union** (evident in its economic policy, adopting the New Economic Policy between 1921 and 1929), Tuva became in 1944 an "autonomous region" of the Soviet Union under the leadership of Party Secretary Toka, relinquishing its de jure independence in what has been described as "dubious circumstances." Soviet industrialization enabled a remarkable expansion of basic utilities to the most remote of villages and ensured rapid urbanization in several centers of population, with the capital, Kyzyl, eventually housing 100,000 citizens. Such industrialization engineered a division between rural, nomadic Tuvans, who retained their Turkic language and mysticism, and urban citizens, who, with the influx of immigrants from other Soviet territories, became Russified, favoring Russian dialects and secularism.

Since 1993, Tuva has been a Republic of the Russian Federation with its own president, retaining a fifty-percent command economy and most Soviet bureaucracies. The successor party has recently introduced nominal market reforms against the wishes of most peasants and *nomenklatura* members, who remain powerful politically and populist and collectivist in sentiment. These reforms have aided the growth of the largely Russian middle class, who hold trade links with Russia, Turkey, China and other central Asian **states**.

– U –

UNIFIED MARIATEGUISTA PARTY. *See* PERUVIAN MARX-ISM.

UNITED STATES OF AMERICA. As a significant political creed, the influence of **Marxism** in the United States has been negligible. The U.S. has, though, provided a string of **socialist** and Marxist pamphleteers, campaigners and intellectuals, chiefly Paul Baran, **Eugene Debs, Daniel De Leon, Michael Harrington**, Jack London**, Paul Sweezy** and William Appleman Williams.

An explanation for the apparent failure of a genuine mass Marxist movement to emerge in the United States came initially from the German economist Walter Sombart in the form of his 1906 essay "Why Is There No Socialism in the USA?" (*Warum gibt es in den Vereinigten Staaten keinen Sozialismus?*). This cited multitudinous reasons for the failure of the doctrine to enter the public imagination, from the favorable attitudes of American workers to the **capitalist** system, and the civil integration offered by full suffrage, to the relative wealth of the U.S. **proletariat** in comparison with its European counterparts. Over the subsequent century, numerous other explanations for the American Marxist malaise have been put forward, such as the strength of the Democratic and Republican parties in a fiercely nonmalleable two-party system, the absence of genuine and mass solidarity among the American working class, and the strength of Catholicism.

In terms of Marxist organizational structures, in the first quarter of the 20th-century left-wing groups, chiefly Debs' **Socialist Party of America**, enjoyed fleeting if marginal popularity. However, a schism in that party over support for the **Bolsheviks** in the 1917 **Russian Revolution** meant they were never as strong again, and resulted in the formation of what became the **Communist Party of the United States of America**. In the 21st century, both maintain little more than pariah status, though they are influential within the U.S. anti-war movement. A brief Marxist intellectual renaissance occurred through the 1960s and into the 1970s with the emergence of New Left thinkers such as Baran, Sweezy and Williams, but this was more a reflection of the **ideology**'s popularity among the intelligentsia than the manifestation of a popular hankering for Marxism.

USE VALUE. *See* COMMODITY.

– V –

VANGUARD PARTY. The notion of a vanguard party was developed and applied by the **Bolsheviks** and by **Vladimir Ilich Lenin** in particular. Lenin believed that revolutionary **class consciousness** would not develop spontaneously within the **proletariat**, and that it was the role of the party to bring such consciousness to the people. The party must consist of thoroughly trained, full-time revolutionaries, an elite of dedicated professional revolutionaries who would guide and lead the people. Critics have suggested that the notion of a vanguard party provides a ready rationale for a minority dictatorship, although defenders have argued that it is a legitimate organizational principle particularly in repressive conditions.

VIENNA UNION. *See* INTERNATIONAL WORKING UNION OF SOCIALIST PARTIES.

VIETMINH. *See* INDOCHINESE COMMUNIST PARTY.

VIETNAM, SOCIALIST REPUBLIC OF. The 1976 reunification of North and South Vietnam saw the launch of the Socialist Republic of Vietnam (*Cong Hoa Xa Hoi Viet Nam*), a **Marxist–Leninist** state led by the **Communist Party of Vietnam** (CPV). Following the close of World War II, **Ho Chi Minh**'s **Vietminh** guerrilla forces seized power and declared Vietnamese independence. This was done in the face of the French, who invaded Vietnam in 1946 with the aim of re-asserting their colonial hold on the country. The conflict that ensued was halted in 1954 with the signing of the Geneva Accords, a peace agreement that partitioned Vietnam into two zones, the North and the South. Having assumed overall control of North Vietnam, Ho's Vietnam Workers' Party set about constructing **socialism** in its own **state** and engendering a **revolution** in South Vietnam. Alarmed by the potential "domino effect" of successive countries adopting **communism**, a Cold War–fixated **United States** invaded North Vietnam in 1964 on the side of the South Vietnamese government, triggering the devastating Vietnam War. As the 1970s began, U.S. involvement decreased, until the January 1973 ratification of the Paris Peace Accords prompted a ceasefire and the rapid exit of American troops from Vietnamese soil. The northern communists, determined to bring about reunification, continued to fight against the southern government. By 1975, they had assumed control in South Vietnam and ousted the incumbent leader, President Duong Van Minh. The following year, the reunified Socialist Republic of Vietnam (SRV) was proclaimed, and the Vietnam Workers' Party transformed into the **vanguard** CPV.

A fervently Marxist–Leninist constitution aimed at realizing "socialism and communism in Vietnam" was hastily sanctioned by the Vietnamese Politburo. The economy was restructured according to strict collectivist principles that were underpinned by the introduction of a heavily managed and target-driven centralized planning system. Strong ties were brokered with the **Soviet Union**, with the culmination being Moscow's underwriting of the SRV's first economic five-year plan. The constitution also saw the CPV formally commit itself to a variety of **democratic centralism** that left state action entirely subordinate to party doctrine and opposition organizations illegal. Bolstered by considerable Soviet military aid, the CPV government was able in 1979 to overthrow the **Khmer Rouge** regime in **Cambodia**, and repel retaliatory attacks by **China**. With Vietnamese self-confidence accordingly at its zenith, the CPV used the 1980 constitution to reaffirm its paramount status as "the only force leading the state and society, and the main factor determining all successes of the revolution."

Despite this portrayal of infallibility, economic malaise meant the CPV's hold on power was less than secure. In 1986 the sluggish pace of development forced the government of moderate leader Nguyen Van Linh to announce a program of "renovation" that encouraged private enterprise and opened the economy to free market influence. The 1989 **collapse of the Soviet Union** meant the loss of the SRV's largest aid contributor, and most prolific trading partner. Coupled with the tide of will for market reform inside the country, the government bowed to the inevitable, announcing in 1992 a new constitution guaranteeing further economic freedom, and relegating Marxist **ideology** to a poor second behind rapid development. Eight years later, Vietnamese acceptance of elements of **capitalism** culminated in the opening of a stock exchange. Nonetheless, the landmark constitution of 1992 did attest one vital remnant of orthodox Marxism–Leninism, namely, that of the foremost role of the CPV as the "leading force" in society. In retaining both its single-party status and stranglehold over political developments, the CPV, like the **Lao People's Revolutionary Party** in neighboring **Laos**, steadfastly held the notion of the all-consuming democratic centralist party. That much of their Marxism–Leninism remains, even if little else does.

The Marxism of the SRV simultaneously borrowed elements of Confucianism, **Maoism** and orthodox Soviet communism, and added in a populist nationalism. Establishing socialism and communism through pure ideological allegiance to Marxism took a back seat first to the struggle for national autonomy, and, once that had been established, to economic survival and development. Lacking an industrialized, urbanized **proletariat** to accomplish the revolutionary transition to socialism, it was left for the ideologues in the CPV to mold Marxism to suit the agrarian and underdeveloped terrain they inhabited. This meant initially clinging to patriotic sentiment, and subsequently permitting the infiltration of capitalism into state ideology.

VIETNAMESE COMMUNIST PARTY. *See* INDOCHINESE COMMUNIST PARTY.

VO NGUYEN GIAP (1910–). Vo Nguyen Giap was a **communist** Vietnamese military commander who led the Vietnam People's Army in victories over the Japanese, French and Americans. Born in Quang Binh province in Vietnam, he was a political activist from an early age. He wrote for various radical journals in the late 1930s and was active in various communist organizations before fleeing Vietnam and joining **Ho Chi Minh** in China in 1939. In 1944 Giap was responsible for creating and organizing what became the Vietnam People's Army. In 1945 he became minister of defense of the **Socialist Republic of Vietnam** and he was commander-in-chief of the Vietnam People's Army in the wars against France and the **United States**. From 1951 to 1982 he served on the Vietnamese Workers' Party Politburo.

Giap wrote extensively on **revolutionary** warfare, and drew heavily on the work of **Mao Zedong**. He noted the crucial role of the **peasantry** and the importance of coordinating the political and the military struggle, claiming to combine the lessons of the **Russian** and **Chinese revolutions** in a unique Vietnamese approach.

– W –

WARSAW PACT. Officially named the Treaty of Friendship, Cooperation and Mutual Assistance, the pact was a military and economic alliance of the **Marxist–Leninist** Eastern Bloc countries signed in 1955 to consolidate resistance to the North Atlantic Treaty Organization (NATO). The founding signatories were **Albania, Bulgaria, Czechoslovakia, Hungary, Poland, Romania** and the **Soviet Union**, with the **German Democratic Republic** joining in 1956. **Yugoslavia** was the only local **communist** country omitted, having been jettisoned from the Warsaw Pact's predecessor, the **Cominform**, in 1948. The Pact allowed Moscow to plant **Red Army** troops across the region, though guaranteeing the sovereignty of its individual members in state affairs. Despite this, the Soviet Union twice invoked the Pact to put down dissent, first during the 1956 **Hungarian Uprising**, and then the 1968 **Prague Spring**, moves that prompted the already recalcitrant Albanians to leave the agreement. By the early 1990s the collapse of the communist regimes in most of the Pact member countries rendered it superfluous, and it was declared "nonexistent" in July 1991.

WESTERN MARXISM. This very broad school of thought originated in the 1920s and ended its development around 1970. Notable figures associated with Western Marxism include **Georgii Lukács**, **Karl Korsch**, **Antonio Gramsci**, **Max Horkheimer**, **Theodor Adorno**, **Herbert Marcuse**, and **Jean-Paul Sartre**. This represents a role call of some of the greatest and most innovative of Marxist thinkers, all linked by their rejection of the orthodox **Marxism** of the **Soviet Union** and of the **Second International**. Typical themes of Western Marxism are humanism, conceiving of Marxism as philosophy not science, and an openness to **Hegelian dialectical** philosophy and other non-Marxist sources for inspiration. The **Frankfurt School** represents an important school within Western Marxism, and also highlights the often academic character of Western Marxism and the tendency of its exponents not to involve themselves directly in working-**class** movements and the **revolutionary** struggle (Gramsci being a notable exception). Some of the most inventive and sophisticated developments of Marxist theory have come out of Western Marxism, but, arguably, this has involved an implicit critique and undermining of Marxism.

WOLPE, HAROLD (?–1996). Wolpe was a leading member of the **South African Communist Party** (SACP) and a radical lawyer and academic active in the underground movement to resist and overcome apartheid. He joined the SACP while studying for his LL.B. at Witwatersrand University. On graduating he was called to the Side Bar, representing activists other lawyers were unwilling to take on, for example Nelson Mandela. Wolpe's underground political activities made him a target for the government, and he was arrested soon after the Sharpeville massacre of 1960, and then again in 1963 as he attempted to flee the country following the arrest of SACP leaders at Lilliesleaf Farm. Wolpe's flight allowed him to escape a lengthy sentence at the Rivonia trial, a show trial that saw other leaders in the resistance to apartheid ruthlessly dealt with. Having arrived in Great Britain, Wolpe worked for both the African National Congress (ANC) and the SACP, and taught sociology in a number of British universities. Following the end of apartheid and the resultant amnesty for previously banned political activists, Wolpe returned to South Africa in 1991.

Perhaps Wolpe's greatest legacy to **Marxism** was his assistance in the foundation of the journal *Economy and Society*. In 1972 he penned an article entitled *Capitalism and cheap labour power in South Africa from Segregation to Apartheid*, which inspired a rethinking within the black consciousness movement, as Wolpe argued that apartheid was not a response to racism, but a response instead to the exploitation of cheap labor that **capital** required.

– Y –

YAMAKAWA, HITOSHI (1880–1958). Born in Okayama prefecture on 20 December 1880, he quit school in 1897 in protest over reform of the education system and left for Tokyo. There he published a magazine *Abundant Sound of Youth* but in the third issue a piece on the "human tragedy" of the crown prince's marriage was judged to be guilty of the crime of lese-majesté and he was given three years' hard labor and ordered to pay a substantial fine. In 1901 Yamakawa was put in Sugamo prison. After his release, he joined the Japanese Socialist Party in February 1906 and became the editor of the *Daily Commoners News* in January 1907. He was jailed again for his part in the Red Flag incident of 1908 but as a result avoided a death sentence meted out to other enemies of the state in a sweep of opponents of the government in 1910. After his release from prison he ran a pharmacy and married but his wife became ill and died in 1923. In 1916 he closed his pharmacy and returned to Tokyo where he resumed his **socialist** movement activities. He remarried Kikuei in the same year.

Yamakawa's **Marxism** became clear in the aftermath of the 1917 **Russian Revolution** when he criticized the official theory of people-based government which was an emperor-centered alternative to democracy. In 1919 he published *Socialist Studies* and was a major figure in the formation of the **Japanese Communist Party** (JCP) in 1922. In the July/August issue of the party journal *Vanguard* he contributed an influential article "Changing the Direction of the **Proletarian** Class Movement" under the slogan "We should be among the masses" in which he criticized Japanese socialists who acted independently of the bulk of the working class and the masses, and argued that they needed to enter into struggle among the masses while maintaining theoretical purity. This argument had a big influence on social movements of the time and was later known as "Yamakawaism." In 1923 he was arrested and tried in the First Communist Party incident but found not guilty.

He was attacked by fellow **communist** theoretician Kazuo Kukamoto, and as a result of these criticisms and the publications of the 1927 theses which denied the role of the JCP as a **vanguard party**, Yamakawa cut his ties with the JCP and did not participate in the reorganization of the party in 1927. Instead, he created the journal *Labor-Farmer* with others who left the party in order to promote the idea of a party of mass struggle in the labor and tenant movements. For 10 years he was able to operate legally as a leading member of the Labor-Farmer group until he was investigated by the police once again in the People's Front incident of 1937. In this incident the police investigated ties of university professors, including **Itsuro Sakisaka** (1897–1985) of Kyushu Imperial University and Kozo Uno (1897–1977) of Tohoku Imperial University. Even though the professors involved were later found not guilty, they lost their posts and Yamakawa and his fellow activist defendants were found guilty in their first trials. Eventually, however, the case was dropped during the appeal process when the Peace Preservation Laws, upon which their convictions were based, were abolished in 1945 at the end of the Pacific War.

In 1946 Yamakawa became chairman of the Committee for a Democratic People's Front which advocated a joint front of all leftist parties. However, his activities were hampered by illness and as confrontation between the socialist and communist parties became more intense in 1947, he abandoned the Front and eventually joined the Socialist Party. In 1950, when he and others created the *Shakaishugi*

Kyokai, he was put in charge along with Tokyo University Professor Hyoei Ouchi, and the group became the premier theoretical body of the left wing of the Japanese Socialist Party. Yamakawa died on 23 March 1958 at the age of 78.

YEMEN, PEOPLE'S DEMOCRATIC REPUBLIC OF. Having played a pivotal part in an often violent struggle to halt colonial rule over south Yemen, the **socialist** National Liberation Front (NLF) assumed power upon the British departure in 1967, and announced the birth of the People's Democratic Republic of South Yemen, later the People's Democratic Republic of Yemen (PDRY).

After overseeing the early years of NLF rule as president and party general secretary, the moderate Qahtan Mohammad al-Shaabi was ousted by radical **Marxist–Leninist** factions within the party in 1969. They put into power Salim Ali Rubayi, made the name change mentioned above a year later, and steered the PDRY toward a Marxist–Leninist system of government based on that of the **Soviet Union**. Ideological ties that bore economic and military fruit were brokered with Moscow, as well as **Cuba** and **China**. All political parties were obliterated and amalgamated into the NLF, which became the Yemen Socialist Party (YSP) in 1978, and the state became wholly subordinate to the will of the party. Foreign and domestic-owned means of production were nationalized in their entirety, and a heavily centralized, planned economy was established, while two sets of Agrarian Reform Laws demanded the forceful confiscation of private land and its equal redistribution among workers' cooperatives. The **ruling class** was destroyed, as landowners, former rulers and tribal leaders were stripped of their means of societal domination. Meanwhile, the position of **women** was enhanced as decreed by the government's Orthodox Socialist Program and its egalitarian tone. Mass organizations such as the General Union of Yemeni Workers were instituted for people to become involved in the revolutionary climate, though in reality these amounted to little more than mouthpieces with which the NLF could filter down party doctrine. In accordance with the atheism of Marxism–Leninism, the former dominance of Islam was constantly undermined by the state, for example in the reclamation and nationalization of existing religious endowments. As in the Soviet Union, all of this was maintained against a backdrop of persecution, as religious and political figures deemed to be enemies of the new state frequently "disappeared."

By 1978 Rubayi's authority had been so destabilized by the factional maneuverings of his rival Abdel Fattah Ismail, since 1969 the second most influential man in the PDRY, that after an ill-advised bid to attain outright control of the country against the will of the Central Committee he was deposed and executed. Predictably, his successor was Ismail, and as champion of the orthodox, Soviet-loyal wing of the newly named YSP, he immediately encouraged further Muscovite influence, and made his party's commitment to Marxism–Leninism more pronounced. The PDRY had always espoused a desire to bring about unification with north Yemen, since 1967 the Yemen Arab Republic (YAR), and aside from during border skirmishes in 1979, its northern counterparts were not unfavorable to such a concept. Ismail's administration, though, wanted not an equal union of PDRY and YAR, but a **communist** puppet state to be ruled from the south. To this end and with Soviet backing, the YSP surreptitiously sponsored **Marxist** groups inside the YAR, an initiative only decelerated with the April 1980 resignation and exile of Ismail. He had been the casualty of further factional rivalries within the YSP, and with his exit the presidency passed to Ali Nasir Muhammad Husani, prime minister since 1971. Ali Nasir oversaw a period of relative calm as the YSP continued to pursue its own interpretation of Marxism, until in 1986 Ismail returned to the PDRY with the intention of winning back his presidency, but in effect prompting a fierce 12-day civil war. This resulted in the loss of over a 1,000 Yemeni lives, most notably that of Ismail himself, and the jettisoning from power of Ali Nasir, who was replaced by Haydar Bakr al-Attas, regarded by many as an ideological pragmatist.

With relations between the YAR and PDRY ever more conciliatory, and the effects of the policies of *glasnost* and *perestroika* that would ultimately engender the **collapse of the Soviet Union** sorely felt by a YSP so firmly under the yoke of Moscow, unification was nigh. On 22 May 1990 the two countries confirmed the inevitable, with the present-day Republic of Yemen pronounced and a raft of **capitalist** measures introduced. To the dismay of many of its left-wing members, the YSP shed its Marxist–Leninist rhetoric and embraced a social democratic-style manifesto that saw it summarily beaten in the multiparty elections of 1992, 1997 and 2003.

Marxism in the PDRY was always subject to local conditions and interpretations. Despite inhabiting an overtly agricultural economy bereft of genuine industry, the NLF/YSP attempted to negate the ramifications of stage theory and immediately bring about their own localized version of Marxism. At the center of this, though, was the staunchly orthodox Marxist–Leninist concept of the mass party. The NLF/YSP hierarchy sought to marry the cross-class appeal they had garnered in the past as a liberation movement with the all-encompassing influence of an organization that has systematically destroyed all other power bases. The result of this was a party which was as hegemonic as any other in the communist world. Southern Yemeni Marxism was a mixture of orthodox theory tailored to meet actual conditions, and as such when Marxist–Leninist orthodoxy died elsewhere, and local conditions took hold (for example in the perennial, often tribal-based factional struggles inside the NLF/YSP), it capitulated as an **ideology**.

YUGOSLAVIA, PEOPLE'S REPUBLIC OF. After the end of German occupation in World War II, Yugoslavia emerged deeply split along ethnic and national lines. **Josip Tito** and his **Communist Party of Yugoslavia** (CPY) succeeded in uniting the country behind the cause of **communism**, and one of the few **Marxist** states to veer significantly from Soviet orthodoxy came into being.

Tito's communists had risen to prominence during the battle to free Yugoslavian lands from the clutches of the Third Reich, receiving Allied assistance along the way. This had left them in a far superior position to other pretenders to Yugoslavian governance, principally the Karadjordjević dynasty. Accordingly, the CPY won 90 percent of votes in the elections of November 1945, banished the Karadjordjević regime from the country, and announced the beginning of the People's Republic of Yugoslavia. Paramount in the CPY's attainment of political stewardship was their uniting of the many factions in the country, replacing it instead with recognition of the uniqueness of each group, and placing a stress on the importance of mutual equality. They overcame the two ideological mainstays of the first half of the 20th century, Serbian primacy and Yugoslavian unitarism, by replacing them with a coalescing creed of Marxism. To match ideological unity with practical unity, the KCP's 1946 constitution created a federal state, based largely on the Soviet model, that embodied the six republics of Croatia, Bosnia and Herzegovina, Macedonia, Montenegro, Slovenia and Serbia, and recognized the relative autonomy of the Serbian provinces of Kosovo and Vojvodina. In a further similarity with the Soviet system, this federal framework was in reality subordinated entirely to the directives of the CPY.

Having gained power in 1945, the CPY initially pursued a fairly orthodox **Stalinist** approach to the economy. Industry and banks were nationalized, a five-year plan was adopted in 1947, and in 1949 moves began to **collectivize** the countryside. However, the split between the **Soviet Union** and Tito's Yugoslavia in 1948 and strong resistance from peasants meant the drive for collectivization was soon relaxed. The division between the two nations, which was to have a determining effect on the development of the Yugoslav route to communism, had occurred over the issue of foreign policy. Tito's brand of aggressive, self-autonomous foreign relations sat uncomfortably with **Josef Stalin** who wanted the Soviet Union to be the commanding power in the communist bloc. Having tolerated the initial differences between the Soviet way to communism and the Yugoslav one of "national communism," Stalin finally decreed that Tito's insistence on pursuing his own foreign policy merited Yugoslavia's expulsion from the **Communist Information Bureau** (Cominform), and accordingly the termination of relations between the two regimes.

Faced with the problems caused by this economic, political and military isolation from the Soviet Union–dominated Eastern Bloc, the CPY was forced to conceive and tread its own "separate road to socialism," through the creation of workers' councils and by introducing elements of self-management into enterprise. This ideological about-face represented a rejection of orthodox **Marxism–Leninism**, and according to the CPY a return to an original form of Marxism that had been distorted by Stalin and the **Communist Party of the Soviet Union** (CPSU). The self-management scheme shifted the means of production into the hands of workers and out of those of the **state**. Price fixing was abandoned and collectivization reversed as the Yugoslavian government sought to create an economy situated somewhere between centralized planning and the free market.

However, the party, as of 1952 renamed the **League of Communists of Yugoslavia** (LCY) to signify their disconnection from the Soviet Union, in allowing economic freedoms but stifling debate so that all decisions remained in its hands, trod a path different from the Moscow one, but like the CPSU retained tight control of society. Further reforms were carved out in the first half of the 1960s, following an intraparty split between secret police chief Aleksandaer Ranković's authoritarian group, and **Edvard Kardelj**'s reformist band of LCY members. The 1963 party constitution had seen the principle of self-management extended to workers in the public sector, and this further decentralizing measure had the effect of prompting a call from Kardelj and others for similar measures to be put in place in the financial and industrial sectors. In spite of opposition from Ranković's conservative faction, in 1964 Tito decreed that the federal control of many economic and political departments should shift to republic level. To further parry the threat of Yugoslavian fragmentation, the LCY followed up these decentralizing measures by enshrining them in the constitution of 1974. While authority was distributed among the members of the federation, at each level and in each country it was still the all-powerful LCY that directed policy, with the party line centrally formulated and filtered outwards via local LCY branches. This was perhaps the basis on which Tito affirmed at its Tenth Party Conference that the LCY was still pursuing the Leninist concept of **democratic centralism**, despite the maintenance of a federal model.

Internationally, Yugoslavia became a leading player in the Non-Aligned Movement (NAM), standing apart from both sides of the Cold War and retaining relationships with East and West depending on which was most advantageous at any given time. By 1961, there were 51 officially nonaligned states, primarily from colonized or formally colonized Asian and African countries, with each consenting to promulgate three core principles: a repudiation of colonialism, a strong condemnation of apartheid, and a demand that military action against national liberation movements be halted. Following the Yugoslavian split with the Soviet Union, Belgrade received economic assistance from the **United States**, and, in contrast to other Eastern Bloc states, maintained trade with the Western world. There was a brief reconciliation with Moscow following Stalin's death, but the two powers remained at arms distance, no more so than when Tito condemned **Warsaw Pact** military intervention in the 1968 **Prague Spring** and the **Brezhnev Doctrine** as an act of **imperialism**. Yugoslavia's standing in the nonaligned world remained strong throughout the communist years, with African regimes such as Idi Amin's Uganda providing ardent support for Tito. However, membership in the NAM alienated the country from the West, eventually playing a part in the collapse of the government as Western European nations increasingly began to shun Yugoslavia, leading to a dramatic increase in its trade deficit.

The beginning of the end for the communist regime in Yugoslavia came when Tito died on 4 May 1980. The collective leadership that took the reins of power inherited a Yugoslavian economy in turmoil and perpetual decline, with an end to growth, crippling foreign debts and food shortages adding to simmering ethnic tensions to create a hugely volatile landscape. Sensing this, the nationalist Serbian League of Communists leader Slobodan Milošević hatched a plot that resulted ultimately in the breakup of the Yugoslavian union. By appealing to the nationalistic tendencies of the populations of the individual republics and mobilizing mass support, in 1988 Milošević succeeded in bringing about leadership changes in Kosovo, Vojvodina and Montenegro, which in turn led to the neutralization of the weak Titoist leaderships of Slovenia, Croatia, Bosnia-Herzegovina and Macedonia.

The breakup of the federation was hastened by events elsewhere, as communist regimes fell one by one, robbing Titoists of potential allies and moreover trading partners. A year later, the Slovene and Croatian communist parties moved toward democratization, scheduling multiparty free elections for 1990. The election results provided a mandate for the disaffiliation of the two countries from Yugoslavia, and coupled with the strengthening of Serbian independence and Milošević's abolishment of Kosovo and Vojvodina, the collapse of the federal system was nigh. Civil war ensued, until by 1992 each of the former republics of Tito's communist Yugoslavia had attained independence, with the rump country now consisting of just Serbia and Montenegro. Successor parties, often espousing a more social democratic approach, replaced the communist parties and the republics started out on the long road to westernization.

The Marxism practiced in the former Yugoslavia represented the most radical departure in Eastern Europe from the Soviet model of Marxism–Leninism. The break with Stalin in 1948 allowed the country freedom of actions other nations in the Soviet bloc did not have. The key difference was the market-based approach to economics that worker self-management fostered, as Tito led the country away from the centrally planned, command systems of the rest of the Soviet bloc in a firm rejection of Stalinist bureaucracy.

– Z –

ZAPATISTAS. Deriving their inspiration from Mexican revolutionary Emiliano Zapata's Liberation Army of the South (*Ejército Libertador del Sur*—ELS), the Zapatista Army of National Liberation (*Ejército Zapatista de Liberación Nacional*—ELZN) was founded in 1983, though it did not come to prominence until 1994.

The ELS had achieved brief popularity in Mexico between 1910 and 1919, rallying the **peasantry** behind its campaign for the redistribution of agricultural land. The ELZN brought these ideas to a new generation, and on New Year's Day 1994 burst forth in a popular uprising in the impoverished southern Mexican region of Chiapas. Calling for agrarian and social reform, it seized a number of regional municipalities and entered into an armed battle with government troops that came to a nervy ceasefire at the end of January. The Zapatistas soon renounced violence as a means of achieving their goals, namely to promote the cause of the indigenous population through eradicating poverty and installing health and education systems, and opposing wider neo-liberal political and economic systems. By 2003 the ELZN was able to claim that so successfully had it constructed its own "state within a state" in Chiapas, that it now boasted a communitarian system of food production, successful state-autonomous education and health programs, and transparent, frequently rotating "Committees of Good Government," whose scrutiny guaranteed the corruption-free administration of affairs.

In its strongly worded writings against neo-liberalism, the ELZN asserted that privatization acts as an exploitative agent against the vulnerable, and in its championing of universal healthcare and education, the ELZN has displayed **Marxist** credentials. However, the Zapatistas have never openly advocated Marxism. Their rejection of orthodox Marxian concepts such as the **dictatorship of the proletariat** has been reflected in their reluctance to aim for total power, as they have preferred instead to build equality in their own Chiapas region while simultaneously calling for localized resistance to globalization in the wider world. In transforming **socialist** and Marxist ideas onto "Indianist" (the prioritizing of the local indigenous population over one particular social class) notions informed by guerrilla army tactics, the ELZN has offered a post-modernist take on Marxism. In addition, its reluctance to pursue the **Leninist** concept of total power and instead a preference to construct a communitarian pocket within a wider state offers a form of neo-**communist** governing system that is largely untried.

ZASULICH, VERA (1852–1919). One of the founders of the first Russian **Marxist** organization, the **Emancipation of Labor Group**, Zasulich was a key figure in early Russian Marxism and a close collaborator of **Georgii Plekhanov** and **Paul Axelrod**. She was the recipient of a famous letter in 1881 from **Karl Marx** suggesting that Russia need not follow the same path of **capitalist** development taken by Western Europe on the way to **socialism**. **Vladimir Ilich Lenin** took up this idea in arguing against the **Mensheviks** that Russia could have a **proletarian revolution**.

ZETKIN, CLARA (1857–1933). Born in Saxony, Zetkin was one of the foremost figures in the German workers' movement, and an activist in the campaign for **women's** rights. Zetkin had her political baptism as a member of the **German Social Democrat Party** (SPD), serving as a left-wing member of the National Executive from 1895. In 1896, despite German laws decreeing that women were to be prevented from joining trade unions, she became the provisional international secretary of the Tailors and Seamstresses Union. In the same year, when speaking at the SPD conference, Zetkin espoused for the first time her rejection of contemporary **bourgeois** feminism of the time that advocated the restriction of votes by property or income. Here Zetkin began the mobilization of the first mass emancipation movement for working-**class** women in the world, the policies of which were expounded in *Die Gleichheit* magazine under her editorship from 1892 to 1917. In 1899 Zetkin gave an account of the struggle of working women under **capitalism** at the founding congress of the **Second International** in Paris. Zetkin then assisted in the formation of the International Women's Socialist Congress in 1907, a radical group poles apart from the reformist SPD, so much so that when in 1908 a new law was passed granting women the right to organize politically with men, the party saw fit to end separate women's associations. Zetkin worked tirelessly to convert **socialist** parties across Europe to the cause of universal suffrage, and she created the Conference of Socialist Women whose earliest achievement was the establishment of International Women's Day (8 March) in 1910. The outspoken German's opposition to World War I led to her expulsion from the SPD, and in 1917 she joined the newborn **German Independent Social Democratic Party** (USPD). Zetkin's membership, however, lasted just two years, as in 1919 she left the party to play a key role in the formation of the **German Communist Party** (KPD) alongside **Rosa Luxemburg** and **Karl Liebknecht** with whom she had worked as a member of the **Spartacists** during World War I. She was soon elected to the KPD leadership, and appointed editor-in-chief of the party newspaper, *Die Kommunistin*, and in 1920 she was elected a Reichstag deputy. Zetkin's activism was ended only by her death in 1933, up to which point she had been steering the women's movement within the **Third International** (Comintern) from the **Soviet Union**, where she had moved in 1924.

The foremost activist and theoretician of the "women question" in her time, Zetkin was regarded as a **Marxist–Leninist**, a perception given credence by the publishing in 1929 of her fond reminiscences of her meetings with **Vladimir Ilich Lenin**. Zetkin bridged the gap between the struggle for women's liberation and **Marxism**, linking the rise of patriarchal order to the rise of private **property**, and placing emphasis on the class-based nature of the women's movement. She was committed to the principle of a general strike as a prologue to social revolution rather than reformism, though in 1923 she persuaded Lenin not to support left-wing uprisings in Germany.

ZHAO ZIYANG (1919–2005). Served as premier of the **People's Republic of China** (PRC) from 1980 until 1987 and then general secretary of the party. A successful administrator and effective economic policy maker, he achieved note outside of China primarily through his stand against the violent repression of the Tiananmen Square protests.

Born in Henan province Zhao joined the Young Communist League at the age of 13 in 1932 and the **Chinese Communist Party** in 1938. He rose to become first secretary of the Guangdong area party organization, but was purged during the **Cultural Revolution**. Rehabilitated, he became chief administrator of Sichuan province in

1975, a full member of the Politburo in 1979 and premier of the PRC in 1980. He resigned as premier and became general secretary of the party in 1987, and was ousted from this position in 1989 during the pro-democracy demonstrations. Arguing for a moderate line against the student protestors in Tiananmen Square he defied party discipline when he was voted down and went to meet the protestors. He was forced to retire from public life, prohibited from speaking in public, and had his traveling restricted, but was allowed to retain his comfortable lifestyle until his death.

ZHOU ENLAI (1898–1976). One of the major Chinese communist leaders in the 20th century and the first premier of the **People's Republic of China** (PRC). Born in the Jiangsu province Zhou studied at Nankai University and in Japan (1917–19) and France (1920–24). In Europe he helped organize branches of the **Chinese Communist Party** (CCP), and when he returned to China in 1924 he played a significant part in the first United Front. In 1927 he was elected to the CCP Central Committee and Politburo, and he was one of the leaders of the **Long March** in 1934–35. He was a key representative of the CCP in negotiations with the Kuomintang mediated by the **United States**, and after the communists came to power in 1949 he was appointed premier and foreign minister. As foreign minister (until 1958) he helped to improve China's standing and its foreign relations with a number of countries. He attended the 1954 Geneva Conference on Indochina and the 1955 Asian–African Conference in Indonesia, and he negotiated the five principles of peaceful coexistence with the Indian leader Jawaharlal Nehru that formed the basis of China's foreign policy up until 1958. He was also involved in the policy of dialogue with the United States and Japan in the early 1970s that saw the signing of the1972 Shanghai Communiqué with President Richard Nixon. As premier he generally had a moderating, stabilizing influence, for example endeavoring to limit the disruption of the **Cultural Revolution**. After the death of **Lin Biao** in 1971, Zhou was number two in the Chinese leadership hierarchy after **Mao**. Zhou died in office in 1976.

ZIMBABWE AFRICAN NATIONAL UNION–PATRIOTIC FRONT. The Zimbabwe African National Union–Patriotic Front (ZANU-PF) came into being in 1963 with the aim of freeing Southern Rhodesia (now Zimbabwe) from British colonial rule. From 1976 it worked alongside the Zimbabwe African Patriotic Union (ZAPU) as part of the Patriotic Front alliance to put pressure on its colonizers. They were victorious in their liberation fight, ensuring free elections in 1980 that allowed ZANU-PF (then just ZANU) to form the government and declare independence from the United Kingdom. Central to all this was the **Marxist**-influenced Robert Mugabe, party leader from 1976, prime minister from 1980 and president from 1987 following a merger with electoral rivals ZAPU that led to the words "Patriotic Front" being suffixed to ZANU's name. Mugabe was reelected president of Zimbabwe in 1990, 1996 and 2002. ZANU-PF advocated **Marxism–Leninism** throughout its battle for liberation and into the formative years of its governing of the young Zimbabwe. Perhaps uniquely, despite this promotion of Marxism–Leninism, it strenuously denied being **communist**, and yet still modeled its party on the **Communist Party of the Soviet Union**. Owing to a crippling economic downturn, by 1991 it had dropped its early Marxist rhetoric entirely, embracing free market economics with zest. In Mugabe's words "we gave in on **socialism** and yielded to **capitalism**." ZANU-PF's March 2005 election victory marked the beginning of its 25th successive year in power, in which time it has been transformed from a moderate Marxist party to a deeply controversial nationalist movement presiding over an economy in terminal decline.

ZINOVIEV, GRIGORI YEVSEYEVICH (1883–1936). Zinoviev was an important figure in the early life of the **Soviet Union**, and was chairman of the **Third International** (Comintern) from 1919 to 1926. Born Ovsel Gershon Aronov Radomyslsky in the Russian town of Yelisavetgrad (later Kirovgrad), Zinoviev joined the **Russian Social Democratic Labor Party** in 1901. He sided with the **Bolshevik** faction from its inception in 1903, and was involved in the unsuccessful 1905 **Russian Revolution**. Zinoviev at this juncture became inextricably linked with **Vladimir Ilich Lenin**, and in 1912 was elected by the party congress to the all-Bolshevik Central Committee. However, Zinoviev did part with Lenin for a period, as he, along with Lev Kamenev, voted against the seizure of power in October 1917. Nonetheless, as a key Bolshevik Zinoviev was made chairman of the Petrograd Soviet following the **revolution**. He then led the opposition to World War I, helping to form the Zimmerwald Left group that called for what they perceived to be an **imperialist** conflict to be turned into a civil war. Alongside Lenin he wrote a pamphlet entitled *Socialism and the War*, and published articles in a collection entitled *Against the Current*, attacking reformist parties such as the **German Social Democratic Party** which had backed the conflict.

In 1921, having been appointed Comintern chairman two years previously, Zinoviev was made a full member of the Politburo. After Lenin died, he sided with Kamenev and **Josef Stalin** to form the "troika" opposition to **Leon Trotsky**, but following Trotsky's expulsion from the party, Stalin turned on his former ally and compelled him to resign from the Politburo and Comintern in 1926. Zinoviev then entered into a "United Opposition" with Trotsky to oppose Stalin, and was duly expelled from the party in 1927. He was readmitted after yielding to Stalin, before a further expulsion and readmission again in 1932, and final eviction from the party in 1934. In 1935, with Stalin's political purges in full swing, Zinoviev was arrested and charged with being complicit in the killing of Sergei Kirov, and handed a 10-year sentence for treason. Zinoviev was just a year into that sentence when in 1936 he was charged with plotting to kill Stalin, and at the first Moscow "Show Trial," sentenced to death by execution.

Zinoviev, even while in league with Trotsky as part of the United Opposition, was always unreceptive to the concept of **permanent revolution**, and was a strong advocate of the **dictatorship of the proletariat**. In 1924 he inadvertently assisted in the demise of the Labour government in Great Britain, as the infamous "Zinoviev Letter," a piece supposedly penned by the Russian calling for British comrades to embroil themselves in revolutionary activity, was printed in the British press creating a moral panic, the backlash of which was defeat for the **socialists**.

Bibliography

CONTENTS

INTRODUCTION

The chief problem in compiling a bibliography on Marxism is the sheer volume of sources. The literature produced by and about Marxists, Marxist organizations, movements and regimes is vast. This abundance of material testifies to the immense spread and influence of Marxism. The list of Marxist parties and organizations around the world is extensive—some 80 listed in this dictionary. The list of Marxist regimes is also lengthy. In the 1970s and 1980s there were, at any given time, two dozen or more Marxist states in the world. These included: Afghanistan, Albania, Angola, Benin, Bulgaria, China, Congo, Cuba, Czechoslovakia, East Germany, Ethiopia, Guinea-Bissau and Cape Verde, Hungary, Kampuchea, Laos, Mongolia, Mozambique, North Korea, Poland, Romania, Somalia, the Soviet Union, Vietnam, Yemen, and Yugoslavia. In China and the Soviet Union Marxist regimes governed two of the most populated countries in the world and, at the time, two of the world's three superpowers.

Huge though the literature is on Marxist political organizations and governments, there is, if anything, even more that has been written on Marxist ideas. As well as a revolutionary activist Marx was a great thinker and theorist and this is reflected in the number of publications devoted to explaining, analyzing, criticizing, advocating, extending and revising his ideas. The use of Marxist ideas has spread well beyond the field of politics to not just the more predictable areas of sociology, economics, history and philosophy—areas in which Marx himself wrote significant works—but also to such diverse fields as psychology, anthropology, ecology, geography and even media studies. The following bibliography aims to reflect both the influence of Marxism on political movements and regimes around the world, and the diversity of subjects and disciplines to which Marxist ideas and perspectives have been applied.

The vastness and the diversity of literature on Marxism make it difficult to generalize about, particularly with regard to its strengths and weaknesses. It is difficult to think of any topic, let alone one of significance, that has not been addressed in the literature on Marxism or from a Marxist perspective (however variable the quality of work may have sometimes been). Any significant Marxists, Marxist movements or governments, concepts or events have been covered. Omissions tend to be of the order of such topics as Tuva, the third country in the world to gain a Marxist government (after Russia, into which it was absorbed, and Mongolia). Tuva has achieved a very small renown for its throat singers, but otherwise has, understandably, not attracted the attention of scholars.

The enormous breadth of Marxism related literature might in itself be considered a strength: Marxism has clearly inspired work in a vast number of domains and across a wide range of disciplines. A further strength of Marxism, at least for the English speaker, is the amount of material on Marxism available in English. Not only have all the works of Marx and his collaborator Friedrich Engels been authoritatively translated into English, but so also have the non-English-language works of legions of other Marxists and writers on Marxism. So, for example, we have the works of Vladimir Lenin, Leon Trotsky, Josef Stalin, Mao Zedong, Deng Xiaoping, Ernesto Guevara, Amilcar Cabral, Rosa Luxemburg, and Eduard Bernstein readily available in English to name but a few notable Marxists from around the world. This, of course, is in no small measure due to the efforts of the Soviet Union and Marxist China to promote Marxism by funding translation and foreign language publication of works by "approved" Marxists (the Soviet Union notably did not fund translations of Trotsky's works). There are still a few interesting and significant sources not available in English translation, for example some Latin American writings in Spanish, but there are no gaping holes in the work available. Overall, as James C. Doherty suggests in his *Historical Dictionary of Socialism*, the Marxist tradition has been well served by the scholarly literature, particularly when compared with the democratic socialist tradition.

Given the immense literature on Marxism this bibliography is inevitably selective. Three considerations in the selection process have been whether or not a book has been of great significance or lasting influence; whether or not a book covers a topic not covered elsewhere; and how up-to-date a book is. So, the aim has been to choose the best recently published books on Marxism, but also to include any books that have been important in the history of Marxism or that have had a significant impact or significance. For example, Franz Mehring's biography of Marx, *Karl Marx*, was first published in 1918 and is now dated, but has been included as, in David McLellan's words "the classical biography of Marx." A further example is M.M. Bober's *Karl Marx's Interpretation of History*, first published in 1927, but included as a landmark study of historical materialism which is still a useful read. Others, such as Massimo Quaini's *Geography and Marxism*, or Maurice Godelier's *Perspectives in Marxist Anthropology*, have been included partly because they cover more unusual and less discussed aspects of Marxist thought.

Other selection criteria concern non-English sources and journal articles. A difficult decision had to be made to exclude articles. To have included articles would have easily led to a tripling in length of the bibliography. In defense of the decision, it should be noted that many key articles can be found collected into books (for example, the excellent *Marx, Justice and History* edited by M. Cohen et al. is largely a collection of articles first published in the journal *Philosophy and Public Affairs*, and Bob Jessop's *Karl Marx: Social and Political Thought, Critical Assessments* volumes contain an impressive number of high-quality, significant and stimulating articles from various sources), and other bibliographical sources that will direct the reader to relevant articles have been included. In addition, a list of journals containing many important articles on Marxism is included below. Non-English sources have by and large been ignored as there is a wealth of sources in English including excellent translations of a great number of texts written in other languages. The few foreign language sources included have largely been selected on the basis that they are both significant works and not yet available in English translation (for example, José Mariategui's *Historia de la Crisis Mundial*). In addition to these, the German-language editions of the principal writings of Karl Marx and Friedrich Engels and important German-language selections and collections have been included for those who wish to study the works of the founders of Marxism in the language in which they were written.

The starting point of the bibliography is the starting point of Marxism: Karl Marx himself and his close collaborator Friedrich Engels. In addition to sources containing their actual writings, notable biographies and secondary sources on them are listed. This is followed by a selection of the best introductions to Marxism and Marxist ideas, and some sources on the key influences on Marx's thought. The bibliography then moves on to Marxism around the world. Marxism is an ideology that has influenced individuals, movements and regimes all over the globe, and the cultures and politics of different regions have, in turn, influenced and shaped Marxist ideas. For example, the Marxisms that have developed in Asia are significantly different in character and content to those found in Europe. The six areas identified—Europe, the Soviet Union, Asia, Latin America, Africa and North America—cover most of the planet, and in each one there have arisen significant Marxist movements, regimes and/or schools of thought. Each region has, where appropriate, been sub-divided into sections covering smaller areas or individual countries, key thinkers and schools of thought, leading Marxists and Marxist leaders, and themes of particular significance to the region. The final part of the bibliography concerns subjects and issues found in the literature on and debates within Marxism. A selection of literature on Marxist philosophy and theory is provided here with specific topics such as aesthetics and culture, justice and ethics, feminism, nationalism, imperialism and international communism all focused on in sub-sections.

The first section covers Marx and Engels, the founders of Marxism. It contains their writings, biographies on them and secondary sources on aspects of their lives, work and relationship. In terms of their writings, the co-authored *Communist Manifesto* is the best and most accessible place to start. Another relatively straightforward piece on Marx's central theory is the *Preface to a Critique of Political Economy*. This is a brief and clear schematic summary of Marx's materialist conception of history (historical materialism). The *German Ideology* (co-authored with Engels) goes into the materialist conception in more detail and with greater philosophical depth, but remains reasonably lucid. On Marx's theory of alienation the key text is his *Economic and Philosophical Manuscripts* (also known as the *1844 Manuscripts* and as the *Paris Manuscripts*). On economics and the workings of capitalism Marx's great work is of course *Capital*, with volume one particularly important. While of enormous importance, *Capital* can also be a little daunting, and those wishing to grasp the key ideas without working their way through *Capital* should read Marx's *Value, Price and Profit* (also published as *Wages, Price and Profit*), a much briefer and very clear exposition of his views intended for trade unionists of the time.

Other significant writings include the *Theses on Feuerbach*, which is a terse, slightly enigmatic set of theses containing the essence of Marx's materialist philosophy and the basis for his historical materialism—a key text, considered a turning point in Marx's intellectual development by many commentators. The *Critique of Hegel's Philosophy of Right* is a difficult text, but shows Marx working out his position in relation to G.W.F. Hegel and Hegelianism. *On the Jewish Question*, again not an easy text, conveys criticisms by Marx of liberalism, while *The Poverty of Philosophy* is an attack on Pierre-Joseph Proudhon, particularly for his ahistorical views, and provides more on Marx's materialist conception of history. Of his other writings (and there are many) the most important are *The Class Struggles in France*, *The Eighteenth Brumaire* and *The*

Civil War in France, which all represent Marx's analyses of specific historical events, that is, the application of his theories to contemporary happenings (France 1848–49; Louis Bonaparte's seizure of power in France in 1851; 1871 Paris Commune). Finally, the *Grundrisse*, a difficult piece, nevertheless warrants a mention both as the groundwork for Marx's *Capital* and as a key text linking his early and later works and incorporating important dialectical themes.

Engels also wrote prolifically and his key solo writings are *The Condition of the Working Class in England*, *Revolution and Counter-Revolution in Germany*, *Anti-Dühring* (an easier very abridged version was published as *Socialism: Utopian and Scientific*), *Dialectics of Nature*, *The Origin of the Family, Private Property and the State*, and *Ludwig Feuerbach and the End of Classical German Philosophy*. In general Engels' works are more accessible than Marx's, though he has been criticized for oversimplifying Marx's ideas and in so doing distorting them. Engels wrote particularly on philosophy and spent much time outlining materialist philosophy and contrasting it with idealist philosophy.

The *Collected Works* of Marx and Engels published by Lawrence and Wishart is a reliable and near comprehensive English translation of their works, while the *Historisch-kritische Gesamtausgabe. Werke/Schriften/Briefe.* (*MEGA¹*) and *Marx-Engels-Gesamtausgabe* (*MEGA²*) are authoritative collections in German. Of the selections of writings of Marx and Engels there are a number of good books with David McLellan's *Karl Marx: Selected Works* a particularly fine example, and Eugene Kamenka's *Portable Marx*, Jon Elster's *Karl Marx: A Reader*, and Christopher Pierson's *The Marx Reader* of a similarly high quality and usefulness for readers seeking the key texts and main ideas of Marx. Joseph O'Malley's *Marx: Early Political Writings* and Terrell Carver's *Marx: Later Political Writings* are very good selections of pre- and post-1848 writings respectively. Two reliable and widely used multi-volume collections are Saul Padover's *Karl Marx Library* (seven volumes) and the Penguin eight-volume collection. These highlighted selections and collections of Marx and Engels' writings are but a few of the considerable number that have been published, more being listed below. Some are helpfully focused on specific themes or areas of Marx's/Engels' thought, for example, religion and colonialism.

David McLellan's *Marx* and Terrell Carver's *Engels* provide the best brief introductions to the lives and main ideas of Marx and Engels respectively. McLellan's *Karl Marx: His Life and Thought* is an extremely good, thorough and detailed intellectual biography. Francis Wheen's *Karl Marx* is the most interesting and readable of the very many biographies of Marx, bringing out Marx as a real person and not just an icon. Carver's longer biography of Engels, *Friedrich Engels: His Life and Thought*, is the best so far on Marx's vital collaborator. Carver is also to be recommended for his book *Marx and Engels: The Intellectual Relationship*.

The second section contains some of the best introductions to Marx, Marxism and Marxist ideas. As so often McLellan stands out for the clarity and authority of his writing. His *The Thought of Karl Marx* cannot be bettered as an introduction to Marx's ideas and contains very useful extracts from Marx's writings on each key topic. Mike Evans' *Karl Marx* provides an excellent and more detailed introduction with particular focus on Marx's views on politics and history.

The third section of the bibliography concerns the influences on Marx's (and Engels') thought. The crucial thinker here is Georg Hegel. Marx counted himself a disciple of Hegel for a while and even late in his intellectual development acknowledged the influence of Hegel. An excellent, extremely clear and brief introduction to Hegel's thought is to be found in Peter Singer's *Hegel*. Shlomo Avineri's *Hegel's Theory of the Modern State* is the best account of Hegel's political views, while Chris Arthur's scholarly *Dialectic of Labour: Marx and his Relation to Hegel* is strong on the intellectual relationship between Marx and Hegel.

The following sections address Marxism in different parts of the world: Europe, the Soviet Union/Russia, Asia, Latin America, Africa and North America. Europe, as well as the birth and dwelling place of Marx, has also been home to many of the most influential and penetrating of Marxist thinkers and a number of important Marxist movements. As such it has generated a wealth of material on and by Marxists. From the range of sources it is difficult to select particularly outstanding works. However, in the section on early European Marxism Peter Gay's *The Dilemma of Democratic Socialism*, Norman Geras' *The Legacy of Rosa Luxemburg* and Jeremy Jennings' *Georges Sorel: The Character and Development of His Thought* are seminal works on their respective subjects. On Western Marxism and Marxists Perry Anderson's *Considerations on Western Marxism*, Russell Jacoby's *Dialectic of Defeat*, David Held's *Introduction to Critical Theory*, Joseph Femia's *Gramsci's Political Thought*, Vincent Geoghegan's *Reason and Eros: The Social Theory of Herbert Marcuse*, and G. Parkinson's edited book *Georg Lukacs: The Man, His Work and His Ideas* are all particularly recommended. On Eurocommunism R. Kindersley's *The Communist Movement: From Comintern to Cominform* is worth reading, and M. Rakovski's *Toward an East European Marxism* is particularly interesting on East European Marxism.

On the Soviet Union and Russian Marxism, as one would expect, there is again a wealth of material, and merely a few of the classic works are highlighted here: Robert Conquest's *The Great Terror: Stalin's Purge of the Thirties*, Isaac Deutscher's trilogy on Trotsky, Stephen Cohen's *Bukharin and the Bolshevik Revolution*, and, if not quite classics then probably the most reliable and authoritative sources, Neil Harding's books on Lenin.

Asian Marxism is dominated by sources on Chinese Marxism and of these Bill Brugger, Stuart Schram and Dick Wilson are important and profound

348 • BIBLIOGRAPHY

authors, while on Latin American Marxism and African Marxism Harry Vanden and Basil Davidson are the vital authors to consult on each area respectively. On Marxism in the United States Albert Fried's *Communism in America: A History in Documents* contains both a good selection of source material and a useful bibliographical essay.

The Subjects and Issues section represents another huge area of Marxist writings. In this final section of the bibliography a very wide range of topics is covered including philosophy, theory, economics, science, the arts, religion, ethics, crime, feminism, and nationalism. This area is too extensive to give detailed guidance on so only a few of the long-standing books and authors that have made major contributions to the study of Marxism and to Marxist studies are mentioned here. M. M. Bober's *Karl Marx's Interpretation of History* is the oldest extended consideration of historical materialism in English, and remains a useful and insightful critical study. Milovan Djilas' *The New Class: An Analysis of the Communist System* is a penetrating, critical analysis of communism in practice. Gerry Cohen's *Marx's Theory of History: A Defence* is a landmark work on historical materialism by one of the foremost political theorists of the 20th century. Alvin Gouldner's *The Two Marxisms* deserves a wide audience for its clarity and insight into an inherent tension between science and philosophy running throughout Marxist thought and movements. Leszek Kolakowski's *Main Currents of Marxism: Its Origin, Growth and Dissolution* is an impressive, insightful and influential work on the history and development of Marxism. Bertell Ollman's *Alienation* is a brilliant and original study of Marx's dialectical approach and theory of alienation. John Plamenatz's *German Marxism and Russian Communism* contains a superb discussion of historical materialism by a leading political theorist. Listed in the miscellaneous section is Robert A. Gorman's extremely useful and extensive pair of bibliographical volumes featuring numerous Marxists and neo-Marxists. Finally, it is worth noting the contributions of Maurice Dobb, Paul Sweezy and Ernest Mandel on economics, and those of Terry Eagleton, Frederic Jameson and Raymond Williams on literature and culture.

Further bibliographical sources are listed here. Of these, David McLellan's *Karl Marx: Selected Writings* contains a very useful selection of sources with brief comments on each, and *A Dictionary of Marxist Thought* edited by Tom Bottomore et al. has quite an extensive bibliography. More specific in subject matter are the Hoover Institution's publications from the late 1960s and early 1970s including Anna Bourguina's *Russian Social Democracy: The Menshevik Movement Bibliography*, R. H. McNeal's *Stalin's Works: An Annotated Bibliography*, Sydney Heitman's *Nikolai I. Bukharin: A Bibliography with Annotations*, and Louis Sinclair's *Leon Trotsky: A Bibliography*. Other bibliographies listed are Jaddish S. Sharma's *Indian Socialism: A Descriptive Bibliography*, Harry E. Vanden's *Latin American Marxism: A Bibliography*, Dione Miles'

Something in Common: An IWW Bibliography, and Maurice F. Neufeld, Daniel J. Leab and Dorothy Swanson's *American Working Class History: A Representative Bibliography*. In addition, on Chinese Marxism Bill Brugger and David Kelly's *Chinese Marxism in the Post-Mao Era* and Mark Selden's *China in Revolution: The Yenan Way Revisited* together provide a wide-ranging list of sources including a number of Chinese and Japanese language sources.

Other useful reference sources include the informative, albeit dated, Bogdan Szajkowski's *Marxist Governments: A World Survey* and the previously mentioned *Historical Dictionary of Socialism* by James C. Doherty. In addition, the internet is now a valuable research resource and there is a large number of websites devoted to Marxism and Marxist groups. However, many of these belong to small Marxist parties and are of very limited interest. Rather than list them all the selection below contains the most useful ones in terms of content and links to other websites:

Fourth International Links: http://www.zoo.co.uk/~z8001063/International-Socialist-Group/FI/FI%20Links.htm (very good for links to Trotskyist organizations)

Hegel Society of America: http://www.hegel.org/ (good for links to other websites on Hegel)

Hegel Society of Great Britain: http://www.shef.ac.uk/misc/groups/hsgb/index.html (good for links to other websites on Hegel)

In Defence of Marxism: http://www.marxist.com/ (very good links to Marxist groups' websites world wide)

Industrial Workers of the World: http://iww.org

Marx and Engels' Writings: http://eserver.org/marx/ (good for Marx and Engels' writings)

Marxism Made Simple: http://flash.to/marxismmadesimple/

Marxism Page: http://www.anu.edu.au/polsci/marx/rd_star.gif

Marxist.Org Internet Archive: http://www.marx.org/archive/index.htm (especially useful for writings of important Marxists and includes an encyclopedia of Marxism)

The MarX-Files: http://www.appstate.edu/~stanovskydj/marxfiles.html (good for Marxist writings)

MARX AND ENGELS: THE FOUNDERS OF MARXISM

The following lists of writings are not comprehensive but do include all the major works. In particular they do not include the numerous articles written for such publications as the *Neue Rheinische Zeitung* and the *New York Daily Tribune*.

Principal Writings of Marx

Note: Not all of these works were published in the lifetime of Marx; the dates in parentheses are dates of composition not publication.

Critique of Hegel's "Philosophy of Right" (1843)
On the Jewish Question (1843)
Critique of Hegel's Philosophy of Right: Introduction (1844)
Economic and Philosophical Manuscripts (1844)
Critical Notes on 'The King of Prussia and Social Reform' (1844)
The Holy Family (1844)
Theses on Feuerbach (1845)
The German Ideology (1846)
The Poverty of Philosophy (1847)
The Communist Manifesto (1848)
Wage, Labour and Capital (1849)
The Class Struggle in France (1850)
The Eighteenth Brumaire of Louis Bonaparte (1852)
Grundrisse (1857/8)
Preface to a Critique of Political Economy (1859)
Critique of Political Economy (1859)
Herr Vogt (1860)
Theories of Surplus Value (1862/3)
Value, Price and Profit (1865)
Capital, vol. I (1867)
Civil War in France (1871)
Critique of the Gotha Programme (1875)
Notes on Adolph Wagner (1880)

Principal Writings of Engels

The Condition of the Working Class in England (1845)
Revolution and Counter-Revolution in Germany (1851/2)
Anti-Dühring (1877/8)
Socialism: Scientific and Utopian (1880)
Dialectics of Nature (1878–82)
The Origin of the Family, Private Property and the State (1884)
Ludwig Feuerbach and the End of Classical Philosophy (1886)

Writings of Marx and Engels: Selections and Collections

Marx, Karl. *The Eastern Question.* Ed. by Eleanor Marx Aveling and Edward Aveling. London: S. Sonnenschein, 1897.

———. *The First Indian War of Independence, 1857–1859*. Moscow: Foreign Languages Publishing House, 1959.

———. *Oeuvres: Économie*. vols. I and II. Ed. and intro. Maximilien Rubel. Paris: Gallimard (Bibliothèque de la Pléiade), 1965 and 1968.

———. *Karl Marx on Colonialism and Modernization*. Ed. and intro. Shlomo Avineri. Garden City, N.Y.: Doubleday, 1968.

———. *Marx on China 1853–60*. London: Lawrence and Wishart, 1951.

———. *The Early Texts*. Ed. by David McLellan. Oxford: Oxford University Press, 1971.

———. *The Ethnological Notebooks of Karl Marx*. Ed. by Lawrence Krader. Assen: Van Gorcum, 1972.

———. *Karl Marx: The Early Writings*. Trans. by Rodney Livingstone and Gregor Benton. London: Pelican, 1975.

———. *Karl Marx: Texts on Method*. Ed. by Terrell Carver. Oxford: Basil Blackwell, 1975.

———. *The Portable Karl Marx*. Ed. by Eugene Kamenka. New York: Penguin, 1983.

———. *Karl Marx: A Reader*. Ed. by Jon Elster. Cambridge: Cambridge University Press, 1986.

———. *Marx: Early Political Writings*. Ed. by Joseph O'Malley. Cambridge: Cambridge University Press, 1994.

———. *Karl Marx: Selected Writings*. Ed. by L. Simon. Indianapolis, Ind.; Cambridge: Hackett Pub. Co., 1994.

———. *Marx: Later Political Writings*. Ed. by Terrell Carver. Cambridge: Cambridge University Press, 1996.

———. *The Marx Reader*. Ed. by Christopher Pierson. Oxford: Polity Press, 1997.

Marx, Karl, and Friedrich Engels. *Reminiscences of Marx and Engels*. Moscow: Foreign Languages Publishing House, no date.

———. *Historisch-kritische Gesamtausgabe. Werke/Schriften/Briefe. (MEGA¹)*. Various places: various publishers, 1927–35.

———. *Selected Works*. Moscow: Progress Publishers, 1935.

———. *Revolution in Spain*. New York: International Publishers, 1939.

———. *On Religion*. Moscow: Foreign Languages Publishing House, 1957.

———. *Werke*. Berlin: Dietz Verlag, 1957–67.

———. *American Journalism of Marx and Engels*. New York: New American Library, 1966.

———. *Marx und Engels über Kunst und Literatur*. 2 vols. Ed. by Manfred Kliem. Frankfurt am Main: Europäische Verlagsanstalt, 1968.

———. *Marx-Engels-Gesamtausgabe (MEGA²)*. Various places: various publishers, 1960s onwards.

———. *Articles on Britain*. Moscow: Progress, 1971.

———. *Articles from the Neue Rheinische Zeitung 1848–1849*. Moscow: Progress Publishers, 1972.

———. *On Literature and Art.* Ed. by L. Baxandall and S. Morawski. New York: International General, 1973.

———. *Marx-Engels über Sprache, Stil und Übersetzung.* Ed. by H. Ruscinski and B. Retzlaff Kress. Berlin: Dietz, 1974.

———. *Collected Works.* 50 vols. London: Lawrence and Wishart, 1975–2005.

———. *On Communist Society.* Moscow: Progress Publishers, 1978.

———. *On the United States.* Moscow: Progress Publishers, 1979.

Marx, Karl, Friedrich Engels, and Vladimir Lenin. *Anarchism and Anarchosyndicalism.* Moscow: Progress Publishers, 1972.

German-Language Editions of the Writings of Marx and Engels

The following list includes editions of some of the major individual works of Marx and Engels, but not German-language collections listed in the previous section. MEGA¹ and MEGA² listed above contain a much fuller (soon to be complete in the case of MEGA²) collection of the writings of Marx and Engels in German.

Engels, Friedrich. *Die Lage der Arbeitenden Klasse in England.* Stuttgart: Dietz, 1892. ·

———. *Revolution und Kontre-Revolution in Deutschland.* Stuttgart: Dietz, 1896.

———. *Herr Eugen Dührings Umivalzung Wissenschaft: Anti-Dühring.* Berlin: Dietz, 1953.

———. *Dialetik der Natur.* Berlin: Dietz, 1962.

———. *Die Entwicklung des Sozialismus von der Utopiezur Wissenschaft.* Berlin: Dietz, 1973.

———. *Der Ursprung der Familie, des Privateigentums und des Staats.* Berlin: Dietz, 1975.

Marx, Karl. *Der Burgerkrieg in Frankeich.* Berlin: Internationales Arbeitverlang, 1931.

———. *Grundrisse der Kritik der Politischen Ökonomie.* Moscow: Verlag für fremdsprachige Literatur, 1939–41.

———. *Lohnarbeit und Kapital.* Berlin: Neuer Weg, 1949.

———. *Zur Kritik der Politischen Ökonomie.* Berlin: Dietz, 1951.

———. *Die Ökonomisch-Philosophische Manuskipte.* Berlin: Akademie, 1955.

———. *Die Heilige Familie.* Berlin: Dietz, 1959.

———. *Die Klassenkampfe in Frankreich 1848 bis 1850.* Berlin: Dietz, 1960.

———. *Der 18. Brumaire des Louis Bonaparte.* Frankfurt: Insel-Verlag, 1965.

———. *Theorie über den Mehrwert.* Frankfurt: Europaishe Verlagsanst, 1968.

———. *Thesen über Feuerbach*. Berlin: Dietz, 1969.

———. *Vorwort zur Kritik der Politischen Ökonomie*. Berlin: Dietz, 1971.

———. *Das Elend der Philosophie*. Berlin: Dietz, 1972.

———. *Kritik des Gothaer Programms*. Berlin: Verlay Neuer Weg, 1973.

———. *Zur Kritik der Hegelschen Rechtsphilosophie*. Berlin: Dietz, 1976.

———. *Zur Judenfrage*. Berlin: Dietz, 1976.

———. *Zur Kritik der Hegelschen Rechtsphilosophie: Einleitung*. Berlin: Dietz, 1976.

———. *Kritische Randglossen zu dem Artikel "Der König von Preussen."* Berlin: Dietz, 1976.

———. *Das Kapital: Kritik der Politischen Ökonomie*. Eist Band. Berlin: Dietz, 1983.

Marx, Karl, and Friedrich Engels. *Manifest der Kommunistischen Partei*. Stuttgart: Philipp Jun, 1969.

Biographies of Marx and Engels

Berlin, Isaiah. *Karl Marx. His Life and Environment*. London: Thornton Butterworth, 1939.

Blumenberg, Werner. *Karl Marx*. London: Verso, 1972.

Carr, E.H. *Karl Marx: A Study in Fanaticism*. London: J.M. Dent and Sons, 1934.

Carver, Terrell. *Engels*. Oxford: Oxford University Press, 2003.

———. *Friedrich Engels: His Life and Thought*. London: Macmillan, 1989.

Henderson, W.O. *The Life of Friedrich Engels*. 2 vols. London: Frank Cass, 1976.

Korsch, Karl. *Karl Marx*. New York: John Wiley and Sons, 1936.

Lewis, J. *The Life and Teaching of Karl Marx*. London: Lawrence and Wishart 1965.

Liebknecht, Wilhelm. *Karl Marx: Biographical Memoirs*. Chicago: C.H. Kerr, 1901.

Mayer, Gustav. *Friedrich Engels: A Biography*. Trans. by Gilbert and Helen Highet. Ed. by R.H.S. Crossman. London: Chapman and Hall, 1936.

McLellan, David. *Karl Marx: His Life and Thought*. London: Macmillan, 1973.

———. *Engels*. London: Collins, 1977.

Mehring, Franz. *Karl Marx*. London: John Lane, 1918.

Nicolaievsky, Boris, and Otto Maenchen-Helfen. *Karl Marx: Man and Fighter*. London: Methuen, 1936.

Padover, Saul. *Karl Marx, An Intimate Biography*. New York: New American Library, 1980.

Payne, Robert. *Marx, A Biography*. London: W.H. Allen, 1968.

Raddatz, Fritz J. *Karl Marx: A Political Biography*. Trans. by Richard Barry. London: Weidenfeld and Nicolson, 1978.

Ryazanov, D. *Karl Marx, Man, Thinker and Revolutionist*. New York: International Publishers, 1927.

Rubel, Maximilien. *Marx: Life and Works*. London: Macmillan, 1980.

Schwarzschild, Leopold. *Karl Marx: The Red Prussian*. New York: Charles Scribner and Sons, 1947.

Wheen, Francis. *Karl Marx*. London: Fourth Estate, 1999.

Secondary Sources on Aspects of the Lives and Work of Marx and Engels

Arthur, Christopher J., ed. *Engels Today: A Centenary Appreciation*. Basingstoke, England: Macmillan, 1996.

Carver, Terrell. *Marx and Engels: The Intellectual Relationship*. Brighton, England: Harvester, 1983.

———, ed. *The Cambridge Companion to Marx*. Cambridge: Cambridge University Press, 1991.

Carver, Terrell, and Manfred B. Steger, eds. *Engels after Marx*. Manchester: Manchester University Press, 1999.

Collins, H., and C. Abramsky. *Karl Marx and the British Labour Movement. Years of the First International*. London: Macmillan and Co., 1965.

Hampden Jackson, J. *Marx, Proudhon and European Socialism*. New York: Collier Books, 1962.

Hunt, Richard N. *The Political Ideas of Marx and Engels*. London: Macmillan, 1974.

Lea, John, and Geoff Pilling, eds. *The Condition of Britain: Essays on Frederick Engels*. London: Pluto, 1996.

Levine, N. *The Tragic Deception: Marx contra Engels*. Santa Barbara, Calif.: Clio, 1975.

Marcus, S. *Engels, Manchester and the Working Class*. New York: Random House, 1974.

McLellan, David. *Karl Marx: Interviews and Recollections*. London: Macmillan, 1981.

Rubel, Maximilien, and Margaret Manale. *Marx without Myth*. New York: Harper and Row, 1975.

Thomas, Paul. *Karl Marx and the Anarchists*. London: Routledge and Kegan Paul, 1980.

INTRODUCTIONS TO MARX, MARXISM AND MARXIST IDEAS

Burns, Emile. *Introduction to Marxism*. London: Lawrence and Wishart, 1966.

Elster, Jon. *An Introduction to Marx*. Cambridge: Cambridge University Press, 1986.

Evans, Michael. *Karl Marx*. London: Allen and Unwin, 1975.
Hook, Sydney. *Towards the Understanding of Karl Marx*. New York: John Day, 1933.
Mazlish, B. *The Meaning of Karl Marx*. New York/Oxford: Oxford University Press, 1984.
McLellan, David. *The Thought of Karl Marx*. London: Papermac, 1980.
Suchting, Wal. Λ. *Marx: An Introduction*. Brighton, England: Wheatsheaf Books, 1983.
Wolff, Jonathan. *Why Read Marx Today?* New York: Oxford University Press, 2001.
Woodfin, Rupert, et al. *Introducing Marxism*. Royston, England: Icon, 2004.

INFLUENCES ON MARX: HEGEL, HEGELIANISM AND FEUERBACH

Arthur, C.J. *Dialectic of Labour: Marx and His Relation to Hegel*. Oxford: Blackwell, 1986.
Avineri, S. *Hegel's Theory of the Modern State*. Cambridge: Cambridge University Press, 1972.
Beiser, F.C, ed. *The Cambridge Companion To Hegel*. Cambridge: Cambridge University Press, 1993.
Burbidge, John. *Historical Dictionary of Hegelian Philosophy*. Lanham, Md.: Scarecrow Press, 2001.
Burns, Tony, and Ian Fraser eds. *The Hegel-Marx Connection*. London: Macmillan, 2000.
Colletti, Lucio. *Marxism and Hegel*. Trans. by Lawrence Garner. London: New Left, 1973.
Cooper, R. *The Logical Influence of Hegel on Marx*. Seattle, Wash.: University of Wash. Press, 1925.
Feuerbach, Ludwig. *The Essence of Christianity*. Trans. by Marian Evans. New York: Harper and Row, 1957.
———. *Principles of the Philosophy of the Future*. Trans. and intro. by Manfred H. Vogel. Indianapolis, Ind.: Bobbs and Merrill, 1966.
Fraser, Ian. *Hegel and Marx: The Concept of Need*. Edinburgh: Edinburgh University Press, 1998.
Hegel, G.W.F. first published 1807. *The Phenomenology of Spirit*. Trans. by A.V. Miller. Oxford: Oxford University Press, 1977.
———. first published 1812. *The Science of Logic*. Trans. by A.V. Miller. London: George Allen and Unwin, 1969.
———. first published 1821. *Philosophy of Right*. Trans. by T.M. Knox. Oxford: Oxford University Press, 1952.

———. first published 1830. *Encyclopaedia of the Philosophical Sciences*: Volume I, *The Logic of Hegel*. Trans. by W. Wallace. London: Oxford University Press, 1975. Volume II, *Philosophy of Nature*. Trans. by A.V. Miller. Oxford: Oxford University Press, 1970. Volume III, *Philosophy of Mind*. Trans. by W. Wallace and A.V. Miller. Oxford: Oxford University Press, 1971.

———. *Philosophy of History*. Trans. by J. Sibree. New York: Dover Publications, 1956.

Hook, Sydney. *From Hegel to Marx*. London: Victor Gollancz, 1936.

Hyppolite, Jean. *Studies on Marx and Hegel*. London: Heinemann, 1969.

Kamenka, Eugene. *The Philosophy of Ludwig Feuerbach*. London: Routledge and Kegan Paul, 1970.

Lamb, D., ed. *Hegel and Modern Philosophy*. Beckenham, England: Croom Helm, 1987.

Lichtheim, George. *From Marx to Hegel and Other Essays*. London: Orbach and Chambers, 1971.

Lowith, Karl. *From Hegel to Nietszche: The Revolution in Nineteenth-Century Thought*. London: Constable, 1964.

Lukács, György. *The Young Hegel*. London: Merlin, 1975.

MacGregor, D. *Hegel and Marx: After the Fall of Communism*. Cardiff: University of Wales Press, 1998.

Marcuse, Herbert. *Reason and Revolution: Hegel and the Rise of Social Theory*. New York: Oxford University Press, 1941.

McLellan, David. *The Young Hegelians and Karl Marx*. London: Macmillan, 1969.

———. *Marx Before Marxism*. London: Macmillan, 1980.

Norman, Richard, and Sean Sayers. *Hegel, Marx and Dialectic: A Debate*. Brighton, England: Harvester, 1980.

O'Malley, J.J., K.W. Algozin, H.P. Kainz, and L.C. Rice, eds. *The Legacy of Hegel: Proceedings of the Marquette Hegel Symposium, 1970*. The Hague: Martinus Nijhoff, 1973.

Rosenthal, J. *The Myth of Dialectics: Re-interpreting the Hegel-Marx Relation*. Basingstoke: Macmillan, 1998.

Singer, P. *Hegel*. Oxford: Oxford University Press, 1983.

Toews, J.E. *Hegelianism: The Path Toward Dialectical Humanism 1805–1841*. Cambridge: Cambridge University Press, 1980.

Solomon, R.C. *In the Spirit of Hegel: A Study of G.W.F. Hegel's Phenomenology of Spirit*. Oxford: Oxford University Press, 1983.

Stace, W.T. *The Philosophy of Hegel: A Systematic Exposition*. New York: Dover Publications, 1955.

Stepelevich, L.S., ed. *The Young Hegelians: An Anthology*. Cambridge: Cambridge University Press, 1983.

Uchida, Hiroshi. *Marx's Grundrisse and Hegel's Logic*. Ed. by Terrell Carver. London: Routledge, 1988.

Wartofsky, Marx W. *Feuerbach*. Cambridge: Cambridge University Press, 1977.

EUROPEAN MARXISM

Early European Marxism: Orthodoxy and Revisionism

Abraham, R. *Rosa Luxemburg. A Life for the International*. Oxford: Berg, 1989.

Basso, L. *Rosa Luxemburg. A Reappraisal*. London: Deutsch, 1975.

Bebel, August. *Woman Under Socialism*. New York: Labor News, 1904.

Bernstein, E. *Evolutionary Socialism*. Trans. by E.C. Harvey. New York: Schocken, 1961.

———. *Documente des Socialismus: Hefte für Geschichte, Urkunden und Bibliographie des Socialismus*. Frankfurt: Saur und Auvermann, 1968. 5 vols.

———. *The Preconditions of Socialism*. Ed. and trans. Henry Tudor. Cambridge: Cambridge University Press, 1993.

———. *Selected Writings of Eduard Bernstein, 1900–1921*. Ed. and trans. Manfred Steger. Atlantic Highlands, N.J.: Humanities Press, 1996.

Donald, Moira. *Marxism and Revolution: Karl Kautsky and the Russian Marxists. 1900–1924*. New Haven, Conn.: Yale University Press, 1993.

Footman, David. *The Primrose Path: A Life of Ferdinand Lassalle*. London: Cresset, 1946.

Frölich, Paul. *Rosa Luxemburg: Her Life and Works*. London: Pluto, 1970.

Gay, Peter. *The Dilemma of Democratic Socialism: Eduard Bernstein's Challenge*. New York: Collier, 1962.

Geary, R. *Karl Kautsky*. Manchester: Manchester University Press, 1987.

Geras, N. *The Legacy of Rosa Luxemburg*. London: New Left, 1976.

Girault, Jacques. *Paul Lafague: textes choisis*. Paris: Éditions sociales, 1970.

Goode, Patrick, ed. and trans. *Karl Kautsky: Selected Political Writings*. London: Macmillan Press, 1983.

Howard, Dick, ed. *Selected Political Writings of Rosa Luxemburg*. New York: Monthly Review Press, 1971.

Jackson, J. Hampden. *Jean Jaurès, His Life and Work*. London: Allen and Unwin, 1943.

Jacob, Mathilde. *Rosa Luxemburg: An Intimate Portrait*. Trans. Hans Fernbach. London: Lawrence and Wishart, 2000.

Jaurès, Jean. *Studies in Socialism*. Trans. M. Minturn. London: Independent Labour Party, 1906.

Jennings, Jeremy. *Georges Sorel: The Character and Development of His Thought*. London: Macmillan, 1985.

Kautsky, J.H. *Karl Kautsky: Marxism, Revolution and Democracy.* New Brunswick, N.J.: Transaction Publishers, 1994.

Kautsky, Karl. *The Social Revolution.* Chicago: Kerr, 1916.

———. *Terrorism and Communism.* London: National Labour Press, 1920.

———. *The Labour Revolution.* New York: Dial Press, 1925.

———. *Dictatorship of the Proletariat.* Ann Arbor: University of Michigan Press, 1964.

———. *The Road to Power: Political Reflections on Growing into the Revolution.* Ed. John H. Kautsky. Trans. Raymond Mayer. Atlantic Highlands, N.J.: Humanities Press, 1996.

Labedz, L., ed. *Revisionism.* London: Allen and Unwin, 1962.

Lafargue, Paul. *The Right to be Lazy.* Chicago: Charles H. Kerr, 1883.

———. *The Evolution of Property from Savagery to Civilization.* Chicago: Charles H. Kerr, 1895.

Looker, R., ed. *Rosa Luxemburg: Selected Political Writings.* London: Cape, 1972.

Luxemburg, R. *The Junius Pamphlet.* London: Merlin Press, n.d.

———. *The Mass Strike, The Political Party and The Trade Unions.* Detroit, Mich.: Marxian Educational Society, 1925.

———. *The Russian Revolution and Leninism or Marxism?* Ann Arbor: University of Michigan Press, 1961.

———. *Selected Political Writings.* Ed. by Robert Locker. London: Cape, 1972.

———. *Reform or Revolution.* New York: Pathfinder Press, 1973.

Nettl, J.P. *Rosa Luxemburg.* 2 vols. London: Oxford University Press, 1966.

Pannekeok, Antonie. *Workers' Councils.* Somerville, Mass.: Kont and Branch, 1970.

———. *Lenin as Philosopher.* London: Merlin, 1975.

Pease, Margaret. *Jean Jaurès, Socialist and Humanitarian.* London: Headley, 1916.

Pelz, William A., ed. *Wilhelm Liebknecht and German Social Democracy: A Documentary History.* Trans. Erich Hahn. Westport, Conn.: Greenwood Press, 1994.

Renton, Dave. *Classical Marxism: Socialist Theory and the Second International.* Cheltenham, England: New Clarion Press, 2002.

Rogers, Homer K. *Before the Revisionist Controversy: Kautsky, Bernstein, and the Meaning of Marxism.* New York: Garland Press, 1992.

Salvadori, M. *Karl Kautsky and the Socialist Revolution.* London: New Left, 1979.

Steenson, Gary P. *Karl Kautsky, 1854–1938: Marxism in the Classic Years.* Pittsburgh: Pittsburgh University Press, 1978.

Steger, M.B. *The Quest for Evolutionary Socialism: Eduard Bernstein and Social Democracy.* Cambridge: Cambridge University Press, 1997.

Tudor, H., and Tudor, J.M., eds. and trans. *Marxism and Social Democracy: The Revisionist Debate, 1896–1898*. Cambridge: Cambridge University Press, 1988.

Western Marxism

Adorno, Theodor. *Negative Dialectics*. London: Routledge and Kegan Paul, 1970.

Adorno, Theodor, and Max Horkheimer. *Dialectic of Enlightenment*. London: Allen Lane, 1978.

Adorno, Theodor, et al. *The Authoritarian Personality*. New York: Harper and Row, 1974.

Agger, Ben. *Western Marxism: An Introduction*. Santa Monica, Calif.: Goodyear, 1979.

Althusser, Louis. *Lenin and Philosophy and Other Essays*. London: New Left, 1971.

———. *For Marx*. Trans. by B. Brewster. London: New Left, 1977.

Althusser, Louis, and Etienne Balibar. *Reading "Capital."* Trans. by B. Brewster. London: New Left, 1970.

Anderson, Perry. *Considerations on Western Marxism*. London: New Left, 1976.

Balibar, Etienne. *On the Dictatorship of the Proletariat*. London: New Left, 1977.

Benton, Ted. *The Rise and Fall of Structuralist Marxism*. London: Hutchinson, 1984.

Boggs, Carl. *Gramsci's Marxism*. London: Pluto Press, 1976.

Breines, Paul, ed. *Critical Interruptions: New Left Perspectives on Herbert Marcuse*. New York: Herder and Herder, 1970.

Buci-Glucksmann, C. *Gramsci and the State*. London: Lawrence and Wishart, 1979.

Callinicos, Alex. *Althusser's Marxism*. London: Pluto Press, 1976.

Davidson, A. *Antonio Gramsci: Towards an Intellectual Biography*. London: Merlin, 1977.

Femia, Joseph V. *Gramsci's Political Thought: Hegemony, Consciousness and the Revolutionary Process*. Oxford: Oxford University Press, 1981.

Fiori, Giuseppe. *Antonio Gramsci: Life of a Revolutionary*. London: New Left, 1970.

Fry, J. *Marcuse: Dilemma on Liberation: A Critical Analysis*. New Jersey: Humanities Press, 1978.

Geoghegan, Vincent. *Reason and Eros: The Social Theory of Herbert Marcuse*. London: Pluto, 1981.

———. *Ernst Bloch*. London: Routledge, 1996.

Goode, Patrick. *Karl Korsch*. London: Macmillan, 1979.

Gramsci, Antonio. *The Modern Prince and Other Writings*. London: Lawrence and Wishart, 1957.

———. *Selections from the Prison Notebooks*. Ed. by Quinton Hoare and Geoffrey Nowell Smith. London: Lawrence and Wishart, 1971.

———. *Selections from Political Writings 1910–1920*. London: Lawrence and Wishart, 1977.

———. *Selections from Political Writings 1921–1926*. London: Lawrence and Wishart, 1978.

———. *Pre-Prison Writings*. Ed. Richard Bellamy. Trans. Virginia Cox. Cambridge: Cambridge University Press, 1994.

Habermas, Jurgen. *Toward a Rational Society*. London: Heinemann, 1970.

———. *Theory and Practice*. London: Heinemann, 1974.

———. *Legitimation Crisis*. London: Heinemann, 1976.

Held, David. *Introduction to Critical Theory: Horkheimer to Habermas*. London: Hutchinson, 1980.

Heller, Agnes, ed. *Lukács Revalued*. Oxford: Basil Blackwell, 1983.

Hoffman, J. *The Gramscian Challenge*. Oxford: Blackwell, 1984.

Holub, R. *Antonio Gramsci: Beyond Marxism and Postmodernism*. London: Routledge, 1992.

Horkheimer, Max. *Critical Theory*. New York: Herder and Herder, 1972.

Horkheimer, Max, and Theodor W. Adorno. *Dialectic of Enlightenment*. Trans. John Cumming. London: Allen Lane, 1973.

Hudson, Wayne. *The Marxist Philosophy of Ernst Bloch*. New York: St. Martin's Press, 1982.

Jacoby, Russell. *Dialectic of Defeat: Contours of Western Marxism*. Cambridge: Cambridge University Press, 1981.

Jay, Martin. *The Dialectical Imagination: A History of the Frankfurt School and the Institute of Social Research 1923–1950*. Boston, Mass.: Little Brown, 1973.

Jessop, Bob. *Nicos Poulantzas: Marxist Theory and Political Strategy*. London: Macmillan, 1985.

Joll, James. *Gramsci*. London: Fontana, 1977.

Katz, B. *Herbert Marcuse and the Art of Liberation*. London: NLB, 1982.

Kellner, D., ed. *Karl Korsch: Revolutionary Theory*. Austin: University of Texas Press, 1977.

Korsch, Karl. *Marxism and Philosophy*. Trans. by F. Halliday. London: New Left, 1970.

Lewis, William S. *Louis Althusser and the Traditions of French Marxism*. Lanham, Md.: Lexington Books, 2005.

Lichtheim, George. *Lukács*. London: Fontana, 1970.

Lowy, M. *Georg Lukács: From Romanticism to Bolshevism.* London: NLB, 1979.

Lukács, Georgii. *History and Class Consciousness.* Trans. by R. Livingstone. London: Merlin Press, 1971.

———. *Political Writings 1919–1929.* London: New Left, 1972.

———. *The Young Hegel: Studies in the Relations between Dialectics and Economics.* Trans. by Rodney Livingstone. London: Merlin Press, 1975.

MacIntyre, A. *Marcuse.* New York: Collins, 1970.

Marcuse, Herbert. *Eros and Civilization.* Boston, Mass.: Beacon, 1955.

———. *One-Dimensional Man.* London: Routledge and Kegan Paul, 1964.

———. *Negations: Essays in Critical Theory.* Boston, Mass.: Beacon, 1968.

Martin, James. *Gramsci's Political Analysis: A Critical Introduction.* Basingstoke, England: Macmillan, 1998.

Mattick, P. *Critique of Marcuse: One Dimensional Man in Class Society.* London: Merlin Press, 1972.

McCarthy, T. *The Critical Theory of Jurgen Habermas.* London: Hutchinson, 1978.

Merleau-Ponty, Maurice. *Humanism and Terror.* Trans. John O'Neill. Boston: Beacon, 1969.

———. *Adventures of the Dialectic.* London: Heinemann, 1973.

Mészáros, István, ed. *Aspects of History and Class Consciousness.* London: Routledge and Kegan Paul, 1971.

Mouffe, Chantal, ed. *Gramsci and Marxist Theory.* London: Routledge and Kegan Paul, 1979.

Parkinson, G. *Georg Lukacs.* London: Routledge and Kegan Paul, 1977.

———, ed. *Georg Lukacs: The Man, His Work and His Ideas.* London: Weidenfeld and Nicolson, 1970.

Poulantzas, Nicos. *Political Power and Social Classes.* London: New Left, 1973.

———. *Fascism and Dictatorship: The Third International and the Problems of Fascism.* London: New Left, 1974.

———. *Classes in Contemporary Capitalism.* London: New Left, 1975.

———. *State, Power, Socialism.* London: New Left, 1978.

Ransome, P. *Antonio Gramsci: A New Introduction.* New York: Harvester Wheatsheaf, 1992.

Sartre, Jean-Paul. *Literary and Philosophical Essays.* New York: Collier, 1962.

———. *The Problem of Method.* London: Methuen, 1963.

———. *Between Existentialism and Marxism.* London: New Left, 1972.

———. *Critique of Dialectical Reason.* London: New Left, 1976.

Sassoon, Anne Showstack. *Gramsci's Politics.* London: Croom Helm, 1980.

———, ed. *Approaches to Gramsci.* London: Writers and Readers Publishing Cooperative, 1982.

Eurocommunism

Bogg, Carl, and D. Plotke, eds. *The Politics of Eurocommunism: Socialism in Transition*. Montreal: Black Rose Books, 1980.

Brown, B.E., ed. *Eurocommunism and Eurosocialism*. New York: Cyrco Press, 1979.

Bull, Martin J., and Paul Heywood eds. *West European Communist Parties after the Revolutions of 1989*. Basingstoke, England: Macmillan, 1994.

Carillo, Santiago. *Eurocommunism and the State*. London: Lawrence and Wishart, 1977.

Claudin, Fernando. *Eurocommunism and Socialism*. London: New Left, 1979

Della Torre, P.F., E. Mortimer, and J. Story, eds. *Eurocommunism: Myth or Reality?* Harmondsworth, England: Penguin, 1979.

Kindersley, R., ed. *In Search of Eurocommunism*. London: Macmillan, 1981.

———. *The Communist Movement: From Comintern to Cominform*. Harmondsworth, England: Penguin, 1975.

Lange, Peter, and Maurizo Vannicelli, eds. *The Communist Parties of Italy, France and Spain: Postwar Change and Continuity. A Casebook*. London: George Allen and Unwin, 1981.

Mandel, Ernest. *From Stalinism to Eurocommunism: The Bitter Fruits of "Socialism in One Country."* London: New Left, 1978.

Middlemas, Keith. *Power and the Party: Changing Faces of Communism in Western Europe*. London: Andre Deutsche, 1980.

Thompson, Willie. *The Communist Movement Since 1945*. Oxford: Blackwell, 1998.

East European Marxism

Auty, P. *Tito: A Biography*. London: Penguin, 1970.

Beloff, N. *Tito's Flawed Legacy: Yugoslavia and the West: 1939–1984*. London: Gollancz, 1985.

Broekmeyer, M.J., ed. *Yugoslav Workers' Self-Management*. Dordrecht: Reidel, 1970.

Bromke, Adam, and John Strong, eds. *Gierek's Poland*. New York: Praeger, 1973.

Callinicos, Alex. *The Revenge of History: Marxism and the East European Revolutions*. Cambridge: Polity, 1991.

Golan, G. *Reform Rule in Czechoslovakia: The Dubcek Era 1968–69*. London: Cambridge University Press, 1973.

Gruenwald, O. *The Yugoslav Search for Man: Marxist Humanism in Contemporary Yugoslavia*. South Handley, Mass.: JF Bergin, 1983.

Hoxa, Enver. *Our Policy Is an Open Policy, the Policy of Proletarian Principles*. Tirana: 8 Nëntori Publishing House, 1978.

Ionescu, G. *Communism in Rumania 1944–62*. London: Oxford University Press, 1964.

Johnson, A. *The Transformation of Communist Ideology: The Yugoslav Case, 1945–1953*. Cambridge, Mass.: MIT Press, 1972.

Kardvelj, Edvard. *Democracy and Socialism*. London: Summerfield Press, 1979.

Kusin, V.V. *The Intellectual Origins of the Prague Spring*. London: Q. Press, 1971.

———, ed. *The Czechoslovak Reform Movement*. London: Q. Press, 1973.

Lydall, Harold. *Yugoslav Socialism: Theory and Practice*. Oxford: Clarendon Press, 1984.

Markovic, M., and R.S. Cohen. *The Rise and Fall of Socialist Humanism*. Nottingham, England: Spokesman, 1975.

Oren, N. *Bulgarian Communism—The Road to Power 1934–1944*. New York: Columbia University Press, 1971.

Pano, N.C. *The People's Republic of Albania*. Baltimore, Md.: Johns Hopkins Press, 1968.

Programme of the League of Communists of Yugoslavia 1958. Belgrade.

Rakovski, M. *Toward an East European Marxism*. London: Allison and Busby, 1978.

Rothschild, J. *The Communist Party of Bulgaria—Origins and Development 1883–1936*. New York: Columbia University Press, 1959.

Shawcross, William. *Crime and Compromise: Janos Kadar and the Politics of Hungary Since Revolution*. London: Weidenfeld and Nicholson, 1974.

Sher, Gerson S. *Praxis: Marxist Criticism and Dissent in Socialist Yugoslavia*. Bloomington: Indiana University Press, 1977.

Silnitsky, F., et al. *Communism and Eastern Europe*. New York: Karz, 1979.

Starr, Richard F. *Poland 1944–62: The Sovietization of a Captive People*. Baton Rouge: Louisiana State University Press, 1962.

Steele, J. *Socialism with a German Face*. London: Cape, 1978.

Stehle, Hansjakob. *Poland: The Independent Satellite*. London: Pall Mall, 1965.

Swain, Geoffrey, and Nigel Swain. *Eastern Europe Since 1945*. London: Macmillan, 1993.

Tismaneau, Vladimir. *The Crisis of Marxist Ideology in Eastern Europe: The Poverty of Utopia*. London: Routledge, 1988.

Tokés, Rudolf, *Béla Kun and the Hungarian Soviet Republic*. New York: Praeger-Pall Mall, 1967.

Windsor, P., and A. Roberts. *Czechoslavkia 1968*. London: Chatto and Windus for the Institute for Strategic Studies, 1969.

Zukin, S. *Beyond Marx and Tito: Theory and Practice in Yugoslav Socialism*. Cambridge: Cambridge University Press, 1975.

Other Works on European Marxism

Anderson, W.K. *James Connolly and the Irish Left*. Dublin: Irish Academic Press and the National Centre for Australian Studies, 1994.

Aron, Raymond. *Dialectics of Violence*. Oxford: Basil Blackwell, 1975.

Beckett, F. *Enemy Within: The Rise and Fall of the British Communist Party*. London: John Murray, 1995.

Bottomore, Thomas B., and Patrick Goode, eds. *Austro-Marxism*. Oxford: Oxford University Press, 1978.

Bricianer, Serge. *Pannekoek and the Workers' Councils*. St. Louis, Mo.: Telos, 1978.

Burkhard, Fred. *French Marxism Between the Wars: Henri Lefebvre and the "Philosophies."* Amherst, N.Y.: Humanity Books, 2000.

Collins, Henry, and Chimen Abramsky. *Karl Marx and the British Labour Movement: Years of the First International*. London: Macmillan, 1965.

De Grand, Alexander. *The Italian Left in the Twentieth Century: A History of the Socialist and Communist Parties*. Bloomington: Indiana University Press, 1989.

Gottfried, Paul. *The Strange Death of Marxism: The European Left in the New Millennium*. Columbia: University of Missouri Press, 2005.

Guttsman, W. L. *The German Social Democratic Party, 1875–1933: From Ghetto to Government*. London: George Allen and Unwin, 1981.

Heywood, Paul. *Marxism and the Failure of Organized Socialism in Spain, 1879–1936*. Cambridge: Cambridge University Press, 1990.

Judt, Tony. *Marxism and the French Left: Studies in Labour and Politics in France. 1830–1981*. Oxford: Clarendon Press, 1986.

Kelly, Michael. *Modern French Marxism*. Oxford: Basil Blackwell, 1982.

Kenny, Mike. *The First New Left*. London: Lawrence and Wishart, 1995.

Koelble, Thomas A. *The Left Unravelled: The Impact of the New Left on the British Labour Party and the West German Social Democratic party, 1968–1988*. Durham, N.C.: Duke University Press, 1991.

Lee, A.H. *The Revolutionary Left in Europe: A Research Guide*. New York: New York Public Library, 1992.

Machin, H., ed. *National Communism in Western Europe: A Third Way for Socialism?* London: Methuen, 1983.

Pierson, Stanley. *Marxist Intellectuals and the Working Class Mentality in Germany, 1887–1912*. Cambridge, Mass.: Harvard University Press, 1993.

Sasson, Donald. *One Hundred Years of Socialism: The West European Left in the Twentieth Century*. New York: I.B. Tauris, 1996.

Smart, D.A. *Pannekoek and Gorter's Marxism*. London: Pluto, 1978.

Sorel, Georges. *The Illusions of Progress*. Berkeley: University of California Press, 1969.

———. *Reflections on Violence*. New York: Macmillan, 1972.

Steenson, Gary P. *"Not One Man! Not One Penny!" German Social Democracy, 1865–1914*. Pittsburgh, Penn.: University of Pittsburgh Press, 1981.

———. *After Marx, before Lenin: Marxism and Socialist Working-Class Parties in Europe, 1884–1914*. Pittsburgh, Penn.: University of Pittsburgh Press, 1991.

Stuart, Robert C. *Marxism at Work: Ideology, Class, and French Socialism during the Third Republic*. Cambridge: Cambridge University Press, 1992.

Williams, G. *Proletarian Order: Antonio Gramsci, Factory Councils and the Origins of Italian Communism*. London: Pluto Press, 1975.

Williams, Stuart, ed. *Socialism in France: From Jaurès to Mitterand*. New York: St. Martin's Press, 1983.

THE SOVIET UNION AND RUSSIAN MARXISM

Early Russian Marxism: Plekhanov and Legal Marxism

Baron, S.H. *Plekhanov: The Father of Russian Marxism*. London: Routledge and Kegan Paul, 1963.

Haimson, L.H. *The Russian Marxists and the Origins of Bolshevism*. Cambridge, Mass.: Harvard University Press, 1955.

Kindersley, R. *The First Russian Revisionists: A Study of Legal Marxism in Russia*. Oxford: Oxford University Press, 1962.

Mendel, A.P. *Dilemmas of Progress in Tsarist Russia: Legal Marxism and Legal Populism*. Cambridge, Mass.: Harvard University Press, 1961.

Plekhanov, Georgii V. *The Role of the Individual in History*. London: Lawrence and Wishart, 1940.

———. *In Defence of Materialism: The Development of the Monist View of History*. London: Lawrence and Wishart, 1945.

———. *Fundamental Problems of Marxism*. London: Lawrence and Wishart, 1969.

The Mensheviks

Ascher, Abraham. *Pavel Axelrod and the Development of Menshevism*. Cambridge, Mass.: Harvard University Press, 1972.

———, ed. *The Mensheviks in the Russian Revolution*. London: Thames and Hudson, 1976.

Bourguina, Anna. *Russian Social Democracy: The Menshevik Movement Bibliography*. Stanford, Calif.: Hoover Institution, 1968.

Broido, V. *Lenin and the Mensheviks*. Aldershot, England: Gower, 1987

Brovkin, V. *The Mensheviks After October: Socialist Opposition and the Rise of the Bolshevik Dictatorship*. Ithaca, N.Y.: Cornell University Press, 1987.

Getzler, I. *Martov: A Political Biography of a Russian Social Democrat.* Cambridge: Cambridge University Press, 1967.

Haimson, L.H. *The Mensheviks: From the Revolution of 1917 to the Outbreak of the Second World War.* Chicago: University of Chicago Press, 1976.

Lenin and Leninism

Besançon, Alain. *The Intellectual Origins of Leninism.* Oxford: Basil Blackwell, 1981.

Cliff, Tony. *Lenin.* 4 vols. London: Pluto, 1975–79.

Deutscher, Tamara, ed. *Not by Politics Alone.* London: Allen and Unwin, 1973.

Hammond, T.T. *Lenin on Trade Unions and Revolution.* New York: Columbia University Press, 1957.

Harding, Neil. *Lenin's Political Thought.* 2 vols. in one. London: Macmillan, 1982.

———. *Leninism.* Durham, N.C.: Duke University Press, 1996.

Lane, D.S. *Leninism: A Sociological Interpretation.* Cambridge: Cambridge University Press, 1981.

Lenin, Vladimir I. *Collected Works.* 45 vols. Moscow: Progress Publishers, 1964–70.

———. *Selected Works.* London: Lawrence and Wishart, 1969.

Lewin, Moshe. *Lenin's Last Struggle.* London: Faber and Faber, 1969.

Liebman, Marcel. *Leninism under Lenin.* London: Cape, 1975.

Lukács, György. *Lenin: A Study on the Unity of His Thought.* London: New Left, 1970.

Meyer, Alfred G. *Leninism.* Cambridge, Mass.: Harvard University Press, 1957.

Payne, Robert. *The Life and Death of Lenin.* London: W.H. Allen, 1964.

Polan, A.J. *Lenin and the End of Politics.* London: Methuen, 1984.

Rigby, H. *Lenin's Government Sovnarkom 1917–1922.* Cambridge: Cambridge University Press, 1979.

Schapiro, Leonard, and Peter Reddaway, eds. *Lenin.* London: Pall Mall, 1967.

Shub, David. *Lenin.* London: Penguin, 1966.

Shukman, Harold. *Lenin and the Russian Revolution.* London: Longman, 1977.

Trotsky, Leon. *The Young Lenin.* Harmondsworth, England: Penguin, 1974.

Ulam, Adam B. *Lenin and the Bolsheviks.* London: Collins, 1965.

Volkogonov, Dmitri. *Lenin: Life and Legacy.* Trans. Harold Shukman. London: HarperCollins, 1994.

Stalin and Stalinism

Alesandrov, G.F., et al. *Joseph Stalin: A Short Biography.* Moscow: Foreign Languages Publishing House, 1952.

Alliluyeva, Svetlana. *Twenty Letters to a Friend*. London: Hutchinson, 1967.
Brackman, Roman. *The Secret File of Joseph Stalin: A Hidden Life*. London: Frank Cass, 2001.
Carr, Edward H. *Stalin: (vol. 1 of Socialism in One Country, 1924–1926)*. London: Macmillan, 1958.
Conquest, Robert. *The Great Terror: Stalin's Purge of the Thirties*. London: Macmillan, 1968.
Deutscher, Isaac. *Stalin: A Political Biography*. London: Oxford University Press, 1967.
Elleinstein, Jean. *The Stalin Phenomenon*. London: Lawrence and Wishart, 1976.
Killingray, David. *Stalin*. London: Harrap, 1976.
McNeal, R.H., ed. *Stalin's Works: An Annotated Bibliography*. Stanford, Calif.: Hoover Institution, 1967
Medvedev, Roy. *Let History Judge: The Origins and Consequences of Stalinism*. New York: Alfred A. Knopf, 1971.
Rigby, Thomas H., ed. *Stalin*. Englewood Cliffs, N.J.: Prentice-Hall, 1966.
Souvarine, Boris. *Stalin: A Critical Survey of Bolshevism*. London: Secker and Warburg, 1935.
Stalin, Josef V. *Problems of Leninism*. Moscow: Foreign Languages Publishing House, 1947.
———. *The Essential Stalin: Major Theoretical Writings, 1905–1952*. Ed. Bruce Franklin. Garden City, N.Y.: Anchor, 1972.
Tucker, Robert C. *Stalin as Revolutionary, 1879–1929: A Study in History and Personality*. New York: Norton, 1973.
———, ed. *Stalinism: Essays in Historical Interpretation*. New York: W.W. Norton, 1977.
———. *Stalin in Power. The Revolution from Above, 1928–1941*. London: W.W. Norton, 1990.
Ulam, Adam B. *Stalin: The Man and His Era*. London: Allen Lane, 1974.

Trotsky and Trotskyism

Ali, Tariq. *Introducing Trotsky and Marxism*. Duxford, England: Icon, 2000.
Carmichael, Joel. *Trotksy: An Appreciation of His Life*. London: Hodder and Stoughton, 1975.
Day, R.B. *Leon Trotsky and the Politics of Economic Isolation*. Cambridge: Cambridge University Press, 1973.
Deutscher, Isaac. *The Prophet Armed: Trotsky 1879–1921*. London: Oxford University Press, 1954.
———. *The Prophet Unarmed: Trotsky 1921–1929*. London: Oxford University Press, 1959.

——. *The Prophet Outcast: Trotsky 1929–1940*. London: Oxford University Press, 1963.

Hallas, Duncan. *Trotsky's Marxism*. London: Pluto, 1979.

Knei-Paz, Baruch. *The Social and Political Thought of Leon Trotsky*. Oxford: Oxford University Press, 1978.

Sinclair, Louis. *Leon Trotsky: A Bibliography*. Stanford, Calif.: Hoover Bibliographical Services, 1972.

Smith, Irving H. *Trotsky*. Englewood Cliffs, N.J.: Prentice-Hall, 1973.

Trotsky, Leon. *My Life*. New York: Grosset and Dunlap, 1963.

——. *History of the Russian Revolution*. Ann Arbor: University of Michigan Press, 1967.

——. *1905*. Harmondsworth, England: Penguin, 1971.

——. *The Revolution Betrayed: What Is the Soviet Union and Where Is It Going?* New York: Pathfinder, 1972.

——. *Terrorism and Communism*. London: New Park, 1975.

——. *Our Political Tasks*. London: New Park, 1980.

Trotsky, Leon, John Dewey, and George Novack. *Their Morals and Ours: Marxist versus Liberal Views on Morality*. New York: Pathfinder, 1969.

Bukharin

Bukharin, Nikolai. *Historical Materialism: A System of Sociology*. New York: International Publishers, 1925.

——. *Imperialism and World Economy*. New York: Monthly Review Press, 1973.

Bukharin, Nikolai, and E.A. Preobrazhnsky. *ABC of Communism*. London: Penguin, 1969.

Coates, Ken. *The Case of Nikolai Bukharin*. Nottingham, England: Spokesman, 1978.

Cohen, Stephen F. *Bukharin and the Bolshevik Revolution: A Political Biography 1888–1938*. New York: Knopf, 1974.

Heitman, Sidney. *Nikola I. Bukharin: A Bibliography with Annotations*. Stanford, Calif.: Hoover Institution, 1969.

Khrushchev

Crankshaw, Edward. *Khrushchev*. London: Collins, 1966.

Frankland, Mark. *Khrushchev*. Harmondsworth, England: Penguin, 1966.

Khrushchchev, Nikita. *Khrushchev Remembers*. 2 vols. Harmondsworth, England, 1977.

Linden, Carl A. *Khrushchev and the Soviet Leadership*. Baltimore, Md.: Johns Hopkins University Press, 1977.

Medvedev, Roy A., and Zhores A. Medvedev. *Khrushchev: The Years in Power*. London: Oxford University Press, 1977.
Page, Martin, and David Burg. *Unpersoned: The Fall of Nikita Sergeyevitch Khrushchev*. London: Chapman and Hall, 1966.

Soviet Leaders and Marxism after Khrushchev: Brezhnev, Chernienko, Andropov and Gorbachev

Dornberg, John. *Brezhnev: The Masks of Power*. London: Andre Deutsch, 1974.
Gorbachev, Mikhail. *Perestroika: New Thinking for Our Country and the World*. London: Collins, 1987.
Institute of Marxism-Leninism, CPSU Central Committee. *Leonid Ilyich Brezhnev: A Short Biography*. Oxford: Pergamon Press, 1977.

History

Carr, Edward II. *A History of the Soviet Union*. 11 vols. London: Macmillan, 1950–78.
———. *The Bolshevik Revolution 1917–1923*. London: Penguin, 1966.
Central Committee of the Communist Party of the Soviet Union. *A History of the Communist Party Short Course*. Moscow: Foreign Languages Publishing House, 1939.
Malia, Martin. *The Soviet Tragedy: A History of Socialism in Russia, 1917–1991*. New York: Free Press, 1994.
Pipes, Richard. *The Russian Revolution 1899–1919*. London: HarperCollins, 1990.
Sandle, M. *A Short History of Soviet Socialism*. London: University College Press, 1999.
Service, Robert. *The Bolshevik Party in Revolution 1917–1923*. London: Macmillan, 1979.
White, J.D. *The Russian Revolution 1917–1921. A Short History*. London: Arnold, 1994.

Economics

Dyker, D. *Restructuring the Soviet Economy*. London: Routledge, 1992.
Erlich, Alexander. *The Soviet Industrialization Debate 1924–1928*. Cambridge, Mass.: Harvard University Press, 1960.
Gregory, P.R., and R.C. Stuart. *Soviet Economic Structure and Performance*, 2nd ed. New York: Harper and Row, 1981.
Lewin, M. *Political Undercurrents in Soviet Economic Debates: From Bukharin to the Modern Reformers*. London: Pluto Press, 1975.

Nove, Alec. *Economic Rationality and Soviet Politics: Or, Was Stalin Really Necessary?* London: Allen and Unwin, 1964.

——. *The Soviet Economic System.* London: Allen and Unwin, 1977.

——. *An Economic History of the USSR.* Harmondsworth, England: Penguin, 1992.

Preobrazhensky, Evgeny A. *The New Economics.* Trans. Brian Pearce. Oxford: Oxford University Press, 1965.

——. *From NEP to Socialism.* London: New Park, 1973.

——. *The Crisis of Soviet Industrialization. Selected Essays.* Ed. by Donald A. Filzer. London: Macmillan, 1980.

Other Works on Russian Marxism and the Soviet Union

Bakhurst, D. *Consciousness and Revolution in Soviet Philosophy.* Cambridge: Cambridge University Press, 1991.

Beilharz, Peter. *Labour's Utopia: Bolshevism, Fabianism, Social Democracy.* London: Routledge, 1992.

Bellis, P. *Marxism and the USSR: The Theory of Proletarian Dictatorship and the Marxist Analysis of Soviet Society.* Basingstoke, England: Macmillan, 1979.

Bettelheim, Charles. *Class Struggles in the USSR: First period: 1917–1923.* Brighton, England: Harvester, 1976.

Brown, Archie, ed. *The Demise of Marxism-Leninism in Russia.* Basingstoke, England: Palgrave, 2004.

Byely, B. *Marxism-Leninism on War and Army: A Soviet View.* Honolulu: University Press of the Pacific, 2002.

Cliff, Tony. *Russia: A Marxist Analysis.* London: International Socialism, 1964.

——. *State Capitalism in Russia.* London: Pluto, 1974.

Cohen, S. *Rethinking the Soviet Experience: Politics and History Since 1917.* Oxford: Oxford University Press, 1985.

Daniels, R. *The Conscience of the Revolution: Communist Opposition in Soviet Russia.* New York: Simon and Schuster, 1969.

Donald, Moira. *Marxism and Revolution: Karl Kautsky and the Russian Marxists. 1900–1924.* New Haven, Conn.: Yale University Press, 1993.

Enteen, George M. *The Soviet Scholar-Bureaucrat. M.N. Pokrovski and the Society of Marxist Historians.* University Park: Pennsylvania State Press, 1978.

Evans, A. *Soviet Marxism-Leninism: The Decline of an Ideology.* Westport, Conn.: Praeger, 1993.

Farber, S. *Before Stalinism: The Rise and Fall of Soviet Democracy.* Cambridge: Polity, 1990.

Filtzer, D. *Soviet Workers and De-Stalinization.* London: Pluto, 1986.

———. *Soviet Workers and Stalinist Industrialization.* Cambridge: Cambridge University Press, 1992.

———. *Soviet Workers and the Collapse of Perestroika.* Cambridge: Cambridge University Press, 1994.

Furedi, Frank. *The Soviet Union Demystified: A Materialist Analysis.* London: Junius, 1986.

Graham, Loren R. *Science and Philosophy in the Soviet Union.* New York: Knopf, 1973.

Haberkern, Ernest E., and Arthur Lipow, eds. *Neither Capitalism nor Socialism: Theories of Bureaucratic Collectivism.* Atlantic Highlands, N.J.: Humanities Press, 1996.

Haupt, G., and J.J. Marie. *Makers of the Russian Revolution.* London: George Allen and Unwin, 1974.

Hayward, M. *Writers in Russia: 1917–1978.* London: Harvill, 1983.

Jaworskyj, M., ed. *Soviet Political Thought: An Anthology.* Baltimore, Md.: Johns Hopkins University Press, 1967.

Kagarlitsky, Boris. *Farewell Perestroika: A Soviet Chronicle.* London: Verso, 1990.

Kowlaski, R.I. *The Bolshevik Party in Conflict. The Left Communist Opposition of 1918.* Basingstoke, England: Macmillan, 1991.

Lane, David. *Politics and Society in the USSR.* London: Martin Robertson, 1978.

Lentini, P., ed. *Elections and Political Order in Russia.* Budapest: Central European University Press, 1995.

Lowy, M. *The Politics of Combined and Uneven Development: The Theory of Permanent Revolution.* London: Verso, 1981.

Marcuse, Herbert. *Soviet Marxism.* London: Routledge and Kegan Paul, 1958.

McAuley, Mary. *Politics and the Soviet Union.* Harmondsworth, England: Penguin, 1977.

Meiklejohn, T.S., ed. *Soviet Policy in Eastern Europe.* New Haven, Conn.: Yale University Press, 1984.

Porter, Cathy. *Alexandra Kollantai: A Biography.* London: Virago, 1980.

Pospelow, P.M., et al. *Development of Revolutionary Theory by the CPSU.* Moscow: Progress, 1971.

Rahmani, L. *Soviet Psychology: Philosophical, Theoretical and Experimental Issues.* New York: International Universities Press, 1973.

Robinson, N. *Ideology and the Collapse of the Soviet System: A Critical History of Soviet Ideological Discourse.* Brookfield, Vt.: Edward Elgar, 1995.

Scanlan, J. *Marxism in the USSR.* Ithaca, N.Y.: Cornell University Press, 1985.

Schactman, Max. *The Bureaucratic Revolution: The Rise of the Stalinist State.* New York: Donald Press, 1962.

Schapiro, Leonard. *The Communist Party of the Soviet Union.* London: Methuen, 1970.

——. *The Government and Politics of the Soviet Union.* London: Hutchinson, 1977.

Scherer, John L. *USSR Facts and Figures Annual*, vol. 1. Gulf Breeze, Fla.: Academic International Press, 1977.

Shanin, Theodor, ed. *Late Marx and the Russian Road.* New York: Monthly Review, 1983.

Sirianni, C. *Workers' Control and Socialist Democracy: The Soviet Experience.* London: Verso, 1982.

Smith, S.A. *Red Petrograd: Revolution in the Factories 1917–1918.* Cambridge: Cambridge University Press, 1983.

Stites, R. *The Women's Liberation Movement in Russia: Feminism, Nihilism and Bolshevism, 1860–1930.* Princeton, N.J.: Princeton University Press, 1978.

Struve, G. *Russian Literature under Lenin and Stalin, 1917–1953.* London: Routledge and Kegan Paul, 1972.

The USSR in Figures. Moscow: Statistika, annual.

Ticktin, Hillel. *Origins of the Crisis in the USSR: Essays on the Political Economy of a Disintegrating System.* Armonk, N.J.: M.E. Sharpe, 1992.

Various. *The Road to Communism.* Moscow: Foreign Languages Publishing House, 1961.

Vaughan James, C. *Soviet Socialist Realism: Origins and Theory.* London: Macmillan, 1973.

Waller Mike. *Democratic Centralism: An Historical Commentary.* Manchester: Manchester University Press, 1981.

Wetter, G.A. *Dialectical Materialism: A Historical and Systematic Survey of Philosophy in the Soviet Union.* London: Routledge and Kegan Paul, 1958.

White, S., and A. Pravda, eds. *Ideology and Soviet Politics.* Basingstoke, England: Macmillan, 1988.

ASIAN MARXISMS

China

Bettelheim, Charles, and N. Burton. *China Since Mao.* New York: Monthly Review Press, 1978.

Bianco, L. *Origins of the Chinese Revolution: 1915–1949.* Stanford: University of California Press, 1971.

Brandt, Conrad, Benjamin Schwartz, and John K. Fairbank, eds. *A Documentary History of Chinese Communism.* New York: Atheneum, 1971.

Brook, Timothy, ed. *The Asiatic Mode of Production in China.* Armonk, N.Y.: M.E. Sharpe, 1989.

Breslin, Shaun. *Mao.* Harlow, England: Longman, 2000.

Brugger, Bill, ed. *China: The Impact of the Cultural Revolution*. London: Croom Helm, 1978.

——. *China: Liberation and Transformation*. London: Croom Helm, 1981.

——, ed. *Chinese Marxism in Flux, 1978–1984: Essays on Epistemology, Ideology, and Political Economy*. London: Croom Helm, 1985.

Brugger, Bill, and David Kelly. *Chinese Marxism in the Post-Mao Era*. Stanford, Calif.: Stanford University Press, 1990.

Carrèrre d'Encausse, Hélène, and Stuart R. Schram. *Marxism and Asia: An Introduction with Readings*. London: Allen Lane The Penguin Press, 1969.

Chan, Adrian. *Chinese Marxism*. London: Continuum, 2003.

Chang, Jung, and Jon Halliday. *Mao: The Unknown Story*. New York: Knopf, 2005.

Cheek, Timothy, ed. *Mao Zedong and China's Revolution: A Brief History with Documents*. Basingstoke, England: Palgrave, 2002.

Ch'en, Jerome, ed. *Mao Papers: Anthology and Bibliography*. Englewood Cliffs, N.J.: Prentice Hall, 1969.

——. *Mao and the Chinese Revolution*. Oxford: Oxford University Press, 1967.

Cohen, Arthur A. *The Communism of Mao-Tse-Tung*. Chicago: University of Chicago Press, 1964.

Croll, Elisabeth. *Feminism and Socialism in China*. London: Routledge and Kegan Paul, 1978.

Deng Xiaoping. *Selected Works*. Beijing: Foreign Languages Press, 1984.

Dirlik, Arif. *Revolution and History: The Origins of Marxist Historiography in China 1919–1937*. Berkeley: University of California Press, 1978.

——. *The Origins of Chinese Communism*. New York: Oxford University Press, 1989.

——. *Marxism in the Chinese Revolution*. Lanham, Md.: Rowman & Littlefield, 2005.

Dirlik, Arif, Paul Healy, and Nick Knight, eds. *Critical Perspectives on Mao Zedong's Thought*. Atlantic Highlands, N.J.: Humanities Press, 1997.

Fitzgerald, C. *Mao Tse-Tung and China*. London: Harmondsworth Penguin, 1977.

Goodman, David. *Deng Xiaoping*. London: Cardinal, 1990.

Hsiung, James Chieh. *Ideology and Practice. The Evolution of Chinese Communism*. New York: Praeger, 1970.

Johnson, C. *Peasant Nationalism and Communist Power: The Emergence of Revolutionary China 1937–1945*. Stanford: University of California Press, 1953.

Kampen, Thomas. *Mao Zedong, Zhou Enlai and the Evolution of The Chinese Communist Leadership*. Denmark: NIAS, 2000.

Knight, Nick, ed. *Mao Zedong on Dialectical Materialism: Writings on Philosophy, 1937*. Armonk, N.Y.: M.E. Sharpe, 1990.

Mao Tse-Tung. *Selected Works*. 5 vols. Peking: Foreign Languages Press, 1961–77.

———. *Selected Readings from the Works of Mao Tsetung*. Peking: Foreign Languages Press, 1967.

Meisner, Maurice. *Li Ta-Chao and the Origins of Chinese Marxism*. Cambridge, Mass.: Harvard University Press, 1967.

———. *Marxism, Maoism and Utopianism*. Madison: University of Wisconsin Press, 1982.

Pantsov, Alexander. *The Bolsheviks and the Chinese Revolution, 1919–1927*. Richmond, England: Curzon Press, 2000.

Pye, L. *Mao Tse-Tung: The Man in the Leader*. New York: Basic Books, 1976.

Roy, M.N. *Revolution and Counterrevolution in China*. Calcutta: Renaissance, 1946.

Saitch, Tony, and Hans van de Ven, eds. *New Perspectives on the Chinese Communist Revolution*. Armonk, N.Y.: M.E. Sharpe, 1994.

Schram, Stuart R. *The Political Thought of Mao Tse-Tung*. Harmondsworth, England: Penguin, 1969.

———, ed. *Mao Tse-Tung Unrehearsed*. London: Penguin, 1974.

Schwartz, Benjamin I. *Chinese Communism and the Rise of Mao*. New York: Harper and Row, 1951.

Selden, Mark. *China in Revolution: The Yenan Way Revisited*. Armonk, N.Y.: M.E. Sharpe, 1995.

Snow, Edgar. *Red Star Over China*. New York: Grove Press, 1961.

Solomon, R. *Mao's Revolution and the Chinese Political Culture*. Berkeley: University of California Press, 1971.

Starr, John Bryan. *Continuing the Revolution. The Political Thought of Mao*. Princeton, N.J.: Princeton University Press, 1979.

Su Shaozhi, et al. *Marxism in China*. Nottingham, England: Spokesman Books, 1983.

Suyin, H. *The Morning Deluge: Mao Tse-Tung and the Chinese Revolution 1893–1953*. Boston: Little, Brown and Co., 1972.

Wilson, Dick. *Mao Tse-tung in the Scales of History*. Cambridge: Cambridge University Press, 1977.

Wilson, Dick, and Matthew Grenier. *Chinese Communism*. London: Paladin, 1992.

Womack, Brantly. *The Foundations of Mao Zedong's Political Thought*. Honolulu: Hawaii University Press, 1982.

Yang Zhongmei. *Hu Yaobang: A Chinese Biography*. New York: M.E. Sharpe, 1988.

Zhao Wei. *The Biography of Zhao Ziyang*. Hong Kong: Educational and Cultural Press, 1989.

India

Basu, A.K. *Marxism in an Indian State: An Analytical Study of West Bengal Leftism.* Kolkata, India: Ratna Prakashan, 2003.

Biswas, S.K. *Pathos of Marxism in India.* Calcutta: Orion, 1996.

Dutt, R. Palme. *India Today.* London: Gollancz, 1940.

Ghose, Sanker. *Socialism, Democracy and Nationalism in India.* Bombay: Allied Publishers, 1973.

Gupta, Sobhanlal Datta. *Comintern India and the Colonial Question 1920–37.* Calcutta: K.P. Bagchi, 1980.

Haithcox, John P. *Communism and Nationalism in India: M.N. Roy and Comintern Policy 1920–39.* Princeton, N.J.: Princeton University Press, 1971.

Joshi, Puran Chandra. *Marxism and Social Revolution in India and Other Essays.* New Delhi: Manak, 2002.

Maita, Kiran. *Roy, Comintern and Marxism in India.* Calcutta: Darbar Prokashan, 1991.

Roy, M.N. *India in Transition.* Geneva: J.B. Target, 1922.

Sharma, Jaddish S., ed. *Indian Socialism: A Descriptive Bibliography.* Delhi: Vikas Publishing House, 1975.

Wielenga, Bastiaan. *Marxist Views on India in Historical Perspective.* Madras: Christian Literature Society, 1976.

Indochina

Chandler, David P. *Brother Number One: A Political Biography of Pol Pot.* Boulder, Colo.: Westview, 1999.

Chau, Phan Tien. *Vietnamese Communism: A Research Bibliography.* Westport, Conn.: Greenwood Press, 1975.

Duiker, William. *Ho Chi Minh.* New York: Hyperion, 2000.

Fall, Bernard B. *Ho Chi Minh—On Revolution: Selected Writings, 1920–66.* New York: Frederick A. Praeger, 1967.

Giap, General Vo Nguyen. *Dien Bien Phu.* Revised ed. Hanoi: Foreign Languages Publishing House, 1964.

Ho Chi Minh. *Selected Works.* 4 vols. Hanoi: Foreign Languages Publishing House, 1960–62.

———. *Patriotism and Proletarian Internationalism.* Hanoi: Foreign Languages Publishing House, 1979.

Hodgkin, Thomas. *Vietnam: The Revolutionary Path.* London: Macmillan, 1981.

Kiernan, Ben. *The Pol Pot Regime: Race, Power, and Genocide in Cambodia under the Khmer Rouge.* New Haven, Conn.: Yale Nota Bene, 2002.

Lacoutre, Jean. *Ho Chi Minh*. Harmondsworth, England: Penguin Books, 1967.
McAlister, Jr., John T. *Vietnam: The Origins of Revolution*. New York: Alfred A. Knopf, 1969.
O'Neil, Robert J. *General Giap: Politician and Strategist*. New York: Praeger, 1969.
An Outline History of the Viet Nam Workers' Party (1930–1970). Hanoi: Foreign Languages Publishing House, 1970.
Pol Pot. *Les Grandioses Victoires de la Révolution du Kampuchea sous la Direction Juste et Clairvoyante du Parti Communiste du Kampuchea*. Phnom Penh: Ministère des Affaires Etrangères du Kampuchea Démocratique, 1978.
Short, Philip. *Pol Pot: The History of a Nightmare*. London: John Murray, 2004.
Turner, Robert F. *Vietnamese Communism: Its Origins and Development*. Stanford, Calif.: Hoover Institution Press, 1975.
Vo Nguyen Giap. *People's War, People's Army*. New York: Praeger, 1962.
Zasloff, J.J., and MacAlister Brown. *Communism in Indochina*. Lexington, Mass.: D.C. Heath, 1975.

Korea

Bong Baik. *Kim Il Sung: Biography*. 3 vols. Tokyo: Miraisha, 1969–70.
Dae-Sook Suh. *The Korean Communist Movement 1918–1948*. Princeton, N.J.: Princeton University Press, 1967.
———, ed. *Documents of Korean Communism: 1918–1948*. Princeton, N.J.: Princeton University Press, 1970.
Kim Il Sung. *Selected Works*. 4 vols. Pyongyang: Foreign Languages Press, 1972.
Kim Jong Il. *Let Us Advance the Banner of Marxism-Leninism and the Juche Idea*. Pyongyang: Foreign Languages Press, 1983.
Scalpino, Robert A., and Chong-Sik Lee. *Communism in Korea*. 2 vols. Berkeley: University of California Press, 1973.
Takashi, Nada. *Korea in Kim Jong Il's Era*. Pyongyang: Foreign Languages Publishing House, 2000.

Other Works on Asian Marxisms

Beckman, George M., and Genji Okubo. *The Japanese Communist Party, 1922–1945*. Stanford, Calif.: Stanford University Press, 1969.
Bernstein, Gail Lee. *Japanese Marxist: Portrait of Kawakami Hajime, 1879–1946*. London: Harvard University Press, 1990.
Bradsher, Henry S. *Afghan Communism and Soviet Intervention*. Oxford: Oxford University Press, 1999.

Dunn, Stephen P. *The Fall and Rise of the Asiatic Mode of Production*. London: Routledge and Kegan Paul, 1982.

Kublin, Hyman. *Asian Revolutionary: The Life of Sen Katayama*. Princeton, N.J.: Princeton University Press, 1964.

Kuroda, Hirokazu. *Studies in Marxism in Postwar Japan: Main Issues in Political Economy and the Materialist Outlook of History*. Tokyo: Hatsubaimoto Akane Tosho Hanbai, 2002.

Mackerras, Colin, and Nick Knight, eds. *Marxism in Asia*. Beckenham, England: Croom Helm, 1985.

Mintz, J.S. *Mohammed, Marx and Marhaen: The Roots of Indonesian Socialism*. New York: Praeger, 1965.

Putsagnorov, T., ed. *50 Years of People's Mongolia*. Ulaanbaatar, 1971.

Sanders, A.J.K. *The People's Republic of Mongolia*. London: Oxford University Press, 1968.

Sawer, Marian. *Marxism and the Asiatic Mode of Production*. The Hague: Martinus Nijhoff, 1977.

Scalapino, Robert A., ed. *The Communist Revolution Asia: Tactics, Goals and Achievements*. Englewood Cliffs, N.J.: Prentice-Hall, 1965.

———. *The Japanese Communist Movement, 1920–1966*. Berkeley: University of California Press, 1967.

Traeger, Frank N., ed. *Marxism in Southeast Asia*. Stanford, Calif.: Stanford University Press, 1959.

Tsukahira, Toshio G. *The Postwar Evolution of Communist Strategy in Japan*. Cambridge, Mass.: Center for International Studies, M.I.T., 1954.

Turner, B.S. *Marx and the End of Orientalism*. London: Allen and Unwin, 1978.

LATIN AMERICAN MARXISM

Aguilar, L.E. *Marxism in Latin America*. New York: Knopf, 1968.

Albar, Víctor. *Historia del comunismo en América Latina*. Mexico: Ediciones Occidentales, 1954.

Alexander, R.J. *Communism in Latin America*. New Brunswick, N.J.: Rutgers University Press, 1957.

Barkin, David P., and Nita R. Manitzas, eds. *Cuba: The Logic of the Revolution*. Andover, Mass.: Warner Modular Publications, 1973.

Bazán, Armando. *José Carlos Mariátigui*. Santiago, Chile: Zig-Zag, 1939.

Becker, M. *Mariátigui and Latin American Marxist Theory*. Athens, Ohio: Latin American Series No. 20, Ohio University Center for International Studies, 1993.

Bonachea, R.E., and N.P. Valdes, eds. *Cuba in Revolution*. New York: Doubleday, 1972.

Caballero, M. *Latin America and the Comintern, 1919–1943*. Cambridge: Cambridge University Press, 1996.

Carr, B., and S. Ellner, eds. *The Latin American Left: From the Fall of Allende to Perestroika*. Boulder, Colo.: Westview Press, 1993.

Castañeda, J. *Utopian Unarmed: The Latin American Left after the Cold War*. New York: Random House, 1993.

Castro, Fidel. *Fidel Castro Speaks*. Ed. by Martin Jenner and James Petras. New York: Grove Press, 1969.

Connolly, Sean. *Castro*. London: Hodder and Stoughton, 2002.

D'Angelo, Edward, ed. *Cuban and North American Marxism*. Amsterdam: Gruner, 1984.

Debray, Régis. *Revolution in the Revolution? Armed Struggle and Political Struggle in Latin America*. Trans. Bobbye Ortiz. New York: Grove Press, 1967.

——. *A Critique of Arms*. 2 vols. London: Harmondsworth Penguin, 1977–78.

Dominguez, J.I. *Cuba: Order and Revolution*. Cambridge, Mass.: Harvard University Press, 1978.

Dumont, R. *Is Cuba Socialist?* New York: Viking, 1974.

Fadndez, Julio. *Marxism and Democracy in Chile: From 1932 to the Fall of Allende*. New Haven, Conn.: Yale University Press, 1988.

Frank, André Gunder. *Capitalism and Underdevelopment in Latin America*. New York: Monthly Review Press, 1969.

Garcia, Fernando D., and Oscar Sola, eds. *Che: Images of a Revolutionary*. London: Pluto, 2000.

Gerassi, John, ed. *Venceremos: The Speeches and Writings of Che Guevera*. New York: Macmillan, 1968.

Guevara, Che. *Guevara on Revolution: A Documentary Overview*. Ed. by J. Mallin. Miami: University of Miami, 1969.

——. *Che: Selected Works of Ernesto Guevara*. Ed. by R.E. Bonachea and N.P. Valdes. Cambridge, Mass.: Harvard University Press, 1970.

Harris, R. *Marxism, Socialism and Democracy in Latin America*. Boulder, Colo.: Westview Press, 1992.

Hodges, D.C. *The Latin American Revolution: Politics and Strategy from Apro-Marxism to Guevanism*. New York: William Morrow, 1974.

Horowitz, I.L., ed. *Cuban Communism*. New Brunswick, N.J.: Transaction, 1978.

Huberman, Leo, and Paul Sweezy. *Cuba: Anatomy of a Revolution*. New York: Monthly Review Press, 1960.

Jackson, D.B. *Castro, the Kremlin, and Communism in Latin America*. Baltimore, Md.: Johns Hopkins University Press, 1969.

Karol, K.S. *Guerrillas in Power: The Course of the Cuban Revolution.* New York: Hill and Wang, 1970.

Liss, S. *Marxist Thought in Latin America.* Berkeley: University of California Press, 1984.

Löwy, Michael. *The Marxism of Che Guevara.* New York: Monthly Review Press, 1973.

———, ed. *Marxism in Latin America from 1909 to the Present: An Anthology.* Atlantic Highlands, N.J.: Humanities Press, 1992.

Luther, Eric, with Ted Henken. *The Life and Work of Che Guevara.* Indianapolis, Ind.: Alpha, 2001.

Mariátigui, José. *Defensa de marxismo: La emoción de nuestro tiempo y otros temas.* Santiago, Chile: Edicones Nacionales y Extranjeras, 1934.

———. *Historia de la Crisis Mundial.* Lima, Peru: Amauta, 1973.

Matthew, H.L. *Fidel Castro.* New York: Simon and Schuster, 1969.

———. *Revolution in Cuba.* New York: Charles Scribner's Sons, 1975.

McCaughan, E. *Reinventing Revolution: The Renovation of Left Discourse in Cuba and Mexico.* Boulder, Colo.: Westview Press, 1997.

Munck, Ronaldo. *Revolutionary Trends in Latin America.* Montreal: Occasional Monograph Series No. 20, McGill University, 1984.

O'Connor, J. *The Origins of Socialism in Cuba.* Ithaca, N.Y.: Cornell University Press, 1970.

Petras, J. *The Left Strikes Back: Class Conflict in Latin America in the Age of Neoliberalism.* Boulder, Colo.: Westview Press, 1999.

Poppino, Rollie. *International Communism in Latin America: A History of the Movement, 1917–1963.* New York: Free Press of Glencoe, 1964.

Ramm, H. *The Marxism of Regis Debray: Between Lenin and Guevara.* Lawrence, Kansas: University Press of Kansas, 1978.

Roberts, K. *Deepening Democracy? The Modern Left and Social Movements in Chile and Peru.* Stanford, Calif.: Stanford University Press, 1998.

Vanden, Harry E. *National Marxism in Latin America: José Carlos Mariátegui's Thought and Politics.* Boulder, Colo.: Lynne Rienner, 1986.

———, ed. *Latin American Marxism: A Bibliography.* New York: Garland, 1991.

NORTH AMERICAN MARXISM

Bell, Daniel. *Marxian Socialism in the United States.* Princeton, N.J.: Princeton University Press, 1967.

Bernstein, Irving. *Turbulent Years.* Boston, Mass.: Houghton Mifflin, 1969.

Browder, E.R. *Marx and America.* New York: Duell, Sloan and Pearce, 1958.

Buhle, Paul. *Marxism in the U.S.: Remapping the American Left.* London: Verso, 1991.

Buhle, Mari Jo, Paul Buhle, and Dan Georgakas, eds. *Encyclopedia of the American Left*. New York: Garland, 1990.

Cannon, James P. *First Ten Years of American Communism*. New York: Pathfinder, 1972.

Caute, David. *The Great Fear: The Anti-Communist Purges under Truman and Eisenhower*. New York: Simon and Schuster, 1978.

Clayton, Douglas. *Floyd Dell: The Life and Times of an American Radical*. Chicago: I.R. Dee, 1994.

Debs, Eugene V. *Gentle Rebel: Letters of Eugene V. Debs*, ed. J. Robert Constantine. Urbana: University of Illinois Press, 1995.

Dobbs, Farrell. *Revolutionary Continuity*. New York: Monad, 1983.

Draper, Theodore. *The Roots of Amercian Communism*. New York: Viking, 1957.

———. *American Communism and Soviet Russia*. New York: Viking, 1960.

Dubofsky, M. *We Shall Be All: A History of the IWW*. Chicago: Quadrangle, 1969.

Fernández-Morera, Daria. *American Academia and the Survival of Marxist Ideas*. Westport, Conn.: Praeger, 1996.

Fried, Albert, ed. *Socialism in America from the Shakers to the Third International: A Documentary History*. New York: Columbia University Press, 1992.

———, ed. *Communism in America: A History in Documents*. New York: Columbia University Press, 1997.

Harrington, Michael. *Socialism*. New York: Saturday Review Press, 1972.

Haynes, John Earl. *Communism and Anti-Communism in the United States*. New York: Garland, 1987.

Hillquit, Morris. *History of Socialism in the United States*. New York: Russell and Russell, 5th ed., 1965. First published in 1903.

Howe, Irving. *Socialism and America*. San Diego, Calif.: Harcourt Brace Jovanovich, 1985.

Howe, Irving, and Lewis Coser. *The American Communist Party: A Critical History*. Boston, Mass.: Beacon, 1957.

Isserman, Maurice. *Which Side Were You On?* Middletown, Conn.: Wesleyan University Press, 1982.

Jaffe, Philip J. *The Rise and Fall of American Communism*. New York: Horizon, 1975.

Johanningsmeier, Edward P. *Forging American Communism*. Princeton, N.J.: Princeton University Press, 1994).

JohnPoll, Bernard K., and Harvey Klehr, eds. *Biographical Dictionary of the American Left*. Westport, Conn.: Greenwood Press, 1986.

Klehr, Harvey. *The Heyday of American Communism*. New York: Basic Books, 1984.

Klehr, Harvey, and John Earl Haynes. *The American Communist Movement.* New York: Twayne, 1992.

Kornbluh, Joyce L., ed. *Rebel Voices: An IWW Anthology.* Chicago: Charles H. Kerr, 1988.

Lewy, Guenter. *The Cause That Failed.* New York: Oxford University Press, 1990.

Miles, Dione, ed. *Something in Common: An IWW Bibliography.* Detroit, Mich.: Wayne State University Press, 1986.

Ottonelli, Fraser M. *The Communist Party of the United States from the Depression to World War II.* New Brunswick, N.J.: Rutgers University Press, 1991.

Neufeld, Maurice F., Daniel J. Leab, and Dorothy Swanson, eds. *American Working Class History: A Representative Bibliography.* New York: R.R. Bowker, 1983.

Rossiter, Clinton L. *Marxism: The View from America.* New York: Harcourt and Brace, 1960.

Salvatore, Nick. *Eugene V. Debs: Citizen and Socialist.* Urbana: University of Illinois Press, 1982.

Seretan, L. Glen. *Daniel DeLeon: The Odyssey of an American Marxist.* Cambridge, Mass.: Harvard University Press, 1979.

Sombart, Werner. *Why Is There No Socialism in the United States?* White Plains, N.Y.: International Arts and Sciences Press, 1976.

Warren, Frank A. *Liberals and Communism: The "Red Decade" Revisited.* New York: Columbia University Press, 1994.

Wilcox, L.M., ed. *Guide to the American Left.* Kansas City, Kans.: Editorial Research Service, 1984 to date.

Young, Marguerite. *Harp Song for a Radical: The Life and Times of Eugene Victor Debs.* New York: Alfred Knopf, 1999.

AFRICAN MARXISM

Aaby, P. *The State of Guinea-Bissau: African Socialism or Socialism in Africa?* Uppsala: The Nordic Africa Institute, 1978.

Cabral, Amilcar. *Revolution in Guinea: An African People's Struggle.* London, Stage 1; New York: Monthly Review Press, 1970.

——. *Unity and Struggle: Speeches and Writings.* London: Heinemann, 1979.

Chabal, P. *Amilcar Cabral: Revolutionary Leadership and People's War.* Cambridge: Cambridge University Press, 1983.

Davidson, Apollon, Irina Filatova, Valentin Gordov, and Sheridan Johns, eds. *South Africa and the Communist International.* 2 vols. London: Frank Cass, 2003.

Davidson, Basil. *Which Way Africa? The Search for a New Society*. Revised ed. London: Penguin, 1967.

——. *In the Eye of the Storm—Angola's People*. London: Longman, 1972.

——. *No Fist Is Big Enough to Hide the Sky: The Liberation of Guinea-Bissau and Cape Verde*. London: Zed, 1981.

Jumba-Masagzi, A.H.K, ed. *African Socialism: A Bibliography and a Short Summary*. Nairobi, Kenya: East African Academy Research Information Centre, 1970.

Machel, Samora Moises. *The Tasks Ahead: Selected Speeches of Samora Machel*. New York: Afro-American Information Service, 1975.

Marcum, J.A. *The Angolan Revolution*. 2 vols. Cambridge, Mass.: MIT Press, 1968–69.

McCulloch, J. *In the Twilight of Revolution: The Political Theory of Amilcar Cabral*. London: Routledge and Kegan Paul, 1983.

Ray, Donald I., ed. *Dictionary of the African Left: Parties, Movements and Groups*. Brookfield, Vt.: Gower, 1989.

Rosenberg, C., and T. Callaghy. *Socialism in Sub-Saharan Africa: A New Assessment*. Berkeley: University of California Press, 1979.

Valdes Vivo, Raul. *Ethiopia's Revolution*. New York: International Publishers, 1978.

Zelig, Leo. *Marxism in Africa: The Class Struggle Across the Continent*. Cheltenham, England: New Clarion, 2002.

SUBJECTS AND ISSUES

Marxism and Philosophy: Dialectics and Materialism

Balibar, Etienne. *The Philosophy of Marx*. London: Verso, 1995.

Bhaskar, Roy. *Dialectics*. London: Verso, 1992.

Callinicos, Alex. *Marxism and Philosophy*. London: Oxford University Press, 1983.

Cornforth, Maurice. *Dialectical Materialism: An Introduction*, vol. 1, *Materialism and the Dialectical Method*. London: Lawrence and Wishart, 1968.

Dupré, Louis. *The Philosophical Foundations of Marxism*. New York: Harcourt, Brace and World, 1966.

Fisk, Milton. *Nature and Necessity*. Bloomington: University of Indiana Press, 1973.

Gollobin, I. *Dialectical Materialism: Its Laws, Categories, and Practises*. New York: Petras Press, 1986.

Guest, D. *A Textbook of Dialectical Materialism*. New York: International Publishers, 1939.

Howard, D. *The Development of the Marxian Dialectic*. Carbondale: Southern Illinois University Press, 1972.

Ilyenkov, E.V. *Dialectical Logic: Essays on its History and Theory*. Trans. by H.C. Creighton. Moscow: Progress Publishers, 1977.

———. *The Dialectics of the Abstract and the Concrete in Marx's Capital*. Moscow: Progress, 1982.

James, C.L.R. *Notes on Dialectics*. Westport, Conn.: Lawrence Hill, 1980.

Jay, M. *Marxism and Totality*. Berkeley: University of California Press, 1982.

Jordan, Z.A. *Philosophy and Ideology*. Dordrecht: D. Reidel, 1963.

———. *The Evolution of Dialectical Materialism*. London: Macmillan, 1967.

Kuusinen, O., ed. *Fundamentals of Marxism-Leninism*. London: Lawrence and Wishart, 1961.

Lecourt, D. *Marxism and Epistemology: Bachlard, Foucault, Languilheim*. London: New Left, 1975.

Marquit, E., P. Moran, and W.H. Truitt. *Dialectical Contradictions: Contemporary Marxist Discussions*. Minneapolis, Minn.: Marxist Educational Press, 1982.

Meikle, Scott. *Essentialism in the Thought of Karl Marx*. London: Duckworth, 1985.

Mepham, John, and David-Hillel Ruben, eds. *Issues in Marxist Philosophy*:
Volume I, *Dialectics and Method*. Brighton, England: Harvester, 1979.
Volume II, *Materialism*. Brighton, England: Harvester, 1979.
Volume III, *Epistemology, Science and Ideology*. Brighton, England: Harvester, 1979.
Volume IV, *Social and Political Philosophy*. Brighton, England: Harvester, 1979.

Parsons, H.L., and J. Somerville, eds. *Dialogues on the Philosophy of Marxism*. Westport, Conn.: Greenwood Press, 1974.

Rockmore, Tom. *Marx after Marxism: The Philosophy of Karl Marx*. Oxford: Blackwell, 2002.

Rotenstreich, N. *Basic Problems of Marx's Philosophy*. Indianapolis, Ind.: Bobbs-Merrill, 1965.

Ruben, D.H. *Marxism and Materialism: A Study in Marxist Theory of Knowledge*. Brighton, England: Harvester, 1979.

Rubinstein, D. *Marx and Wittgenstein: Social Praxis and Social Explanation*. London: Routledge and Kegan Paul, 1981.

Sayers, Sean, and P. Osborne, eds. *Socialism, Feminism and Philosophy: A Radical Philosophy Reader*. London: Routledge, 1990.

Schmidt, A. *The Concept of Nature in Marx*. Trans. by B. Fowkes. London: New Left, 1971.

Suchting, Wal A. *Marxism and Philosophy*. New York: New York University Press, 1986.

Timpanaro, Sebastien. *On Materialism*. London: New Left, 1976.

Wilde, Lawrence. *Marx and Contradiction*. Aldershot, England: Avebury, 1989.

Zelen, Jindrich. *The Logic of Marx*. Trans. by T. Carver. Oxford: Basil Blackwell, 1980.

Marxist Theory

Acton, Harold B. *The Illusion of the Epoch: Marxism-Leninism as a Philosophical Creed*. London: Routledge and Kegan Paul, 1955.

Avineri, Shlomo. *The Social and Political Thought of Karl Marx*. Cambridge: Cambridge University Press, 1968.

Barrow, C.W. *Critical Theories of the State: Marxist, Neo-Marxist, Post-Marxist*. Madison: University of Wisconsin Press, 1993.

Bonefeld, Werner, and Sergio Tischler Visqueria. *What Is to Be Done?: Leninism, Anti-Leninist Marxism and the Question of Revolution Today*. Aldershot, England: Ashgate, 2002.

Callari, A., and D. Ruccio, eds. *Postmodern Materialism and the Future of Marxist Theory: Essays in the Althusserian Tradition*. London: Wesleyan University Press, 1996.

Callinicos. Alex. *Against Postmodernism: A Marxist Critique*. London: Lawrence and Wishart, 1989.

———. *The Revolutionary Ideas of Karl Marx*. London: Bookmarks, 1995.

Carew-Hunt, R.N. *The Theory and Practice of Communism*. London: Penguin, 1963.

Carver, Terrell. *Marx's Social Theory*. Oxford: Oxford University Press, 1982.

———. *The Postmodern Marx*. Manchester: Manchester University Press, 1998.

Caudwell, Christopher. *The Concept of Freedom*. London: Lawrence and Wishart, 1965.

Cohen, Gerry A. *History, Labour and Freedom*. Oxford: Clarendon Press, 1988.

Cole, G.D.H. *What Marx Really Meant*. New York: A.A. Knopf, 1934.

Cornforth, Maurice. *The Open Philosophy and the Open Society: A Reply to Karl Popper's Refutations of Marxism*. London: Lawrence and Wishart, 1968.

Corrigan, Philip, Harvie Ramsay, and Derek Sayer. *Socialist Construction and Marxist Theory: Bolshevism and Its Critique*. London: Macmillan, 1978.

Draper, Hal. *Karl Marx's Theory of Revolution*. 4 vols. New York: Monthly Review Press, 1990.

Dunayevskaya, Raya. *Marxism and Freedom from 1776 until Today*. New York: Twayne, 1964.

———. *Philosophy and Revolution: From Hegel to Sartre and from Marx to Mao*. Atlantic Highlands, N.J.: Harvester, 1982.

Elster, Jon. *Making Sense of Marxism*. Cambridge: Cambridge University Press, 1985.

Fetscher. I. *Marx and Marxism*. New York: Herder and Herder, 1971.

Fischer, Ernst. *Marx in His Own Words*. London: Allen Lane, 1970.

Garaudy, Roger. *Karl Marx: The Evolution of His Thought*. London: Lawrence and Wishart, 1967.

Geras, Norman. *Literature of Revolution: Essays on Marxism*. London: Verso, 1986.

Gilbert, A. *Marx's Politics. Communists and Citizens*. Oxford: Robertson, 1981.

Gould, Carol. *Marx's Social Ontology: Individuality and Community in Marx's Theory of Social Reality*. Cambridge, Mass.: MIT Press, 1978.

Gouldner, Alvin W. *The Two Marxisms: Contradictions and Anomalies in the Development of Theory*. London: Macmillan, 1980.

Graham, Keith. *Karl Marx: Our Contemporary. Social Theory for a Post-Leninist World*. London: Harvester Wheatsheaf, 1992.

Heilbronner, Robert L. *Marxism: For and Against*. New York: W.W. Norton, 1980.

Heller, Agnes. *The Theory of Need in Marx*. London: Allison and Busby, 1976.

Hoffman, John. *Marxism and the Theory of Praxis*. London: Lawrence and Wishart, 1975.

Jessop, Bob, and C. Malcolm-Brown, eds. *Karl Marx: Social and Political Thought, Critical Assessments*. 4 vols. London: Routledge, 1990.

Jessop, Bob, with Russell Wheatly, eds. *Karl Marx: Social and Political Thought, Critical Assessments, Second Series*. 4 vols. London: Routledge, 1999.

Johnston, L. *Marxism, Class Analysis and Socialist Pluralism*. London: Allen and Unwin, 1986.

Kain, P. *Marx and Modern Political Theory*. Lanham, Md.: Rowman & Littlefield, 1993.

Kitching, G. *Karl Marx and The Theory of Praxis*. London: Lawrence and Wishart, 1975.

Labriola, Antonio. *Socialism and Philosophy*. Chicago: C.H. Kerr, 1898.

Laclau, E. *Politics and Ideology in Marxist Theory*. London: New Left, 1977.

Levine, Andrew. *A Future for Marxism?: Althusser, the Analytical Turn and the Revival of Socialist Theory*. London: Pluto, 2003.

Lewis, J. *The Marxism of Marx*. London: Lawrence and Wishart, 1972.

Lobkowitz, N. *Theory and Practice. The History of a Marxist Concept*. Notre Dame, Ind.: Notre Dame University Press, 1967.

MacIntyre, A.C. *Marxism: An Interpretation*. London: SCM Press, 1953.

Maguire, John M. *Marx's Paris Writings*. Dublin: Gill and Macmillan, 1972.

———. *Marx's Theory of Politics*. Cambridge: Cambridge University Press, 1978.

Masaryk, T.G. *Masaryk on Marx*. Ed. and trans. by E.V. Kohak. Lewisburg, Pa.: Bucknell University Press, 1972.

McBride, William L. *The Philosophy of Marx*. New York: St. Martin's Press, 1977.

McCarney, Joseph. *Social Theory and the Crisis of Marxism*. London: Verso, 1990.

McLellan, David. *Introduction to "Marx's Grundrisse."* London: Macmillan, second edition, 1980.

———, ed. *Marx: The First Hundred Years*. London: Frances Pinter Publishers, 1983.

Meyer, A.G. *Marxism: The Unity of Theory and Practice*. Cambridge, Mass.: Harvard University Press, 1954.

Miller, R. *Analyzing Marx*. Princeton, N.J.: Princeton University Press, 1981.

Parkin, Frank. *Marxism and Class Theory: A Bourgeois Critique*. London: Tavistock, 1979.

Pierson, Chris. *Marxist Theory and Democratic Politics*. Cambridge: Polity, 1986.

Plamenatz, John. *Karl Marx's Philosophy of Man*. Oxford: Oxford University Press, 1975.

Postone, M. *Time, Labour, and Social Domination*. Cambridge: Cambridge University Press, 1993.

Roberts, M. *Analytical Marxism: A Critique*. London: Verso, 1996.

Roemer, J. *Analytical Foundations of Marxism*. New York: Cambridge University Press, 1981.

———, ed. *Analytical Marxism*. Cambridge: Cambridge University Press, 1986.

Schaff, Adam. *Marxism and the Human Individual*. New York: McGraw-Hill, 1970.

Swingewood, A. *Marx and Modern Social Theory*. London: Macmillan, 1975.

Torrance, J. *Karl Marx's Theory of Ideas*. Cambridge: Cambridge University Press, 1995.

Tucker, D.F.B. *Marxism and Individualism*. New York: St. Martin's, 1980.

Walker, Angus. *Marx: His Theory and Its Context*. London: Longman, 1978.

Webb, Darren. *Marx, Marxism and Utopia*. Aldershot, England: Ashgate, 2000.

Wetherly, Paul. *Marxism and the State: An Analytical Approach*. Basingstoke, England: Palgrave, 2005.

Wood, Allen W. *Karl Marx*. London: Routledge and Kegan Paul, 1981.

Historical Materialism

Acton, H.B. *What Marx Really Said*. New York: Schoken Books, 1967.

Bober, M.M. *Karl Marx's Interpretation of History*. New York: W.W. Norton, 1965.

Cohen, G.A. *Karl Marx's Theory of History: A Defence*. Oxford: Clarendon Press, 1978.

Fleischer, H. *Marxism and History*. London: Allen Lane, 1973.

Giddens, Anthony. *A Contemporary Critique of Historical Materialism*. London: Macmillan, 1981.

Jakubowski, F. *Ideology and Superstructure in Historical Materialism*. London: Pluto Press, 1990.

Labriola, Antonio. *Essays on the Materialist Conception of History*. Chicago: C.H. Kerr, 1895.

Larrain, Jorge. *A Reconstruction of Historical Materialism*. London: Allen and Unwin, 1986.

Leff, Gordon. *The Tyranny of Concepts: A Critique of Marxism*. London: Merlin Press, 1961.

McMurtry, John M. *The Structure of Marx's World-View*. Princeton, N.J.: Princeton University Press, 1978.

Perry, Matt. *Marxism and History*. Basingstoke, England: Palgrave, 2002.

Rader, M. *Marx's Interpretation of History*. Oxford: Oxford University Press, 1979.

Rigby, Steven. *Marxism and History: A Critical Introduction*. Manchester: Manchester University Press, 1998.

Shaw, William H. *Marx's Theory of History*. London: Hutchinson, 1978.

Wetherley, Paul, ed. *Marx's Theory of History: The Contemporary Debate*. Aldershot, England: Avebury, 1992.

Alienation, Human Nature and Humanism

Axelos, K. *Alienation, Praxis and Techne in the Thought of Karl Marx*. Austin, Tex.: University of Texas, 1976.

Forbes, Ian. *Marx and the New Individual*. London: Unwin Hyman, 1990.

Fromm, Erich. *Marx's Concept of Man*. New York: Frederick Ungar, 1961.

———. *Socialist Humanism*. New York: Doubleday, 1965.

Geras, Norman. *Marx and Human Nature: Refutation of a Legend*. London: Verso, 1983.

Kolakowski, Leszek. *Toward a Marxist Humanism*. New York: Grove, 1968.

Koren, H. *Marx and the Authentic Man*. Duquesne, Pa.: Duquesne University Press, 1967.

Mandel, Ernest, and George Novak. *The Marxist Theory of Alienation*. New York: Pathfinder Press, 1973.

Markovic, M. *The Contemporary Marx: Essays on Humanist Communism*. Nottingham, England: Spokesman Books, 1974.

Mészáros, István. *Marx's Theory of Alienation*. London: Merlin Press, 1970.

Ollman, Bertell. *Alienation: Marx's Conception of Man in Capitalist Society.* Cambridge: Cambridge University Press, 1976.

Pappenheim, F. *The Alienation of Modern Man.* New York: Monthly Review, 1959.

Petrovic, Gajo. *Marx in the Mid-Twentieth Century.* Garden City, N.Y.: Doubleday, 1967.

Pines, C. *Ideology and False Consciousness: Marx and His Historical Progenitors.* Albany, N.Y.: State University of New York Press, 1993.

Sayers, Sean. *Marxism and Human Nature.* London: Routledge, 1998.

Schacht, Richard. *Alienation.* Garden City, N.Y.: Doubleday, 1970.

Torrance, J. *Estrangement, Alienation and Exploitation.* London: Macmillan, 1977.

Venable, Vernon. *Human Nature: The Marxian View.* Cleveland, Ohio: Meridian, 1966.

Walton, P., and A. Gamble. *From Alienation to Surplus Value.* London: Sheed and Ward, 1972.

Economics, Political Economy and Capital

Aglietta, M. *A Theory of Capitalist Regulation.* London: New Left, 1979.

Arthur, Chris, and G. Reuten, eds. *The Circulation of Capital.* Basingstoke, England: Macmillan, 1998.

Baran, P., and Paul Sweezy. *Monopoly Capitalism.* New York: Monthly Review Press, 1966.

Bellofiore, R., ed. *Marxian Economics: A Reappraisal. Essays on Volume 3 of Capital. Volume 1: Method, Value and Money.* New York: St. Martin's Press, 1998.

Böhm-Bawerk, L.V. *Karl Marx and the Close of His System.* London: Merlin, 1975.

Bose, A. *Marxian and Post-Marxian Political Economy.* London: Harmondsworth Penguin, 1975.

Boyer, R. *The Regulation School: A Critical Introduction.* New York: Columbia University Press, 1990.

Bradley, I., and M. Howard, eds. *Classical and Marxian Political Economy.* London: Macmillan, 1982.

Brus, Wlodzimierz. *The Market in a Socialist Economy.* London: Routledge and Kegan Paul, 1972.

———. *The Economics and Politics of Socialism.* London: Routledge and Kegan Paul, 1973.

———. *Socialist Ownership and Political Systems.* London: Routledge and Kegan Paul, 1975.

Cowling, Keith. *Monopoly Capitalism.* London: Macmillan, 1982.

Cullenberg, S. *The Falling Rate of Profit: Recasting the Marxian Debate.* London: Pluto Press, 1994.

Cutler, A., et al. *Marx's 'Capital' and Capitalism Today.* London: Routledge and Kegan Paul, 1977.

de Brunoff, Suzanne. *Marx on Money.* London: Pluto, 1976.

Desai, Meghnad. *Marxian Economics*, 2nd ed. Oxford: Basil Blackwell, 1979.

Dmitriev, V.K. *Economic Essays on Value Competition and Utility.* Cambridge: Cambridge University Press, 1974.

Dobb, Maurice. *Marx as an Economist.* London: Lawrence and Wishart, 1943.

———. *Studies in the Development of Capitalism.* New York: International Publishers, 1963.

———. *Political Economy and Capitalism.* Westport, Conn.: Greenwood, 1972.

———. *Theories of Value and Distribution since Adam Smith.* Cambridge: Cambridge University Press, 1973.

———. *Capitalist Enterprise and Social Progress.* Westport, Conn.: Hyperion, 1980.

Elson, Diane, ed. *Value: The Representation of Labour in Capitalism: Essays.* London: CSE Books, 1979.

Emmanuel, Arghiri. *Unequal Exchange: A Study of the Imperialism of Trade.* London: New Left, 1972.

Fine, Ben. *Marx's "Capital."* London: Macmillan, 1975.

Fine, Ben, and L. Harris. *Rereading "Capital."* New York: Columbia University Press, 1979.

Gillman, J.M. *The Falling Rate of Profit. Marx's Law and Its Significance to 20th Century Capitalism.* New York: Cameron Associates, 1958.

Godlier, Maurice. *Rationality and Irrationality in Economics.* London: New Left, 1972.

Hardach, Gerd, and Dieter Karras. *A Short History of Socialist Economic Thought.* London: Edward Arnold, 1978.

Hiferding, Rudolf. *Böhm-Bawerk's Criticism of Marx.* Ed. by Paul Sweezy. London: Merlin, 1975.

———. *Finance Capital: A Study of the Latest Phase of Capitalist Development.* London: Routledge and Kegan Paul, 1981.

Horowitz, D., ed. *Marx and Modern Economics.* London: MacGibbon and Kee, 1968.

Itoh, Makoto. *Value and Crisis, Essays on Marxian Economics in Japan.* London: Pluto, 1980.

Kornai, J. *The Socialist System: The Political Economy of Communism.* Oxford: Clarendon, 1992.

Kühne, Karl. *Economics and Marxism.* 2 vols. London: Macmillan, 1979.

Lallier. A. *The Economics of Marx's Grundrisse.* Basingstoke, England: Macmillan, 1989.

Lange, Oskar. *Political Economy*. Oxford: Pergamon, 1963.

Lavoie, Donald. *Rivalry and Central Planning: The Socialist Calculation Debate Reconsidered*. Cambridge: Cambridge University Press, 1985.

Luxemburg, Rosa. *What Is Economics?* New York: Pioneer, 1954.

Mandel, Ernest. *Marxist Economic Theory*. New York: Monthly Review Press, 1969.

———. *The Formation of Marx's Economic Thought*. London: New Left Books, 1971.

———. *Late Capitalism*. Atlantic Highlands, N.J.: New Left; Humanities Press, 1975.

Mattick, P. *Marx and Keynes: The Limits of the Mixed Economy*. London: Merlin, 1971.

Moseley, F., ed. *Marx's Method in Capital*. Atlantic Highlands, N.J.: Humanities Press, 1993.

Morishima, Michio. *Marx's Economics*. Cambridge: Cambridge University Press, 1973.

Oakley, A. *Marx's Critique of Political Economy: Intellectual Sources and Evolution*. 2 vols. London: Routledge and Kegan Paul, 1985.

Oishis, Takahisa. *The Unknown Marx*. London: Pluto, 2001

Pilling, G. *Marx's "Capital": Philosophy and Political Economy*. London: Routledge and Kegan Paul, 1980.

Resnick, S., and R. Wolff. *Knowledge and Class: A Marxian Critique of Political Economy*. Chicago: Chicago University Press, 1987.

Robinson, Joan. *An Essay on Marxian Economics*. London: Macmillan, 1963.

Rosdolsky, R. *The Making of Marx's 'Capital.'* Trans. by P. Burgess. London: Pluto, 1977.

Rubin, Isaak I. *Essays on Marx's Theory of Value*. Montreal: Black Rose, 1973.

Sayer, D. *Marx's Method: Ideology, Science and Critique in "Capital."* Hassocks, England: Harvester, 1983.

Shortall, F. *The Incomplete Marx*. Aldershot, England: Avebury, 1994.

Sloan, P. *Marx and the Orthodox Economists*. Oxford: Blackwell, 1973.

Smith, T. *The Logic of Marx's Capital*. Albany, N.Y.: State University of New York Press, 1990.

Steedman, I. *Marx after Sraffa*. London: Verso, 1997.

Sweezy, P. *The Theory of Capitalist Development*. New York: Monthly Review Press, 1970.

Wolff, R.D. *Understanding Marx: A Reconstruction and Critique of Capital*. Princeton: Princeton University Press, 1984

Wolff, R.D., and S. Resnick. *Economics: Marxian versus Neoclassical*. Baltimore, Md.: John Hopkins University Press, 1987.

Wolfson, M. *Karl Marx*. New York: Columbia University Press, 1971.

Science and Methodology

Bologh, R.W. *Dialectical Phenomenology: Marx's Method*. London: Routledge and Kegan Paul, 1979.

Habermas, Jurgen. *Knowledge and Human Interests*. London: Heinemann, 1971.

Huxley, Julien. *Soviet Genetics and World Science: Lysenko and the Meaning of Heredity*. London: Chattus and Windus, 1949.

Joravsky, David. *Soviet Marxism and Natural Science 1917–1932*. London: Routledge and Kegan Paul, 1961.

——. *The Lysenko Affair*. Cambridge, Mass.: Harvard University Press, 1970.

Lecourt, D. *Proletarian Science? The Case of Lysenko*. London: New Left, 1977.

Levidow, Les, and Robert M. Young, eds. *Science, Technology and the Labour Process: Marxist Studies*. CSE Books, 1981.

Little, Daniel. *The Scientific Marx*. Minneapolis: University of Minnesota Press, 1986.

Markovic, Mihailo, and Gajo Petrovic, eds. *Praxis: Yugoslav Essays in the Philosophy and Methodology of the Social Sciences*. Dordrecht: D. Reidel, 1969.

McCarthy, G.E. *Marx's Critique of Science and Positivism: The Methodological Foundations of Political Economy*. Dordrecht: Kluwer Academic Publishers, 1988.

Medvedev, Zhores. *The Rise and Fall of T.D. Lysenko*. New York: Columbia University Press, 1969.

Moseley, Fred, and Martha Campbell, eds. *New Investigations of Marx's Method*. Atlantic Highlands, N.J.: Humanities Press, 1997.

Murray, P. *Marx's Theory of Scientific Knowledge*. New York: Humanities Press International, 1988.

Sayer, Derek. *Marx's Method*. Brighton, England: Harvester, 1979.

Walker, David M. *Marx, Methodology and Science: Marx's Science of Politics*. Aldershot, England: Ashgate, 2001.

Wilson, H.T. *Marx's Critical/Dialectical Procedure*. London: Routledge, 1991.

Aesthetics, Culture, Literature and the Arts

Arvon, A. *Marxist Esthetics*. Ithaca, N.Y.: Cornell University Press, 1973.

Baxendall, L. *Marxism and Aesthetics*. New York: Humanities, 1968.

Baxendall, L., and S. Morowski. *Marx and Engels on Literature and Art*. New York: International General, 1973.

Benjamin, Walter. *Understanding Brecht*. London: New Left, 1973.

Bennett, Tony. *Formalism and Marxism*. London: Routledge, 2005.

Bisztray, George. *Marxist Models of Literary Realism*. New York: Columbia University Press, 1974.

Bloch, Ernst, et al. *Aesthetics and Politics*. London: New Left, 1977.

Brecht, Bertolt. *Plays*. Ed. Eric Bentley. New York: Grove, 1961.

——. *Brecht on Theater*. Ed. John Willett. New York: Hill and Wang, 1964.

——. *Collected Plays*. Ed. Ralph Mannheim and John Willett. New York: Random House, 1971.

——. *Poems 1913–56*. Ed. John Willett and Ralph Mannheim. New York: Random House, 1976.

Bullock, Chris, and David Peck. *Guide to Marxist Literary Criticism*. Bloomington: Indiana University Press, 1980.

Craig, D., ed. *Marxists on Literature*. Harmondsworth, England: Penguin, 1975.

Demetz, Peter. *Marx, Engels and the Poets: Origins of Marxist Literary Criticism*. Chicago: University of Chicago Press, 1967.

Eagleton, Terry. *Criticism and Ideology: A Study in Marxist Literary Theory*. London: New Left, 1976.

——. *Walter Benjamin or, Towards a Revolutionary Criticism*. London: New Left, 1981.

——. *Marxism and Literary Criticism*. London: Routledge, 2002.

Ewen, Frederic. *Bertolt Brecht*. New York: Citadel, 1967.

Fuegi, John. *The Essential Brecht*. Los Angeles: Hennessy and Ingalls, 1972.

Goldmann, Lucien. *Towards a Sociology of the Novel*. London: Tavistock, 1975.

Jameson, Frederic. *Marxism and Form: Twentieth-Century Dialectical Theories of Literature*. Princeton, N.J.: Princeton University Press, 1971.

Laing, David. *The Marxist Theory of Art*. Brighton, England: Harvester, 1978.

Lenin, Vladmir I. *On Literature and Art*. Moscow: Progress Publishers, 1967.

Leslie, Esther. *Walter Benjamin, Overpowering Conformism*. London: Pluto, 2000.

Lifshitz, Mikhail. *The Philosophy of Art of Karl Marx*. London: Pluto, 1973.

Lukács, György. *History of the Development of Modern Drama*. London: Merlin, 1911.

——. *Aesthetic Culture*. (In Hungarian.) Budapest: Athenaum, 1913.

——. *The Historical Novel*. Boston, Mass.: Beacon, 1962.

——. *Realism in Our Time: Literature and the Class Struggle*. New York: Harper and Row, 1964.

——. *The Theory of the Novel*. Cambridge, Mass.: MIT Press, 1971.

Marcuse, Herbert. *The Aesthetic Dimension*. Boston, Mass.: Beacon, 1978.

Mulhearn, F. *Contemporary Marxist Literary Theory*. London: Longmans, 1992.

Munk, Erika. *Brecht: A Collection of Critical Pieces*. New York: Bantam, 1972.

Nelson, G., and L. Grossberg, eds. *Marxism and the Interpretation of Culture*. London: Longmans, 1989.

Plekhanov, Georgii. *Art and Social Life*. London: Lawrence and Wishart, 1956.

Prawer, S.S. *Karl Marx and World Literature*. Oxford: Oxford University Press, 1976.

Raphael, Max. *Proudhon, Marx, Picasso: Three Studies in the Sociology of Art*. London: Lawrence and Wishart, 1933.

Regula, Qureshi. *Music and Marx: Ideas, Practice and Politics*. New York: Routledge, 2002.

Roberts, Julian. *Walter Benjamin*. London: Macmillan, 1982.

Schoeps, Karl H. *Bertolt Brecht*. New York: Frederick Ungar, 1977.

Slaughter, C. *Marxism, Ideology and Literature*. Brighton, England: Harvester, 1980.

Solomon, M., ed. *Marxism and Art*. Brighton, England: Harvester, 1979.

Vázquez, Adolfo Sanches. *Art and Society: Essays in Marxist Aesthetics*. London: Merlin, 1973.

Willett, John. *Theater of Bertolt Brecht*. New York: New Directions, 1968.

Williams, Raymond. *Marxism and Literature*. Oxford: Oxford University Press, 1977.

Religion

Bociurkiw, B.R., and J.W. Strong, eds. *Religion and Atheism in the USSR and Eastern Europe*. London: Macmillan, 1975.

Bordeaux, Michael. *Opium of the People*. London: Faber, 1965.

Carlebach, Julius. *Karl Marx and the Radical Critique of Judaism*. London: Routledge and Kegan Paul, 1978.

Collier, Andrew. *Christianity and Marxism: A Philosophical Contribution to Their Reconciliation*. London: Routledge, 2001.

Girardi, G. *Marxism and Christianity*. Dublin: M.H. Gill and Son, 1968.

McLellan, David. *Marxism and Religion: A Descriptive Assessment of the Marxist Critique of Christianity*. London: Macmillan, 1987.

Ethics and Justice

Ash, W. *Marxism and Moral Concepts*. New York: Monthly Review Press, 1964.

Brenkert, George. *Marx's Ethics of Freedom*. London: Routledge and Kegan Paul 1983.

Buchanan, Allen E. *Marx and Justice: The Radical Critique of Liberalism*. Totowa, N.J.: Rowman and Littlefield, 1982.

Cohen, Marshall, Thomas Nagel, and Thomas Scanlon, eds. *Marx, Justice and History*. Princeton, N.J.: Princeton University Press, 1980.

Kamenka, Eugene. *Marxism and Ethics*. London: Macmillan, 1969.

———. *The Ethical Foundations of Marxism*. London: Routledge and Kegan Paul, 1972.

Lukes, Stephen. *Marxism and Morality*. Oxford: Oxford University Press, 1985.

McLellan, David, and Sean Sayers, eds. *Socialism and Morality*. London: Macmillan, 1990.

Pfeffer, R. *Marxism, Morality and Social Justice*. Princeton, N.J.: Princeton University Press, 1990.

Wilde, Lawrence. *Ethical Marxism and its Radical Critics*. Basingstoke, England: Macmillan, 1998.

———, ed. *Marxism's Ethical Thinkers*. Basingstoke, England: Palgrave, 2001.

Crime and Law

Cain, Maureen, and Alan Hunt, eds. *Marx and Engels on Law*. London: Academic Press, 1979.

Greenberg, David F., ed. *Crime and Capitalism: Readings in Marxist Criminology*. Palo Alto, Calif.: Mayfield, 1981.

Hazard, Hohn N. *Communists and Their Law: A Search for the Common Core of the Legal Systems of the Marxian Socialist States*. Chicago: University of Chicago Press, 1969.

Pashkunis, E.B. *Selected Writings on Marxism and Law*. Trans. by Peter B. Maggs. Intro. by Piers Beirne and Robert Sharlet. London: Academic Press, 1979.

Pearce, Frank. *Crimes of the Powerful: Marxism, Crime and Deviance*. London: Pluto, 1976.

Phillips, Paul. *Marx and Engels on Law and Laws*. Oxford: Martin Robertson, 1981.

Quinney, Richard. *Class, State and Crime*. New York: Longman, 1977.

Women and Feminism

Barrett, Michèle. *Women's Oppression Today: Problems in Marxist Feminist Analysis*. London: Verso, 1980.

Eisenstein, Zillah, ed. *Capitalist Patriarchy and the Case for Socialist Feminism*. New York: Monthly Review Press, 1978.

Firestone, Shulamith. *The Dialectic of Sex: The Case for Feminist Revolution*. New York: Morrow, 1970.

Foreman, Ann. *Femininity as Alienation: Women and the Family in Marxism and Psychoanalysis*. London: Pluto, 1977.

Guettel, Charnie. *Marxism and Feminism*. Toronto: Women's Press, 1974.

Kuhn, Annette, and Annemarie Wolpe, eds. *Feminism and Materialism: Women and Modes of Production*. Boston, Mass.: Routledge and Kegan Paul, 1978.

Mitchell, Juliet. *Women's Estate*. Baltimore, Md.: Penguin, 1971.

Sargent, Lydia, ed. *Women and Revolution: A Discussion of the Unhappy Marriage of Marxism and Feminism*. Boston, Mass.: South End Press, 1981.

Sayers, Janet, M. Evans, and N. Redclift, eds. *Engels Revisited: New Feminist Essays*. London: Tavistock, 1987.

Vogel, Lise. *Marxism and the Oppression of Women: Toward a Unitary Theory*. New Brunswick, N.J.: Rutgers University Press, 1983.

Nationalism

Benner, E. *Really Existing Nationalisms: A Post-Communist View from Marx and Engels*. Oxford: Clarendon, 1995.

Bloom, S.F. *The World of Nations. A Study of the National Implications in the Work of Marx*. New York: Columbia University Press, 1941

Cummins, Ian. *Marx, Engels and National Movements*. London: Croom Helm, 1980.

Davis, Horace Bancroft. *Nationalism and Socialism: Marxist and Labour Theories of Nationalism to 1917*. New York: Monthly Review Press, 1967.

———. *Towards a Marxist Theory of Nationalism*. New York: Monthly Review Press, 1978.

———, ed. *The National Question: Selected Writings by Rosa Luxemburg*. New York: Monthly Review Press, 1976.

Herod, C. *The Nation in the History of Marxian Thought*. The Hague: Martinus Nijhoff, 1976.

Leninism and the National Question. Moscow: Progress, 1977.

Lowy, Michael. *Fatherland or Mother Earth? Essays on the National Question*. London: Pluto, 1998.

Munck, Ronaldo. *The Difficult Dialogue, Marxism and Nationalism*. London: Zed, 1986.

Nimni, E. *Marxism and Nationalism: Theoretical Origins of a Political Crisis*. London: Pluto, 1991.

Shaheen, S. *The Communist Theory of National Self Determination*. The Hague: W. Van Hoeve, 1956.

Simmonds, George W., ed., *Nationalism in the USSR and Eastern Europe*. Detroit, Mich.: University of Detroit Press, 1977.

Szporluck, R. *Communism and Nationalism*. Oxford: Oxford University Press, 1988.

Imperialism and the Developing World

Brewer, Anthony. *Marxist Theories of Imperialism: A Critical Survey.* London: Routledge and Kegan Paul, 1980.

Fagen, R., C.D. Deere, and K.L. Coraggio, eds. *Transition and Development: Problems of Third World Socialism.* New York: Monthly Review Press, 1986.

Kay, G. *Development and Underdevelopment: A Marxist Analysis.* London: Macmillan, 1975.

Melotti, Umberto. *Marx and the Third World.* London: Macmillan, 1977.

Warren, B. *Imperialism: Pioneer of Capitalism.* London: Verso, 1980.

White, G., R. Murray, and C. White, eds. *Revolutionary Socialist Development in the Third World.* London: Macmillan, 1983.

The Communist Internationals and International Socialism

Braunthal, Julius. *History of the International.* Trans. Henry Collins and Kenneth Mitchell. Vol.1, 1864–1914; Vol.2, 1914–1943; Vol.3, 1943–68. London: Nelson, 1966; Gollancz, 1980. Originally published in German in 1961, 1963, and 1971.

Butler, William E., ed. *A Sourcebook on Socialist International Organizations.* Dordrecht: Kluwer Academic Publishing, 1980.

Carr, Edward H. *The Comintern and the Spanish Civil War.* New York: Pantheon Books, 1984.

Claudin, Fernando. *The Communist Movement: From Comintern to Cominform.* London: Penguin, 1975.

Degras, Jane, ed. *The Communist International 1919–1943: Documents.* 3 vols. London: Oxford University Press, 1956–65.

Devin, Guillaume. *L'Internationale Socialiste: Histoire et sociologie du socialisme international 1945–1990.* Paris: Presses de la Fondation Nationale des Sciences Politiques, 1993.

Documents of the First International. 5 vols. London: Lawrence and Wishart, 1963–68.

Documents of the Fourth International: The Formative Years (1933–1940). New York: Pathfinder, 1973.

Dutte, R. Palme. *The Internationale.* London: Lawrence and Wishart, 1964.

Hallas, Duncan. *The Comintern.* London: Bookmarks, 1985.

Haupt, Georges. *Aspects of International Socialism, 1871–1914.* Cambridge: Cambridge University Press, 1986.

Joll, James. *The Second International, 1889–1914.* London: Routledge and Kegan Paul, 1975.

Lazitch, Branko, and Milorad M. Drachovitch, eds., *Biographical Dictionary of the Comintern.* Stanford, Calif.: Hoover Institution Press, 1986.

Morgan, R. *The German Social Democrats and the First International 1864–1872.* Cambridge: Cambridge University Press, 1965.

Socialist International. *The Socialist International: A Short History.* London: Socialist International, 1969.

Soholev, A.L., et al. *Outline History of the Communist International.* Moscow: Progress, 1971.

Wrynn, J.E. *The Socialist International and the Politics of European Reconstruction, 1919–1930.* Amsterdam: University of Amsterdam, 1976.

Miscellaneous

Aronson, R. *After Marxism.* New York: Guildford Press, 1995.

Ball, T., and J. Farr, eds. *After Marx.* Cambridge: Cambridge University Press, 1984.

Beetham, David, ed. *Marxists in the Face of Fascism.* Manchester: Manchester University Press, 1984.

Bertram, C., and A. Chitty, eds. *Has History Ended? Fukuyama, Marx and Modernity.* Aldershot, England: Avebury, 1994.

Blackburn, Robin, ed. *After the Fall: The Failure of Communism and the Future of Socialism.* London: Verso, 1991.

Boggs, Carl. *The Socialist Tradition: From Crisis to Decline.* New York: Routledge, 1995.

Bottomore, Thomas B. *Marxist Sociology.* London: Macmillan, 1975.

——, ed. *Karl Marx.* Oxford: Oxford University Press, 1979.

——, ed. *Modern Interpretations of Marx.* Oxford: Blackwell, 1981.

——, ed. *A Dictionary of Marxist Thought.* Oxford: Blackwell, 1991.

Callari, Antonio, Stephen Cullenberg, and Carole Biewener, eds. *Marxism in the Postmodern Age: Confronting the New World Order.* New York: Guilford Press, 1995.

Cole, G.D.H. *A History of Socialist Thought.* 5 vols. New York: St. Martin's Press, 1956.

Colletti, Lucio. *From Rousseau to Lenin.* London: New Left, 1973.

Cowling, Mark, ed. *The Communist Manifesto—New Interpretations.* Edinburgh: Edinburgh University Press, 1998.

Cowling, Mark, and Paul Reynolds, eds. *Marxism, the Millennium and Beyond.* Basingstoke, England: Palgrave, 2000.

Cullenberg, S., C. Biewener, and A. Callari, eds. *Marxism in a Postmodern Age: Confronting the New World Order.* New York: Guilford Press, 1994.

Derrida, Jaques. *Spectres of Marx.* London: Routledge, 1994.

Diamond, Stanley, ed. *Toward a Marxist Anthropology.* The Hague: Mouton, 1979.

Djilas, Milovan. *The New Class: An Analysis of the Communist System.* London: Thames and Hudson, 1957.

Doherty, James C. *Historical Dictionary of Socialism.* Lanham, Md.: Scarecrow, 1997.

Draper, Hal. *The Adventures of the Communist Manifesto.* Berkeley, Calif.: Centre for Socialist History, 1994.

Foster, J. *Marx's Ecology: Materialism and Nature.* New York: Monthly Review Press, 2000.

Fromm, Erich. *Fear of Freedom.* London: Routledge and Kegan Paul, 1942.

Gamble, Andrew, David Marsh, and Tony Tant, eds. *Marxism and Social Science.* London: Macmillan, 1999.

Gandy, G. Ross. *Marx and History: From Primitive Society to the Communist Future.* Austin: University of Texas Press, 1979.

Garaudy, Roger. *Marxism and the Twentieth Century.* London: Collins, 1970.

Geoghegan, Vincent. *Utopianism and Marxism.* London: Methuen, 1987.

Gibson-Graham, K., S. Resnick, and R.D. Wolff, eds. *Re/Presenting Class: Essays in Postmodern Marxism.* Durham, N.C.: Duke University Press, 2001.

Godelier, Maurice. *Perspectives in Marxist Anthropology.* Cambridge: Cambridge University Press, 1977.

Gorman, Robert A. *Biographical Dictionary of Neo-Marxism.* London: Mansell, 1985.

———. *Biographical Dictionary of Marxism.* London: Mansell, 1986.

Gorz, Andre. *Farewell to the Working Class: An Essay on Lost Industrial Socialism.* London: Pluto, 1982.

Grundmann, R. *Marxism and Ecology.* Oxford: Clarendon, 1991.

Hall, Stuart, and Martin Jacques, eds. *New Times.* London: Lawrence and Wishart, 1990.

Hobsbawm, Eric, ed. *The History of Marxism.* Brighton, England: Harvester, 1978–82.

Howe, Irving, ed. *A Handbook of Socialist Thought.* London: Victor Gollancz, 1972.

Hughes, Jonathan. *Ecology and Historical Materialism.* Cambridge: Cambridge University Press, 2000.

Hunt, Alan, ed. *Marxism and Democracy.* London: Lawrence and Wishart, 1980.

Hussain, Athar, and Keith Tribe. *Marxism and the Agrarian Question.* 2 vols. London: Macmillan, 1981.

Hyman, R. *Marxism and the Sociology of Trade Unionism.* London: Pluto, 1971.

McLemee, Scott, and Paul LeBlanc. *C.L.R. James and Revolutionary Marxism: Selected Writings of C.L.R. James 1939–1949.* Amherst, N.Y.: Humanity Books, 2000.

Kilroy-Silk, Robert. *Socialism since Marx*. London: Allen Lane Penguin Books, 1972.

Kisson, S.F. *War and the Marxists: Socialist Theory and Practice in Capitalist War*. London: Andre Deutsch, 1988, 1989. 2 vols.

Kolakowski, Leszek. *Marxism and Beyond*. London: Pall Mall, 1969.

———. *Main Currents of Marxism: Its Origin, Growth and Dissolution*. 3 vols. Trans. by P.S. Falla. Oxford: Oxford University Press, 1978.

Larraine, Jorge. *Marxism and Ideology*. London: Macmillan, 1983.

Lerner, Warren. *A History of Socialism and Communism in Modern Times: Theorists, Activists, and Humanists*. Englewood Cliffs, N.J.: Prentice-Hall, 2nd ed., 1993.

Levin, M. *Marx, Engels and Liberal Democracy*. Basingstoke, England: Macmillan, 1989.

Lichtheim, George. *Marxism: An Historical and Critical Study*. London: Routledge and Kegan Paul, 1961.

Lovell, David. *Marx's Proletariat: The Making of a Myth*. London: Routledge, 1988.

Lozovsky, A. *Marx and the Trade Unions*. London: Martin Lawrence, 1935.

Magnus, B., and S. Cullenberg, eds. *Whither Marxism? Global Crises in International Perspective*. London: Routledge, 1995.

McCarthy, G. *Marx and the Ancients*. Savage, Md.: Rowman and Littlefield, 1990.

———, ed. *Marx and Aristotle: Nineteenth-Century German Social Theory and Classical Antiquity*. Savage, Md.: Rowman and Littlefield, 1992.

Miliband, Ralph. *The State in Capitalist Society*. New York: Basic Books, 1969.

———. *Marxism and Politics*. Oxford: Oxford University Press, 1977.

———. *Capitalist Democracy in Britain*. Oxford: Oxford University Press, 1982.

———. *Socialism for a Sceptical Age*. London: Verso, 1994.

Mills, C. Wright. *The Marxists*. New York: Dell, 1962.

Mitrany, D. *Marx against the Peasant*. London: Weidenfeld and Nicolson, 1951.

Molyneaux, John. *Marxism and the Party*. London: Pluto, 1978.

Moore, Stanley. *Marx on the Choice between Socialism and Communism*. Cambridge, Mass.: Harvard University Press, 1980.

Mount, Ferdinand, ed. *Communism*. London: Harvill, 1995.

Munck, Ronaldo. *Marx@2000: Late Marxist Perspectives*. London: Macmillan, 2000.

Nove, Alec. *Marxism and Really Existing Socialism*. Chur, Switzerland: Harwood Academic Publishers, 1986.

Ollman, Bertell. *Dialectical Investigations*. London: Routledge, 1993.

———. *How to Take an Exam . . . And Remake the World*. Montreal: Black Rose, 2001.

Parsons, H.L., ed. *Marx and Engels on Ecology*. Westport, Conn.: Greenwood, 1977.

Pike, Jon. *From Aristotle to Marx*. Aldershot, England: Avebury, 1998.

Plamenatz, John. *German Marxism and Russian Communism*. London: Longman, 1963.

Quaini, Massimo. *Geography and Marxism*. Oxford: Basil Blackwell, 1974.

Reich, Wilhelm. *The Mass Psychology of Fascism*. London: Penguin, 1942.

———. *The Sexual Revolution*. New York: Orgone Institute, 1945.

Robinson, Cedric J. *Black Marxism: The Making of Black Radical Tradition*. Chapel Hill, N.C.: University of North Carolina, 2000.

———. *An Anthropology of Marxism*. Aldershot, England: Ashgate, 2001.

Roemer, John. *A Future for Socialism*. London: Verso, 1994.

Ryan, M. *Marxism and Deconstruction: A Critical Articulation*. Baltimore, Md.: Johns Hopkins University Press.

Seddon, D., ed. *Relations of Production: Marxist Approaches to Economic Anthropology*. London: Frank Cass, 1978.

Seliger, Martin. *The Marxist Conception of Ideology*. Cambridge: Cambridge University Press, 1977.

Selucky, Radoslav. *Marxism, Socialism and Freedom*. London: Macmillan, 1979.

Sim, Stuart, ed. *Post-Marxism: A Reader*. Edinburgh: Edinburgh University Press, 1998.

———. *Post-Marxism, An Intellectual History*. London: Routledge, 2000.

Smith, Cyril. *Marx at the Millenium*. London: Pluto, 1996.

Stedman Jones, G. *Languages of Class: Studies in English Working Class History*. Cambridge: Cambridge University Press, 1983.

Szajkowski, Bogdan. *Marxist Governments: A World Survey*. 3 vols. London: Macmillan, 1981.

Thompson, Edward P. *The Making of the English Working Class*. London: Gollancz, 1963.

———. *The Poverty of Theory*. London: Merlin Press, 1978.

Townshend, Jules. *The Politics of Marxism: The Critical Debates*. London: Cassell, 1996.

Vaillancourt, P.M. *When Marxists Do Research*. New York: Greenwood Press, 1986.

Van den Berg, A. *The Immanent Utopia: From Marxism on the State to the State of Marxism*. Princeton, N.J.: Princeton University Press, 1988.

Van Parijs, P. *Marxism Recycled*. Cambridge: Cambridge University Press, 1993.

Voloshinov, V.N. *Marxism and the Philosophy of Language*. Trans. by Ladislav Matejka and I.R. Titunik. Cambridge, Mass.: Harvard University Press, 1986.

Wayne, Mike. *Marxism and Media Studies: Key Concepts and Contemporary Trends*. London: Pluto, 2003.

Wesson, R. *Why Marxism? The Continuing Success of a Failed Theory*. New York: Basic Books, 1996.

Westoby, A. *Communism Since World War II*. Brighton, England: Harvester, 1985.

Wilczynski, Joseph. *An Encyclopedic Dictionary of Marxism, Socialism and Communism*. London: Macmillan, 1981.

Wilson, Edmund. *To the Finland Station*. London: Macmillan, 1972.

Wood, Ellen Meiskins. *The Retreat From Class: The New, True Socialism*. London: Verso, 1986.

——. *Democracy Against Capitalism: Renewing Historical Materialism*. Cambridge: Cambridge University Press, 1995.

Worsley, Peter. *Marx and Marxism*. London: Tavistock, 1982.

Zavarzadeh, Mas'ud, Teresa L. Ebert, and Donald Morton, eds. *Post-Ality: Marxism and Postmodernism*. Washington, D.C.: Maisonneuve Press, 1995.

JOURNALS

Capital and Class London, 1977 to date.

Critique Glasgow, 1973 to date.

East European Studies formerly *Soviet Studies* Oxford, 1949 to date.

Historical Materialism London, 1997 to date.

History of Political Thought Exeter, 1980 to date.

International Labor and Working Class History Los Angeles, 1976 to date.

International Socialism London, 1960–78 1st series, 1978 to date 2nd series.

International Socialist Review New York, 1956–1975.

Mediations: Journal of the Marxist Literary Group Chicago, 1971–1991.

New Left Review London, 1960 to date.

Political Studies Oxford, 1952 to date.

Political Theory Newbury Park, California, 1972 to date.

Post-Ality: Marxism and Postmodernism Washington, D.C., 1995 to date.

Problems of Communism Washington, D.C., 1952 to date. London, 1974–1991.

Race and Class London, 1974 to date.

Rethinking Marxism Amherst, Mass., 1988 to date.

Revolutionary Russia London, 1975 to date.

Slavonic and East European Review London, 1922 to date.

Socialist Register London, 1964 to date.

Socialist Review London, 1960 to date.

Studies in Marxism Middlesbrough, England, 1994 to date.

Studies in Soviet Thought Dordrecht, 1961 to date.

About the Authors

David M. Walker (B.A. University of Lancaster; M.A. University of Kent; Ph.D. University of Manchester) is lecturer in politics at the University of Newcastle. For the last 15 years he has taught courses on a range of aspects of political theory, including socialism and Marxism. He is a member of the United Kingdom Political Studies Association Marxism Specialist Group, and his publications include the book *Marx, Methodology and Science* and articles for the journal *Studies in Marxism*. He has just completed a booklet on historical materialism for British A-Level students, and is currently editing a book on Marxist thought in the 20th century.

Daniel Gray has a degree in politics and history from the University of Newcastle, England, and has written on the practical application of Welsh socialist pioneer Robert Owen's ideas at New Lanark, and on German intervention in the Spanish civil war. He is currently on a sabbatical from academia working for the National Library of Scotland and writing on politics for *Holyrood Magazine* and on football for Middlesbrough Football Club's award-winning magazine *Fly Me to the Moon*.